DISCIPLING THROUGH ROMANS

Verse-by-verse
through the book of Romans

by Don Krow

with Life for Today Commentary by Andrew Wommack

Discipling Through Romans
Copyright © 2012 Andrew Wommack Ministries Inc.

ISBN: 978-1-59548-031-6

Andrew Wommack Ministries
PO Box 3333
Colorado Springs CO 80934-3333

awmi.net

Introduction

Recently, a prisoner shared with me how he and a group of men would gather around in the penitentiary and read Andrew Wommack's *Life for Today* commentary notes. This generated a lot of discussion, and many people were helped through this men's Bible study.

The truths in the book of Romans are foundational to Christianity and have greatly impacted my life. It has been my desire to help people understand these truths, so we put together a study-tool that would take a person using expositional (that is, verse-by-verse) teaching through the book of Romans. Through a verse-by-verse study of the book of Romans, I have developed questions to be asked where the answers are found in the Scriptures. For example, in a home Bible study, I would take a person to a verse, have them read it out loud, and then ask them a question. We continued to do this, verse-by-verse, all the way through the book of Romans and it prompted much discussion. I also developed an answer key so that the person leading the group could not only ask the question, but would have a concrete answer to start the discussion.

I decided to put together a combination of Andrew Wommack's *Life for Today* footnotes from the book of Romans along with the questions and answer keys that I developed and called it "Discipling Through Romans." I believe this can be used as another teaching method and tool for the body of Christ. The beauty of this particular study is that it takes a person verse-by-verse through an entire book of the Bible. In this way, we avoid many of the pitfalls of denominationalism that would emphasize only one particular truth at the expense of another. Expositional teaching is by far a safer approach to examining the Scriptures.

I believe that you can adapt this method of study and teaching to your own particular group. You may read Andrew's footnotes and then create a discussion. You could read the notes and then ask the prepared questions. Or you could go directly to the scriptures (read the scripture) and then ask a question. There's a freedom to adapt this study and personalize it for your own particular study.

Don Krow

Discipling Through Romans

Verse-by-verse
through the book of Romans

TABLE OF CONTENTS

OVERVIEW OF ROMANS CHAPTER 1

by Andrew Wommack

Welcome to our Discipleship Evangelism teaching through the book of Romans. I'm really excited about what God is going to do in your life through this study. In my estimation, the book of Romans is the most profound teaching on grace in the Word of God. The book of Galatians basically makes the same points, but there Paul is angry, because the Galatians at one time had been into grace but through legalistic teaching, had left it and gotten back into guilt and condemnation. Paul took the gloves off and beat them with the truth in the book of Galatians. There are times that ministers to me, but the book of Romans is like a scholarly approach. It isn't written to deal with a specific problem, and it lays out the truths of the Gospel in a powerful way.

Some of the verses in Romans 1 are introductory. It's a shame we have to skip over them, but as you go through the study we will actually deal in more detail with these truths. The Apostle Paul got right to the point beginning in Romans 1:16:

"I am not ashamed of the gospel of Christ: for it [the gospel] *is the power of God unto salvation to every one that believeth; to the Jew first, and also to the Greek."*

That is a tremendous statement, but it has lost a lot of its power today because the word "Gospel" has become just a religious cliché that people use to apply to anything having to do with the Christian religion. The word "Gospel," if you look it up in the Greek, literally means "good news." Actually, it means even more than that because the word was used outside of the Bible in Greek literature prior to the time the Bible was written. It was so obscure that of all the references I have studied, there were only two uses in all of Greek literature outside of the Bible.

The reason for that is because it meant not only good news, but actually meant something like "nearly-too-good-to-be-true" news. It was an exaggeration saying that basically this is nearly too good to believe, more than anyone could comprehend. Therefore, it wasn't used often, but when Jesus came along, loved us unconditionally, and died for our sins—not imputing them to us but reconciling us to God on a free, unearned, undeserved basis—this word "Gospel" became appropriate, and it is used constantly throughout the New Testament.

The point I'm trying to make is that we have lost some of this in our churches today, because we use the word to describe all kinds of things. Literally, Paul is talking about the nearly-too-good-to-be-true news of the grace of Christ. It is the power of God unto salvation. That is a great statement—one of the great things that is missing in the Christian church today. They are not really preaching the good news. Instead they are condemning people, basically telling them that there is a God… there is a devil… there is a heaven… there is a hell… sin has separated us from God, and if we don't repent, we will go to hell.

All of those statements are true, but they are not the Gospel. Again, the word means nearly-too-good-to-be-true news. It is true that there is a God and a devil, a heaven and a hell, a heaven to gain and a hell to shun, but that isn't good news. The thing that makes the Gospel specifically good news is the grace of God. His grace is involved in these statements about the Gospel. In Acts 20:24 Paul held a ministers' conference, called a bunch of the preachers from Ephesus together, and said,

> *"But none of these things move me, neither count I my life dear unto myself, so that I might finish my course with joy, and the ministry, which I have received of the Lord Jesus, to testify the gospel of the grace of God."*

Notice in this verse he used the word "gospel" and "grace of God" interchangeably.

Let me say some radical things here. If a person isn't preaching the grace of God… and that word literally means "unearned, undeserved, unmerited favor"… if they aren't preaching that you receive all God has and everything Jesus purchased for us on an unearned, undeserved basis, they aren't preaching the true Gospel. This same point is made again in Galatians 1:6 where Paul says,

> *"I am amazed that you are so soon removed from the grace of God unto another gospel:"*

He is again using this term "grace" … unearned, unmerited, undeserved favor… interchangeably with the word "Gospel." So the word "Gospel" is literally referring to the grace of God.

In other words, you could say it is talking about the way you receive these things. For example, if I told you I had a million dollars for you and had deposited it in your bank account, would that be good news—nearly-too-good-to-be-true news? Most of you would be excited and say, "Yes, that's wonderful." But if I put a condition on it and said, "And all you have to do to draw the money out is to live without sin. If you sin, you can't take advantage of it." That would totally change the whole picture. Instead of being excited and blessed by my having deposited this money in your account, you would actually become angry. Some people would respond by saying, "You know what? It would have been better if you had never put that money in my account, because you're asking something of me that I can't do. I'm going to fail … I feel condemnation… I missed this great opportunity."

In a very real sense, this is what has happened with the way people are presenting relationship with God. They say, "Sure, Jesus is the Son of God. Sure, Jesus died for your sins. Sure, there has been an atonement made, and your sins can be forgiven." They are saying that is the Gospel, but it isn't the Gospel if they tack onto it, "What you have to do is start living holy, go to church, pay your tithes, and live a proper life. If you will do these things, then God will move in your life."

That isn't the Gospel the Apostle Paul preached. They are saying some of the elements of the Gospel, the fact that Jesus died for our sins, but if qualifications are put on it that people have to be holy to some measure to be able to appropriate it, they aren't preaching the Gospel the Apostle Paul preached.

As a matter of fact, four different times after Paul made these great statements about the grace of God, how God offers us relationship with Him, and all those benefits free of charge, Paul says, "Now what am I saying? Am I saying you can continue in sin so grace may abound? God forbid!" The point is that when Paul preached the Gospel, a constant question came up, "Are you saying that you can just live in sin, and God will still do these things?" No, that wasn't what he was saying, but if you aren't preaching the grace of God and talking about Him loving you independent of your performance to the degree that someone asks you the question, "Are you saying I can just live in sin?" then you aren't preaching the same Gospel the Apostle Paul preached.

That's how strong it is, and the truth is that the modern-day Christian church is again saying some of these elements of the Gospel—that Jesus died for our sins—but tacking onto it that God only answers your prayers proportional to your goodness and holiness. That is wrong! That is not the Gospel, and it's the reason we aren't seeing the power of the Gospel.

Notice again in verse 16,

"I am not ashamed of the gospel of Christ (the unearned, undeserved, unmerited favor of God—the grace of God)*, for it is the power of God unto salvation."*

Salvation here doesn't mean only the forgiveness of sins. It includes forgiveness, but healing is a part of salvation … deliverance is a part of salvation … prosperity is a part of salvation. If you are having problems in any of those areas, if it doesn't seem like you have the power to obtain and receive the benefits that were provided for you by Jesus, then I can promise you the reason is because you haven't fully understood the gospel.

So, do you know what you have to do? You have to do what the book of Romans is presenting and get a revelation of the Gospel of the grace of Christ. That's what the book is about, and I believe God is going to change your life through this teaching.

Romans 1:1-32
Discipleship Commentary

....

Read the entire lesson, and then answer the questions that follow.

Romans 1:1 - Paul, a servant of Jesus Christ, called to be an apostle, separated unto the gospel of God,

(Rom. 1:1) Out of the six Greek words for "servant" used in the New Testament, Paul used one of the most slavish terms possible. The word used in this passage is "doulos" and comes from the root word "deo," which means "bind." So, Paul is literally speaking of himself as being a bondman or slave of Jesus Christ, a slave by free choice, yet owned and purchased by Jesus Christ (1 Cor. 6:19-20).

The idea of being a love-slave by choice comes from Old Testament passages such as Exodus 21:2-6 and Deuteronomy 15:12-17. If an Israelite bought a Hebrew slave, he must set him free in the seventh year. However, if the slave loved his master and said, "I will not go away from thee," then a hole was to be bored through the lobe of his ear pronouncing him a bond-slave forever.

By the use of this word, Paul is declaring Jesus as his absolute Master, yet indicating the idea of his expression of love and free choice to the one whom he serves.

Notice that Paul spoke of his servitude to Christ before he mentioned his apostleship. This reveals Paul's priorities and humility, which were key factors in his success.

Romans 1:2 - (Which he had promised afore by his prophets in the holy scriptures,)

(Rom. 1:2) The concept of the Gospel was not new. Galatians 3:8 says that the Lord preached the Gospel unto Abraham. Also, Moses gave the conditions of the Gospel in Deuteronomy 30:11-14, which Paul quoted in Romans 10:6-8 as he explained faith as the only condition to receiving God's grace. Jesus Himself said that the law of Moses, the prophets, and the psalms were full of prophecies concerning Him (Luke 24:44).

The Gospel was woven throughout the Old Testament scriptures. Indeed, the job of the Old Testament law was to "shut us up" or constrain us toward the Gospel (Gal. 3:23). In this sense, there is no conflict between the Old Testament law and the New Testament grace. The Old Testament ministry of law was only temporary (Gal. 3:19) until the Gospel could be put into effect by the sacrifice of Jesus.

The conflict between law and grace comes when people try to mix the two. As Jesus described in His parables about the new wine in the old wine skin and the new patch on the old garment, the two covenants are not compatible.

✗ The Old Testament law paved the way for the Gospel and pointed men toward the Gospel. If the law is used to point out man's need and bring him to his knees through hopelessness of self-salvation, then the Gospel is used to provide salvation and relationship. There is no conflict. Conflict arises only when individuals refuse to use faith in God's grace as the only means of salvation, and insist that some degree of adherence to law is required for justification.

Romans 1:3-4 - Concerning his Son Jesus Christ our Lord, which was made of the seed of David according to the flesh; 4) And declared to be the Son of God with power, according to the spirit of holiness, by the resurrection from the dead:

(Rom. 1:4) The resurrection of Jesus from the dead is the greatest witness of all to the validity of Jesus' claims.

Romans 1:5 - By whom we have received grace and apostleship, for obedience to the faith among all nations, for his name:

(Rom. 1:5) This is the first of twenty-four times the term "grace" is used in Paul's epistle to the Romans. The Greek word for grace is "charis" and is translated many different ways throughout the New Testament. It is translated: favor, thanks, gracious, thankworthy, thank, thanked, pleasure, liberality, and acceptable. The most common way it is translated is by the word "grace" which is used 129 times in the New Testament.

According to Thayer's Greek-English Lexicon, "the word 'charis' (grace) contains the idea of kindness which bestows upon one what he has not deserved. The New Testament writers used 'charis' pre-eminently of that kindness by which God bestows favors even upon the ill-deserving."

Another form of the Greek word "charis" (grace) is "charisma" and is translated "gift." Vine's Expository Dictionary defines "charisma" as "a gift of grace, a gift involving grace on the part of God as the donor." In other words, "charisma" is a specific form or manifestation of the grace of God. It is used to describe as a free gift: righteousness (Rom. 5:16-17); spiritual gifts (1 Cor. 12:28-31, Rom. 12:6-8); eternal life (Rom. 6:23); celibacy (1 Cor. 7:7); healings (1 Cor. 12:9, 28, 30); and miraculous intervention (2 Cor. 1:11).

The Greek word used here for "obedience" is "hupakoe" and means "attentive hearkening; that is by implication compliance or submission."

Many times in the New Testament faith and obedience are linked together (Acts 6:7, Rom. 16:26, and Jas. 2:14-22). This is because the origin and historical development of the words "believe" and "obey" are closely related. What you believe is what you will do.

If you really believed that the building you were in was on fire, you would do something. Different people might do different things, but it is inconceivable that anyone who really believed the building was on fire would do nothing. The New Testament calls this a "work of faith" (1 Th. 1:2-3, 2 Th. 1:11), which is an action corresponding to and induced by what a person believes. This differs from a work of the law in that a work of the law requires no faith and is a works of one's own resources without any reference, reliance, or trust in God (Gal. 2:16, 3:12, 5:4, Rom. 3:28, 4:15-16, and 9:30-32).

Romans 1:6 - Among whom are ye also the called of Jesus Christ:

(Rom. 1:6) This verse states that we are "the called of Jesus Christ." The next verse states to what Jesus has called us. He called us to be saints. God's grace has extended the call (or invitation) to every person to become saints through salvation (Titus. 2:11), but not everyone chooses to respond positively to this call. If an individual rejects God's call, then God chooses to reject that person (Luke 12:9, 1 John. 2:23). Matthew 22:14 says, "For many are called, but few are chosen."

Romans 1:7 - To all that be in Rome, beloved of God, called to be saints: Grace to you and peace from God our Father, and the Lord Jesus Christ. _____

(Rom. 1:7) It is one of the greatest truths of the Bible and also one of the hardest to comprehend, that we are the objects of God's love. God didn't just pity us or feel some sense of moral obligation to save us. He saved us because of His infinite love for us (John 3:16).*An experiential understanding of God's love is the key to being filled with all the fullness of God (Eph. 3:19).

Romans 1:8 - First, I thank my God through Jesus Christ for you all, that your faith is spoken of throughout the whole world.

(Rom. 1:8) This is quite a statement! It is to be understood that this is speaking of the known Roman world, but this is still an astounding fact. These believers who had never had an apostolic visit and, as far as we know, had very little teaching, had such a strong faith in the Lord that stories of that faith had spread throughout the world. This is quite a contrast with many churches today that haven't even impacted their neighborhoods with the Gospel of Christ.

Romans 1:9-11 - For God is my witness, whom I serve with my spirit in the gospel of his Son, that without ceasing I make mention of you always in my prayers; 10) Making request, if by any means now at length I might have a prosperous journey by the will of God to come unto you. 11) For I long to see you, that I may impart unto you some spiritual gift, to the end ye may be established;

(Rom. 1:11) Two things are very significant in Paul's statement here. First, we see that spiritual gifts can be imparted or passed from one person to another. This is the whole purpose of the presbytery laying hands on an individual during ordination, as Paul reminds Timothy of in 1 Timothy 4:14.

Second, spiritual gifts help establish, or strengthen, an individual. This is in stark contrast to what some critics of the gifts of the Holy Spirit claim. As Paul said in 1 Corinthians 14:3-4, the gifts of the Spirit operating in the church produce edification, exhortation, and comfort; in private use, they edify the individual.

Romans 1:12-13 - That is, that I may be comforted together with you by the mutual faith both of you and me. 13) Now I would not have you ignorant, brethren, that oftentimes I purposed to come unto you, (but was let hitherto,) that I might have some fruit among you also, even as among other Gentiles.

(Rom. 1:13) The word "let" that was used here is an old English word which means "hindered." It is still used in that sense in the sports of tennis and table tennis.

Paul was saying that he had purposed many times to travel to Rome, but he had been hindered up to this point. In Romans 15:21-22 Paul clearly states what his hindrance was. That others closer to where he was had not heard the Gospel yet. In other words, he was hindered from bringing the gospel to Rome because there were so many other places that needed him just as much. However, in Romans 15:23 Paul says that he had presented the Gospel to every region in those parts, and he was now ready to begin his journey to Rome.

Romans 1:14 - I am debtor both to the Greeks, and to the Barbarians; both to the wise, and to the unwise.

(Rom. 1:14) Paul was making this statement in a spiritual sense. He was expressing his sense of obligation to share the Gospel of Jesus Christ with all men. This was one of the attitudes of Paul that motivated him to travel to the ends of the known world and constantly lay his life on the line for the sake of Christ. Likewise, those who seek to be used of God today need to recognize that their duty to share Christ with a dying world is not optional.

In Paul's day, the term "barbarian" was not an offensive term. It was simply used to distinguish anyone who did not speak the Greek language or, later, to identify anyone who was not of the Hellenic race.

Romans 1:15 - So, as much as in me is, I am ready to preach the gospel to you that are at Rome also.

(Rom. 1:15) Paul has now dispensed with the preliminaries and is beginning to present his defense of the Gospel, which was his primary purpose of writing.

Romans 1:16 - For I am not ashamed of the gospel of Christ: for it is the power of God unto salvation to every one that believeth; to the Jew first, and also to the Greek.

(Rom. 1:16) The Gospel is the power of God that releases the effects of salvation in our lives. Salvation is much more than just being born again. This refers to every benefit to which the believer is entitled through Jesus. Therefore, if we are not experiencing the abundance that Jesus provided for us in any area of our lives then we are having a problem understanding and/or believing the Gospel.

The term "Gospel" has become so familiar to Christians that the true meaning and understanding has been lost. The truths of the Gospel are not commonly preached or understood in many churches. This is the reason that so many Christians are not walking in all the benefits of their salvation. They don't have the power of the Gospel working in them.

If a person needs healing, it's in the Gospel. If deliverance is needed, it's in the Gospel. Prosperity, answered prayer, joy, peace, love—they are all found through understanding and believing the Gospel.

Most English words that end with the suffix "eth" in the Bible carry the idea of an act or process which continues. So, the man that "believeth" is a man who has believed and is continuing to believe.

In the Greek language, the word that was translated "believeth" here is a present participle which expresses the idea of a continuous and repeated action. Therefore, the faith that results in salvation cannot be abandoned and still produces its results (Heb. 6:4-6, 10:29, and Col. 1:21-23). It may appear to be abandoned, as in the case of Peter when he denied the Lord (Luke 22:57-62), but Jesus had prayed that his "faith fail not."

The Scriptures present true biblical faith as an ongoing experience, not a one-time action.

Romans 1:17 - For therein is the righteousness of God revealed from faith to faith: as it is written, The just shall live by faith.

(Rom. 1:17) The expression "from faith to faith" describes the means whereby righteousness is given and retained. God's righteousness cannot be earned; it can only be acquired through faith. As proof that righteousness received by faith is not a new idea or concept, Paul quotes Habakkuk 2:4, "The just shall live by faith" (also quoted in Gal. 3:11 and Heb. 10:38).

The just shall live by faith. They don't just visit faith every once in a while, or vacation there once a year; they live in and by faith.

Romans 1:18 - For the wrath of God is revealed from heaven against all ungodliness and unrighteousness of men, who hold the truth in unrighteousness;

(Rom. 1:18) Paul's purpose in writing verses 18-20 is to explain why the Gospel is the power of God unto salvation (v. 16). The problem was that then, just as now, most people felt the way to get people to come to God was to condemn them and scare them out of Hell. People doubted that Paul's good news of the love of God would be enough to cause repentance.

Therefore, Paul begins to prove that every person already has an instinctive knowledge of God's wrath against their sin. We don't need to prove God's wrath. God has already done that. What people need to know is the good news that God placed His wrath for our sins upon His own Son so that we could be completely forgiven. This good news will draw men to God more than the bad news will ever drive men to God.

In Romans 1:18-20, Paul is declaring that God has revealed Himself to all mankind. Old Testament scriptures proclaim that God has revealed Himself to everyone through nature (Ps. 19:1-3), but Paul is stating here that there is an intuitive revelation of God within every man.

There are five words used in these three verses to describe the extent to which God has revealed Himself to mankind that are worth special note. Any one of these five words used by itself would have made a strong argument for Paul's case. However, the combination of these words in just two sentences emphasizes the certainty of Paul's claims.

The use of the word "all" in verse 18 shows the extent to which God has revealed Himself. God has placed a witness within every man against all ungodliness and unrighteousness.

In verse 19, the Greek word that was translated "manifest" is related to the word that was translated "shewed" in this same verse. The word is "phaneroo," and it means, "to render apparent; manifestly declare; make manifest; shew." This word makes it very clear that this instinctive, or intuitive knowledge, is not so subtle that it can be overlooked. God gives every individual the right to choose, but there can be no doubt that every person has, at one time, clearly seen and understood (v. 20) the basic truths of God's existence.

In verse 20, Paul says this inner witness of God causes the individual to "clearly see" the invisible things of God and even "understand" the Godhead. The Greek word that was translated "clearly seen" is the word "kathorao" and means, "to behold fully; i.e. distinctly apprehend." This leaves no doubt that every person who has ever walked the earth has had a clear revelation of God. The use of the word "understand" emphatically states that God not only gave them knowledge but the understanding to use that knowledge.

Therefore, no one will be able to stand before God on judgment day and say "God is not fair." He has given every person who has ever lived, regardless of how remote or isolated they may have been, the opportunity to know Him. They are without excuse.

Someone might say, "If all this is true, then why can't you observe more of this intuitive knowledge of God in the lives of those who have not heard the Gospel?" Paul gives the answer to this in verses 21-23.

Romans 1:19-20 - Because that which may be known of God is manifest in them; for God hath shewed it unto them. 20) For the invisible things of him from the creation of the world are clearly seen, being understood by the things that are made, even his eternal power and Godhead; so that they are without excuse:

(Rom. 1:20) The dictionary definition of the word "Godhead" is, "God, or the essential and divine nature of God." Therefore, Paul is stating that God has given every person an intuitive revelation of His divine nature. What a statement! And what a responsibility when men will have to stand before God and answer for the perversions they had perpetrated in the name of God. In their hearts, they knew better.

Romans 1:21-23 - Because that, when they knew God, they glorified him not as God, neither were thankful; but became vain in their imaginations, and their foolish heart was darkened. 22) Professing themselves to be wise, they became fools, 23) And changed the glory of the uncorruptible God into an image made like to corruptible man, and to birds, and fourfooted beasts, and creeping things.

(Rom. 1:21) As Paul explained in Romans 1:18-20, every person who has ever lived has had God reveal Himself to them, but this verse is explaining that revelation is not always received. Each individual has the freedom of choice.

In verses 21-23, Paul describes different characteristics of those who reject God's revelation. These could also be descriptive of progressive steps that one takes away from the true revelation of God.

The first step in rejecting God is not to glorify Him as the supreme, all knowing, unquestionable God. This is what happened with Adam and Eve in the Garden of Eden. They questioned God's intent behind His command (Gen. 3:1-6). They ceased to magnify and honor God as they once did. Submission to God as supreme is always humbling and therefore "self" rebels. This is very prevalent today.

Second, they were not thankful. This is always a sign that self is exalting itself above God. A selfless person can be content with very little. A self-centered person cannot be satisfied. Thankfulness is a sign of humility, and cultivating a life of thankfulness will help keep "self" in its proper place.

After these first two steps have been taken, then the individual's mind is freed to begin imagining foolish, wicked, and idolatrous thoughts. This leads to a hardened heart ("foolish heart was darkened") and becoming reprobate.

Romans 1:24 - Wherefore God also gave them up to uncleanness through the lusts of their own hearts, to dishonour their own bodies between themselves:

(Rom. 1:24) This phrase "God gave them up" is used twice in this passage (here and in verse 26) and the phrase "God gave them over" is used once (v. 28). These phrases are drawing on the fact that there is a God-given intuitive knowledge inside of everyone that would prevent them from committing such depraved acts. However, because of our free choice, God will not continue to force that restraint upon us against our will. If a person persists in rebellion against this conviction of God, He will give that person up to his or her own heart's lust.

Therefore, a person who is committing some of the terrible acts spoken of here (idolatry, homosexuality, etc.) and says that he or she has no conviction about it, is either lying (Rom. 1:18-20) or has been given over to a reprobate mind by God.

Romans 1:25-26 - Who changed the truth of God into a lie, and worshipped and served the creature more than the Creator, who is blessed for ever. Amen. 26) For this cause God gave them up unto vile affections: for even their women did change the natural use into that which is against nature:

(Rom. 1:26) Verses 26 and 27 are speaking of lesbianism and homosexuality. If any one could doubt the clear statements of the Old Testament scriptures that this is an abomination to God (Lev. 18:22, 20:13, and Deut. 23:17-18), then these scriptures should forever settle the question.

Romans 1:27 - And likewise also the men, leaving the natural use of the woman, burned in their lust one toward another; men with men working that which is unseemly, and receiving in themselves that recompence of their error which was meet.

(Rom. 1:27) This is speaking of the emotional and physical consequences of homosexuality. Paul here says these consequences are "meet." The word that Paul used (Gk.-"dei") is found in 100 verses, but it is only translated "meet" one other time in the New Testament (Luke 15:32). All other times the translation clearly denotes something that is necessary (behoved, must, need, needful, ought, oughtest, and should).

This implies that these consequences (such as disease) are prescribed payment for such acts. Add to this the use of the word "recompense" (meaning "payment or compensation for an act") in this same verse, and it clearly looks as if physical and emotional scars are God's judgment upon this sin.

These natural consequences of sin are not necessarily God's direct punishment on the individuals who commit these acts. Anyone who participates in homosexuality, which is expressly forbidden by God, is bringing punishment on himself. It's like the law of gravity. Many people are killed when they violate this God-given law, but it is not accurate to say God killed them. They killed themselves. There was no malice on God's part.

Likewise, God established natural laws governing sexual behavior. Marriage was given while man was still in a perfect state (Gen. 2), and it is very possible that God never imagined man perverting such a beautiful gift (Jer. 7:31). When one violates God's sexual order, that person is destroying him or herself just as surely as someone who tries to breathe under water or walk off a cliff.

This verse is saying that the devastation that many homosexuals experience in their bodies is an appropriate payment for someone who has willfully perverted the perfect gift of marriage that God gave to us before the Fall. But this does not mean that God hates homosexuals and is personally punishing them. If that were so, some of the diseases we see would not be selective. All homosexuals would contract these diseases.

No, these maladies occur naturally when God's perfect order is perverted. God hates homosexuality, but loves the individuals who are homosexuals. If homosexuals will turn to God and put faith in Jesus as their Savior, they can be saved just the same as anyone else.

Romans 1:28 - And even as they did not like to retain God in their knowledge, God gave them over to a reprobate mind, to do those things which are not convenient;

(Rom. 1:28) The reason they did not like to retain God in their knowledge is because the knowledge of God would have convicted them and restrained them from committing such acts. This is the same motivation behind the actions of those who oppose Christianity so strongly today. People want to sin without anyone convicting them.

The Greek word translated "reprobate" is "adokimos," and it means "undiscerning; not distinguishing; void of judgment." In this text it may be understood as "an abominable mind, a mind to be abhorred by God and man" (KSB).

This is describing the state of a person who has "passed the point of no return" with God. As the context explains, God has revealed Himself to every person who has ever walked the earth. But there comes a point where God's Spirit will not strive with man any longer (Gen. 6:3). When that happens, the individual is hopelessly damned, because no one can come to the Father except the Spirit draws him.

Therefore, a reprobate person is a person whom God has abandoned, and there is no hope of salvation for that person. Paul applied this term to Christians who had renounced their faith in Christ.

Some people may fear that they are reprobate because of some sin or blasphemy that they have uttered. However, as these verses describe, a reprobate person is past feeling, remorse, or conviction. If a man is repentant over some terrible action, then that is proof alone that the Spirit of God is still drawing him, and he is not reprobate. A reprobate person wouldn't care.

Romans 1:29 - Being filled with all unrighteousness, fornication, wickedness, covetousness, maliciousness; full of envy, murder, debate, deceit, malignity; whisperers,

(Rom. 1:29) It is very interesting to see some of the things included in this list of abominations that many people would not consider sin, or certainly not a "bad" sin like others on the list. For instance, the word "debate" means "to quarrel or argue." Some people think that is perfectly okay, but Paul lists it right along with murder and sexual sins.

The word "whisperers" means "gossips." A "backbiter" is a person who slanders the character, or reputation, of another when they are not present. Pride is listed among these sins that are an abomination to God as well as being disobedient to parents. A "covenant-breaker" is a person who cannot be trusted to keep his or her word.

The truth is, there are no little sins or acceptable sins. All unrighteousness is sin (1 John 5:17) and should be rejected.

Romans 1:30-31 - Backbiters, haters of God, despiteful, proud, boasters, inventors of evil things, disobedient to parents, 31) Without understanding, covenantbreakers, without natural affection, implacable, unmerciful:

(Rom. 1:31) Although this phrase "without natural affection" has been interpreted by many to mean homosexual acts, the Greek word suggests something different. The Greek word that is used is "astorgos" which literally means "hard-hearted towards kindred." This describes someone who is unloving and without the natural tenderness that a mother would express for her child. Therefore, Paul is describing a hardhearted person who is void of love and tenderness.

Romans 1:32 - Who knowing the judgment of God, that they which commit such things are worthy of death, not only do the same, but have pleasure in them that do them.

(Rom. 1:32) When God turns an individual over to a reprobate mind, they do not lose their knowledge of what's right and wrong; they just lose God's conviction about it. They still know they are wrong, but they don't care.

Romans 1:1-32
Discipleship Questions

. . . .

Answer the following questions by reading the corresponding discipleship commentary lesson and using your Bible.

1. In Romans 1:1, what three ways does Paul identify himself to the church at Rome?
   _____
   _____

2. Read Romans 1:1. What does the word "servant" imply?
   _____

3. What does the word "Lord" imply?
   _____

4. Read Romans 1:1. What is an apostle?
   _____

5. Read Romans 1:1. What does the phrase "separated unto the gospel of God" mean?
   _____
   _____

6. Read Romans 1:2. Notice that in the King James Version verse 2 is in parenthesis. What is Paul trying to amplify in verse 2?_____
   _____

7. Read Romans 1:3. According to this verse, what is the Gospel?
   _____

8. Read Romans 1:3. Concerning Jesus Christ's human nature, He was a descendant of whom?_____

9. Read Romans 1:4. According to this verse, who was Jesus Christ?
   _____

10. Read Romans 1:5. According to this verse, God granted Paul grace and apostleship for what purpose?_____
    _____

11. Romans 1:6 says that we are called to belong to Jesus Christ. What does the word "call" mean?_____

12. Read Romans 1:7. How did Paul describe these Roman Christians?_____
    _____
    _____

13. Read Romans 1:8. How was the Romans' Christian faith affecting the world?

_____

14. How did Paul serve God according to Romans 1:9?

_____

_____

15. Read Romans 1:9. What kind of prayer life did Paul have on behalf of others?

_____

16. Read Romans 1:11. Paul wanted to come to the Christians in Rome so that he might do what?_____

17. Read Romans 1:11. What was his desired result?

_____

_____

18. What else did Paul want to do according to Romans 1:12?

_____

_____

19. Read Romans 1:13. What was the purpose of Paul visiting Rome?

_____

_____

20. Read Romans 1:14-15. To whom did Paul want to communicate the Gospel?

_____

_____

21. Read Romans 1:16 (KJV). The Gospel is referred to as what?

_____

_____

22. Read Romans 1:16. The Gospel of Christ is the power of God to save whom?

_____

23. Read Romans 1:17. What is revealed within the Gospel?

_____

24. Read Romans 1:17. A right relationship with God is revealed, or made known, through what? _____

25. What is faith? _____

_____

_____

_____

_____

26. Read Romans 1:18. God's wrath is an expression of His goodness. For whatever stands against evil is good. According to Romans 1:18, the wrath of God is against what?

_____

27. What two things have been revealed in Romans 1:17-18?

_____

_____

28. Men hold the truth, or know the truth, even in their unrighteousness. Why is this so, according to Romans 1:19?

_____

_____

29. Read Romans 1:20 and Romans 2:14-15. Romans 1:20 can be described as revealing "general revelation." "General revelation" is what God has revealed to all mankind, to every individual. What two things is general revelation based upon?

_____

_____

30. Read Romans 1:20. What two things does God show about Himself through created things?

_____

_____

31. Read Romans 1:20. Does this make mankind, in some respect, accountable before God?

_____

32. Read Romans 1:21. How did mankind respond to this revelation about God?

_____

_____

_____

33. Read Romans 1:22. What did mankind now profess? To "profess" means, "to declare publicly." _____

34. Read Romans 1:22. In reality, what was mankind?

_____

35. Read Romans 1:23. Man changed the glory, splendor, and beauty of the incorruptible God into an image and likeness of what?

_____

_____

_____

36. Read Romans 1:24. Man turned from God, and God gave them up to what?

_____

37. Read Romans 1:24. This uncleanness manifested in what form? Also read Psalms 81:11-16._____

_____

38. According to Romans 1:25, man gave up divine truth for what?

_____

_____

39. Read Romans 1:25. What did men worship and serve more than the Creator?

_____

40. Read Romans 1:26. Romans 1:26 states, "For this cause," or "Because of this," God gave them up. To what does this phrase refer?

_____

_____

41. Read Romans 1:26-27. The consequence of these people's decisions resulted in what?

_____

_____

42. How is this behavior described in Romans 1:26-27?

_____

_____

43. Read Romans 1:28. According to Romans 1:28, what did man not want to do?

_____

44. What does the word "retain" mean?

_____

45. Read Romans 1:28. As a result of man's choice, what did God do?

_____

_____

_____

46. What is the result of having one's mind depraved?

_____

_____

47. Read Romans 1:29-31. As a result of man not glorifying God, not being thankful, and not wanting to keep God in their knowledge, mankind became **filled** with what?

_____

_____

_____

_____

_____

48. God gave a revelation of Himself through creation. His eternal power and deity was made known. What other revelation does mankind have according to Romans 1:32?

    _____

    _____

49. Read Romans 1:32. Man's actions described in Romans 1:29-31 carry what penalty?

    _____

50. Not only does mankind continue in his own sinful lifestyle (in the light of knowing his wrong), but he also has pleasure in what?

    _____

Romans 1:1-32
Discipleship Answer Key

. . . .

Do not look at the answer key until you have completed the questions.
Compare your answers with the following answers.

1. In Romans 1:1, what three ways does Paul identify himself to the church at Rome?
   1. As a servant.
   2. As an apostle.
   3. As one separated unto the Gospel.

2. Read Romans 1:1. What does the word "servant" imply?
   Someone who expresses submission, obedience or debt to another.

3. What does the word "Lord" imply?
   The opposite of the word "servant." Someone who is the master.

4. Read Romans 1:1. What is an apostle?
   "One who is sent" with a message from Divine authority.

5. Read Romans 1:1. What does the phrase "separated unto the gospel of God" mean?
   Specially chosen to preach the good news of God.

6. Read Romans 1:2. Notice that in the King James Version verse 2 is in parenthesis. What is Paul trying to amplify in verse 2?
   Paul is stating that the Gospel is not some kind of new religion, but was promised long ago by God's prophets in the Scriptures.

7. What is the Gospel according to Romans 1:3? Also read Romans 1:16 (KJV).
   It is the good news about God's Son, Jesus Christ.

8. Read Romans 1:3. Concerning Jesus Christ's human nature, He was a descendant of whom? Also read Isaiah 9:6-7.
   David.

9. Who was Jesus Christ, according to Romans 1:4?
   The Son of God with power.

10. According to Romans 1:5, God granted Paul grace and apostleship for what purpose?
    To call people from among all the nations to obedience to the Christian faith.

11. Romans 1:6 says that we are called to belong to Jesus Christ. What does the word "call" mean?
    Invited by God to belong to Jesus Christ and obtain eternal salvation.

12. How did Paul describe the Christians in Romans 1:7?
   1. As "beloved of God" i.e. the ones God loves or the object of His love.
   2. As "saints," i.e., designated to be set apart unto God.

13. How was the Romans' Christian faith affecting the world? See Romans 1:8.
   The whole world was hearing of their faith.

14. How did Paul serve God according to Romans 1:9?
   1. With his spirit, i.e., with his whole heart.
   2. In the Gospel of His Son, or in preaching the Gospel of His Son.

15. Read Romans 1:9. What kind of prayer life did Paul have on behalf of others?
   He always made mention of others in his prayers.

16. Read Romans 1:11. Paul wanted to come to the Christians in Rome so that he might do what?
   Impart unto them some spiritual gift.

17. Read Romans 1:11. What was his desired result?
   That they would be strengthened.

18. What else did Paul want to do according to Romans 1:12?
   Be mutually encouraged by each other's faith. Paul was not a one-man show needing no one else.

19. Read Romans 1:13. What was the purpose of Paul visiting Rome?
   To see fruit produced. Today's English Version says, "to win converts among you... as I have among other Gentiles" (Romans 1:13b).

20. Read Romans 1:14-15. To whom did Paul want to communicate the Gospel?
   To everyone: Greeks and non-Greeks, educated and ignorant, and to the people of Rome.

21. Read Romans 1:16 (KJV). The Gospel is referred to as what?
   The Gospel of Christ. The good news is Jesus Christ and His redemptive work.

22. Read Romans 1:16.The Gospel of Christ is the power of God to save whom?
   Everyone that believeth.

23. Read Romans 1:17. What is revealed within the Gospel?
   Righteousness, or right-relationship with God.

24. Read Romans 1:17. A right relationship with God is revealed, or made known through what?
   Faith.

25. What is faith?

To place confidence in, to trust, to rely upon, to commit something trustfully to, to deliver a person into the charge of another. The Amplified Bible states, "Believe in the Lord Jesus Christ [give yourself up to Him, take yourself out of your own keeping and entrust yourself into His keeping] and you will be saved..." (Acts 16:31).

26. Read Romans 1:18. God's wrath is an expression of His goodness. For whatever stands against evil is good. According to Romans 1:18, the wrath of God is against what?

All ungodliness and unrighteousness.

27. What two things have been revealed in Romans 1:17-18?

1. Righteousness through the Gospel.
2. Wrath against the ungodliness and unrighteousness of men.

28. Men hold the truth, or know the truth, even in their unrighteousness. Why is this so, according to Romans 1:19?

For God has shown a certain amount of truth to them—enough to make them accountable before Him.

29. Read Romans 1:20 and Romans 2:14-15. Romans 1:20 can be described as revealing "general revelation." "General revelation" is what God has revealed to all mankind, to every individual. What two things is general revelation based upon?

1. Created things.
2. The conscience (the inward knowledge of right and wrong).

30. Read Romans 1:20. What two things does God show about Himself through created things?

1. His eternal power.
2. The Godhead i.e. His Deity.

31. Read Romans 1:20. Does this make mankind, in some respect, accountable before God?

Romans 1:20 says, "so they (mankind) are without excuse."

32. Read Romans 1:21. How did mankind respond to this revelation about God?

1. They glorified Him not as God.
2. They were not thankful.
3. They became vain (empty, lacking substance) in their imaginations (thought processes).
4. Their foolish heart (mind, thoughts) was darkened (because they had shut out the light).

33. Read Romans 1:22. What did mankind now profess? To "profess" means, "to declare publicly."

To be wise.

34. Read Romans 1:22. In reality, what were mankind?

Fools. Lacking discernment and understanding.

35. Read Romans 1:23. Man changed the glory, splendor, and beauty of the uncorruptible God into an image and likeness of what?
    1. Corruptible (depraved) man.
    2. Birds.
    3. Fourfooted beasts i.e. animals.
    4. Creeping things, i.e., reptiles. Idolatry is not a form of man seeking for God but rather a result of man turning from God.

36. Read Romans 1:24. Man turned from God, and God gave them up to what?
    Uncleanness (to be morally defiled).

37. Read Romans 1:24. This uncleanness manifested in what form? Also read Psalms 81:11-16.
    Men dishonoring their own bodies between themselves. Sin will take you farther than you want to go.

38. According to Romans 1:25, man gave up divine truth for what?
    A lie. The Living Bible states, " Instead of believing what they knew was the truth about God, they deliberately chose to believe lies" (Rom. 1:25a).

39. Read Romans 1:25. What did men worship and serve more than the Creator?
    The creature, i.e., created things.

40. Read Romans 1:26. Romans 1:26 states, "For this cause," or "Because of this," God gave them up. To what does this phrase refer?
    It refers to Romans 1:25:
    1. Because they changed the truth about God into a lie.
    2. Because they worshipped and served what God had created instead of the Creator.

41. Read Romans 1:26-27. The consequence of the people's decisions resulted in what?
    Vile affections. The Greek word is "PATHOS," from which we get our word "pathological," or a disorder in behavior.

42. How is this behavior described in Romans 1:26-27?
    Perversion. Being inflamed with lust, natural relations were exchanged for unnatural ones.

43. Read Romans 1:28. According to Romans 1:28, what did man not want to do?
    Retain God in their knowledge.

44. What does the word "retain" mean?
    To keep.

45. Read Romans 1:28. As a result of man's choice, what did God do?
He gave them over to a reprobate mind. Reprobate in Greek is "ADOKIMOS" and means "not standing the test, rejected." It is used of land that bears thorns and thistles (Vine's). It's a mind that God cannot approve, and must be rejected by Him. It is like God is saying, "If this is what you want, then you can have it."

46. What is the result of having one's mind depraved?
To do those things which are not convenient. The words "not convenient" mean "not fitting, proper, or appropriate."

Statement: When you choose sin, you must put God out of your mind.

47. Read Romans 1:29-31. As a result of man not glorifying God, not being thankful, and not wanting to keep God in their knowledge, mankind became **filled** with what?
Unrighteousness, fornication, wickedness, covetousness (greed), maliciousness (the desire to harm others or to see others suffer, ill will, spite), envy (jealously), murder, debate (quarrel, argue), deceit (deception, to trick), malignity (intense ill will or hatred, great malice), whisperers (gossips), backbiters (to slander the character or reputation of others), haters of God, despiteful (an act of defiance, insult, offense), proud (arrogant), boasters (brag, pride), inventors of evil things, disobedient to parents, without understanding, covenant breakers (untrustworthy), without natural affection, (unloving), implacable (incapable of appeasement), unmerciful.

48. God gave a revelation of Himself through creation. His eternal power and deity was made known. What other revelation does mankind have according to Romans 1:32?
A revelation of accountability before God. Romans 1:32 says, "Who knowing the judgment of God."

49. Read Romans 1:32. Man's actions described in Romans 1:29-31 carry what penalty?
Death (separation from God forever, 2 Thessalonians 1:9).

50. Not only does mankind continue in his own sinful lifestyle (in the light of knowing his wrong), but he also has pleasure in what?
Others that do the same things.

OVERVIEW OF ROMANS CHAPTER 2

by Don Krow

"Therefore, thou art inexcusable, O man, whosoever thou art that judgest: for wherein thou judgest another, thou condemnest thyself; for thou that judgest doest the same things. But we are sure that the judgment of God is according to truth against them which commit such things." (Romans 2:1-2).

In Romans 1 we have seen that God gave a revelation of Himself through creation to mankind. Two things were revealed: God's eternal power and His deity. Man did not respond to that in a positive way; therefore, he turned from light and went into darkness. Paul said in Romans 1 that man became filled with unrighteousness, fornication, and all kinds of sin.

When we begin Romans 2, what we see is a person who is saying, "That's right, Paul, these people turned away from the truth about God's creation and revelation about God Himself, but I'm not like that. I'm a religious person; I have the law, and I keep it." Paul is beginning here to prosecute the religious person, and the way he does it is to say "You are inexcusable because when you judge another person, you yourself do the same things."

I have often thought, "Do I really do the things done by all the people in the world? I was raised in a religious setting … in a church. Do I do those things?" When Jesus interprets the law in Matthew 5:22, He said if you become angry with a brother without cause, it is the spirit of murder—the same as committing a murder. The Bible says if you, in your heart, lust after a woman, it is the same as committing adultery with her in your heart. In Exodus 20 the law says that we shouldn't even covet, which means we shouldn't even have a desire.

Paul is saying that when we judge other people and say, "God, look what that person is doing," we ourselves are coming under judgment in the sense that when we look down on others, we need to realize that we do the same kind of thing. If we haven't done it outwardly, we have done it inwardly in our hearts. Paul says in Romans 2:2 that God's judgment is going to be according to truth, according to the way things really are.

Verse 3: *"And thinkest thou this, O man, that judgest them which do such things, and doest the same, that thou shalt escape the judgment of God?"* The answer is no.

Verse 4: *"Or despisest thou the riches of his goodness and forbearance and longsuffering; not knowing that the goodness of God leadeth thee to repentance?"* The reason God's goodness (a word that means kindness) is leading people to repentance is that He doesn't want to bring judgment. There will be a day, according to Acts 17:31, in which God will judge the world in righteousness by the man Christ Jesus, but right now is a day of grace, a day when God is not bringing judgment upon mankind. He brought that judgment on Jesus Christ on the cross, and now He is operating in forbearance. He is withholding judgment on man.

Paul is saying that God's goodness, forbearance, and longsuffering are giving man time to repent. God's kindness right now is to lead you to repentance. He is not willing that any should perish, but that all should come to repentance.

Verse 5: *"But after thy hardness and impenitent heart treasurest up unto thyself wrath against the day of wrath and revelation of the righteous judgment of God."* Paul is talking here about a person who is rejecting the truth … the Gospel … and it says in one's hardness and unrepentant heart that person is treasuring up for him or herself wrath against the day of wrath. There will be a day of wrath and a revelation of the righteous judgment of God and, because of the hardness of their unrepentant hearts, people are storing up wrath for a revelation against the day of wrath. That's not happening to them now, but in the day of judgment, this is what is going to happen.

Verse 6: *"Who will render to every man according to what he has done."* Salvation is by grace, but judgment is according to what people have done. No one is going to get away with anything. We have injustice in our systems in the United States. Many times an innocent person may go to prison or a guilty person will fail to serve any sentence at all. But in the day of God's judgment, the Bible says here that God will render to every man according to what he has done. The only way to escape is to come through the blood of the Lord Jesus (Romans 5:9) and be justified … declared righteous by His blood … and we shall be saved from this wrath.

Verses 7-11: *To them who by patient continuance in well doing seek for glory and honour and immortality, eternal life: But unto them that are contentious, and do not obey the truth, but obey unrighteousness, indignation and wrath, Tribulation and anguish, upon every soul of man that doeth evil, of the Jew first, and also of the Gentile; But glory, honour, and peace, to every man that worketh good, to the Jew first, and also to the Gentile: For there is no respect of persons with God."* There is a contrast here between the unbeliever, who in his unrepentant state and hardness of heart will receive in judgment according to what he or she has done, and the believer, who in patient continuance has done what is right, i.e., he or she has a heart of repentance. He is seeking glory, honor, and immortality, and God will give to that person eternal life. But to those who are contentious and do not obey the truth, there will be unrighteousness, indignation, and wrath against the day of wrath in the revelation of the righteous judgment of God. Verse 11 says there is no partiality, no respect of persons with God.

Verse 12: *"For as many as have sinned without law shall also perish without law: and as many as have sinned in the law shall be judged by the law."* There are two kinds of people here: One has the law and the other doesn't. Paul says those who have sinned without the law will perish, but those who have the law and have not obeyed it, also will perish. This means that no one has ever adequately lived up to the light that God has given them. The Jew who had the law of Moses had never lived up to it. The Gentile, who had not the law of Moses, had the work of the law—that person's conscience revealed right and wrong, but he or she did not live up to that law.

Verse 13: *"(For not the hearers of the law are just before God, but the doers of the law shall be justified."* A person must turn from one's own way, to God and His way, in repentance, in order to be declared righteous before God.

Verses 14-16: *For when the Gentiles, which have not the law, do by nature the things contained in the law, these, having not the law, are a law unto themselves; Which shew the work of the law written in their hearts, their conscience also bearing witness, and their thoughts the mean while accusing or else excusing one another;) In the day when God shall judge the secrets of men by Jesus Christ according to my gospel."* Again this is basically saying that the Jew had the law, and the Gentiles did not have the law but had something that worked like the law in their hearts, their conscience. That conscience never declared them right but always condemned them of the things they were not doing. They were found guilty through their conscience.

Paul is trying to bring all men, regardless of who they are, under guilt and condemnation so they might come and see their need of a Savior and flee to the grace of God as a means of being righteous before Him.

Verses 17-20: *Behold, thou art called a Jew, and restest in the law, and makest thy boast of God, And knowest his will, and approvest the things that are more excellent, being instructed out of the law, And art confident that thou thyself art a guide of the blind, a light of them which are in darkness, An instructor of the foolish, a teacher of babes, which hast the form of knowledge and of the truth in the law."* This religious person had the law, embraced it, showed people how they must live, and bragged that he or she had a relationship with God. Let's look at the questions Paul asked this person.

Verses 21-22: *"Thou therefore which teachest another, teachest thou not thyself? thou that preachest a man should not steal, dost thou steal? Thou that sayest a man should not commit adultery, dost thou commit adultery? Thou that abhorrest idols, dost thou commit sacrilege?"* He said, "You are teaching other people, but you yourself are not living up to what you teach, what you preach. You who preach that a man should not steal, do you steal? You who say a man should not commit adultery, do you commit adultery? You who abhor idols, do you commit sacrilege?"

Paul is saying that even though people have understood what God required, no one lived up to the requirements He demands; therefore, this has brought them, even their conscience within them, to an understanding of guilt before God. This is the foundation of coming to a Savior and saying, "God, I can't keep your law, I'm unable to do this. I need a Savior."

Verses 23-24: *"Thou that makest thy boast of the law, through breaking the law dishonourest thou God? For the name of God is blasphemed among the Gentiles through you, as it is written."* Paul is saying, "The way you live is causing people to think less of God by your actions."

Verse 25: *"For circumcision verily profiteth, if thou keep the law: but if thou be a breaker of the law, thy circumcision is made uncircumcision."* Circumcision is an outward action of the inward reality of righteousness by faith. Romans 4 will tell us that. But if you have the outward act, the religious symbol and don't have the reality in your heart—a changed heart toward God—then you really have nothing.

Verse 26: *"Therefore if the uncircumcision keep the righteousness of the law, shall not his uncircumcision be counted for circumcision?"* If a person has the inward reality of true faith towards God, yet doesn't have the outward religious act of circumcision, baptism, or some of these other ordinances, the reality of that which symbolizes them in the heart will make him or her acceptable before God.

Verses 27-29: *"And shall not uncircumcision which is by nature, if it fulfil the law, judge thee, who by the letter and circumcision dost transgress the law? For he is not a Jew, which is one outwardly; neither is that circumcision, which is outward in the flesh. But he is a Jew, which is one inwardly; and circumcision is that of the heart, in the spirit, and not in the letter; whose praise is not of men, but of God."* What Paul is saying is that a true person of God, a true Christian, is not one outwardly (by doing outward things) but is one inwardly (has had a change of heart inwardly, circumcision of the heart in the person's spirit). This is what makes a true child of God —an inward change that has turned to Jesus Christ in faith and had a change of heart. That is how Paul concludes Romans 2.

Romans 2:1-29
Discipleship Commentary

Read the entire lesson and then answer the questions that follow.

Romans 2:1 - Therefore thou art inexcusable, O man, whosoever thou art that judgest: for wherein thou judgest another, thou condemnest thyself; for thou that judgest doest the same things.

(Rom. 2:1) In the preceding chapter, Paul had conclusively proved that the Gentiles were guilty before God. They had no excuse for their vile actions (Rom. 1:20). This, no doubt, pleased the Jews. That's exactly what they believed and what they had been arguing. They maintained that unless these Gentiles converted to Judaism and observed the law of Moses (specifically the law of circumcision), they could not be saved.

However, after Paul had taken full advantage of the Jews' prejudice, he turns his arguments to the Jews, showing them that they are just as guilty or even more guilty than the Gentiles. He ends this chapter with statements about the Gentiles' faith being superior to the Jews' circumcision and concludes that a true Jew is born of faith, not of the flesh (Rom. 2:28-29).

Thus, the second chapter proves the Jews, or religious person, just as guilty before God as the heathen. Then in the third chapter Paul draws this all together by proclaiming that since everyone, Jew and Gentile, is in "the same boat," then all can be saved by one method of salvation, through faith.

From a human perspective, some people have obtained a level of holiness that gives them the right to judge others. However, when viewed from God's standpoint, we are all sinners and one sinner has no justification for condemning a fellow sinner. We may not be doing the exact same transgressions, but we are guilty of being lawbreakers (Jas. 2:10) and are, therefore, disqualified from being the judge.

Also, whenever a man condemns another, he is showing that he has a knowledge of right and wrong and therefore can no longer claim ignorance for his own offenses. As verse two explains, we are better off to leave the judging to God.

The Greek word that is rendered "judgest" three times in this verse and once in verse three is the word "krino." It is speaking of a harsh, condemning type of judging that was warned against in Matthew 7:1. There is a Greek word "anakrino," which signifies discernment, which is encouraged in Scripture

Romans 2:2-3 - But we are sure that the judgment of God is according to truth against them which commit such things. 3) And thinkest thou this, O man, that judgest them which do such things, and doest the same, that thou shalt escape the judgment of God?

(Rom. 2:3) These pious Jews could have argued with Paul that they were not committing the same sins that these heathens were, but in reality they were committing the same sins. They may not have worshiped idols, but they were covetous, which Colossians 3:5 reveals is idolatry. They may not have committed adultery, but they had lusted in their hearts, which Jesus said was equal to adultery (Matt. 5:28). They may not have murdered anyone, but they had hated, which was the same root sin (Matt. 5:21-22).

When viewed in this way, judgment for others disappears and mercy comes to light.

Romans 2:4 - Or despisest thou the riches of his goodness and forbearance and longsuffering; not knowing that the goodness of God leadeth thee to repentance?

(Rom. 2:4) This is a radical statement that the Jews of Paul's day and the religious legalists of our day reject. They refuse to accept that the goodness of God is sufficient motivation for people to turn from sin. They insist that fear of punishment is a superior motivator.

It is true that fear is a more familiar motivator to most people. Even a lost man or carnal Christian can identify with fear and respond to it. But as 1 John 4:18 states, "fear hath torment." Those who respond to God through fear will also be tormented with thoughts of doubt and condemnation, as to whether they have done enough. Fear will move some toward God, but it is inferior to love. There is nothing that fear can do that love can't do better and without the side effect of torment.

Those who were motivated to seek God because of fear if they didn't, will cease to be motivated when things are going good. They become the ones who only pray when they are in trouble. Those who come to God because of His goodness will see God as the source of their success and continue to serve God in the good and the bad times.

The world, and especially religion, has used negative reasons to motivate people. The Gospel uses the positive reason of God's great love to draw men unto God. We need to renew our minds to line up with God's thinking.

Romans 2:5 - But after thy hardness and impenitent heart treasurest up unto thyself wrath against the day of wrath and revelation of the righteous judgment of God;

(Rom. 2:5) The Apostle James said, "For he shall have judgment without mercy, that hath shewed no mercy; and mercy rejoiceth against judgment" (James 2:13). Those who show mercy will be shown mercy; but those who are hardhearted and unmerciful will reap the same when they stand before the judgment seat of God.

Romans 2:6-13 - Who will render to every man according to his deeds: 7) To them who by patient continuance in well doing seek for glory and honour and immortality, eternal life: 8) But unto them that are contentious, and do not obey the truth, but obey unrighteousness, indignation and wrath, 9) Tribulation and anguish, upon every soul of man that doeth evil, of the Jew first, and also of the Gentile; 10) But glory, honour, and peace, to every man that worketh good, to the Jew first, and also to the Gentile: 11) For there is no respect of persons with God. 12) For as many as have sinned without law shall also perish without law: and as many as have sinned in the law shall be judged by the law; 13) (For not the hearers of the law are just before God, but the doers of the law shall be justified.

(Rom. 2:6) Verses 6-16 are speaking of the final judgment of God at the end of this world. The Lord will judge us and render a due reward according to every man's work. Although this is true, some have taken these scriptures to mean the opposite of what Paul is saying in context here.

In context, we see that Paul is preaching that Jews and Gentiles alike have all sinned and come short of the glory of God (Rom. 3:23). Therefore, no one can be saved by works (Rom. 3:20). The only way to be saved is through faith in Jesus and what He did for us (Rom. 3:24-28). Therefore, these verses cannot be contradicting everything else that Paul is saying by proclaiming that acceptance by God is based on performance.

No, the action that will be rewarded with eternal life is the action of faith (John 3:16). Faith alone saves, but saving faith is never alone. True faith has actions (James 2:17-20). The Greek word that is translated "do not obey" in verse 8 means, "to disbelieve (willfully and perversely): not believe; unbelieving." So it is faith that is the issue, even though actions are being spoken of.

Therefore, to those whose faith is causing them to patiently continue in well doing (v. 7), they will receive eternal life. But to those whose rejection of God's mercy causes them to disobey (disbelieve) the truth, they will receive indignation and wrath, tribulation and anguish (vv. 8-9).

Romans 2:14 - For when the Gentiles, which have not the law, do by nature the things contained in the law, these, having not the law, are a law unto themselves:

(Rom. 2:14) This is speaking of this intuitive knowledge of God described in chapter 1.

Romans 2:15 - Which shew the work of the law written in their hearts, their conscience also bearing witness, and their thoughts the mean while accusing or else excusing one another;)

(Rom. 2:15) Our conscience is the part of us that bears witness as to what is right and wrong. This happens through our thoughts either accusing or excusing us. Our conscience is a part of our soul, which can be deduced from the fact that even a Christian's conscience can be defiled (1 Cor. 8:7), evil (Heb. 10:22), and weak (1 Cor. 8:7,10), which the born-again spirit cannot be (see note 3 at Mt. 26:41, p. 507).

A good conscience is essential to faith. Without a good conscience, our faith is made shipwrecked (1 Tim. 1:19). A good conscience produces confidence (1 John 3:21, Heb. 10:35). An evil conscience condemns us (1 John 3:20).

It is possible that God created man without a conscience and that the conscience was acquired through the tree of the knowledge of good and evil. The name of that tree is descriptive of the function of the conscience.

The conscience is referred to by name 32 times in 30 verses in the New Testament (John 8:9; Acts 23:1, 24:16; Rom. 2:15, 9:1, 13:5; 1 Cor. 8:7, 10, 12, 10:25, 27-29; 2 Cor. 1:12, 4:2, 5:11; 1 Tim. 1:5, 19, 3:9, 4:2, 2 Tim. 1:3; Titus 1:15; Heb. 9:9, 14, 10:2, 22, 13:18; and 1 Pet. 2:19, 3:16, 21).

Romans 2:16 - In the day when God shall judge the secrets of men by Jesus Christ according to my gospel.

(Rom. 2:16) This is quite a statement of authenticity for the Gospel which Paul preached. God didn't get His understanding of the Gospel from Paul, but Paul received his revelation of the Gospel from God. He was so sure of this that he could make statements like this, and that of Galatians 1:8-12.

Romans 2:17 - Behold, thou art called a Jew, and restest in the law, and makest thy boast of God,

(Rom. 2:17) It is true that the Jews had been given the Word of God which gave them a superior knowledge of God. However, since they had not kept the law, their superior knowledge had just made them more accountable than other people.

Romans 2:18-21 - And knowest his will, and approvest the things that are more excellent, being instructed out of the law; 19) And art confident that thou thyself art a guide of the blind, a light of them which are in darkness, 20) An instructor of the foolish, a teacher of babes, which hast the form of knowledge and of the truth in the law. 21) Thou therefore which teachest another, teachest thou not thyself? thou that preachest a man should not steal, dost thou steal?

(Rom. 2:21) The Jews took pride in their keeping of the law but there wasn't any Jew who could boast that he or she had kept the law perfectly. "All have sinned, and come short of the glory of God" (Rom. 3:23). Paul highlights three areas in which they boasted of their own holiness, but he reveals that they were actually sinners in these very things.

They boasted that they didn't steal, but Paul reveals that they did steal. Jesus also rebuked the Pharisees for stealing. This is not the typical type of theft but what we would call "white-collar crime."

Paul says that they were adulterers even though they prided themselves on not committing adultery. They were guilty of spiritual adultery if nothing else (James 4:4) and Jesus had revealed that adultery was also a sin of the heart, even if there was no action (Matt. 5:28).

They also thought they were not idolatrous, but Paul convicts them on this count also. He uses the word "sacrilege," which refers to them being temple robbers, thereby making direct reference to their covetousness, which is idolatry (Col. 3:5).

Therefore, even though they had a form of godliness, they were sinners just like the Gentiles, and their hypocrisy gave the Gentiles a reason to blaspheme God. This leads Paul to proclaim that the Jews' claim to some kind of special covenant with God is made void through their breaking of the law. In the third chapter of Romans, he goes on to draw the conclusion that everyone, Jew and Gentile, is in the same condition of sin and needs salvation through Christ.

Romans 2:22-25 - Thou that sayest a man should not commit adultery, dost thou commit adultery? thou that abhorrest idols, dost thou commit sacrilege? 23) Thou that makest thy boast of the law, through breaking the law dishonourest thou God? 24) For the name of God is blasphemed among the Gentiles through you, as it is written. 25) For circumcision verily profiteth, if thou keep the law: but if thou be a breaker of the law, thy circumcision is made uncircumcision.

(Rom. 2:25) If a Jew could keep the law perfectly, then the Jewish covenant that was sealed with the sign of circumcision would give that person an advantage over others. But that has never and can never happen. No one can keep the law, and the law was not given to provide a way to God. Therefore, because no Jew has ever kept the law perfectly, they are the same as uncircumcised in the sight of God.

Romans 2:26 - Therefore if the uncircumcision keep the righteousness of the law, shall not his uncircumcision be counted for circumcision?

(Rom. 2:26) Notice that Paul did not say that the uncircumcision kept the law. Instead he mentions them keeping the "righteousness" of the law and "fulfilling" the law (v. 27). There is a difference. A person can fulfill the righteousness of the law through faith in Jesus, but no one, Jew nor Gentile, can keep the law.

Romans 2:27-28 - And shall not uncircumcision which is by nature, if it fulfil the law, judge thee, who by the letter and circumcision dost transgress the law? 28) For he is not a Jew, which is one outwardly; neither is that circumcision, which is outward in the flesh:

(Rom. 2:28) As with so many commandments of the Old Testament, circumcision was an outward sign of a greater inward reality. Paul uses this term "sign" in referring to the circumcision of Abraham in Romans 4:11. The Jews of the first century had ignored the circumcision of the heart and had focused all their attention on the flesh (1 Sam. 16:7). Paul is clarifying that it is the condition of the heart that makes someone a child of God, not the flesh.

Romans 2:29 - But he is a Jew, which is one inwardly; and circumcision is that of the heart, in the spirit, and not in the letter; whose praise is not of men, but of God.

(Rom. 2:29) This is a remarkable statement. Paul is saying that those who have been born again through faith in Jesus have been circumcised in their hearts (Col. 2:11-12) and are the true Jews. They aren't Jews in nationality or religion, but they are the true people of God. Paul deals with this in more detail in Romans 9 and clearly makes a case that Gentiles who are united with Christ in the new birth are now God's people. Paul makes the same point in Galatians 3, saying that anyone who is saved through faith in Jesus is now Abraham's seed and heirs according to the promise (Gal. 3:16, 22, 26-29). This leaves no doubt that the church is now God's chosen people on earth.

This does not mean that God has forsaken the Jews. Paul once again deals with that issue in Romans 9. There are still prophesies which apply to the physical nation of Israel, which will be fulfilled. However, the New Testament church composed of Jews and Gentiles, is now God's kingdom on earth.

Paul's statement here definitely places the spirit in the heart of man. This has led some to believe that the heart and spirit are the same, but 1 Peter 3:4 refers to the spirit of man as the hidden man of the heart, implying that the spirit comprises only a part of the heart. The heart of man is actually made up of two parts, the soul and the spirit. This is the reason the Scripture speaks of having two minds in our hearts (James 4:8) and why we must believe with all our hearts (Acts 8:37), not just a part.

The Greek word that is used here for "letter" is "gramma" and literally means, "a writing; i.e. a letter, epistle, book, etc." Paul is saying that circumcision is spiritual rather than natural. True circumcision is a born-again nature and not a mark in the flesh.

Romans 2:1-29
Discipleship Questions

. . . .

Answer the following questions by reading the corresponding
discipleship commentary lesson and using your Bible.

1. Read Romans 2:1. Why are we inexcusable when we judge others?

   _____

2. Read Romans 2:2-3. God will judge those who do wrong. We know that His judgment is right. We judge others who do wrong, but we do wrong ourselves. Do you think we can avoid God's judgment?

   _____

   _____

3. Read Romans 2:4. Many people think they will avoid judgment. Why? Also read 2 Peter 3:9.

   _____

   _____

4. Read Romans 2:5. What four things is Romans 2:5 stating?

   _____

   _____

   _____

   _____

5. How is a person saved according to Ephesians 2:8?

   _____

6. Read Romans 2:6. Judgment is according to what?

   _____

   _____

7. Some say that God will only deal with the sin of unbelief. Does Romans 2:6 teach this?

   _____

   _____

   _____

8. Sometimes when the Bible speaks of salvation it speaks in terms of the good works that every saved person shows in his or her life (Matthew 7:21). What fruit is being expressed in the believer in Romans 2:7?

   _____

   _____

9. Read Acts 26:20 in The New International Version. What is the fruit of repentance according to Acts 26:20?

_____

_____

10. What two groups of people are mentioned in Romans 2:8-10?

_____

_____

_____

11. According to Romans 2:11, does God show partiality in His judging?

_____

_____

_____

12. In Romans 2:12, what two kinds of people are mentioned?

_____

13. Read Romans 2:13. What must a person do if he or she is going to be saved by the law?

_____

14. Has anyone lived up to God's law, or even the law of one's own conscience?

_____

15. How does Romans 2:15 show that people cannot live up to the law?

_____

_____

16. Read Romans 2:16. What will God bring to light in judgment?

_____

17. Read Romans 2:17. What is the person in Romans 2:17 called?

_____

_____

18. Read Romans 2:17. On what did this person's faith rest?

_____

19. Read Romans 2:17. This person bragged about what?

_____

_____

20. Read Romans 2:18. According to Romans 2:18, did this religious person know God's will?

_____

21. Read Romans 2:18. Did this religious person know the difference between good and evil, moral and immoral? _____

22. Read Romans 2:18. How was this religious person instructed?

_____

_____

23. What are the claims of the religious person in Romans 2:19?

_____

_____

24. Read Romans 2:20. What else did the religious person claim?

_____

_____

_____

25. What two questions does the Apostle Paul ask the religious person in Romans 2:21?

_____

_____

26. What two questions does the Apostle Paul ask in Romans 2:22?

_____

_____

27. What question does the Apostle Paul ask the religious person in Romans 2:23?

_____

_____

_____

28. Romans 2:24 is a quotation from Isaiah 52:5 (LXX). How could we paraphrase the meaning of Romans 2:24?

_____

_____

29. Read Romans 2:25. What scriptural principle can we learn from the phrase, "Circumcision verily profiteth, if thou keep the law"?

_____

_____

_____

30. Read Romans 2:25. What scriptural principle can we derive from the phrase, "If thou be a breaker of the law, thy circumcision is made uncircumcision"?

_____

_____

31. Read Romans 2:26. What scriptural principle do we learn from Romans 2:26?

_____

_____

32. Read Romans 2:27. What scriptural principle do we learn from Romans 2:27?

_____

_____

33. Read Romans 2:28-29. What does it mean to be a true Jew according to Romans 2:28-29?

_____

34. Read Romans 2:28-29. What is the meaning of Romans 2:28-29?

_____

_____

_____

Romans 2:1-29
Discipleship Answer Key

. . . .

Do not look at the answer key until you have completed the questions.
Compare your answers with the following answers.

1. Read Romans 2:1. Why are we inexcusable when we judge others?
   For we that judge do the same things.
   Consider murder and anger (Matthew 5:21-22), adultery and lust (Matthew 5:27-28), and coveting (Exodus 20:17).

2. Read Romans 2:2-3. God will judge those who do wrong. We know that His judgment is right. We judge others who do wrong, but we do wrong ourselves. Do you think we can avoid God's judgment?

3. Read Romans 2:4. Many people think they will avoid judgment. Why?
   Because God is patient and longsuffering. In His goodness He patiently waits for men to repent (See 2 Peter 3:9).

4. Read Romans 2:5. What four things is Romans 2:5 stating? Also read Acts 17:30-31 and Acts 24:25).
   1. Men have stubborn, unyielding, and unrepentant hearts.
   2. They're storing up against themselves wrath (divine retribution, eternal punishment) on the day of wrath.
   3. There will be a revealing of God's righteous judgment. (It is not revealed now; God's goodness, patience, and longsuffering are).
   4. There will be a Day that man without Christ will be accountable.

5. How is a person saved according to Ephesians 2:8?
   Salvation is by grace through faith.

6. Read Romans 2:6. Judgment is according to what?
   Judgment is according to what people have done (their works). People who have not accepted God's deliverance from judgment through faith in Jesus' blood (Romans 5:9) will be judged for the things they have done (their deeds).

7. Some say that God will only deal with the sin of unbelief. Does Romans 2:6 teach this?

8. Sometimes when the Bible speaks of salvation it speaks in terms of the good works that every saved person shows in his or her life (Matthew 7:21). What fruit is being expressed in the believer in Romans 2:7?
   Patient continuance in doing what is right. Seeking glory, honor and immortality, those will be given eternal life. This is the fruit of a saved person.

9. What is the fruit of repentance according to Acts 26:20? See Acts 26:20 in The New International Version.
Good works, i.e., works of faith (works produced as a byproduct of faith).

10. What two groups of people are mentioned in Romans 2:8-10?
The believer and the unbeliever. One group fights against the truth (Rom. 2:8). One group obeys the truth, leading to a change that produces works meet for repentance (Acts 26:19-20), i.e., they proved their repentance by their deeds.

11. According to Romans 2:11, does God show partiality in His judging?
No. Those who have repented and turned to God and His mercy will be saved. For those who have not repented but have obeyed unrighteousness, there will be tribulation and anguish upon every one that practices evil.

12. In Romans 2:12, what two kinds of people are mentioned?
Those without the law and those with the law.

13. Read Romans 2:13. What must a person do if he or she is going to be saved by the law?
Keep all the law without one slip. See Galatians 3:10.

14. Has anyone lived up to God's law or even the law of one's own conscience?
No.

15. How does Romans 2:15 show that people cannot live up to the law?
Their consciences accuse and condemn them.

16. Read Romans 2:16. What will God bring to light in judgment?
Everything, even the secrets of men.

17. Read Romans 2:17. What is the person in Romans 2:17 called?
A Jew. The word "Jew" is derived from the word "Judah" (meaning "praise"), and was used to denote God's chosen people. Our religious man could have been called a Baptist, Presbyterian, Methodist, or Pentecostal.

18. Read Romans 2:17. On what did this person's faith rest?
The law. He knew the Word of God. He knew the stories of the Bible.

19. Read Romans 2:17. This person bragged about what?
He bragged about a relationship with God. He was not a heathen; he believed in God.

20. Read Romans 2:18. According to Romans 2:18, did this religious person know God's will?
Yes.

21. Read Romans 2:18. Did this religious person know the difference between good and evil, moral and immoral?
Yes. He approved what is superior.

22. Read Romans 2:18. How was this religious person instructed?
He was instructed out of the law. He heard the Bible, went to church, paid tithes, etc. This is our religious person.

23. What are the claims of the religious person in Romans 2:19?
1. He is a guide to the (spiritually) blind.
2. He's a light to them that are in darkness. (He's not the blind leading the blind; he knows the way, just ask him!).

24. Read Romans 2:20. What else did the religious person claim?
1. To be an instructor, or corrector, to those who are foolish or ignorant.
2. To be a teacher to babes, or those who are immature.
3. Within the law (or Bible) he has an embodiment of knowledge and truth.

25. What two questions does the Apostle Paul ask the religious person in Romans 2:21?
1. You who teach another, don't you teach yourself?
2. You who preach a man should not steal, do you steal?

26. What two questions does the Apostle Paul ask in Romans 2:22?
1. You say a man should not commit adultery, but do you? (See Jesus' interpretation of this command in Matthew 5:27-28).
2. You abhor idols, do you commit sacrilege? Sacrilege is the misuse, or theft, of anything sacred that belongs to God.

27. What question does the Apostle Paul ask the religious person in Romans 2:23?
You who brag about the law, don't you know you dishonor God by breaking it?

28. Romans 2:24 is a quotation from Isaiah 52:5 (LXX). How could we paraphrase the meaning of Romans 2:24?
Men and women who claim to be the people of God, but do shady things, cause people to think less of God.

29. Read Romans 2:25. What scriptural principle can we learn from the phrase, "Circumcision verily profiteth, if thou keep the law"?
Religious rites (such as circumcision, baptism, church membership, etc.) only have value if what they symbolize is present and real in a person's life.

30. Read Romans 2:25. What scriptural principle can we derive from the phrase, "If thou be a breaker of the law, thy circumcision is made uncircumcision"?
If the reality of what a religious rite represents is not present in a person's life, the religious rite means nothing. (It's as if the person has not been baptized, circumcised, or gone through catechism, etc..)

31. Read Romans 2:26. What scriptural principle do we learn from Romans 2:26?
If the reality of a religious rite is present in a person's heart and life, it is acceptable to God, even if the person has not performed the religious rite.

32. Read Romans 2:27. What scriptural principle do we learn from Romans 2:27?
A man with the reality of the religious rite in his heart, condemns the man who has performed the rite (circumcision, baptism, etc.), but does not possess the reality of it.

33. Read Romans 2:28-29. What does it mean to be a true Jew according to Romans 2:28-29?
A real Jew is anyone whose heart is right with God, or belongs to God in heart.

    Example: A wedding ring symbolizes something sacred (faithfulness and commitment). To be unfaithful makes the wedding ring meaningless even thought it's on one's hand.

34. Read Romans 2:28-29. What is the meaning of Romans 2:28-29?
God doesn't want outward regulations—He wants men's hearts. A circumcised heart is one that has turned from Satan and his ways, to God and His ways (Acts 26:18). This person receives praise from God, not men. True Christianity is inward, not outward.

OVERVIEW OF ROMANS CHAPTER 3

by Don Krow

Turn to Romans 3:1: *"What advantage then hath the Jew? or what profit is there of circumcision?"* Paul has just said in Romans 2 that a real Jew, one of God's people, is not someone who is born to a certain nationality; a real Jew is one inwardly, who has had a change of heart toward God, who puts faith in God and the Lord Jesus Christ. Now the Jews are objecting and saying, "What benefit is there in being a physical Jew, a descendant of Abraham physically. What advantage is there?"

I would answer that with something like, "You don't have any advantage at all. Now that Jesus Christ has died on the cross for all the world, both Jew and Gentile come on the same basis. You have no advantage at all."

The Apostle Paul answers that question just the opposite in Romans 3:2: *"Much in every way: chiefly, because that unto them were committed the oracles of God."* First of all, they were entrusted with the oracles of God, which means the very Word of God. In other words, what Paul is saying, if I can say it very briefly, that the Gentiles do not produce Scripture. God entrusted His Word, the Scripture, to the Jewish nation … our Old Testament. The inspired Word of God came through the Jews … our New Testament writers were basically Jews.

Muslims have their Koran, Christian Scientists have their Keys to Understanding Scripture, Mormons have The Book of Mormon. The problem is the Bible says the oracles of God have come through the Jewish nation. They have a great advantage in that.

Verses 3-4: *"For what if some did not believe? shall their unbelief make the faith of God without effectt? God forbid: yea, let God be true, but every man a liar; as it is written, That thou mightest be justified in thy sayings, and mightest overcome* (this is a quotation from Psalm 51) *when thou art judged."* Paul is saying: what if the Jews have the Word of God, but don't believe it? Will that nullify God's promises? Basically he says that God will be faithful to His Word regardless of the unfaithfulness of man.

Verses 5-6: *"But if our unrighteousness commend the righteousness of God, what shall we say? Is God unrighteous who taketh vengeance? (I speak as a man)."* When people, with their own distorted reasoning, begin to abandon the Word of God, this is what happens: They begin to justify their actions through perverted thinking, which is what is happening here.

Paul said, "I am speaking in human terms. What if my unrighteousness brings out God's righteousness more clearly? God had no right to judge me," and then said that is ridiculous. It is like a criminal standing before a judge saying, "Judge, the reason I'm here is actually to support you and the police officers, because without me you wouldn't have a job." How ridiculous and distorted is that kind of thinking?

Verses 6-8: *"God forbid: for then how shall God judge the world? For if the truth of God hath more abounded through my lie unto his glory; why yet am I also judged as a sinner? And not rather, (as we be slanderously reported, and as some affirm that we say,) Let us do evil, that good may come? whose damnation is just."* Paul again is using the twisted, distorted thinking of man to say, "Man is saying that because I preach grace, that righteousness and right-standing before God is a free gift, I am saying to go out and sin, because it somehow benefits God. That is not what I am saying. That is a distorted and perverted way of thinking about grace."

Verse 9: *"What then? are we better than they? No, in no wise: for we have before proved both Jews and Gentiles, that they are all under sin."* Paul is coming to a conclusion in this verse saying, "Are we Jews or Gentiles any better? No, if you read Romans 1-3, the conclusion will be this: we are all under sin. Now I'm going to call God to the judgment stand, and He Himself is going to testify about the perversion of man." That is what we see in the next few verses.

Verses 10-12: *"As it is written, There is none righteous, no, not one: There is none that understandeth, there is none that seeketh after God. They have all gone out of the way, they are together become unprofitable; there is none that doeth good, no, not one."* This is a quotation from Psalm 14:1-3.

Verses 13-18: *"Their throat is an open sepulchre; with their tongues they have used deceit; the poison of asps is under their lips; Whose mouth is full of cursing and bitterness: Their feet are swift to shed blood; Destruction and misery are in their ways: And the way of peace they have not known. There is no fear of God before their eyes."* Paul is using Old Testament scriptures by quoting about four passages in Psalms, one in Ecclesiastes, and one from Isaiah 59, totally bringing man under guilt and condemnation to say, "No one seeks after God; there is none righteous, not even one." There is not even one person down through all the time mankind has been alive who ever met God's standard, or law. Therefore, God is going to give a new way, a new dimension, of coming into right-relationship with Him.

Verse 19: *"Now we know that what things soever the law saith, it saith to them who are under the law: that every mouth may be stopped, and all the world may become guilty before God."* What is this saying? God never gave the law so man could be right, justified, or declared righteous. God gave the Law to show man how ungodly and sinful he really is, that he might go to a Savior and say, "God, I can't keep this law ... I can't live this way ... I can't meet this standard. I need mercy ... I need grace ... I need pardon ... I need a Savior, and that Savior is you." So the Law condemns man. It was never meant to make him right before God but to shut his mouth and show him to be guilty before Him.

Verses 20-23: *"Therefore by the deeds of the law there shall no flesh be justified in his sight: for by the law is the knowledge of sin. But now the righteousness of God without the law is manifested, being witnessed by the law and the prophets; Even the righteousness of God which is by faith of Jesus Christ unto all and upon all them that believe: for there is no difference. For all have sinned, and come short of the glory of God."* Paul is saying that now, apart from the law, apart from doing, earning, achieving, God is offering righteousness—not man's righteousness, not the best man can do, but the very righteousness of God—to all mankind, unto all and upon all who will believe.

This is described in verse 22 as the righteousness of God, a right relationship with Himself, that He is offering mankind. It is not by performance of the law, by works of righteousness man does, but it is a "through faith in Jesus Christ" righteousness that will make men and women acceptable before God. Why do we need this righteousness? Because verse 23 says we have all sinned and come short of the glory of God.

Verse 24: *"Being justified freely."* The new American Standard says "being justified as a gift," declared righteous as a gift, freely without charge. If I give you a gift and then ask you to give me something in return, it wouldn't be a true gift. God justifies, declares people righteous before Him, truly as a gift. He freely gives it. How? Verse 24 continues, *"by his grace through the redemption that is in Christ Jesus."* He does it as a favor because of His kindness.

Does He do this justly? Of course He does. Redemption means that He paid the price to give us this righteousness, to buy us, to purchase us. He paid the wages of sin so we might freely have this gift of righteousness. Everything God did was righteous and just. He didn't ignore sin, sweep it under the carpet. He said, "It must be judged; the wages of sin is death, but I tell you what I'll do. I will pay the penalty of death Myself, in the person of Jesus Christ."

Verse 25: *"Whom God hath set forth to be a propitiation through faith in his blood, to declare his righteousness for the remission of sins that are past, through the forbearance of God."* This is saying that Jesus is the propitiation for our sins. What does the word "propitiation" mean? The Greeks used it as something men did to appease or try to please the gods, because they thought their nature was not very loving or kind. They constantly worked to appease and please the gods.

The Bible never says that man has to do anything to appease or please God. It says Jesus did something to appease and please Him. In 1 John 2 it says that Jesus was the propitiation for our sins, and not for our sins only but for the sins of the whole world. Jesus did something that appeased and pleased God. He took the judgment of our sins so men would never have to work their way to God again. Righteousness is given to us freely as a gift.

Verse 26: *"To declare, I say, at this time his righteousness: that he might be just, and the justifier of him which believeth in Jesus."* God gave Jesus as a sacrifice of atonement, of redemption, to demonstrate that He was a righteous God. He dealt with sin in the person of Jesus so He could freely forgive us, to demonstrate that He was righteous.

Verse 27: *Where is boasting then? It is excluded. By what law? of works? Nay: but by the law of faith."* One thing salvation by grace has done is remove the boasting of any man. We will never hear anyone in heaven say, "Look what I did; look at the great things I did." All of our boasts will be in Jesus, for salvation is totally of Him and what He did for us on the cross. So boasting is excluded in man's works; it is excluded by the law of faith, because the law of faith rests upon the work of another—the person and work of Jesus Christ and what He did on our behalf. Truly that is amazing grace. Throughout eternity we will be praising Him for that grace.

Verses 28-29: *"Therefore we conclude that a man is justified by faith without the deeds of the law. Is he the God of the Jews only? Is he not also of the Gentiles? Yes, of the Gentiles also."* The Jews say, "There must be one God—a God of works; and there must be another God—a God of grace that comes to the Gentiles." Paul is saying, "No, there is only one God."

Verse 30: *"Seeing it is one God, which shall justify the circumcision by faith, and uncircumcision through faith."* There is one God, one way of righteousness before Him, and that is through faith in Jesus Christ's righteousness. We don't have to work or perform for it; it is given to us freely through faith in Jesus Christ.

Verse 31: *"Do we then make void the law through faith? God forbid: yea, we establish the law."* How do we establish the Law through being justified by faith? The Law demanded perfect righteousness, and because man could not perform perfectly, or offer to God perfect righteousness, Jesus Christ Himself bore our sin and imputed to us a perfect righteousness that the Law demanded.

Therefore, we aren't saying the Law is no good; we're saying God offered the perfect righteousness the Law demands through faith in Jesus Christ. The Law is stunned … it can say nothing … it can no longer condemn, because the perfect righteousness that it demanded has been imputed to us through faith in Jesus Christ. It is the righteousness of God unto all who will believe.

Romans 3:1-31
Discipleship Commentary

. . . .

Read the entire lesson and then answer the questions that follow.

Romans 3:1 - What advantage then hath the Jew? or what profit is there of circumcision?

(Rom. 3:1) Paul had just proven that the Jews were just as guilty as the pagans whom they disdained. This led to the question, "What advantage is there in being a Jew then?" Paul gives the most important answer to that question in verse two and then addresses the issue more in Romans 9:4-5.

Romans 3:2 - Much every way: chiefly, because that unto them were committed the oracles of God.

(Rom. 3:2) The main advantage that the Jews had over others was that God had committed His Word unto them. They not only had the intuitive knowledge of God, but they had a written record of God's instructions, which should have served as an added restraint from departing from God. They, however, had missed the true intent of God's law and, therefore were not taking advantage of the benefits God's Word afforded them.

The Greek word for "oracles" is "logion," which means, "an utterance of God." Therefore, this is speaking of the Word of God that was committed to the Jews. In the Old Testament, the word "oracle" was also used to designate the innermost part of the temple since the ark of the covenant was kept.

The word "oracles" is used four times in the New Testament (Acts 7:38, Rom. 3:2, Heb. 5:12, and 1 Pet. 4:11). In each of these instances, the word is clearly referring to the Word of God.

Romans 3:3 - For what if some did not believe? shall their unbelief make the faith of God without effect?

(Rom. 3:3) Paul is using the phrase "the faith of God" in this verse interchangeably with the word "oracle" in verse two. He is saying that the unbelief of the Jews did not make the Word of God or the promises of God without effect. Therefore, the Word of God is the faith of God. No wonder faith comes by hearing God's Word; God's Word contains His faith.

Paul is asking the question, "If some of the Jews did not believe God's Word, does that make God's Word of no effect?" The answer to this question is a resounding "no" in verse four. However, Mark 7:13 says we make the Word of God of none effect through our tradition. What's the harmony between these two verses?

An individual can make God's Word of no effect in his or her personal life. Hebrews 4:2 says God's Word will not profit us unless we mix it with faith. So the Word will not profit anyone who doesn't believe it, but God's Word itself doesn't lose any power. That is what Paul is stating here. The unbelief of the Jewish nation as a whole did not void the promises of God concerning salvation through a savior. The promises of salvation were of no effect to the individuals who rejected Jesus, but to anyone who will put his faith in Jesus as Messiah, the Word of God still has its power to save.

Romans 3:4 - God forbid: yea, let God be true, but every man a liar; as it is written, That thou mightest be justified in thy sayings, and mightest overcome when thou art judged.

(Rom. 3:4) This is the first of ten times that Paul uses this expression in the book of Romans (here; Rom. 3:6, 3, 6:2, 15; 7:7, 13, 9:14, and 11:1, 11). He also uses this expression four other times in his other epistles (1 Cor. 6:15; Gal. 2:17, 3:21, and 6:14).

The Greek words that are used are "me ginomai," meaning "let it not be! far be it! God forbid," they express emphatic denial of the false conclusion that someone might draw from his teaching.

This phrase "let God be true, but every man a liar" is given in response to the question of verse 3 (see note at Rom. 3:3, above). Paul is stating that God and His promises are always true even if men don't believe Him. However, there can be other applications of this truth which will benefit us greatly.

When anyone or anything contradicts a promise to us in God's Word, we need to reckon God to be true and that person or thing to be lying. We need to believe that what God's Word says about our prosperity is true (2 Cor. 8:9, 3 John 2), instead of what our checkbook says. We need to believe that we were healed by His stripes (Isa. 53:5, Matt. 8:17, and 1 Pet. 2:24), instead of believing what the x-rays show. In every aspect of our lives, we need to believe God's Word above what we see or hear.

This is a quotation from David out of Psalm 51:4 when he was repenting of his sin with Bathsheba and the murder of her husband. David was admitting his sinfulness and proclaiming God's complete justification in judging his sin in whatever way He saw fit. David's sin had not made God unholy it made him unholy. In David's sinfulness, he now saw the holiness of God clearer than ever.

This is what Paul is drawing from this Old Testament passage. He was saying that in a similar manner, God retained His holiness even when His people were unholy. It was the Jews who suffered from not believing God's Word, not God.

Romans 3:5 - But if our unrighteousness commend the righteousness of God, what shall we say? Is God unrighteous who taketh vengeance? (I speak as a man)

(Rom. 3:5) Paul had just explained that the Jews' faithlessness did not make God unfaithful to His Word. Therefore, when you consider how unfaithful we have been to God, it makes God's mercy and faithfulness appear even greater. So this brings up new questions like, "If my unrighteousness reveals God's righteousness, or causes it to be seen in an even greater way, then am I actually helping God? Would it be right for God to judge me for something like that?" Of course, Paul's answer to that is another "God forbid."

It is true that we would never have seen the love and goodness of God as clearly if we had not sinned, but that does not mean our sin was a good thing. This is one piece of information that the Lord never wanted us to know by experience. No one will be able to tell God on judgment day that his sin just helped God reveal how great His mercy was. The Lord will be totally just in bringing His judgment on all those who refuse His offer of mercy given through Jesus, His Son.

Paul is saying that this logic he had just spoken was not from God but was carnal. He was not saying this as God's spokesman but was expressing a thought that opponents of the Gospel had so he could expose the error in it. Therefore, he gave a disclaimer in parenthesis that this was not God's wisdom, but man's.

Romans 3:6 - God forbid: for then how shall God judge the world?

(Rom. 3:6) Paul is saying that if that were true (v. 5), God couldn't judge the world, and it is a well-established fact in Scripture that God will judge the world. Therefore, that argument has to be rejected.

Romans 3:7-8 - For if the truth of God hath more abounded through my lie unto his glory; why yet am I also judged as a sinner? 8) And not rather, (as we be slanderously reported, and as some affirm that we say,) Let us do evil, that good may come? whose damnation is just.

(Rom. 3:8) Paul preached the grace of God as no one else recorded in Scripture. This led many people to slander him and his teaching by accusing him of encouraging people to sin. This was totally untrue. The grace of God teaches us to deny ungodliness and worldly lust (Titus 2:11-12). Here, Paul shows his total rejection of those allegations by saying that the damnation of those people is just. He also "raises the stakes" for anyone who wants to criticize those who proclaim the grace of God. According to Paul, they will be damned.

Romans 3:9 - What then? are we better than they? No, in no wise: for we have before proved both Jews and Gentiles, that they are all under sin;

(Rom. 3:9) In Romans 1:18-32, Paul proved that the Gentiles were guilty before God for their actions because of an intuitive knowledge of God. In Romans 2, Paul proved that the Jews were even worse off than the Gentiles, because they had been given the Word of God and yet had not kept it.

Now, in chapter three, he brings all this together and concludes that everyone (Jew and Gentile, religious and pagan, moral and immoral) is guilty before God. Paul cites many Old Testament scriptures to verify this and to show that this is not some new doctrine. Faith in the sacrificial death of a savior was God's plan of redemption all along.

Paul's arguments in Romans 3:9-18 provide the reason for salvation by grace through faith (Eph. 2:8), and refute the doctrines of every other religion.

Man is so destitute that he cannot save himself; he has to have a savior. Therefore, every other religion is wrong, because it doesn't provide a savior. To some degree or another, the other religions of the world teach that the burden of salvation is upon our own shoulders.

In contrast, Christianity has a Savior, and not just some man. God Himself provided salvation for mankind. Within the ranks of those who claim Christianity, this is also the pivotal issue. Any deviation from trust in Jesus and His imputed righteousness, to reliance on our own holiness for right-standing with God is error.

Therefore, the truth expressed in these verses is critical to understanding God's plan of salvation. Since man could never "make up" for his sins, God did what man could not do. He paid the price Himself. No other method of payment is acceptable.

Romans 3:10-20 - As it is written, There is none righteous, no, not one: 11) There is none that understandeth, there is none that seeketh after God. 12) They are all gone out of the way, they are together become unprofitable; there is none that doeth good, no, not one. 13) Their throat is an open sepulchre; with their tongues they have used deceit; the poison of asps is under their lips: 14) Whose mouth is full of cursing and bitterness: 15) Their feet are swift to shed blood: 16) Destruction and misery are in their ways: 17) And the way of peace have they not known: 18) There is no fear of God before their eyes. 19) Now we know that what things soever the law saith, it saith to them who are under the law: that every mouth may be stopped, and all the world may become guilty before God. 20) Therefore by the deeds of the law there shall no flesh be justified in his sight: for by the law is the knowledge of sin.

(Rom. 3:19) Paul had conclusively proven that both Jews and Gentiles were sinners and, therefore, incapable of saving themselves through their own works of righteousness. They both needed a savior. He now begins to reveal that the means of that salvation is through faith in Jesus the Messiah, and not through our moral goodness.

This very clear statement by Paul comes as a complete shock to most Christians. Christianity as a whole has embraced the Old Testament Law, and most Christians have never thought that the Law was not intended for them. However, Paul is saying that the Law was given to the Jews. The purpose of that Law was to produce guilt; therefore, anyone who is denying their guilt before God can profit from its condemning effect (2 Cor. 3:9, 1 Tim. 1:9). But a Christian who embraces the Old Testament Law (not everything that is in the Old Testament is law) as God's gift to them has misunderstood its purpose.

That is not to say that a Christian should reject the Old Testament as God's holy Word. God forbid. It certainly is God's Word and is, therefore, profitable for doctrine, reproof, etc. (2 Tim. 3:16). However, it needs to be interpreted in light of the New Covenant. Jesus not only set us free from the curse of the Law (Gal. 3:13), He also set us free from the Law itself (Rom. 4:16, 6:14-1, 7:4-6; 8:2; 2 Cor. 3:7; Gal. 2:19, 3:24-25, 4:21, 5:18; Eph. 2:14-15; Col. 2:14; 1 Tim.1:9; Heb. 7:18-19, 8:7-13, and 10:8-9). A desire to live under the commands of the Old Testament Law is a return to bondage and a misunderstanding of our new covenant in Jesus.

Paul begins to make a series of radical statements here. Radical because the Jews of his day, just like many church people of our day, thought that the Law of God was given so that we could earn our salvation through keeping it. That wasn't its purpose. The Law was not given for the purpose of producing justification (Rom. 3:20, 28, 4:13; Gal. 2:16, 3:11, 5:4; and Titus 3:5).

The Law was given to kill (2 Cor. 3:7) and condemn (2 Cor. 3:9). The Law strengthened sin (1 Cor. 15:56) and made sin come alive (Rom. 7:9). The Law gave sin an occasion against us to deceive us and work all manner of lust in us (Rom. 7:8,11). In short, the Law strengthened our enemy, sin, not us.

Why would God give us something that strengthened our enemy? Because sin had already beaten us, and we didn't know it. Mankind was deceived into thinking that although we weren't perfect, surely our sins weren't that bad. We really are pretty good people, and the outcome would be "okay." The only thing that is wrong with that thinking is that God doesn't grade on a curve. It doesn't matter if you are better than someone else. All have sinned and come short of the glory of God (Rom. 3:23), and the wages for sin (any sin) is death (Rom. 6:23).

James 2:10 says, "For whosoever shall keep the whole law, and yet offend in one point, he is guilty of all." If a person commits any sin he oe she is guilty of them all. It's similar to breaking a window. It doesn't matter how big a hole you make in the window. If it's broken, the whole window has to be replaced. If we break even the slightest command, we are guilty of breaking them all.

So God had to break the deception that people had fallen into, of thinking they were surely good enough to be accepted by God. The way He did this was to give the Law. It made sin and its lust come alive in us. To those who would receive it, it became obvious that if this holy perfection of the Law was what God demanded, no one could be saved by his or her own goodness.

That was the point that God wanted to make, and that is the point that Paul is making here. No one can be saved by keeping the Law, because all have sinned and come short of the Law's perfection (Rom. 3:23).

Therefore, the Law stripped us of every excuse and made us guilty before God. The Law gave us a knowledge of just how sinful we were and removed any deception of us ever being saved because we were such "nice guys" in comparison to others. As Paul said in Galatians 3:23, "But before faith came, we were kept under the law, shut up unto the faith which should afterwards be revealed." The Law took away every hope of salvation except faith in a savior. That was the purpose of the Law.

Romans 3:21 - But now the righteousness of God without the law is manifested, being witnessed by the law and the prophets;

(Rom. 3:21) This is another one of Paul's radical statements that was diametrically opposed to the Jewish thinking of his day. Mercy and grace were present in the Old Testament, but it was typified in the Old Testament sacrifices, which were incorporated in the Law. Therefore, the Jews had come to think that the only way God would grant any forgiveness was through fulfilling the Law as much as possible and then offering the appropriate sacrifice prescribed in the Law for any sins. For Paul to say that a person could be righteous apart from the Law was unthinkable.

Paul didn't end there though, he went on to say that this method of receiving right-standing with God was promised under the Old Testament Law and Prophets. This meant that Paul was not putting forth a new doctrine but expounding the true doctrine, which the Old Testament law and Prophets had advocated all along. This left no doubt that the Jews' trust in the Old Testament Law for justification was never God's intent. They had misunderstood and misapplied the Law in this area.

Likewise today, many religious people misunderstand the true intent of the Old Testament law.

Romans 3:22 - Even the righteousness of God which is by faith of Jesus Christ unto all and upon all them that believe: for there is no difference:

(Rom. 3:22) Paul makes an even clearer presentation of this truth in Romans 9:30-10:9. The Jews were seeking to produce their own righteousness that was according to their holy actions that conformed to the Law. Paul is speaking of a different type of righteousness, not a human righteousness that was flawed, but the perfect righteousness of God Himself.

Through faith in Jesus, we can receive the very righteousness of God as a gift (2 Cor. 5:21). God's righteousness is infinitely more in quality and quantity than man's puny righteousness (Isa. 64:6). No one can ever be justified in the sight of God based on one's own righteousness which comes through acts of holiness. One must have God's righteousness, which only comes through faith in the Lord Jesus Christ as Savior. Paul said in Philippians 3:9, "And be found in him, not having mine own righteousness, which is of the law, but that which is through the faith of Christ, the righteousness which is of God by faith." This is "the righteousness of God," which Paul is referring to here.

Notice that Paul did not say that this righteousness of God came by faith in Jesus Christ. No, it comes by the faith of Jesus Christ. There is a big difference.

Our faith does not produce our righteousness. Jesus obtained righteousness (the perfect righteousness of God) through His faith, and offers it to everyone who will believe on Him as Lord. Therefore, our faith (which is also a gift from God Eph. 2:8) just receives what Jesus has already obtained for us through His faith. Jesus obtained our justification and righteousness through His faith (Gal. 2:16).

The only difference between Jew and Gentile, or the moral and immoral, is in the sight of men. From God's point of view, there is no difference. All have sinned and come short of the glory of God (Rom. 3:23, Jas. 2:10).

Romans 3:23 - For all have sinned, and come short of the glory of God;

(Rom. 3:23) This is one of the pivotal doctrines of Scripture. Jesus only came to save sinners (1 Tim. 1:15). Unless an individual acknowledges that he or she is a sinner, that person cannot be saved. Romans 4:5 says that God justifies the ungodly. Therefore, until a person admits he is ungodly, that person cannot be saved.

A person has to be stripped of all other means of salvation (John 14:6) before he or she can receive Jesus as his Savior. That was the purpose of the Old Testament Law, and that is the argument that Paul has given in Romans 1:21-23. Therefore, the truth of universal guilt before God that is expressed in this verse is true in all its applications.

However, in context, this verse is just a stepping stone to an even greater truth that is expressed in verses 24-26. Because the whole world is guilty before God, He has provided one way of salvation for everyone. In the same way that everyone is guilty, so everyone has already been justified freely by God's grace.

That does not mean everyone is saved. Everyone has had the sacrificial offering of Jesus made for their sins by grace (1 Tim. 4:10, 1 John 2:2), but grace alone doesn't save. We have to put faith in what God has provided for us by grace (Eph. 2:8). Therefore, although the price has been paid for the sins of the whole world, only those who receive it by faith will benefit from the salvation that Jesus offers.

The Greek word that was translated "glory" here is "doxa," and according to W.E. Vine, it means "the manifested perfection of His character, especially His righteousness of which all men fall short." A simple way of saying this is that all men fall short of Jesus. Jesus is the glory of the Father (John 1:14, 2 Cor. 4:6, Heb. 1:3, and Rev. 21:23).

A common mistake that people make is comparing themselves with other people (2 Cor. 10:12). Nearly everyone has heard, "if the hypocrites down there at church make it, then I'll make it." The only thing that is wrong with that thinking is that the hypocrites down there at church aren't God's "measuring stick." Everyone is going to be compared to Jesus, the glory of God, and therefore, everyone will come up short. We all need a savior.

Romans 3:24 - Being justified freely by his grace through the redemption that is in Christ Jesus:

(Rom. 3:24) Justification is not something to be earned but a gift to be received. Seeking to earn salvation is the only sin that will prevent a person from being saved, because you cannot submit yourself to the righteousness of God, which comes as a gift through faith, as long as you are seeking to establish your own righteousness (Rom. 10:3).

Grace is God's ability given to us on an unearned, undeserved basis. However, this grace comes through the redemption that Jesus provided. Therefore, there can be no grace in our lives apart from faith in Jesus. Romans 5:2 says, "By whom also we have access by faith into this grace wherein we stand, and rejoice in hope of the glory of God."

Romans 3:25 - Whom God hath set forth to be a propitiation through faith in his blood, to declare his righteousness for the remission of sins that are past, through the forbearance of God;

(Rom. 3:25) This verse is speaking of the sins that were committed under the Old Covenant, before the sacrifice of Jesus was made. Those sins were also paid for by the blood of Jesus. The Old Testament sacrifices were only types and shadows of the true sin offering that Jesus made. It was impossible for the blood of bulls and of goats to ever take away sins (Heb. 10:4).

The Lord dealt with sins under the Old Testament through His forbearance. In a similar way that a person gives a check or credit card in exchange for the real currency desired, so the Lord gave the Old Testament sacrifices. However, just as these substitutes would be unacceptable if there was no reality to back them up, so the Old Testament sacrifices only served as a token of the real sacrifice of Jesus that would pay for sin (Heb. 9:13-14).

Romans 3:26 - To declare, I say, at this time his righteousness: that he might be just, and the justifier of him which believeth in Jesus.

(Rom. 3:26) Paul restates this amazing fact that it is the righteousness of Jesus that has been given to us. We don't just have enough righteousness to let us slip into heaven. We have been given Jesus' righteousness. First Corinthians 1:30 says, "But of him are ye in Christ Jesus, who of God is made unto us wisdom, and righteousness, and sanctification, and redemption." Jesus is my righteousness! Second Corinthians 5:21 says, "For he hath made him to be sin for us, who knew no sin; that we might be made the righteousness of God in him."

Romans 3:27 - Where is boasting then? It is excluded. By what law? of works? Nay: but by the law of faith.

(Rom. 3:27) Boasting, bragging, or pride about our holiness, or spiritual accomplishments, is a sure sign that we don't understand justification by grace through faith as Paul was teaching it here. If we acknowledge that we are no better than anyone else, regardless of our conduct, and that the only way we obtained peace with God was through putting faith in what Jesus did for us, then there is no room for boasting about our achievements. It was the accomplishments of Jesus that saved us.

Pride is the root of all divisions in the church today. Therefore, the prevalence of division in the church is a painful testimony of the lack of this foundational truth of justification by grace through faith.

Notice that Paul refers to the law of faith. Faith is governed by law, just as gravity or electricity is. If we would view faith as a law rather than something that sometimes works and other times doesn't, we would begin to get very different results.

The law of electricity has been here on earth since creation. Man has observed it in such things as lightening and static electricity, but it was not until someone believed that there were laws that governed the activity of electricity that progress began to be made in putting it to use. Likewise, none deny the existence of faith, but it is only when an individual begins to understand that there are laws that govern faith, and then begins to learn what those laws are, that faith begins to work for the individual.

Romans 3:28 - Therefore we conclude that a man is justified by faith without the deeds of the law. 29) Is he the God of the Jews only? is he not also of the Gentiles? Yes, of the Gentiles also: 30) Seeing it is one God, which shall justify the circumcision by faith, and uncircumcision through faith.

(Rom. 3:30) There is no reason to believe that Paul is making any distinction between the way the Jews and the Gentiles are justified by his use of the words "by" and "through." The same end (justification) is achieved, and faith is the way for both Jew and Gentile to receive it.

Romans 3:31 - Do we then make void the law through faith? God forbid: yea, we establish the law.

(Rom. 3:31) Paul had just systematically taken away the Jews' trust in the Law for the purpose of justification. This led to the question, "Is the Law then useless?" Paul emphatically answers, "God forbid."

The real purpose of the Law was established by the Gospel. The problem with the Jews was that they were using the Law for something that God never intended. The Law was useless to produce justification. God didn't give the Law so that we could keep it and, thereby, earn justification. The Law was given to reveal to us that we could never live up to such a holy standard and, thereby, drive us to God to call out for mercy (Gal. 3:22-24).

The true purpose of the Law is still functional today. As 1 Timothy 1:8-10 says, "But we know that the law is good; if a man use it lawfully; Knowing this, that the law is not made for a righteous man." The Law is God's way of revealing to man his need. It is powerless to make provision for that need. It's the Gospel that provides the power to produce salvation.

In chapter 4, Paul goes on to use two great men of the Old Testament (Abram and David) as examples of how justification came through faith, not through the Law.

Romans 3:1-31
Discipleship Questions

. . . .

Answer the following questions by reading the corresponding discipleship commentary lesson and using your Bible.

1. Read Romans 3:1. What are the two questions being asked in Romans 3:1?

   _____

   _____

   _____

2. Read Romans 3:2. How does Paul answer the questions asked in Romans 3:1?

   _____

   _____

3. Read Romans 3:2. How is the word "oracles" used in Scripture?

   _____

   _____

   _____

4. Read Romans 3:3. What are the questions being asked in Romans 3:3?

   _____

   _____

5. Read Romans 3:4. How did Paul answer the questions of Romans 3:3?

   _____

   _____

6. Read Romans 3:5. What is it that brings out God's righteousness more clearly?

   _____

   _____

7. Read Romans 3:6. Is God unrighteous to punish, or judge, mankind?

   _____

8. Read Romans 3:7. What is the question being asked in Romans 3:7?

   _____

9. Read Romans 3:8. What is the question being asked in Romans 3:8?

   _____

10. Read Romans 3:8. How did Paul answer that question?

   _____

   _____

11. Read Romans 3:9. What are the questions being asked in Romans 3:9?

_____

_____

12. Read Romans 3:9. How are the questions in Romans 3:9 answered?

_____

_____

13. Read Romans 3:10. In Romans 3:10, the phrase "as it is written," translated in Greek, is in the perfect tense. What does this mean?

_____

14. Read Romans 3:10. According to Romans 3:10, how are both Jew and Gentile alike?

_____

_____

15. "There is none that understandeth" (Rom. 3:11). Why is this so, according to Ephesians4:18?_____

16. "There is none that seeketh after God" (Rom. 3:11). Why is this so, according to Philippians 2:21? _____

17. Read John 6:44. If none seeketh after God, then what must God do?

_____

18. What does the word "draw" mean?

_____

_____

_____

_____

19. What must the Lord do for us, according to Acts 16:14?

_____

20. Read Romans 3:12. According to Romans 3:12, how many have turned away from God?

_____

21. According to Isaiah 53:6, how many have turned away from God?

_____

22. Is this true of you? _____

23. What idea does the word "unprofitable" carry in Romans 3:12?

_____

_____

24. Read Romans 3:12. How many of us have kept on doing what is right?

_____

25. Read Romans 3:13. Mankind's throat is like a what?

_____

26. How did Jesus state this in Matthew 12:34?

_____

27. Read Romans 3:13. With their tongues, what do men do?

_____

_____

28. Read Romans 3:13. According to Romans 3:13, men's lips can be likened to what?

_____

_____

29. Mankind's mouth is full of cursing and bitterness (Rom. 3:14). How would you define "cursing"? _____

_____

30. How would you define "bitterness"? Rom. 3:14.

_____

31. How can Romans 3:15 be compared to Matthew 5:21-22?

_____

_____

32. Read Romans 3:16. Destruction and misery mark mankind's ways. How would you define the word "destruction"?

_____

_____

33. Read Romans 3:16. How would you define the word "misery"?

_____

34. The way of peace mankind does not know (Rom. 3:17). How does Isaiah 57:21 state this?

_____

_____

35. Read Romans 3:18. What is the cause of sin according to Romans 3:18?

_____

_____

36. Read Romans 3:19. What effect does the Law have upon every individual?

_____

37. Read Romans 3:20. How many people will be declared right before God by keeping the Law? _____

38. Why? _____
_____
_____

39. Read Romans 3:21. What righteousness is being offered to us in Romans 3:21?
_____
_____

40. Read Romans 3:21. The source of this righteousness is that it is without what?
_____

41. Read Romans 3:21. This righteousness from God is now what?
_____

42. Read Romans 3:21. Does the Old Testament tell us about this righteousness?
_____
_____

43. Read Romans 3:22. What kind of righteousness makes people acceptable to God?
_____

44. Read Romans 3:22. Who is this righteousness offered to?
_____

45. Read Romans 3:22-23. The phrase, "for there is no difference," is really a phrase that means, "there is no difference or distinction." In what way is there no difference or distinction in mankind? _____
_____

46. In Romans 3:23 the phrase, "come short of the glory of God," is in the present tense in Greek. This means that it is a continuous action. It happens over and over again. It's an habitual action. The phrase, "Being justified," in Romans 3:24, is also in the present tense and has the same meaning. Grace is greater than sin (Rom. 5:20). How would you define what it means to be justified? _____
_____

47. Read Romans 3:24. Justification is not an attainment of man; it is a gift of God. What word in Romans 3:24 (besides the word "grace") proves this statement?
_____
_____
_____

48. Read Romans 3:24. God declares us righteous. He does it freely, and how is this done? (by His what)? _____

_____

49. Read Romans 3:24. How could God bestow righteousness upon a sinner and still be just?

_____

50. Read Romans 3:24. In whom was this redemption?

_____

51. Read Romans 3:25. According to Romans 3:25, What did God publicly display Jesus to be?

_____

52. What does "propitiation" mean?

_____

_____

_____

_____

53. Read Romans 3:25. What was the price that brought man into a favorable and righteous standing before God?

_____

54. According to Romans 3:25-26, why was it necessary for Christ to die? Read Romans 3:25-26 from the Today's English Version or New American Standard Version.

_____

55. Read Romans 3:25. How could we define God's "forbearance"?

_____

56. If sin had not been paid for until the time of Jesus, how could a holy God justly forgive a man such as David, who had committed adultery?_____

_____

57. How can God justify a guilty person?

_____

58. Read Romans 3:26. In Romans 3:26, Paul states that through redemption God has been shown to be just (i.e. righteous). What else is He?

_____

59. Read Romans 3:27. What are the questions being asked in Romans 3:27?

_____

_____

_____

60. Read Romans 3:28. What is the conclusion of Paul's argument in Romans 3:28?

_____

_____

61. Read Romans 3:29-30. What is the argument of Romans 3:29-30?

_____

_____

_____

62. Read Romans 3:31. What is the question being asked in Romans 3:31?

_____

_____

63. Read Romans 3:31. How do we establish the Law by justification through faith?

_____

_____

_____

_____

Romans 3:1-31
Discipleship Answer Key

. . . .

Do not look at the answer key until you have completed the questions.
Compare your answers with the following answers.

1. Read Romans 3:1. What are the two questions being asked in Romans 3:1?
   What is the advantage of being a Jew, or of being circumcised? (I would answer this question by saying, "None at all! Now that the Old Testament prophecy of the Messiah is fulfilled, now that Jesus has died for our sins, we all are on the same ground. Jew and Gentile, all must accept Christ." Paul now answers the questions the opposite of the way I did).

2. Read Romans 3:2. How does Paul answer the questions asked in Romans 3:1?
   "The Jews have great advantage in every way! Most importantly, to them were committed the oracles of God" (Romans 3:2).

3. Read Romans 3:2. How is the word "oracles" used in scripture?
   In Acts 7:38 it is used for the contents of the Mosaic law. In Hebrews 5:12 it is used for the substance of Christian doctrine. In 1 Peter 4:11, of utterances of God through Christian teachers. In Romans 3:2 it is used of all the written utterances of God through the Old Testament scriptures.

4. Read Romans 3:3. What are the questions being asked in Romans 3:3?
   If the Jews are unfaithful and break their promises, does that mean God will break His promises?

5. Read Romans 3:4. How did Paul answer the questions of Romans 3:3?
   By the expression, "God forbid!" (An expression of horror to an improper conclusion). Man may be unfaithful to God, but God will always be faithful and true to His promises.

   The Contemporary English Version states, **"No, indeed! God tells the truth, even if everyone else is a liar. The Scriptures say about God, 'Your words will be proven true, and in court you will win your case' "** Ps. 51:4 (Rom. 3:4).

   Statement: The context of Romans 3:4 is a quote from Psalms 51:4. In this context David's sin of adultery has just been exposed. Just before this, God had given the promise that David's seed would set on the throne and reign forever (the Messiah). The question is, Will David's faithlessness cancel God's promise? David is basically saying from Psalms 51:4, "I've been faithless to you God, but you will always prove to be true to your word."

6. Read Romans 3:5. What is it that brings out God's righteousness more clearly?
   Our unrighteousness (by way of contrast).

7. Read Romans 3:6. Is God unrighteous to punish, or judge, mankind?
"God forbid!" (An expression of horror to an improper conclusion).

8. Read Romans 3:7. What is the question being asked in Romans 3:7?
Why am I judged as a sinner if it advances the glory of God?

   Statement: Perverted practices lead to perverted thinking. Example: A criminal robs a bank and steals a car. After being caught he stands before a judge and says, "Judge, it is only because of guys like me that you and the police officers have jobs. My unrighteousness serves you."

9. Read Romans 3:8. What is the question being asked in Romans 3:8?
Why not do evil so that good may come?

10. Read Romans 3:8. How did Paul answer that question?
I am not saying to do evil so that good may result. That is perverted and twisted thinking!

11. Read Romans 3:9. What are the questions being asked in Romans 3:9?
   1. What then? What is the point of further testimony?
   2. Are we any better than the other groups of people shown to be condemned in Romans 1-3?

12. Read Romans 3:9. How are the questions in Romans 3:9 answered?
No, in no way is anyone better than anyone else. All are under the power, authority and control of sin (1 John 5:19).

   Statement: Six times in the following verses the Apostle Paul uses the word "none" or phrase "no, not one" to reveal man's total lack of righteousness before God. Romans 3:10-12 quotes Psalm 14:1-3, Psalm 53:1-3, and Ecclesiastes 7:20 to reassure this truth.

13. Read Romans 3:10. In Romans 3:10, the phrase "as it is written," translated in Greek, is in the perfect tense. What does this mean?
That there is continuity and permanence to what's written.

14. Read Romans 3:10. According to Romans 3:10, how are both Jew and Gentile alike?
There is none righteous, no, not one. No person who ever lived could be characterized as righteous by God's standard. To prevent some from thinking so, Paul said, "no, not one!"

15. "There is none that understandeth" (Rom. 3:11). Why is this so, according to Ephesians 4:18?
Sin has darkened man's understanding.

16. "There is none that seeketh after God" (Rom. 3:11). Why is this so, according to Philippians 2:21?
People are more interested in themselves than in Jesus Christ.

17. Read John 6:44. If none seeketh after God, then what must God do?
Draw individuals to Himself.

18. What does the word "draw" mean?
Literally "to drag." The word is used in John 21:11, referring to Peter drawing fishes to shore. It is used in Acts 16:19, referring to Paul and Silas being drawn into a market place unto the rulers of the city. It is used in James 2:6, referring to rich men drawing poor people before judgment seats.

19. What must the Lord do for us, according to Acts 16:14?
Open our hearts to respond to Him.

20. Read Romans 3:12. According to Romans 3:12, how many have turned away from God?
All have turned away.

21. According to Isaiah 53:6, how many have turned away from God?
All.

22. Is this true of you?
Yes. In theology, this is called the total depravity of man.

23. What idea does the word "unprofitable" carry in Romans 3:12?
This word is used to describe something that once was good, but now is corrupt. Example: meat that is now rotten, milk that has soured.

24. Read Romans 3:12. How many of us have kept on doing what is right?
Not even one.

25. Read Romans 3:13. Mankind's throat is like a what?
An open grave.

26. How did Jesus state this in Matthew 12:34?
A bad heart produces a bad mouth.

27. Read Romans 3:13. With their tongues, what do men do?
Lie and deceive. In Greek this phrase is in the imperfect tense meaning it is continual. Lying and being deceitful is normal to sinful man.

28. Read Romans 3:13. According to Romans 3:13, men's lips can be likened to what?
The poison in a diamondback rattlesnake.

29. Mankind's mouth is full of cursing and bitterness (Rom. 3:14). How would you define "cursing"?
Cursing is desiring the worst for a person by criticizing him or her openly.

30. How would you define "bitterness"? Rom. 3:14.
Bitterness is having open hostility against others.

31. How can Romans 3:15 be compared to Matthew 5:21-22?
When in anger you say to someone, "I wish you were not here," that is where murder begins.

32. Read Romans 3:16.Destruction and misery mark mankind's ways. How would you define the word "destruction"?
In Greek this word means "breaking in pieces, shattering, total devastation." This could take the form of divorce, abuse, rape, etc.

33. Read Romans 3:16.How would you define the word "misery"?
By the word "pain."

34. The way of peace mankind does not know (Rom. 3:17). How does Isaiah 57:21 state this?
"There is no peace, saith my God, to the wicked" (Isa. 57:21).

35. Read Romans 3:18. What is the cause of sin according to Romans 3:18?
No fear of God. To fear God means to have such an appreciation of the Majesty of God, the holiness of God and the justice of God, that you do not want to offend Him.

36. Read Romans 3:19. What effect does the Law have upon every individual?
It silences every mouth and makes all stand guilty before God.

37. Read Romans 3:20. How many people will be declared right before God by keeping the Law?
No person will be declared right before God by keeping the Law.

38. Why?
Because the Law only brings the knowledge of sin; it does not bring the ability to be declared right. The Law is like a mirror; it can show the dirt on one's face, but it was not meant to remove it.

39. Read Romans 3:21. What righteousness is being offered to us in Romans 3:21?
The righteousness of God, or from God. The righteousness that man needs comes from God Himself.

40. Read Romans 3:21. The source of this righteousness is that it is without what?
Without the law, or apart from the Law.

41. Read Romans 3:21.This righteousness from God is now what?
Manifested, or made known.

42. Read Romans 3:21. Does the Old Testament tell us about this righteousness? Also read Genesis 3:15 and Isaiah 53:11.
Yes. The Law is the first five books of the Old Testament. The Prophets are the second main section of the Old Testament.

43. Read Romans 3:22. What kind of righteousness makes people acceptable to God?
A through faith in Jesus Christ righteousness.

44. Read Romans 3:22. Who is this righteousness offered to?
Unto all and upon all them that believe.

45. Read Romans 3:22-23. The phrase, "for there is no difference," is really a phrase that means, "there is no difference or distinction." In what way is there no difference or distinction in mankind?
There is no distinction in that all have sinned and fall short of the glory of God.
Example; jumping contest across the lake. All fall short.

46. In Romans 3:23 the phrase, "come short of the glory of God," is in the present tense in Greek. This means that it is a continuous action. It happens over and over again. It's an habitual action. The phrase, "Being justified," in Romans 3:24, is also in the present tense and has the same meaning. Grace is greater than sin (Rom. 5:20). How would you define what it means to be justified?
To treat, reckon, or account someone in right-relationship, right-standing, or righteous before God.

47. Read Romans 3:24. Justification is not an attainment of man; it is a gift of God. What word in Romans 3:24 (besides the word "grace") proves this statement?
Freely. "Freely" is the Greek word "DOREAN" and literally means "without a cause, freely" (Strong). Many translations translate it "gift" or "free gift" (RSV, JB). There is nothing in you or me that caused God to put righteousness to our account—it's a gift.

48. Read Romans 3:24. God declares us righteous; He does it freely, and how is this done? (by His what)?
By His grace. Grace is the free, unmerited, undeserved favor toward those who deserve the opposite.

Example: My son breaks his arm and I rush him into the hospital. On the way to the hospital I am picked up for speeding. The police officer could deal with me in one of two ways: First, he could deal with me in justice (there would be no doubt of the outcome, I am guilty. Second, he could deal with me in grace (not because there is anything good in me, but because of my son).

God can deal with us in justice (there is no doubt of the outcome because we are guilty), or God can deal with us in grace (with no cause in you or me, but because of His Son).

49. Read Romans 3:24. How could God bestow righteousness upon a sinner and still be just?
Only through the redemption that is in Christ Jesus.

There are several Greek words for "redemption." 1. AGORAZO: a common word used in a marketplace. It means "to pay a price whereby something is purchased." 2. EX AGORAZO: the prefix "ex" means "out of." This word means not just to purchase with a price, but to purchase out of. It removes the thing redeemed. 3. LUTROO: "a setting at liberty, to free, release or deliver." To release from what it was: to function and accomplish what it was made for.

Example: I see a lamp I want in a Green stamp magazine. I go to the redemption center and pay the purchase price, set by the company. I now remove the lamp from its state of uselessness in the box. I put it on the table and plug it into an outlet. It now has a very useful function. In a sense, it was released from what it was, so that it might function and accomplish what it was made to accomplish.

Statement: We were purchased in the marketplace of sin (Eph. 2:1-3). We were purchased "out of" the authority of darkness (Col. 1:13; Acts 26:18). We were "freed" or "released" to have a useful function - to glorify God (See 1 Cor. 6:20).

50. Read Romans 3:24. In whom was this redemption?
In Christ Jesus. He is the one who paid the price.

51. Read Romans 3:25. According to Romans 3:25, What did God publicly display Jesus to be?
A propitiation.

52. What does "propitiation" mean?
Propitiation is a word that was used among the Greeks, and has the significance of doing something that would please the gods, appease the gods, or make the gods propitious. The reason being, is that the gods were not thought of as having a very loving nature, so men had to appease them. The Bible never speaks of man making God propitious. The Bible states, "Jesus is the propitiation for our sins: and not for ours only, but also for the sins of the whole world" (1 John 2:2). God was propitiated through the sacrifice of Jesus. "Propitiation" refers to both the payment of sin (sacrifice) and the place of payment (the place of mercy, the mercy seat).

53. Read Romans 3:25. What was the price that brought man into a favorable and righteous standing before God?
Christ's blood (See Eph. 1:6-7).

54. According to Romans 3:25-26, why was it necessary for Christ to die? See Romans 3:25-26 from the Today's English Version or New American Standard Version.
To demonstrate He is a righteous God.

Example: The argument goes like this: If your child does something wrong and asks forgiveness, because you are a loving parent, wouldn't you forgive him? If a sinner comes to God and asks for forgiveness, because God is a loving God, will He not forgive him?

Conclusion: There would be no need for Christ's death.

Why was it necessary for Christ to die? Because God is more than a loving God: He is also a just and righteous God. Christ's death demonstrates that God is righteous, by not overlooking sin, but by judging sin at the cross.

Read Romans 3:25. How could we define God's "forbearance"?
Forbearance means, "to restrain oneself in the face of being provoked."

Example: You tell your children not to do certain things when you have company. Your children misbehave. They look over at you, and nothing happens. You must not have meant it, or you forgot what you said. The children think this until the company leaves; that's when the action begins.

For 4,000 years man has provoked God by his sin. God has restrained Himself and seems to have overlooked sin (ignored sin), but He has not forgotten it. In demonstrating that He is righteous, He took all the judgment that man has escaped from for 4,000 years, and laid it upon Jesus on the cross.

55. If sin had not been paid for until the time of Jesus, how could a holy God justly forgive a man such as David, who had committed adultery?
David was forgiven on credit. God was looking ahead to Calvary to pay the payment for David's sins.

56. How can God justify a guilty person?
God has made a payment for sin.

57. Read Romans 3:26. In Romans 3:26, Paul states that through redemption God has been shown to be just (i.e. righteous). What else is He?
The justifier of the one who puts faith in Jesus.

Example One: You tell your children to be in by 6:00 p.m. or they can't watch TV that evening. They come in at 6:05 p.m. You now have two options: First, you can be loving and forgiving by saying, "Well you were close, so let's just forget about it. Second, you can be righteous and say, "Because you did not do what I said, there will be no TV tonight." As a parent, I can be loving and forgiving, BUT NOT righteous and forgiving. Righteousness demands that I live according to the standard I set. God can be BOTH, righteous and forgiving because Christ has paid the price for our sins. So on the basis of Christ's death for us, God can righteously declare us righteous because our sins have been paid for. This is a, "through-faith-in-Jesus-Christ-righteousness" (Rom. 3:22).

Example two: You have a debt to the electric company and I know your electricity is going to be cut off tomorrow. As a concerned neighbor, I go down and pay your bill of $99.95.

The next day you go down to the electric company and say, "I'm sorry, I do not have the $99.95 to pay my bill. Will you grant me an extension? Will you somehow ignore the rule this once?" The secretary says, "I think one of your neighbors came down and paid your bill. Yes, Don Krow is his name."

You now have a choice: You can reject the offer by saying, "I'm not accepting charity from anyone; if anyone pays the bill, I'll pay it myself!" (You are a proud man and can't accept grace) or, you may accept the payment. It's the same with Christ. You may reject the payment He made for your sin, or accept the redemption and He'll be your redeemer.

Example three: I was driving west one day on highway 18, near my old home town in northeastern Oklahoma. As I was exceeding the speed limit driving to my father's ranch I suddenly looked back and saw a flashing red light. It was an Oklahoma Highway patrolman. I was stopped and summoned to appear before a judge at the Pawnee County Courthouse. When I stood before the judge, I discovered he was an old friend of my family's. I was sure that my ill fortune was going to be turned for the better. As the judge greeted me he kindly said, "You know I would like to show you mercy, to show you grace, but I cannot, in order to be a just judge." He sentenced me to pay a fine of $100 or spend one day in jail. Knowing that I did not have the money, I was ready to serve one day in jail. The judge did something quite unusual. He took off his robe as judge, stepped down from the bench, and reached into his pocket. He gave me $100 and said, "Pay your fine!" In his justice he sentenced me, but in his mercy he paid my debt.

God, in His justice, has sentenced us (the wages of sin is death: Rom. 6:23) but in His mercy, He paid our debt.

58. Read Romans 3:27. What are the questions being asked in Romans 3:27? **What can we boast about doing to earn salvation? Nothing at all! It is wiped out! By what principle? Of works? No. If it were of works we would have something to brag about. If it is of faith, then we simply rest on the object of our faith, Jesus Christ.**

59. Read Romans 3:28. What is the conclusion of Paul's argument in Romans 3:28? **People are declared righteous before God by faith in Christ without the work of trying to keep the Law.**

60. Read Romans 3:29-30. What is the argument of Romans 3:29-30? **Are there two Gods? One for the Jews and one for the Gentiles? Are there two ways of salvation? One way by Law and one way by faith? No. There is only one God and one way of salvation—through faith.**

61. Read Romans 3:31. What is the question being asked in Romans 3:31?
Are we throwing out the Law because we are justified by faith? God forbid! We establish the Law.

62. Read Romans 3:31. How do we establish the Law by justification through faith?
1) By putting the Law to its proper use (Rom. 3:20), revealing the knowledge of sin. The Law is like a mirror, fire alarm, or a light on your car's dashboard. It shows there's a problem, but in itself, it is not the answer.

2) By confirming what the Law has always taught: justification is by faith (Abraham—Gen. 15:6).

3) By offering the righteousness that the Law demands (through faith in Jesus Christ—Rom. 3:22, Rom. 1:17).

4) By executing the penalty for breaking the Law (that's how laws are established).

Example: If a Jew in the Old Testament was gathering sticks on the Sabbath, the Law said, Thou shalt not kindle a fire on the Sabbath... and if you do, you will be stoned to death (Ex. 35:2-3). On one hand you have the Law; on the other hand you have the man breaking the Law. How is it that the Law is established? By forgiving the man? No! The Law is established when the man is taken and stoned to death. It is the execution of the penalty of the broken law on the lawbreaker that establishes the law.

Example: The law states that no cameras are allowed in a courtroom, but a newspaper man brings one in anyway. How is that law established? Only by executing the penalty of that broken law on the man (a fine or jail time).

Statement: On the day the Old Testament law of death for sin was executed upon Jesus Christ for our transgressions, the law was established. Justification through faith, establishes the law because it involves the execution of the broken law upon our substitute: Jesus Christ (Gal. 3:13).

OVERVIEW OF ROMANS CHAPTER 4

by Don Krow

Romans 4:1: *"What shall we say then that Abraham our father, as pertaining to the flesh, hath found?"* In other words, what has Abraham discovered in this matter of being justified, being declared right before God? This is really the question that is being asked here.

Verse 2: *"For if Abraham were justified by works* [if he were declared righteous by his works, by something he did], *he hath whereof to glory* [he has a reason to boast], *but not before God."* Abraham could never boast before God. Why? What does the scripture say?

Verse 3: *"For what saith the scripture? Abraham believed God* [a quotation from Genesis 15:6], *and it was counted to him for righteousness."* Abraham was justified through faith, and when he believed God, God put something to his account that he did not have before—righteousness.

Verse 4: *"Now to him that worketh is the reward not reckoned of grace, but of debt."* Paul is contrasting something we are all familiar with: When you work on a job, you earn wages. They don't pay you because you're good looking, because they like your personality, or because they think you're great. They pay you because you do a job. You work and get wages for the things you do. We all understand that. They don't pay you by grace, as a favor. That is the principle of works. Paul says God uses the principle of grace to make people right before him.

Verse 5: *"But to him that worketh not, but believeth on him that justifieth the ungodly, his faith is counted for righteousness."* Paul is saying that the first thing a person must do who wants to be made righteous before God is to stop working for it. Look at this … *"to him that worketh not, but believeth"* on God (or Christ), God justifies, declares righteous. Who? Look at your Bible. Who does God declare righteous here? God declares righteous ungodly people through their faith in Jesus Christ.

Justification is a sovereign act of God whereby He declares the believing sinner righteous even though he is still in a sinning state. I repented—that means I've had a change of heart; I want to do things God's way. I have turned to Jesus Christ for God's righteousness through faith in Him. I want to do what's right, but do you know that I will fail? Each day at different times, I fail. It may be in my thoughts, what I say, or by my actions. God has designed salvation through faith in Jesus Christ, so He can declare ungodly people righteous. That's the good news of the Gospel.

Look at it here … to him or her who will quit working to try to be saved, but will put faith in God, and believe on Christ, God will justify, and declare them righteous; it's the ungodly who are made right by their faith. It's faith that is counted as righteousness. Isn't that good news? I don't have to be perfect. God accepts me as perfect, as righteous, because of my faith in Jesus Christ who has paid the price for my righteousness.

Verse 6: David also described this blessedness, a person who understands this. *"Even as David also describeth the blessedness of the man, unto whom God imputed righteousness without works."* That person will truly be happy, truly rejoice, when he realizes this: God will put righteousness to his account without him working for it.

Verses 7-8: *"Saying* [quotation from Psalm 32]*, Blessed are they whose iniquities are forgiven and whose sins are covered. Blessed is the man to whom the Lord will not impute sin."* Do you see what the synonym is here? God imputing righteousness without you working for it is synonymous with your iniquities being forgiven and your sins covered. Isn't that amazing? When God forgave my sins, He also put righteous (right standing) to my account without me working for it.

Something even greater is where verse 8 says, *"Blessed is the man to whom the Lord will not impute sin."* God has given me a covenant called the new covenant. It's not based on my performance but on Him and what He has done through Jesus Christ. Through that new covenant, He says, "This is what I promise. I will be merciful to you in your unrighteousness, and your sins and iniquities I will remember no more." That is what Paul is saying here. He will not count sin against an individual, because He has counted that sin against Jesus Christ, our substitute. Isn't it amazing that I have a relationship with Jesus Christ that will never fluctuate according to my good works or bad works, but because of what He has done and because I put faith in Him?

Verse 9: *"Cometh this blessedness then upon the circumcision* [Jews] *only, or upon the uncircumcision* [Gentiles] *also? for we say that faith was reckoned to Abraham for righteousness."* Is this blessedness of having your sins forgiven, of having righteousness put to your account without you working for it, just for Jews? No. It's also for Gentiles, for everyone, because it's faith in Jesus Christ that is accounted for righteousness. It's not by the works of righteousness we do, but through His mercy that He saves us (Titus 3:5).

Verse 10: *"How was it then reckoned? when he was in circumcision, or in uncircumcision? Not in circumcision, but in uncircumcision."* What is that saying? It is saying that it wasn't religious symbols that brought him the righteousness, but a heart that turned to God in faith.

Verse 11: *"And he received the sign of circumcision, a seal of the righteousness of the faith which he had yet being uncircumcised: that he might be the father of all them that believe, though they be not circumcised; that righteousness might be imputed unto them also.* This says that circumcision was only a seal, a sign, that God had accepted him as righteous through his faith.

For the sake of time I will go to verses 19-22: *"And being not weak in faith, he considered not his own body now dead, when he was about an hundred years old, neither yet the deadness of Sara's womb: He staggered not at the promise of God through unbelief; but was strong in faith, giving glory to God; And being fully persuaded that, what he had promised, he was able also to perform. And therefore it was imputed to him for righteousness."* Now here it is. Righteousness comes through faith. It didn't come through Abraham's works, performance, or keeping the Law. It says here that God gave a promise, which is simply His word on something. Abraham took God at His word, and the Bible tells us that we must take God at His word, because we have a promise. The promise is that Jesus paid a perfect price.

I want you to see this in verses 22-23: *"Therefore it was imputed to him for righteousness. Now it was not written for his sake alone, that it was imputed to him."* This was not just a good story from the Old Testament about Abraham being made righteous through his faith. It is saying that this is for us—an instruction to us in the New Testament.

Look at verses 23-24: *"Now it was not written for his sake alone, that it was imputed to him, But for us also, to whom it shall be imputed."* The same righteousness that was put to Abraham's account will be put to our accounts as well, when we exercise faith the same way Abraham did.

Verses 24-25: *"But for us also, to whom it shall be imputed, if we believe on him that raised up Jesus our Lord from the dead; Who was delivered for our offences, and was raised again for our justification."* God is asking us to be made righteous the same Abraham was, by trusting His promise that Jesus Christ has paid a perfect price for our sins.

Will you trust Him now? Will you rely on Him now? Will you cling to Him and His perfect work now? If you do, the very righteousness of God will be laid to your account through faith in Jesus Christ.

Romans 4:1-25
Discipleship Commentary

. . . .

Read the entire lesson and then answer the questions that follow.

Romans 4:1 - What shall we say then that Abraham our father, as pertaining to the flesh, hath found?

(Rom. 4:1) The question is, "What good then were Abraham's works?" Paul answers this indirectly. Paul states what Abraham's works were not good for—they were not good enough to grant him justification in the sight of God. Justification came by faith. He shows that Abraham's works, or efforts, didn't earn him anything from God. Abraham was justified by faith for over thirteen years before he performed the act of circumcision that the Jews were insisting was necessary for right-standing with God (vv. 10-11).

Romans 4:2 - For if Abraham were justified by works, he hath whereof to glory; but not before God.

(Rom. 4:2) Our own good works will only allow us to boast if we are comparing ourselves with other people (2 Cor. 10:12). However, in the sight of God, none of us have anything to brag about. We have all come short of the glory of God.

Romans 4:3 - For what saith the scripture? Abraham believed God, and it was counted unto him for righteousness.

(Rom. 4:3) Paul is showing an inspired revelation of the Old Testament scriptures. All devout Jews knew the story of Abraham, but they had missed this simple truth that Paul brings out. In Genesis 15:6, the scripture clearly says Abraham believed God and that God counted Abraham's faith for righteousness. It can't get any clearer than that. Later in this same chapter, Paul refers to the interval of time (over thirteen years) between when Abraham's faith counted him righteous and the time when he was circumcised as further proof that Abraham's righteousness was given to him before he performed the righteous acts of the Law.

Paul had just made a series of radical statements which were hard for these Jews to swallow. He is now going back to Old Testament scripture and the founder of the Jewish nation to prove his assertions. He skillfully uses the very scriptures they had misunderstood to verify his Gospel of grace. He also quotes David to draw on two of the most revered men of the Old Testament as examples of salvation by grace through faith.

Hebrews 11:6 says, "But without faith it is impossible to please him." It was Abraham's faith that pleased God. The Lord promised Abraham that his seed would be as numerous as the stars in the sky and the sand on the seashore, and Abraham believed God. That pleased Him so much that he counted Abraham righteous right then, even though Abraham had not yet fulfilled the rite of circumcision and was not living such a holy life.

According to Leviticus 18:9, it was an abomination (Lev. 18:26) for a man to marry a half sister. Sara, Abraham's wife, was his half sister (Gen. 20:12). Therefore, Abraham's marriage to Sara was not what pleased God. Abraham had already lied about Sara being his wife so that he could save his own neck. He was willing to let a man commit adultery with his wife without objecting. Immediately after this instance when the Lord counted Abraham's faith for righteousness (Gen. 15:6), Abraham tried to accomplish God's will in the flesh with Hagar (Gen. 16). Then Abraham repeated this terrible sin concerning Sara again (Gen. 20).

Anyone who really looked at the life of Abraham and the favor that he found with God would have to conclude that it was Abraham's faith that pleased God. It's the same with any of us. The only thing that we can do to please God is put faith in Jesus as our Savior.

The Greek word that was translated "counted" in this verse is the word "logizomai," which means, "to take an inventory, i.e. estimate." It is an accounting term that means "to enter in the account book" (Rienecker's A Linguistic Key to the Greek New Testament). This same word is used 11 times in this chapter. It was translated "counted" twice (vv. 3 and 5), "impute" once (v. 8), "imputed" four times (vv. 11, 22, 23, 24), "imputeth" once (v. 6), and "reckoned" three times (vv. 4, 9, 10). By comparing the different ways this same Greek word was translated into English, it becomes very easy to discern an accurate meaning for it.

Romans 4:4 - Now to him that worketh is the reward not reckoned of grace, but of debt.

(Rom. 4:4) Paul is saying that if an individual could be saved by works, then God would be providing that salvation as a payment to that person, and, of course, that doesn't make sense. God is not under obligation or debt to save anyone. Trust in our own works voids grace, and likewise, trust in God's grace makes faith in our own efforts useless. This is repeated by Paul again in Romans 11:6; "And if by grace, then is it no more of works: otherwise grace is no more grace. But if it be of works, then is it no more grace: otherwise work is no more work."

Romans 4:5 - But to him that worketh not, but believeth on him that justifieth the ungodly, his faith is counted for righteousness.

(Rom. 4:5) What a statement!! Paul had been countering the false doctrine that acting righteous could make a person righteous. Now he drops the bomb that God justifies the ungodly! We might add from the context that that is the only kind of person that He justifies. That's because He hasn't got any other kind of people to justify. We've all sinned and come short of the glory of God. This verse should forever dispel any delusions that anyone might have of trying to earn God's favor by his or her performance.

Faith in the atonement of Jesus grants us righteousness. Our actions don't grant us righteousness. However, true faith will produce actions (James 2:17), and these actions, or lack thereof, can be used for others to determine where we stand with the Lord (1 John 3:7-10). Although our actions are an indication of our inner faith, they can be misinterpreted, and therefore any judgments made based on actions need to be for the purpose of discernment only and not condemnation.

Romans 4:6 - Even as David also describeth the blessedness of the man, unto whom God imputeth righteousness without works,

(Rom. 4:6) King David was living under the old covenant of Law. However, this scripture that Paul quotes from Psalm 32, as well as the things David wrote in Psalm 51 when repenting for his sins against Uriah and Bathsheba, show that he had a tremendous revelation of the salvation by grace through faith that was coming with the Messiah.

Romans 4:7-8 - Saying, Blessed are they whose iniquities are forgiven, and whose sins are covered. 8) Blessed is the man to whom the Lord will not impute sin.

(Rom. 4:8) The Greek word that is translated "will not" in this verse is what is called an emphatic negative, and it means "not ever." This is the strongest language possible that those who receive forgiveness will not ever have their sins held against them. He didn't just say "did not" or "does not" but "will not," implying that even future tense sins have been dealt with through the sacrificial offering of Jesus, once for all (Heb. 10:10, 14).

Most Christians have the concept that the sins that they committed before they professed faith in Christ were forgiven at salvation, but any sins that are committed after that time are not forgiven until they are repented of and forgiveness is asked. That is not the case.

All our sins, past, present, and future were forgiven us through the one offering of Jesus. If God can't forgive future tense sins, then none of us can be saved, because Jesus only died once, nearly 2,000 years ago, before we had committed any sins. All our sins have been forgiven.

Why then 1 John 1:9, which says, "If we confess our sins, he is faithful and just to forgive us our sins, and to cleanse us from all unrighteousness." This is not speaking of the eternal salvation of our spirits but rather the salvation of our souls (James 1:21, 1 Pet. 1:9). It's our spirits that were born again at salvation, and sin will never be imputed to our born-again spirits. They have been sanctified and perfected forever (Heb. 10:10, 14, and 12:23) and cannot sin (1 Jn. 3:9).

However, we are still in the process of saving our souls (James 1:21; 1 Pet. 1:9). When we sin, the devil has a legal right to bring his forms of death into our soulish area (Rom. 6:16). How do we get the devil out once he has gotten in? We confess our sins, and God brings the forgiveness that is already a reality in our born-again spirits out into the soulish realm, and the devil has no right to stay.

If we had to confess every sin committed after our born-again experience in order to maintain our salvation, no one would ever make it. What if we forgot to confess some sin? That puts the burden of salvation back on us.

We must remember that "God is a Spirit" (John 4:24), and we must worship Him through our new born-again spirits. Therefore, we truly are blessed because God will not hold any sin against our spirits. Our spirits are clean and pure (Eph. 4:24, Heb. 12:23 and 1 John 4:17) and will not change due to our performance.

Romans 4:9 - Cometh this blessedness then upon the circumcision only, or upon the uncircumcision also? for we say that faith was reckoned to Abraham for righteousness.

(Rom. 4:9) Paul had previously shown in this chapter that Abraham's faith was what granted him right-standing with God, and he used a quote from David to verify salvation by grace through faith. He now returns to the story of Abraham and uses the very religious act which the legalists were demanding compliance with (i.e., circumcision) to further certify that salvation is by grace through faith.

Romans 4:10 - How was it then reckoned? when he was in circumcision, or in uncircumcision? Not in circumcision, but in uncircumcision.

(Rom. 4:10) The time between when God counted Abraham's faith for righteousness and when Abraham was circumcised was over thirteen years. This can be deduced in the following way. The instance where God counted Abraham righteous took place in Genesis 15:6, which was before the birth of Ishmael (Gen. 16:15). Abraham circumcised Ishmael the same day that he was circumcised (Gen. 17:26), which Genesis 17:25 says took place when Ishmael was thirteen years old. Therefore, the circumcision of Abraham was at least thirteen years and nine months after his justification by faith in Genesis 15:6.

This truth is so simple and obvious that it is amazing that the legalistic Jews had missed it. Paul explains that God said Abraham was righteous (Gen. 15:6) over thirteen years before he performed the rite of circumcision. Now if circumcision was necessary for justification with God, as some Jews were advocating, then Abraham could not have been righteous until after the performing of this act. But God Himself said Abraham was righteous. Therefore, the rite of circumcision (or any other act of obedience) cannot be a prerequisite for justification.

In our day, religious people no longer contend that circumcision is essential for salvation, Paul conclusively disproved that. However, many people are still making the same mistake. They have just substituted some other act of holiness for circumcision. They may have changed cars, but they are headed down the same road to the same destination.

For instance, entire denominations are built around the doctrine that water baptism is essential for salvation. There is no disputing that water baptism is a command of Jesus (Matt. 28:19-20) just as circumcision was a command under the Old Testament (Gen. 17:9-14). However, the same logic that Paul uses here to disprove circumcision as a prerequisite to justification can be used to prove that water baptism is not required before a person can be saved.

Any condition that must be met for salvation, except faith in what Jesus did for us, is error (Rom. 3:28). This is what Paul called "another Gospel" or, more accurately, a perversion of the Gospel (Gal. 1:6-7).

Romans 4:11 - And he received the sign of circumcision, a seal of the righteousness of the faith which he had yet being uncircumcised: that he might be the father of all them that believe, though they be not circumcised; that righteousness might be imputed unto them also:

(Rom. 4:11) The rite of circumcision was a confirmation of the righteousness that Abraham had already attained by faith. It was meant to be a constant reminder to him of the covenant between God and himself. It was never intended to be something that Abraham would boast about or use to show others his holiness. This was private!

No doubt one of the reasons the Lord chose this act as a sign of the covenant instead of some other act, was to prevent the very thing that the Jews were doing. How were you to tell if someone else was circumcised? That's not the kind of thing that is public knowledge. It's between God and that individual. God gave the sign of circumcision, because it is a very private act; therefore, He never intended us to use circumcision to judge the righteousness of anyone.

Romans 4:12 - And the father of circumcision to them who are not of the circumcision only, but who also walk in the steps of that faith of our father Abraham, which he had being yet uncircumcised.

(Rom. 4:12) Note that Abraham had faith before he had the action of circumcision. Many people have mistakenly thought that actions produce faith, but that's not so. Acting right doesn't make a person right; you have to be born again.

Romans 4:13 - For the promise, that he should be the heir of the world, was not to Abraham, or to his seed, through the law, but through the righteousness of faith.

(Rom. 4:13) There is no Old Testament scripture that states Abraham would be heir of the world in these words. The closest scriptures would be when the Lord told Abram that all the families of the earth would be blessed through him (Gen. 12:3) and that He had made Abraham the father of many nations (Gen. 17:4-5).

The Jews interpreted God's promises to Abraham as being to his physical descendants only. However, the Old Testament promises to Abraham that the Apostle Paul is referencing remove any doubt about the Jews being the only ones to be blessed through God's covenant with Abraham. Abraham's true seed is anyone of any nation or language who places faith in Christ as his or her Savior.

Romans 4:14 - For if they which are of the law be heirs, faith is made void, and the promise made of none effect:

(Rom. 4:14) We are either justified by faith in our works without faith in Christ, or we are justified by faith in Christ without faith in our works, but not a combination of the two (Rom. 11:6). Trusting in our own goodness as the reason that God would grant us salvation, neutralizes faith and renders God's promise to Abraham useless.

There are Christians who have put their faith in Christ for their eternal salvation, but then fall back into the deception that God is going to bless them and use them based on their performance. This is what happened to the Galatians. Paul told them that Christ had become of no benefit to them if they were trusting in what they did to be justified with God (Gal. 5:4). Likewise today, many Christians do not experience the full effect of their salvation, because they are making faith void by trusting in their own goodness.

Romans 4:15 - Because the law worketh wrath: for where no law is, there is no transgression.

(Rom. 4:15) The Law of God released the wrath of God. Without the Law there was no wrath, because without the Law there was no transgression. First John 3:4 says, "Whosoever committeth sin transgresseth also the law: for sin is the transgression of the law." Therefore, before the Law of God was given, men's sins were not being held against them.

This is why Abraham was not killed for marrying his half sister and Jacob for marrying his wife's sister (Lev. 18:18). God had not given the Law concerning these things yet, and therefore, there was no willful transgression on these men's part. So, when the law of God was introduced, sin revived and we died. The Law produced death by releasing God's wrath against our sins.

Anyone who seeks to keep the Law of God for the purpose of being justified in God's sight will also release the wrath of God on his or her life. Praise God for Jesus who brought us out from under the Law and put us under grace (Rom. 6:14).

Romans 4:16 - Therefore it is of faith, that it might be by grace; to the end the promise might be sure to all the seed; not to that only which is of the law, but to that also which is of the faith of Abraham; who is the father of us all,

(Rom. 4:16) Paul makes it very clear here that the seed of Abraham included more than his physical descendants. Jesus taught on this and Paul mentions this a number of times (Rom. 2:28-29, 4:11-12,16, ch. 9; and Gal. 3).

Since God made salvation available on the basis of faith in what He did, then everyone can be saved. If He would have made our holiness the basis of salvation, then no one could have been saved, "for all have sinned and come short of the glory of God" (Rom. 3:23).

Romans 4:17 - (As it is written, I have made thee a father of many nations,) before him whom he believed, even God, who quickeneth the dead, and calleth those things which be not as though they were.

(Rom. 4:17) The phrase, "and calleth those things which be not as though they were" is referring to what Paul had just cited about when God changed Abram's name to Abraham (Gen. 17:5). The name Abram meant "high father." The name Abraham meant "father of a multitude." The Lord changed Abram's name to Abraham one year before the birth of Isaac, thus confessing that Abraham was the father of a multitude before it happened in the physical.

This illustrates God's faith. God says things are so before there is physical proof that they are so. The same thing was done at creation (Gen. 1). God spoke everything into existence, and then it was so. He spoke light into existence and then, three days later, created a source for that light to come from (Gen. 1:3 with 14-19).

God has given us the power to create with faith-filled words. If we are going to operate in God's kind of faith, we have to learn to call those things which are not as though they were.

Romans 4:18 - Who against hope believed in hope, that he might become the father of many nations, according to that which was spoken, So shall thy seed be.

(Rom. 4:18) There was no hope, in the natural, for Abraham or his wife Sara. They were both as good as dead when it came to having children at their age. Therefore, they rejected the natural and believed God with a supernatural hope. There is a natural hope, which everyone has, and there is a supernatural hope that is imparted by God (1 Cor. 13:13). To receive miracles, we have to reject the limitations of natural hope and press on to obtain God's supernatural hope through faith.

Abraham's faith was based on God's Word. Every word of God is powerful and contains the faith of God to bring that word to pass. If we will only consider God's Word, then we will only believe.

Romans 4:19 - And being not weak in faith, he considered not his own body now dead, when he was about an hundred years old, neither yet the deadness of Sara's womb:

(Rom. 4:19) This verse is telling us how Abraham kept from being weak in faith. The key is what he focused his attention on.

Some translations and many commentators turn this verse around to say the opposite of what the King James Version says. For instance, the New International Version says, "without weakening in his faith, he faced the fact that his body was as good as dead," etc. However, that type of reasoning is missing one of the great scriptural keys to strong faith.

The word "consider" is defined as "1. to deliberate upon; examine; study; 4. to take into account; make allowance for; 5. to have regard for; pay attention to" (New American Heritage Dictionary). The Greek word that was used is "katanoeo," which simply means, "to observe fully."

Therefore, we can see that Abraham did not deliberate upon, examine, or study the age of himself and Sarah and the impact that would have on the promise God had given him. He did not take those things into account or make any allowance for them. That was not what he paid attention to.

That is amazing, and that is exactly the reason many of us would not be able to receive the same miracle. We consider every negative thing that looks contrary to God's promises and then try to overcome the fear and unbelief that comes through those thoughts with our faith. That's not the way Abraham was strong in faith.

Abram was 75 years old when the Lord first promised him that he would have a child and that all the nations of the earth would be blessed through him (Gen. 12:1-4). He was 99 years old in this instance which Paul is citing (Gen. 17:1) and Sara was 90 years old (Gen. 17:17). Yet, he didn't even take into account the impossibility of what God had promised him.

It is true that Abraham was strong in faith (v. 20), but the thing that made him strong in faith is the fact that he kept his mind stayed on God's promise, and equally important, he kept his mind off anything which would have been contrary to God's promise. Many people desire the same strong faith that Abraham had, but very few desire to control their thinking the way Abraham did.

Faith is a direct result of what we think on. If you think on God's Word, faith comes (Rom. 8:6, 10:17). If you think on other things, unbelief and fear come (Rom. 8:6). If you want the faith of Abraham working in you, then think the way he thought and never consider anything except God's Word, and you will be strong in faith.

Romans 4:20 - He staggered not at the promise of God through unbelief; but was strong in faith, giving glory to God;

(Rom. 4:20) From the context of this statement, we can see that the unbelief that Abraham refused to consider was the unbelief that would have come through thinking on the natural facts. Many people don't perceive facts as generating unbelief. We have been led to believe that we have to consider all the facts to make a proper decision, but that's not so with God's Word.

When we have clear direction from God's Word, we shouldn't consider anything else. Considering "facts" contrary to God's promises will make us stagger in our faith.

Jesus had equated praise with strength. Here we see that this is one thing that made Abraham strong in faith. Praise keeps our minds stayed on God and what He is doing. You cannot praise God and keep your mind on the problem. You will fall into complaining every time. This is why praise makes us strong in faith.

A person who believes the promises of God brings glory to God. Conversely, a person who disbelieves the promises of God dishonors God.

Romans 4:21 - And being fully persuaded that, what he had promised, he was able also to perform.

(Rom. 4:21) Notice that Abraham wasn't just persuaded; he was fully persuaded. Many people have been persuaded that the promises of God are true but they stop short of meditating on God's Word until they become fully persuaded. Strong faith belongs to those who continue in God's Word until all doubt is removed.

This is so obvious that it should go without saying, but the truth is, we really do doubt that God can perform His promises to us. How could this be? The answer lies in the way God made our hearts.

Whatever we focus our attention on is what our heart will believe, and whatever we neglect is what our heart will disbelieve. If we allow ourselves to meditate on our problems and all the reasons why it looks impossible for God to move in our situations, then we will believe that our problems are bigger than God. However, when we keep our minds stayed on the promises of God, nothing is too difficult for God (Jer. 32:17, 27).

Romans 4:22 - And therefore it was imputed to him for righteousness. 23) Now it was not written for his sake alone, that it was imputed to him; 24) But for us also, to whom it shall be imputed, if we believe on him that raised up Jesus our Lord from the dead; 25) Who was delivered for our offences, and was raised again for our justification.

(Rom. 4:23) In verses 23-24, Paul applies all these truths he has discussed about Abraham to us. God is no respecter of persons (Rom. 2:11). If He justified Abraham by faith, He will do the same for us.

Romans 4:1-25
Discipleship Questions

. . . .

Answer the following questions by reading the corresponding discipleship commentary lesson and using your Bible.

1. Read Romans 4:1. What is the question being asked in Romans 4:1?
   _____
   _____

2. Read Romans 4:2. If Abraham was justified, or declared righteous, by something he did (his good works), then what does he have reason to do?
   _____

3. Read Romans 4:3. How does this scripture say Abraham was justified?
   _____

4. Read Romans 4:4. To the person who works, his or her wages are not reckoned, or given as a favor but as what?
   _____

5. Read Romans 4:5. A person who wants to be justified by faith must stop doing what?
   _____

6. Read Romans 4:5. According to Romans 4:5, God justifies what kind of person?
   _____

7. Read Romans 4:5. Faith in God is credited to a person as what?
   _____

8. Read Romans 4:6. In Psalms 32, David describes people who are blessed and happy. Why are they blessed and happy? _____
   _____

9. Read Romans 4:7. Righteousness, without working for it, is a synonym for what phrase?
   _____

10. Read Romans 4:7. Happy are the people who have had what happen to them?
   _____

11. Read Romans 4:8. Happy is the man to whom the Lord will not do what?
   _____

12. Read Romans 4:9. Is this happiness of being made right before God just for the Jews, or is it for the Gentiles as well?
   _____

13. Read Romans 4:10. Under what circumstances—circumcision or uncircumcision—was justification, or righteousness, credited to Abraham?

_____

14. Read Romans 4:11. What two words describe circumcision in Romans 4:11?

_____

15. What is a "sign"?

_____

_____

_____

16. What is a "seal"?

_____

17. Read Romans 4:11. What was it a token, or proof, of in Abraham's life?

_____

_____

18. Romans 4:11 states that Abraham is the "father of all them that believe." How does Galatians 3:16 and 3:29 reflect this statement?

_____

_____

19. Read Romans 4:12. What is Romans 4:12 stating?

_____

_____

20. Read Romans 4:13. Romans 4:13 is stating that Abraham and his seed will not be the heirs of Canaan, nor of Palestine. What will they be heirs of?

_____

21. Read Romans 4:13. This promise came not because Abraham obeyed the Law but because he did what?

_____

_____

22. Read Romans 4:14. If any of God's promises are based on the Law, then what two things must be concluded?

_____

_____

23. Read Romans 4:15. The Law does not bring God's gift of salvation. What does it produce?

_____

24. Read Romans 4:15. What is the last part of Romans 4:15 stating?

_____

25. Read Romans 4:16. The promised inheritance, in which Christians share, is of what?

_____

26. Read Romans 4:17. According to Romans 4:17, what was the object of Abraham's faith?

_____

27. Read Romans 4:17. What two things does Romans 4:17 reveal about God?

_____

_____

28. Read Romans 4:18. What specific promise did Abraham believe God for?

_____

_____

29. Read Romans 4:18. Abraham, against hope, believed. What do you think this phrase means?

_____

30. Read Romans 4:19. According to Romans 4:19, what was the truth about Abraham and Sara?_____

31. Read Romans 4:20. How did Abraham respond according to Romans 4:20?

_____

32. Read Romans 4:21. God gave a promise to Abraham (Genesis 15:2-6). How did Abraham respond to that promise?

_____

_____

33. Read Romans 4:22. State in your own words what Romans 4:22 is saying.

_____

_____

34. Read Romans 4:23-25. What is Paul telling us in Romans 4:23-25?

_____

_____

_____

Romans 4:1-25
Discipleship Answer Key

Do not look at the answer key until you have completed the questions.
Compare your answers with the following answers.

1. Read Romans 4:1. What is the question being asked in Romans 4:1?
   What did Abraham our forefather, discover in this matter of being justified by faith?

2. Read Romans 4:2. If Abraham was justified, or declared righteous, by something he did (his good works), then what does he have reason to do?
   Glory, i.e., brag or boast.

3. Read Romans 4:3. How does this scripture say Abraham was justified?
   He believed God, and God put righteousness (right-standing) to his account.

4. Read Romans 4:4. To the person who works, his or her wages are not reckoned, or given, as a favor but as what?
   As a debt, i.e., an obligation.

5. Read Romans 4:5. A person who wants to be justified by faith must stop doing what?
   Stop working for it.

6. Read Romans 4:5. According to Romans 4:5, God justifies what kind of person?
   The ungodly.

7. Read Romans 4:5. Faith in God is credited to a person as what?
   Righteousness, or right-relationship.

8. Read Romans 4:6. In Psalms 32, David describes people who are blessed and happy. Why are they blessed and happy?
   Because God put right-standing to their account without them working for it.

9. Read Romans 4:7. Righteousness, without working for it, is a synonym for what phrase?
   Iniquities forgiven and sins covered.

10. Read Romans 4:7. Happy are the people who have had what happen to them?
    Their sins forgiven and put out of their sight.

11. Read Romans 4:8. Happy is the man to whom the Lord will not do what?
    Put sin to their account.

12. Read Romans 4:9. Is this happiness of being made right before God just for the Jews, or is it for the Gentiles as well?
    It is for both Jews and Gentiles.

13. Read Romans 4:10. Under what circumstances—circumcision or uncircumcision—was justification, or righteousness, credited to Abraham?
When he was uncircumcised.

Statement: Circumcision was introduced in Genesis 17. Ishmael's circumcision was done at the same time as Abraham's, and Ishmael was 13 years old. This indicates that Abraham's circumcision was 14 years after his justification. Fourteen years earlier, before his circumcision, Abraham had gained a status of total acceptance before God.

14. Read Romans 4:11. What two words describe circumcision in Romans 4:11?
1. A sign.
2. A seal.

15. What is a "sign"?
It denotes an outward evidence of something. In Abraham's instance, it was evidence that God had a covenant with him. Water baptism is an outward sign that one has repented and come into union with Jesus Christ.

Statement: Jack was a young Jewish man who married a Methodist girl. He was converted and joined her church. When he was baptized, his parents had a funeral for him. They realized what a lot of Christians don't realize: baptism marks a person as being a child of God. It is an expected accompaniment of conversion, because it confirms something: I am a child of God.

16. What is a "seal"?
A token, or proof, of something.

17. Read Romans 4:11. What was it a token or proof of in Abraham's life?
It was a token, or proof, that Abraham was in a right relationship with God, through faith.

18. Romans 4:11 states that Abraham is the "father of all them that believe." How does Galatians 3:16 and 3:29 reflect this statement?
The promises were made to Abraham and to his one seed, being Christ. In Christ we are Abraham's seed and also inherit the promises through Him.

19. Read Romans 4:12. What is Romans 4:12 stating?
Abraham is the spiritual father of those who are circumcised, but only if they have the same kind of faith that Abraham had before he was circumcised.

20. Read Romans 4:13. Romans 4:13 is stating that Abraham and his seed will not be the heirs of Canaan, nor of Palestine. What will they be heirs of?
The world.

21. Read Romans 4:13. This promise came not because Abraham obeyed the Law but because he did what?
    "This promise was made, not because Abraham obeyed the law, but because he believed and was accepted as righteous by God" (Rom. 4:13b TEV).

22. Read Romans 4:14. If any of God's promises are based on the Law, then what two things must be concluded?
    1. Faith is eliminated, excluded, made void, wiped out.
    2. The promise is nullified or made of none effect. See Romans 11:6.

23. Read Romans 4:15. The Law does not bring God's gift of salvation. What does it produce?
    Wrath, judgment, condemnation. The Law establishes a violation and brings wrath.

24. Read Romans 4:15. What is the last part of Romans 4:15 stating?
    If there is no (only promise), then you can't break it (causing transgression).

25. Read Romans 4:16. The promised inheritance, in which Christians share, is of what?
    Faith.

    Statement: If the Christians' inheritance depended upon the Law, then no one could obtain it because we all fail in obedience. (To depend upon the law is the same as depending upon perfect obedience). To be obtainable, the Christians inheritance must be a matter of grace (a favor): not a debt that is worked for. Law is not a matter of a favor - grace is. Belief is the condition of it.

    Example: A few years ago a large group of people gathered at Niagara Falls to watch a man named Blondand walk across the falls on a tightrope. He went across to the other side and then back again. When he returned, he asked if anyone believed that he could take a man on his back across the falls. The crowd yelled, "Yes!" He then asked for someone to get on his back. Finally, one man did. Many believed Blondand could do it, but only one believed him, to do it.
    Many people believe things about Christ, but only a few are willing to trust Him with their very souls.

26. Read Romans 4:17. According to Romans 4:17, what was the object of Abraham's faith?
    God. "Before Him whom he believed, even God." The object of true faith is, and only is, God.

27. Read Romans 4:17. What two things does Romans 4:17 reveal about God?
    1. He quickeneth (gives life to) the dead.
    2. He calls things that be not as though they were.

    Example: Abram (meaning "father") he called Abraham ("the father of a multitude") even when he had no children.

28. Read Romans 4:18. What specific promise did Abraham believe God for?
To become the father of many nations. Abraham's seed is threefold in the scripture.
1. He has a physical seed: the nation of Israel.
2. He has a Messianic seed: Jesus Christ (Galatians 3:16).
3. He has a spiritual seed: all believers in Jesus Christ (Galatians 3:29).

29. Read Romans 4:18. Abraham, against hope, believed. What do you think this phrase means?
He believed, against any possibility in his own person or his own self.

30. Read Romans 4:19. According to Romans 4:19, what was the truth about Abraham and Sara?
Abraham was too old to be a father, and Sara's womb was dead.

31. Read Romans 4:20. How did Abraham respond according to Romans 4:20?
He believed the promise of God, and gave glory and praise to Him.

32. Read Romans 4:21. God gave a promise to Abraham (Genesis 15:2-6). How did Abraham respond to that promise?
He was fully persuaded that God would keep His promise and perform what He said He would do.

33. Read Romans 4:22. State in your own words, what Romans 4:22 is saying.
Because of a confident trust in God, Abraham became a friend of God, i.e., in right-standing before Him.

34. Read Romans 4:23-25. What is Paul telling us in Romans 4:23-25?
This story is not just about Abraham; it applies to all who desire justification before God. The same kind of faith that brought justification to Abraham is the same kind of faith that brings salvation to men today.

This faith has God as its object. This faith believes God for forgiveness through Jesus Christ. Faith is borne out of need (we have to abandon our own efforts, to trust a Savior).

Statement: While Abraham was in Ur of the Chaldees, God promised him that he would be the heir of the world (Genesis 12:1-3; Romans 4:13). How long he had been a believer in God, we are not told. Years later, God promised him a seed as numerous as the stars in heaven. Abraham believed in God and God counted it to him for righteousness (Genesis 15:5-6). About 15 years later, God promised that Sarah would bear a son. Abraham believed (Genesis 17:15-21). Perhaps 25 years later, God commanded Abraham to offer his son Isaac, upon an altar (Genesis 22:2). Abraham's faith did not fail. James says, "And the scripture was fulfilled which saith, Abraham believed God, and it was imputed unto him for righteousness: and he was called the Friend of God" (James 2:23). Abraham was righteous by faith, and his faith was affirmed on at least four separate occasions. Abraham's faith covered a period of perhaps 50 years. It is this kind of faith that God calls every believer to exercise. A momentary, one-time act of faith is not saving faith according to the Scriptures (Luke 8:13).

OVERVIEW OF ROMANS CHAPTER 5

by Andrew Wommack

Today we come to Romans 5. There have already been so many powerful things in Romans. Paul has made his point about the Gospel. In chapter 1 he started by saying that the Gospel, the nearly-too-good-to-be-true news, is the power of God unto salvation. Then he showed that Jews and Gentiles alike, those who are religious and non-religious, are all guilty before God, which was basically the purpose of the Law. He concluded in Romans 3:23-24 by saying, *"For all have all sinned, and come short of the glory of God; Being justified freely by his grace."*

In chapter 4 he used some of the greatest examples of the Old Testament—Abraham and David—to prove that they were also justified by faith. Even during the period of the Law, all those who actually had a positive relationship with God learned this principle of faith. In the latter part of the fourth chapter he specifically talks about Abraham and says this was not written for his sake alone, that he was justified by grace, but for our sake.

In 5:1 Paul makes a conclusion, saying, *"Therefore being justified by faith, we have peace with God through our Lord Jesus Christ."* There is so much that could be said about this, but this is the only way a person can truly obtain peace. There are millions of people going through what I call "religious calisthenics," doing all of these things—working their fingers to the bone—trying to earn favor with God. But one of the main missing ingredients is that they don't produce peace. The only way to truly have peace and feel the pleasure of God is to understand being justified by faith, not by performance. That is the point Paul is making.

In verse 2 he says, *"By whom* [talking about Christ] *we have access by faith into this grace wherein we stand, and rejoice in hope of the glory of God."* The word "access" here literally means, "to give admission." If you go to a movie theater, there is a price of admission you have to pay to get in. Here is the grace of God, and we have already made this point abundantly that everything God has and everything Jesus purchased and obtained for us is available by the basis of this grace. It is ours in God's grace, but how do you have access to that grace? How do you enter into the grace of God?

This verse says that faith is the payment that grants you access. It is not your Bible reading, your holiness, or your goodness—those things are important, but not to gain or maintain access to God. It takes time to build faith through being in the Word of God. You have to study it, but He isn't impressed with your Bible study. He doesn't answer your prayers more if you read more, pray more, live holy, but if you study more, you will get more faith manifest, because you have been spending time in the Word.

If you pray more, stay in the presence of God, and keep your mind stayed on Him, you will find that faith will increase. So there is a relationship between living right and receiving the blessing of God, but it is absolutely wrong to think your godly living makes Him more prone to answer your prayers. God, by grace (that means unmerited, unearned favor independent of you or anything you deserve), has already granted you everything. The only thing you have to do to access or gain admission to it is believe. You have to study the Word to help you believe, not to make God prone to answer your prayers.

That is a tremendous truth, and there are many benefits to it. One is that this will also diminish the condemnation and guilt that come into your life. As much as you want to do what God wants you to, in order to live a godly life, you will fail sometime or other. You will get angry and lose your temper, you will say or do something that you shouldn't. And if you think God's attitude toward you changes because you fail to be what you were supposed to be, then you will come under guilt and condemnation. It isn't that you will doubt God has the ability, but you will start to doubt His willingness to use His ability on your behalf, because you know you don't deserve it. That isn't true. It isn't your goodness, your holiness that causes God to love you, answer your prayers, and move in your life. God does everything He does by grace, and the only thing you have to add is faith. Faith gives you access into the grace of God.

Paul goes on to say that this is not only good for the future—thinking about heaven—but these principles work here on earth. For time's sake I am going to go to verse 8, which says, *"But God commendeth his love toward us, in that, while we were yet sinners, Christ died for us."* Many people take this verse out of context and use it solely as an evangelistic tool to say that God loves the sinner … that he died for you while you were a sinner.

That is absolutely true. There is nothing inappropriate about that statement, but in context, the point he is making is not really the fact that God loves sinners enough to die for them. Look at it again with verse 9: *"But God commendeth his love toward us, in that, while we were yet sinners, Christ died for us. Much more then, being now justified by his blood, we shall be saved from wrath through him."* It is true that Jesus loves sinners and gave His life for them, but the point here is that if you can accept that Jesus loves you enough to die for you while you were a sinner, God loves you much <u>more</u> now that you are a saint.

What Paul is doing is using an accepted truth that God loves sinners, saying if God loves sinners, He loves saints much more. That is important, because most people actually believe God loves the sinner more than He loves the saint. A person can come to the Lord right in the midst of adultery, drunkenness, or overdosing on drugs, then cry out in repentance, and most people believe He would hear a prayer like that, because He loves sinners. But let the sinner be saved and then mess up, and most people would say, "God won't answer your prayer."

If a lost man came into a church service drunk or high on dope, many people would walk up and begin to tell him about God's love for him. They would extend mercy and grace toward the sinner. But let him get saved and come back next week drunk, and the very people who told him about how God loved him as a sinner, would condemn him and say, "God is angry with you … He is going to judge you …you won't get your prayers answered." That is the opposite of what these verses are saying. I'm not saying the Lord condones those things, because He wants you to live in victory not defeat, but I am saying that if you can accept that God loved you so much that He died for you while you were a sinner, He loves you much more now that you have accepted Him as your Lord and Savior.

This is summarized again in Romans 5:10 in one verse: *"For if, when we were enemies, we were reconciled to God by the death of his Son, much more, being reconciled, we shall be saved by his life."* In the latter part of this chapter Paul makes the argument five times that in the same way you inherited a sin nature that has separated you from God, and holds you under His wrath and punishment. On the other side but same way, now that you are born again, you have been made righteous, not by what you do but by what He did for you.

Here is the logic. It is not what you do—the sins you commit—that makes you a sinner. It is the fact that you were born a sinner, separated from God, that makes you commit individual acts of sin. Not everyone has that concept, but it is true. It is the sin nature you were born with that makes you commit individual acts of sin. You didn't do anything to deserve this sin nature—you were born with it. The fact that you are a human being means you came into this earth with a sin nature.

In contrast, once you are born again, you receive the born-again nature of Jesus that has righteousness and right-standing with God. Paul says this five times through the end of this chapter. In your study, I want you to spend time meditating on this. These verses in Romans 5 literally changed my life. I have never gotten over it and don't ever expect to. I had accepted one side of the coin unconditionally, that I was a sinner. If you accept one side, you must, in all honesty, accept the flip side that when you are born again you become the righteousness of God.

Romans 5:1-21
Discipleship Commentary

Read the entire lesson and then answer the questions that follow.

Romans 5:1 - Therefore being justified by faith, we have peace with God through our Lord Jesus Christ:

(Rom. 5:1) The word "therefore" means "for that reason; consequently; hence." Paul had just proven through the life of Abraham that justification came by faith. He then made the statement that these truths about Abraham were not written in Scripture for his sake alone but so that we could also be justified by faith (Rom. 4:23-24). So, having established justification by faith, he now moves on to some of the benefits of being justified by faith instead of works.

The first benefit that Paul mentions is peace. Peace can only come when we relate to God on the basis of faith in what He did for us instead of what we do for Him. A person who is thinking that he or she must perform to meet some standard in order to be accepted with God will have no peace. Performing for acceptance puts the burden of salvation on our shoulders, and no one can bear that load.

We were incapable of living holy enough to please God before we were saved, and we are incapable of living holy enough to please God now that we are saved (Heb. 11:6). We were saved by faith, and we must continue to walk with God by faith (Col. 2:6). Not understanding this has caused many Christians who love God to not enjoy the peace that was provided them through faith in Jesus. This is the Gospel of peace (Luke 2:14, Rom. 10:15, and Eph. 6:15).

Romans 5:2 - By whom also we have access by faith into this grace wherein we stand, and rejoice in hope of the glory of God.

(Rom. 5:2) The Greek word that was translated "access" here is the word "prosagoge" and literally means "admission." It was only used three times in the New Testament, and it was translated "access" each time (here, Eph. 2:18, and 3:12). Faith is our admission, or ticket, into the grace of God. No one is allowed in without a ticket. Our own good works won't grant us admission. God's grace can only be accessed by faith.

The Greek word that is translated "rejoice" here is the same word that is translated "glory" in the next verse and "joy" in verse 11. That Greek word is "kauchaomai," meaning, "to vaunt (in a good or bad sense)." It is derived from an obsolete root word—"aucheo"—meaning, "to boast." Paul was rejoicing because of the grace that had been given him and the hope of being glorified with Jesus.

Anyone can rejoice because of those good things, but Paul went on to say that he had the same rejoicing even in the midst of tribulation. Not many people rejoice during the hard times. But Paul could make this boast because he was totally convinced of the faithfulness and unconditional grace of God. Those who can't rejoice during tribulation are not convinced.

Rejoicing and hope are very closely related. We cannot rejoice in trying times if we have no hope. Therefore, hope is very important in the Christian life.

The hope that Paul is rejoicing in here is probably what he called the blessed hope in Titus 2:13. In that instance, Paul was clearly referring to the second coming of Jesus. Therefore, what Paul is probably speaking of here is the return of Jesus and becoming like Him (1 John 3:1-2)

Romans 5:3 - And not only so, but we glory in tribulations also: knowing that tribulation worketh patience;

(Rom. 5:3) Paul had just expressed the joy that he had concerning the second coming of Jesus and the glory that would be revealed in us. Anybody can rejoice about heaven, but now Paul begins to say that he has that same rejoicing in the midst of tribulations. This is something that very few people can say, and Paul is presenting this as a direct result of justification by faith.

When we are believing that God loves us because of our faith in Him and not our performance for Him, then we rejoice, not only in the good times and pleasant things, like thoughts of heaven, but also in the hard times. Our faith remains steadfast. However, people who are trusting in their own efforts will be devastated in trouble, because they will know they are getting what they deserve and will feel that they have to get their act cleaned up before they can expect any help. Their attention will be on self instead of Jesus, the author and finisher of their faith (Heb. 12:2).

Paul continues this same thought on through verse 10. In verses 6-8, he illustrates how great the love of God for us was, in that He died for us when we were ungodly. Then he draws a conclusion by way of comparison. If God loved us when we were His enemies, then how much more does He love us now that we are His sons. That's the reason he could rejoice even in tribulation. If God could work in his life while he was a sinner to bring him to justification, then how much more, now that he is reconciled to God, will God work whatever comes against him to his good!

People have taken these scriptures to say that God is the one who brings tribulations to accomplish these positive results in our lives. That is not what these scriptures say.

Tribulations exist not because God creates them but because there is a battle between the kingdom of God and the kingdom of the devil. When we operate in faith, God can grant us such victory that we are actually better off because of the battle.

It's just like when an army goes to war. If they win, there are spoils to be gained. But if those soldiers embraced their enemy because of the spoil they were expecting to receive, they would be killed instead of blessed. First, you have to fight and win the war and then, and only then, will the spoils be available. The enemy doesn't come to be a blessing, but a blessing can be obtained from the enemy if we are victorious.

Likewise, tribulations and adversities are not blessings from God. They are attacks from the enemy, intended to steal away the Word of God out of our lives (Mark 4:16-17). No man should say that the temptation came from God, for God is not the one who tempts any man (James 1:13). However, there are spoils to be gained when we fight and win over our problems.

If problems were the thing that perfected us, then most Christians would have been perfected long ago, and those who experience the greatest problems would be the greatest Christians, but that's not the way it is. God's Word is given to make us perfect and thoroughly furnished unto every good work (2 Tim. 3:17). God's Word does not need to be supplemented with problems to accomplish its work.

This is a pivotal point. Those who believe God has ordained the problems in their lives to work some redemptive virtue will submit to those problems and, therefore, to Satan, the author of those problems. They have to or else they would be rebelling at God, in their way of thinking. Yet James 4:7 tells us to submit ourselves to God and resist the devil. If Satan can reverse our thinking on this issue and get us to submit to problems that he brings into our lives, he's got us (Rom. 6:16).

Paul is simply rejoicing that even in tribulation, he had the opportunity to use and, therefore, strengthen his patience that had already been given him as a fruit of the Spirit (Gal. 5:22-23) and through the Word of God (Rom. 15:4). As he believed that, and stood in patience, he would gain experience that would cause him to hope even more the next time the devil attacked.

Likewise, we can rejoice in tribulation, knowing that regardless of what the devil does we will win and reap the spoils of victory.

The word "worketh" was translated from the Greek word "katergazomai" meaning "to work fully; i.e. accomplish; by implication to finish; fashion." Paul was not saying that tribulations produced patience. Patience comes from the scriptures (Rom. 15:4). But tribulations cause us to use what God has already given us through His Word, and we, therefore, become stronger as a result.

According to the dictionary, patience is "the capacity of calm endurance." The Greek word used for patience here is "hupomone" meaning "cheerful (or hopeful) endurance; constancy." Patience is not a passive word as many people use it, but it is an active word. Patience is actually faith—faith that is sustained over a long period of time. Patience comes from the Scriptures (Rom. 15:4) just as faith does (Rom. 10:17). Patience is a fruit of the Spirit just like faith (Gal. 5:22-23). It was by faith that Moses endured (the definition of patience—Heb. 11:27). It was through faith and patience that Abraham received the promises (Heb. 6:12-15), not just faith, but a faith that was constant over a twenty-five-year period of time.

Therefore, patience is not just passively waiting on God to do something, but it is actively believing for the manifestation of God's promise against all odds, regardless of how long it takes. That kind of faith will make you perfect and complete, not wanting for any good thing (James 1:4).

Patience is a by-product of hope. Romans 8:25 says, "But if we hope for that we see not, then do we with patience wait for it." When people have hope firmly established in them, then no obstacle or length of time can keep them from enduring. That's why the Scriptures produce patience—they give us hope (Rom. 15:4).

Therefore, patience, hope, and faith are all intertwined. You can't have one without the others. A person who claims to be patiently waiting on God and yet has lost hope is deceived. Likewise, a person who isn't believing God, is not operating in patience. First comes hope from a promise of God's Word. Then faith begins to give substance and evidence to those things that were hoped for (Heb. 11:1) and if time is involved before the manifestation comes, then patience does its work (James 1:4).

Romans 5:4 - And patience, experience; and experience, hope:

(Rom. 5:4) The Greek word that was used for "experience" here is the word "dokime" and means "approved character; the quality of being approved as a result of test and trials" (Rienecker). Sanday and Headlam also defined this word in this verse as "the temper of the veteran as opposed to that of the raw recruit." Therefore, this verse is speaking of the character that is produced as a result of having fought battles and won.

Hope by itself will never give us victory. Many people have hoped for things and yet have never realized those hopes, because they never moved into faith. Faith is the victory that causes us to overcome the world (1 John 5:4). Yet faith won't work without hope.

Just as a thermostat activates the power unit on an air conditioner, so hope is what activates our faith. Faith only produces what we hope for (Heb. 11:1). Therefore, hope is the first step towards faith.

"To hope is to desire, usually with confidence in the likelihood of gaining what is desired" (Dict.). So, desiring the things of God with some expectation of obtaining them is the first step in walking in faith. Once this hope is present, then faith can begin to bring the desired thing into manifestation. If a delay is encountered, patience completes the work.

In context, Paul is saying that our experience "worketh" hope. However, he also said in this same epistle (Rom. 15:4) that hope came through the Scriptures. Therefore, it is to be understood that the character that is developed through tribulations just adds to the hope that we have already received through Scripture.

Romans 5:5-6 - And hope maketh not ashamed; because the love of God is shed abroad in our hearts by the Holy Ghost which is given unto us. 6) For when we were yet without strength, in due time Christ died for the ungodly.

(Rom. 5:6) Notice the terms that Paul uses to describe us before the transformation of the new birth. We were weak (this verse), ungodly (this verse), sinners (v. 8), and enemies (v. 10). The Lord didn't save us because we deserved it; it was an act of grace.

As great as this truth is, Paul doesn't stop here. He continues on to make a comparison that if God loved us enough to die for us when we were weak, ungodly, sinners, and enemies, then much more now that we are justified (v. 9) and reconciled (v. 10), He is willing to save us in spite of our actions.

Romans 5:7 - For scarcely for a righteous man will one die: yet peradventure for a good man some would even dare to die.

(Rom. 5:7) Paul is attempting to explain the great love of God shown to us through grace. He draws on the greatest expression of love known to man, which is laying down your life for another (John 15:13), to illustrate this. However, he goes a step further.

It is possible to imagine a person giving up one's life for someone else. That has happened many times. But it is inconceivable that someone would sacrifice one's life for an enemy. Yet that is exactly what God did (v. 10). Since that is so, how could we ever doubt God's goodness to us now? On our worst day as a Christian, we love God infinitely more than our best day as an unbeliever.

Romans 5:8 - But God commendeth his love toward us, in that, while we were yet sinners, Christ died for us.

(Rom. 5:8) This verse is commonly quoted to illustrate the unconditional love that God has toward sinners. While that is certainly true, and this verse does clearly teach that, this is not the point that Paul is making. In context, Paul is talking to Christians about the grace of God. He is making a comparison, and verses 9-10 are the point of his comparison. He is using this truth in verse 8, about God commending His love toward us while we were still sinners, as a step to another truth.

Not viewing this verse in context has caused many people to accept salvation by grace but then to come back under the deception that they have to live good enough for God to use them as a Christian. While realizing one truth, they completely missed the whole point of what Paul was saying. These verses, taken in context, conclusively prove that we begin and continue our walk with God through faith in His grace (Col. 2:6)

Romans 5:9-11 - Much more then, being now justified by his blood, we shall be saved from wrath through him. 10) For if, when we were enemies, we were reconciled to God by the death of his Son, much more, being reconciled, we shall be saved by his life. 11) And not only so, but we also joy in God through our Lord Jesus Christ, by whom we have now received the atonement.

(Rom. 5:9) The phrase "much more" which is used here and in verse 10, is amazing. It would have been wonderful to think that after salvation, God continued to love us with the same love that was manifest toward us through the death of His Son. But Paul is saying that once a person is justified by grace through faith, God loves him or her much more. Being loved the same would be great, more would have been awesome, but much more is beyond our ability to comprehend.

Many Christians accept the love of God for the sinner. They extend love toward a drunk or adulterer as long as he or she is lost, but if the drunk or adulterer receives the forgiveness of God and ever commits one of those sins again, they show no mercy. They actually believe that God loves us much less, now that we are saved. We got by with things before we were saved, but now we have to be holy or else.

These verses clearly teach that is not the truth. God loves us much more now than He did before our salvation. And before our salvation, He loved us so much that He died for us. He loves us even more now.

Does this mean that living a holy life is not necessary? It means that our own holiness is not a requirement. We are accepted with God by grace through faith. But a person who is truly born again has had a change of heart. He or she wants to live holy (1 John 3:3). However, we all fail to be as holy as we want to be. When we fail, this knowledge that God loves us more now than when He sent His Son to die for us, will keep us from being condemned and draw us back to serving God.

Romans 5:12 - Wherefore, as by one man sin entered into the world, and death by sin; and so death passed upon all men, for that all have sinned:

(Rom. 5:12) Paul had already made a strong case for salvation by grace through faith. He used a comparison which illustrated just how great God's grace is. He now uses another comparison to make this same point. He begins making this point in this verse, but inserts a parenthetical phrase in verses 13-17. Therefore, to get the complete thought Paul is bringing, it helps to skip from verse 12 to verse 18.

He is saying that in the same way that we inherited the sin nature independent of our actions, we also inherit God's righteous nature, not based on our actions, through the new birth. The reasoning is that if we became sinners through what one man did, then we can also become righteous through one man, the Lord Jesus Christ.

Romans 5:13 - (For until the law sin was in the world: but sin is not imputed when there is no law.

(Rom. 5:13) Verses 13-17 are a parenthetical phrase. In verse 12, Paul begins likening imputed righteousness to imputed sin. He interrupts that thought to briefly explain how God dealt with the sin nature of man from the time of Adam until the time of the Law of Moses. Therefore, the point that Paul is making can be received by skipping directly from verse 12 to 18. However, some very important information is revealed in this parenthetical phrase.

Paul said that until the time that the law was given, sin was not imputed unto men. The most-used Greek word for "impute" is "logizomai," which is an accounting term meaning God was not entering men's sins in the account book. In this instance, there is a different Greek word used ("ellogeo"—used only one other time in the N.T.—Phile. 18), but it has virtually the same meaning. This is a radical statement.

Most people have interpreted God's dealings with man after the sin of Adam to be immediate rejection and banishment from His presence, in other words, an immediate imputing of man's sins. However, Paul is stating just the opposite. God was not holding men's sins against them until the time that the Law of Moses was given.

With this in mind, it should change the way we think about God's dealings with man between the fall and the giving of the Law. Adam and Eve were not driven from the Garden of Eden because God could not stand them in His presence anymore. God's dealings with Adam and Eve and their children in Genesis 4 prove His presence was still with them. The reason He drove them from Eden is clearly stated in Genesis 3:22- 23. It was to keep them from eating of the tree of life and living forever.

Instead of this being a punitive act, it was actually an act of mercy. It would have been terrible for man to live forever in a sinful body, subject to all the emotions and diseases that sin brings. God had a better plan through Jesus.

In accordance with what Paul was revealing here, God was merciful to the first murderer (Gen. 4:9-15), even to the point of placing a mark on his forehead and promising vengeance if anyone tried to kill him. In contrast, once the Law was given, the first man to break the ordinance of the Sabbath was stoned to death for picking up sticks. That doesn't seem equitable. But the answer is that before the Law, God was not imputing men's sins unto them as He was after the giving of the Law.

It would appear that the destruction of Sodom and Gomorrah and the flood of Noah were two notable exceptions to this. Actually, these were not exceptions. While these two acts of judgment were punitive on the individuals who received the judgment, they were actually acts of mercy on the human race as a whole. In the same way as a limb or organ will sometimes be sacrificed to save a life, so God had to destroy these sinners to continue His mercy on the human race. The people in Noah's day and the inhabitants of Sodom and Gomorrah were so vile that they were like a cancer that had to be killed.

So, for the first 2,000 years after man's fall (approximate time between fall and the giving of the Law), God was not holding man's sins against them. That is why Abram was not killed for marrying his half sister, and Jacob for marrying his wife's sister.

Therefore, we can see that God's immediate reaction to man's sin was mercy and not judgment. It was over 2,000 years before God began to impute man's sins unto them, and according to Galatians 3:19 ,23-24, that was only a temporary way of dealing with sin until Jesus could come. Through Jesus, God is once again reconciling the world unto Himself, not imputing men's sins unto them (2 Cor. 5:19).

Romans 5:14 - Nevertheless death reigned from Adam to Moses, even over them that had not sinned after the similitude of Adam's transgression, who is the figure of him that was to come.

(Rom. 5:14) If God was not bringing judgment upon man's sins until the time of the Law of Moses, then why were men still dying. Isn't death the wages of sin (Rom. 6:23)? Why were men still dying if their sins weren't being counted against them?

Sin has a twofold effect. It is not only a transgression against God, worthy of His judgment, but it is also the inroad of Satan into our lives. Romans 6:16 says, "Know ye not, that to whom ye yield yourselves servants to obey, his servants ye are to whom ye obey; whether of sin unto death, or of obedience unto righteousness?" If we yield to sin, we also submit ourselves to Satan, the author of that sin.

This is why men were still dying even though God was not bringing His judgment on their sins. Satan was the one who had the power of death (Heb. 2:14), and it was Satan through sin who was causing men to die. As sin multiplied on the earth, the life span of man decreased, not because of God's judgment, but because of the effects of sin on the human race.

Therefore, we can see that even when God doesn't judge sin, sin is still deadly. This is why the New Testament believer should resist sin. God doesn't bring judgment on His children for their sins, but Satan will. The Christian doesn't live holy in order to avoid God's judgment but so that our enemy won't have any access to us.

The people from Adam to Moses had not sinned in the same way that Adam had, because they didn't have a direct commandment to violate as Adam did. They were living under their own consciences which was enough to make them guilty. However, it was not until the time that God revealed the commandments through Moses that man once again began to violate direct commands of God (Rom. 4:15).

The Greek word translated "figure" here is "tupos" which means a type, figure, pattern (W.E. Vine). Paul is saying that Adam was a type of Jesus in the sense that in the same way sin entered the world through one man, so righteousness entered the world through one man, Jesus.

Romans 5:15 - But not as the offence, so also is the free gift. For if through the offence of one many be dead, much more the grace of God, and the gift by grace, which is by one man, Jesus Christ, hath abounded unto many.

(Rom. 5:15) Paul proceeds to make a series of comparisons about imputed righteousness through Christ being like imputed sin through Adam. Five times Paul makes this comparison so that there should be no doubt that in the same way that all became sinners through Adam, all who put faith in Christ are made righteousness through Him.

The religious world has basically accepted this truth of inherited sin from Adam, but this truth of inherited righteousness through the new birth is still a mystery to many. Yet, Paul is saying that if one is true, then so is the other. These truths are like two sides to one coin. If you accept one truth, you have to accept the other.

These are five comparisons (vv. 15-19), but they are opposite comparisons. Adam's sin brought things from good to bad, but Jesus brought things from bad to good. The results are opposite extremes, but the principle involved in both is the same. In the same way that Adam was able to pass sin and its consequences on to his descendants, so Jesus is able to pass righteousness and all its benefits on to those who put faith in Him.

The gift by grace spoken of here and in verses 16 and 18 is clearly stated in verse 17. It is the gift of righteousness.

Romans 5:16 - And not as it was by one that sinned, so is the gift: for the judgment was by one to condemnation, but the free gift is of many offences unto justification.

(Rom. 5:16) Adam's one sin produced a sin nature in all men that in turn caused each person to commit individual acts of sin. However, Jesus not only dealt with the original sin that contaminated the human race, but He also dealt with each individual act of sin.

Romans 5:17 - For if by one man's offence death reigned by one; much more they which receive abundance of grace and of the gift of righteousness shall reign in life by one, Jesus Christ.)

(Rom. 5:17) This comparison is repeated again in verse 21.

Romans 5:18-19 - Therefore as by the offence of one judgment came upon all men to condemnation; even so by the righteousness of one the free gift came upon all men unto justification of life. 19) For as by one man's disobedience many were made sinners, so by the obedience of one shall many be made righteous.

(Rom. 5:19) Some people think it is our individual acts of sin that make us a sinner but that is not what Paul is saying in these verses. These scriptures clearly state that Adam's one sin made all men sinners. It is man's sin nature that produces sins, not his sins that produce a sin nature.

Therefore, anyone who is trying to obtain righteousness through their actions is totally missing the point. Even if a man could stop all his sinning, he could not change his sin nature, which he was born with. That's the reason we must be born again.

These scriptures should provide the ultimate argument for righteousness by faith to everyone who believes the Scriptures to be inspired by God. Paul repeatedly says that believers are made righteous through faith in Christ independent of their actions in the same way that everyone was made sinners not through their individual sins but through Adam's one sin.

Romans 5:20 - Moreover the law entered, that the offence might abound. But where sin abounded, grace did much more abound:

(Rom. 5:20) Paul was writing to Jewish Christians who had mistakenly thought that faith in Christ alone was not enough to produce justification. They thought you also had to fulfill a minimum standard of holiness by complying with certain commands of the Old Testament Law. That's what occasioned Paul's whole teaching on justification by faith.

Paul had so conclusively proven justification by faith in Christ alone that he knew the legalistic Jews were wondering, "What was the purpose of the Law then?" He states that purpose in this verse. The Law was given to make sin increase, or superabound.

The purpose of the Law was not to strengthen us in our battle against sin but to strengthen sin in its battle against us. Sin had already beaten us, and we didn't know it. The Law brought that realization to us so that we would quit trusting in ourselves and call out to God for salvation.

So, the Law made sin and all its devastating effects abound, but God's grace abounded even more. The Law gave sin so much dominion against us that the grace of God is the only way out.

Romans 5:21 - That as sin hath reigned unto death, even so might grace reign through righteousness unto eternal life by Jesus Christ our Lord.

(Rom. 5:21) The sin that is being spoken of here is not the individual acts of sin that we commit but rather the propensity for sin itself. The American Heritage dictionary defines propensity as an innate inclination; tendency; bent. It is this inherited inclination to sin that Paul is speaking of.

The word "sin" is used 45 times in the book of Romans (Rom. 3:9, 20; 4:8; 5:12, 13, 20, 21; 6:1, 2, 6, 7, 10, 11, 12, 13, 14, 15, 16, 17, 18, 20, 22, 23; 7:7, 8, 9, 11, 13, 14, 17, 20, 23, 25; 8:2, 3, 10; and14:23). The plural "sins" is used four times (Rom. 3:25; 4:7; 7:5; and 11:2).

Of this total of 49 times that sin or sins is used in Romans, these two English words come from three Greek words. One of these Greek words "hamartema" is only used once in

Romans 3:25 and only three other times in all the New Testament (Mark 3:28, 4:12; 1 Cor. 6:18). Of the remaining 48 times, the Greek word "hamartia" was used 47 times and "hamartano" just once (Rom. 6:15).

This is very significant because the Greek word "hamartia" is a noun, while "hamartano" is a verb. A noun denotes a person, place, or thing, while verbs describe the action of nouns. Therefore, in all but one instance in the book of Romans, the words "sin," or "sins," describe man's tendency toward sin and not the individual acts of sins themselves. If you think of the word "sin" in these chapters as denoting the act of sin, you will miss what Paul is saying.

The believer's fight is not against individual acts of sin but against the inner tendency to sin. If the propensity to sin can be broken, then the actions of sin will cease. Our individual acts of sin are only an expression, or indication, of how well we are doing in our war against this condition of the heart that causes us to sin.

Romans 5:12 says that this propensity to sin (or what many call the sin nature) entered the world through Adam. It is this sin nature that caused us to sin, not our individual acts of sin that gave us a sin nature.

At salvation, our old man (Rom. 6:6), or sin nature, died, but the tendency to sin remained through the thoughts and emotions that the old man left behind. The Christian doesn't have a sin nature any longer that compels a person to sin but he or she is simply dealing with the renewing of one's mind.

Sin ruled through condemnation like a king (v. 16), to bring death upon everyone. Condemnation is like the general of sin that enforced its power. Likewise, now God's grace rules through righteousness, like a king to bring all who are in Christ into eternal life. Righteousness is the general of grace who defends us against all the wiles of the devil.

Sin would ultimately bring death to every individual whether they were condemned or not (Rom. 6:23). But to those who are guilt ridden and condemned over their sins, sin has a particularly devastating effect. Likewise, those who put faith in Christ will ultimately experience God's eternal life. But those who understand righteousness as a gift to be received and not a wage to be earned are the ones who reign as kings in this life over sin and all its effects.

Remove guilt or condemnation, and sin loses its strength to rule (1 Cor. 15:56). Remove the knowledge of righteousness by faith, and grace loses its power to release eternal life in our daily lives.

Romans 5:1-21
Discipleship Questions

. . . .

*Answer the following questions by reading the corresponding
discipleship commentary lesson and using your Bible.*

1. Read Romans 4:25. In the context of Romans 5:1, the basis (a foundation upon which some-thing rests) for our justification is explained. What is the basis of our justification?

   _____

   _____

2. Explain again what justification means.

   _____

3. Read Romans 5:1, Hebrews 12:2, and Acts 16:31. We are not to have faith in faith; faith always has an object. What is the object of our faith?

   _____

4. According to Romans 5:1, how do we have peace with God? "Peace" is defined as "the absence of war or other hostilities."

   _____

   _____

5. Read Romans 5:2. We have access by faith into God's what?

   _____

6. In Romans 5:2 the phrase "by whom" is referring to whom?

   _____

7. Read Romans 5:2. The phrase "wherein we stand" refers to what?

   _____

   _____

8. According to Romans 5:2, what is the reason that a Christian can rejoice?

   _____

9. Read Romans 5:3. As believers, we can also rejoice in what?

   _____

10. Read Romans 5:3. Why can we rejoice in tribulation?

    _____

    _____

11. Read Romans 5:4. According to Romans 5:4, what is the result of patience or persever-ance?_____

    _____

12. Read Romans 5:4. What is the end result of all of this?

_____

13. Read Romans 5:5. What does the phrase "And hope maketh not ashamed" mean?

_____
_____

14. Read Romans 5:5. In this hope, we will not be disappointed. Why?

_____
_____
_____

15. According to Romans 5:6, whom was God's love directed toward?

_____
_____

16. Read Romans 5:7. How often does someone give his or her life for a good person?

_____

17. In Romans 5:6, God directed His love toward the ungodly. In Romans 5:8, whom does God direct His love toward?

_____

18. Read Romans 5:8. How did God demonstrate His love toward the sinner?

_____

19. Read Romans 5:9. What is it that saves us from God's wrath?

_____
_____

20. Read Romans 5:10. In Romans 5:6 God saves the **ungodly**. In Romans 5:8 God saves **sinners**. In Romans 5:10, whom does God save?

_____

21. Read Romans 5:10. According to Romans 5:10, how were we reconciled to God?

_____

22. What does "reconcile" mean?

_____
_____

23. Read Romans 5:10. According to Romans 5:10, how shall we be saved?

_____
_____

24. Read Romans 5:11. According to Romans 5:11, why can the Christian rejoice?

_____

25. Read Romans 5:12. What were the results of Adam's sin, according to Romans 5:12?

_____

_____

26. "Death passed upon all men, for all have sinned" (Rom. 5:12). In what two ways does the Bible speak of death?

_____

_____

27. Read Romans 5:13. Was sin in the world before God gave the Law of Moses?

_____

28. Read Romans 5:13. "But sin is not imputed when there is no law." What does this phrase mean?_____

_____

29. Read Romans 5:14, 12. Why do babies, who have never sinned or broken God's Law, die?

_____

_____

30. Read Romans 5:15. What is being contrasted in the first sentence of Romans 5:15?

_____

_____

31. Read Romans 5:15. How could we paraphrase the first sentence of Romans 5:15?

_____

_____

32. Romans 5:15b states, "For if through the offence [sin] of one [Adam] many be dead [i.e. die]." To whom is the many referring?_____

_____

33. Read Romans 5:15. In Romans 5:15, Adam's sin is contrasted with what?

_____

34. What is God's grace?

_____

_____

35. Read and comment on Romans 5:15 by using a good modern translation.

_____

_____

36. In Romans 5:16 there is a contrast between God's gift of righteousness and Adam's sin. What is the contrast?

_____

_____

37. What kind of righteousness is God offering us, according to Romans 5:17?

_____

38. What does the word "gift" imply?

_____

39. If I bought you some groceries as a gift and then asked you to give me $23.50, would that be a gift?_____

40. If you bought your children bicycles as gifts for Christmas and then asked them to make payments, would they be gifts?_____

41. Romans 5:18a states that through Adam's sin, judgement came upon all men, resulting in condemnation. What is the meaning of condemnation?

_____

_____

42. Read Romans 5:18. By the righteous act of Jesus Christ, what free gift came upon all men?

_____

43. Read Romans 5:19. According to Romans 5:19, how were we made sinners?

_____

44. According to Romans 5:19, how are we made righteous?

_____

45. Read Romans 5:20. According to Romans 5:20, why were the Ten Commandments given?

_____

_____

46. Read Romans 5:20. Where sin increased, what increased more?

_____

47. "Grace did much more abound." What does this mean?

_____

_____

48. According to Romans 5:21, sin ruled over all men, and what did it bring?

_____

49. Grace reigns through righteousness (i.e., giving us right-standing with God) resulting in what?

_____

Romans 5:1-21
Discipleship Answer Key

....

Do not look at the answer key until you have completed the questions.
Compare your answers with the following answers.

1. Read Romans 4:25. In the context of Romans 5:1, the basis (a foundation upon which something rests) for our justification is explained. What is the basis of our justification?
Jesus was put to death for our sins and rose again to make us right with God.

2. Explain again what justification means.
To be declared in right-standing, or in a right-relationship, with God.

3. Read Romans 5:1, Hebrews 12:2, and Acts 16:31. We are not to have faith in faith; faith always has an object. What is the object of our faith?
The Lord Jesus Christ.

4. According to Romans 5:1, how do we have peace with God? "Peace" is defined as "the absence of war or other hostilities."
Through what Jesus Christ our Lord has done for us.

5. Read Romans 5:2. We have access by faith into God's what?
Grace, mercy, or favor.

6. In Romans 5:2 the phrase "by whom" is referring to whom?
Jesus Christ. It is by Jesus Christ that we have this free admission into God's favor.

7. Read Romans 5:2. The phrase "wherein we stand" refers to what?
Our position before God. The place of favor, privilege, and acceptance before God.

8. According to Romans 5:2, what is the reason that a Christian can rejoice?
He can rejoice in the hope (we have) of sharing God's glory.

9. Read Romans 5:3. As believers, we can also rejoice in what?
Tribulations or troubles.

10. Read Romans 5:3. Why can we rejoice in tribulation?
Because the quality of patience, perseverance, endurance, and steadfastness result from being tried.

11. Read Romans 5:4. According to Romans 5:4, what is the result of patience or perseverance?
Experience, or proven character.

12. Read Romans 5:4. What is the end result of all of this?
Hope.

13. Read Romans 5:5. What does the phrase "And hope maketh not ashamed" mean?
"Hope does not disappoint us." In other words, in the hope of glorification (v.2), we will not be disappointed.

14. Read Romans 5:5. In this hope, we will not be disappointed. Why?
1. Because the Holy Spirit has been given to us. See Ephesians 1:13-14 (NIV).
2. Because the love of God is shed abroad in our hearts. I take this to mean that God has shed abroad in our hearts the consciousness of being loved by Him. The New Living Translation states, "And this expectation will not disappoint us. For we know how dearly God loves us, because he has given us the Holy Spirit to fill our hearts with his love."

15. According to Romans 5:6, Whom was God's love directed toward?
1. Those without strength, i.e., the helpless.
2. The ungodly.

16. Read Romans 5:7. How often does someone give his or her life for a good person?
Rarely.

17. In Romans 5:6, God directed His love toward the ungodly. In Romans 5:8, whom does God direct His love toward?
The sinner.

18. Read Romans 5:8. How did God demonstrate His love toward the sinner?
By sending Christ to die for them.

19. Read Romans 5:9. What is it that saves us from God's wrath?
Being justified by His blood. The Jerusalem Bible states, "Having died to make us righteous, is it likely that he would now fail to save us from God's anger?"

20. Read Romans 5:10. In Romans 5:6 God saves the **ungodly**.
In Romans 5:8 God saves **sinners**. In Romans 5:10, whom does God save?
His enemies.

21. Read Romans 5:10. According to Romans 5:10, how were we reconciled to God?
Through the death of God's Son.

22. What does "reconcile" mean?
The American Heritage Dictionary states that reconcile means, "To re-establish friendship between. To settle or resolve, as a dispute." The way to overcome enmity, ill will, or hostility is to take away the cause of the quarrel. We may apologize for the hasty word, we may pay the money that is due, we may make what restitution is appropriate, but in every case, the way to reconciliation is by effectively dealing with the root cause of the enmity. Reconciliation in the New Testament is to change, or exchange, enmity for friendship by the sacrifice of Jesus for our sins.

23. Read Romans 5:10. According to Romans 5:10, how shall we be saved?
By Christ's life. The Amplified Bible says, "Daily delivered from sin's dominion through His resurrection life."

24. Read Romans 5:11. According to Romans 5:11, why can the Christian rejoice?
Because he or she has now received reconciliation, i.e., been made a friend with God.

25. Read Romans 5:12. What were the results of Adam's sin, according to Romans 5:12?
1. Sin entered into the world.
2. Death came by sin.
3. Death passed upon the whole human race.

26. "Death passed upon all men, for all have sinned" (Rom. 5:12). In what two ways does the Bible speak of death?
1. Physical death. See James 2:26.
2. Spiritual death, or the second death. See Revelation 20:12-15;
2 Thessalonians.1:9.

27. Read Romans 5:13. Was sin in the world before God gave the Law of Moses?
Yes.

28. Read Romans 5:13. "But sin is not imputed when there is no law." What does this phrase mean?
"But sin cannot be charged against a man where no law exists" (The Twentieth Century New Testament).

29. Read Romans 5:14, 12. Why do babies, who have never sinned or broken God's Law, die?
Because of the effect of sin that Adam's transgression brought upon us. It was Adam's transgression, or sin, that did this.

The Living Bible states, "[We know that it was Adam's sin that caused this] because although, of course, people were sinning from the time of Adam until Moses, God did not in those days judge them guilty of death for breaking his laws - because he had not yet given his laws to them, nor told them what he wanted them to do. So when their bodies died it was not for their own sins since they themselves had never disobeyed God's special law against eating the forbidden fruit, as Adam had" (Rom. 5:13-14).

30. Read Romans 5:15. What is being contrasted in the first sentence of Romans 5:15?
Adam's sin and God's free gift of righteousness, or forgiveness.

31. Read Romans 5:15. How could we paraphrase the first sentence of Romans 5:15?
What a difference there is between Adam's sin and God's free gift of forgiveness.

32. Romans 5:15b states, "For if through the offence [sin] of one [Adam] many be dead [i.e. die]." To whom is the many referring?
All of mankind. All of mankind will physically die because of Adam's transgression.

33. Read Romans 5:15. In Romans 5:15, Adam's sin is contrasted with what?
God's grace.

34. What is God's grace?
The undeserved, unmerited favor of God displaying itself in mercy and forgiveness to those who actually deserve the opposite.

35. Read and comment on Romans 5:15 by using a good modern translation.
What a difference there is between Adam's sin and God's free gift of forgiveness. For this one man, Adam, brought death to many through his sin. But this other man, Jesus Christ, brought forgiveness to many through God's bountiful grace (Romans 5:15).

36. In Romans 5:16 there is a contrast between God's gift of righteousness and Adam's sin. What is the contrast?
The Contemporary English Version states, "There is a lot of difference between Adam's sin and God's gift. That one sin led to punishment (or condemnation). But God's gift (of righteousness) made it possible for us to be acceptable to him, even though we have sinned many times."

37. What kind of righteousness is God offering us, according to Romans 5:17?
The gift of righteousness.

38. What does the word "gift" imply?
It's free.

39. If I bought you some groceries as a gift and then asked you to give me $23.50, would that be a gift?
No.

40. If you bought your children bicycles as gifts for Christmas and then asked them to make payments, would they be gifts?
No.

Statement: A gift does cost something, but not to those who receive it! God's gift of righteousness (gift of right-relationship with Him) cost God the death of His Son, but it is offered freely as a gift to those who will receive it.

41. Romans 5:18a states that through Adam's sin, judgement came upon all men, resulting in condemnation. What is the meaning of condemnation?
To condemn is to pronounce judgment against; to sentence; to doom (American Heritage Dictionary).

117

42. Read Romans 5:18. By the righteous act of Jesus Christ, what free gift came upon all men? **Justification, which results in life.**

   Today's English Version states, **"So then, as the one sin condemned all men, in the same way the one righteous act sets all men free and gives them life" (Rom. 5:18).**

43. Read Romans 5:19. According to Romans 5:19, how were we made sinners? **Through Adam's disobedience.**

44. According to Romans 5:19, how are we made righteous? **Through Christ's obedience, not ours.**

   "One man disobeyed God, and many became sinners. In the same way, one man obeyed God, and many will be made right" (Rom. 5:19, New Century Version).

45. Read Romans 5:20. According to Romans 5:20, why were the Ten Commandments given? **"The Ten Commandments were given so that all could see the extent of their failure to obey God's laws" (Romans 5:20a - Living Bible).**

46. Read Romans 5:20. Where sin increased, what increased more? **God's grace.**

47. "Grace did much more abound." What does this mean? **"But the more we see our sinfulness, the more we see God's abounding grace forgiving us" (Rom. 5:20b, Living Bible).**

48. According to Romans 5:21, sin ruled over all men, and what did it bring? **Death.**

49. Grace reigns through righteousness (i.e., giving us right-standing with God), resulting in what? **Eternal life (by Jesus Christ our Lord).**

OVERVIEW OF ROMANS CHAPTER 6

by Don Krow

In Romans 6 we come to the second main section of the book. The beginning section was the guilt and condemnation of mankind. Then we saw Jesus Christ being introduced to produce the justification, the righteousness that mankind needed. In chapter 6 we see how to live out this right-standing with God that we enjoy. How do we live a righteous life? How do we live a life that is honoring to God? That is what we will be dealing with in the next few chapters.

Verse 1: *"What shall we say then? Shall we continue in sin, that grace may abound?"* Why does Paul ask a question like that? It comes because he had just made the statement about grace in Romans 5:20 when he said, *"Where sin abounded, grace did much more abound."* He also said that through one man's (Adam's) disobedience, we were all made sinners, and by one man's (Jesus Christ's) obedience in going to the cross of Calvary, living a perfect sinless life, and being a sacrifice for us, He justified us and made us righteous. We were made righteous not based on *our* righteousness but on Jesus Christ's righteousness and what He did on our behalf.

Romans 6:1 is saying that someone said, "Well, if grace is greater than sin, if grace swallows up sin, let's just go out and live in sin, let's live like the devil." Paul is saying, "You don't understand. You have a wrong understanding of grace." Suppose I acted in ways that were loving toward my wife, I brought her flowers and said, "Honey, here are a dozen roses to let you know how much I love you." Would she say "Get out of here, you jerk, I'm going to divorce you" if I showed her expressions of love and kindness? Absolutely not; she would respond in loving ways.

The grace of God does not lead us to live sinful, lawless lives. It causes us to live lives pleasing to the very one who has justified us and declared us righteous. We will live more holy under grace than we ever would under the Law, trying to work for and earn it. So here is the question. Somebody again wants to pervert grace, saying, "Shall we continue in sin, shall we live a lifestyle of sin because grace is greater?" Paul says, "Absolutely not!"

Verse 2: *"God forbid. How shall we, that are dead to sin, live any longer therein?"* There has been a death to sin, and I can no longer live in it. How is that death to sin taking place in my life?

Verses 3-4: This is how we came to a place of death to sin. *"Know ye not, that so many of us as were baptized into Jesus Christ were baptized into his death? Therefore we are buried with him by baptism into death: that like as Christ was raised up from the dead by the glory of the Father, even so we also should walk in newness of life."* Paul is saying there has been a death to sin through our union with and baptism into Jesus Christ. No longer will we even want to live in sin. No longer are we slaves to sin. The Bible tells us here that now we should walk and live in a new kind of life—a newness of life.

Verses 5-6: *"For if we have been planted together in the likeness of his death, we shall be also in the likeness of his resurrection: Knowing this, that our old man is crucified with him, that the body of sin might be destroyed, that henceforth we should not serve sin."* Paul is saying that when we identify with Jesus, when we come into union with Him, into His death, into His burial, into His resurrection, sin no longer is our master. We have come under a new master, the Lord Jesus Christ, a new master, righteousness, a new master, God. Verse 6 says that the body of sin, the power of sin, has been destroyed through the crucifixion of the Lord Jesus Christ so that we should, henceforth, no longer live under the bondage of sin as our master.

Verses 7-10: *"For he that is dead is freed from sin. Now if we be dead with Christ, we believe that we shall also live with him: Knowing that Christ being raised from the dead dieth no more; death hath no more dominion over him. For in that he died, he died unto sin once; but in that he liveth, he liveth unto God."* This entire first part of Romans 6 is telling the believer that there is a union with Jesus Christ in His death, burial, and resurrection, and we need to identify with that union.

Then verse 11 tells us this: *"Likewise reckon ye also yourselves to be dead indeed unto sin, but alive unto God through Jesus Christ our Lord."* "Likewise" means what happened to Jesus happened to us. We were in Him; He was our substitute so that from now on, we no longer have to allow sin to be our master.

Verse 12: *"Let not sin therefore reign in your mortal body, that ye should obey it in the lusts thereof."* We make a decision to say, "No. We aren't going to let sin reign and rule." How is it going to rule? It wants to rule in our mortal bodies, but I don't have to obey it in its desires. We have come under a new Lord, a new master. It's not sin, not the devil—it's Jesus Christ.

Verse 13: *"Neither yield ye your members as instruments of unrighteousness unto sin: but yield yourselves unto God, as those that are alive from the dead, and your members as instruments of righteousness unto God."* There are two things going on here which are very important that we understand. The first is that through being baptized into Jesus Christ, we have been baptized into His death, burial, and resurrection. We have identified with Jesus in union with Him; sin is no longer our master. We need to identify with those facts.

The second thing we need to do is yield. The Bible says yield—give place to what? Yield now my members, the members of my body, as instruments of righteousness, right doing, to God. No longer yield these members to sin, but yield them to God. I can do it because I'm in union with Christ. He has set His love upon me and I'm in right-standing with God. Now He is asking me to yield these members of my body that have been paid for, bought with a price—the blood of Jesus Christ—to Him. As we yield them to Him, we can no longer yield them to sin. We don't have to yield them to sin any longer. We can yield them to God.

Verse 14: *"For sin shall not have dominion over you: for ye are not under the law, but under grace."* For you to sin under the Law would result in your death. You sin—you die a spiritual death, separation from God forever. But under grace, He will never impute to you, or put to your account, sin. Therefore, sin will never have dominion over you again.

Verse 15: *"What then? shall we sin, because we are not under the law, but under grace? God forbid."* The first question was "shall we continue in sin?" This question is "shall we even do sin?" No, we should not sin, because we are under grace and not under Law.

Verses 16-18: Again it goes back to that principle, *"Know ye not, that to whom ye yield yourselves servants to obey, his servants ye are to whom ye obey; whether of sin unto death, or of obedience unto righteousness? But God be thanked, that ye were the servants of sin, but ye have obeyed from the heart that form of doctrine which was delivered you. Being then made free from sin, ye became the servants of righteousness."* Again he is saying we used to be under slavery to Satan, under slavery to sin, but we have repented, we've had a change of heart, we've changed masters, and we have obeyed from our hearts the Gospel of Jesus Christ that has been delivered to us.

Verse 19: *"I speak after the manner of men because of the infirmity of your flesh: for as ye have yielded your members servants to uncleanness and to iniquity unto iniquity; even so now yield your members servants to righteousness unto holiness."* He is saying, "I am speaking in a way that you can understand. Just as you used to yield your members to sin and iniquity, now yield your members as servants to righteousness and right doing."

Verses 20-21: *"For when ye were the servants of sin, ye were free from righteousness. What fruit had ye then in those things whereof ye are now ashamed? for the end of those things is death."* We have all done things in the past that we are ashamed of, and those things would lead us unless we had turned to Jesus Christ for His mercy. They would have led us to eternal death, separation from God.

Verses 22-23: *"But now being made free from sin, and become servants to God, ye have your fruit unto holiness, and the end everlasting life. For the wages of sin is death; but the gift of God is eternal life through Jesus Christ our Lord."*

I want to emphasize two things in Romans 6: Through baptism into Jesus Christ, we are identifiying with our union with Him in His death, burial, and resurrection. Because we are now in union with Jesus Christ and have been bought with a price—His very blood that purchased us—we are no longer under slavery to sin. God is calling us each day, in our daily walk with Him, to yield the members of our bodies, our mortal bodies, to Him and to righteousness and to express the fruit of the Holy Spirit that God has placed on the inside of us as we yield to Him and count on His power to live a godly, holy life.

Romans 6:1-23
Discipleship Commentary

· ·

Read the entire lesson and then answer the questions that follow.

Romans 6:1 - What shall we say then? Shall we continue in sin, that grace may abound?

(Rom. 6:1) Paul had stated God's grace in such way that it was inevitable that someone would ask, Can we just keep on sinning since we are saved by grace? Of course, that is not what Paul was saying at all. He had already answered this argument before (Rom. 3:8), and he does it again in Romans 6:15, making it a total of three times in this epistle that he had to overcome misunderstandings about his grace teaching encouraging sin.

Paul spoke this revelation of God's grace under the inspiration of the Holy Ghost with perfect balance, yet he was still misunderstood.

Therefore, anybody teaching grace who does not encounter the same arguments, having to explain that they are not advocating a life of sin, has not preached grace the way that Paul did. If, in our efforts to prevent misuse, we present grace in such a way that no one ever accuses us of giving people a license to sin, we haven't presented grace correctly.

Romans 6:2 - God forbid. How shall we, that are dead to sin, live any longer therein?

(Rom. 6:2) Paul had so convincingly proven salvation by grace that there was not any theological argument left against it. Yet, the most common complaint against grace is not theological. It concerns the practical application. Most people can't handle grace, because they think, If I'm saved by grace, then why resist sin? Paul answers this question in two ways in this chapter. First, Christians don't live a life of sin, because they are dead to sin. This is the point Paul is making in verses 1-14. Second, although God is not imputing our sins unto us, Satan is. Beginning with verse 15, Paul clearly states that sin is an inroad of the enemy into our lives.

Therefore, Paul states that sin is still deadly and something to be resisted, but he changes the motivation for living holy. No longer do we resist sin to try to be accepted with God, but we live holy because our nature has been changed and because actions of sin give place to the devil.

What does it mean that we are dead to sin? From the context and also from personal experience, we can easily see what it doesn't mean. It clearly doesn't mean that a Christian is incapable of committing sins.

Once again, the Greek word translated "sin" here is "hamartia," which is a noun describing the propensity for sin or what many call the sin nature. The New International Version calls this the old self. Our old self was the driving force behind our acts of sin. Paul is saying that since our old self that loved to sin is dead, it is not our nature as a Christian to commit acts of sin, like it was before we were born again. That's the number one reason that Christians don't sin. They don't want to sin.

However, by Paul saying that the part of us that compelled us to sin is dead, new questions are raised. If we no longer have a sin nature that compels us to sin, then why do we do it? Some Christians believe they are still driven to sin and quote Paul's statements in Romans 7 to justify this. Paul goes on to answer this question in verse 6.

Romans 6:3 - Know ye not, that so many of us as were baptized into Jesus Christ were baptized into his death?

(Rom. 6:3) Our spirit is the part of us that was born again, and this is the part of us that Paul is referring to as being baptized into Jesus and His death. Our physical man is not dead, and our soul is not dead. But our old man died with Christ.

The baptism that is being spoken of in verses three and four is not water baptism. Hebrews 6:2 speaks of the doctrine of baptisms (plural), clearly stating that there is more than one kind of baptism.

It is easy to see that there is a difference between the baptism of the Holy Spirit and the baptism into the body of Christ. When John the Baptist spoke of the baptism of the Holy Ghost in Matthew 3:11, he said Jesus is the baptizer and that the Holy Spirit is the one that we are being baptized with. In 1 Corinthians 12:13, Paul says the Holy Spirit is the baptizer and that the body of Christ is what we are being baptized into. So, there are two different baptizers and two different elements that we are being baptized into, leaving no doubt that these are two different baptisms.

The mistake of always associating the word "baptism" with water baptism has led many people to incorrectly interpret Romans 6:3-4 as speaking of water baptism. Some have even attempted to use these verses to prove that water baptism is the act that causes salvation. However, that is not what Paul is saying, but is in fact, exactly the opposite of every point that he has been making in the book of Romans for salvation by grace through faith. This is not speaking of the sign of water baptism.

Paul is speaking of the act where every person, who puts saving faith in Jesus as their Lord, is automatically and instantaneously baptized into Jesus and all that He purchased for us (1 Cor. 12:13, Col. 2:12). He is simply stating that every believer has become dead to sin (v. 6) through the death of Jesus. Jesus didn't die for His own sins; He had none. He died for our sins (1 Pet. 2:24). Therefore, His death was for us, and all the benefits to be obtained through His death and resurrection are our benefits.

Romans 6:4 - Therefore we are buried with him by baptism into death: that like as Christ was raised up from the dead by the glory of the Father, even so we also should walk in newness of life.

(Rom. 6:4) This verse states our death with Christ as an accomplished fact and our resurrection with Christ as what should be the result of that death. That might lead some to speculate that our death with Christ to sin has already been accomplished, while our resurrection with Him (in context, spiritual resurrection) has yet to be accomplished. Yet comparison with other scripture will reveal that is not so.

Ephesians 2:5-6 states our spiritual resurrection with Christ as an accomplished fact that happens at salvation. Colossians 2:12-13 makes the same claim. In Colossians 3:1, Paul uses the reasoning that if we are risen with Christ, we should seek those things which are above. Just as surely as all Christians are to seek heavenly things, likewise all Christians have been risen with Christ.

Our spirits died to sin and are already resurrected with Christ unto newness of life. These things are already realities in our new spirits. Yet, to see these facts become realities in our physical lives, we have to first know what happened to us in our spirits at salvation and then believe this good news. To the degree that we think, believe, and act like who we are in our spirit,, to that degree we will experience the life of Christ in our flesh.

Romans 6:5-6 - For if we have been planted together in the likeness of his death, we shall be also in the likeness of his resurrection: 6) Knowing this, that our old man is crucified with him, that the body of sin might be destroyed, that henceforth we should not serve sin.

(Rom. 6:6) Our spirits have already died with Christ unto sin and are already resurrected unto newness of life. Yet, this newness of life, which is a reality in our spirits, does not automatically manifest itself in our flesh. Verse 6 makes it very clear that we have to know some things before this resurrection life flows from our spirit into our flesh.

Facts, whether spiritual or natural, don't govern our lives. It's our knowledge or perception of truths that control our physical emotions and experiences (Prov. 23:7). If someone lied to you about a family member having just died, you would experience sorrow or other negative emotions, even though there was no factual basis to feel that way. In the same way, if you were told that a family member had died, and it was true, but you didn't believe the report, you would be spared those emotions.

Likewise, we have had the power of sin broken in our lives by our death to sin, and we have the resurrection power of Christ's life in our spirits. But these facts won't change our experiences until we know them and begin to act accordingly. All Christians are already blessed with all spiritual blessings (Eph. 1:3), but few Christians know that, and even fewer understand it to a degree that it impacts their lives. "My people are destroyed for lack of knowledge" (Hosea 4:6).

Walking in resurrection power in our physical lives is dependent on knowing that our old man (old self, NIV) is crucified. If we don't believe that, then there won't be newness of life (v. 4) or victory for us.

Our old self is already crucified. Yet some people have effectively voided the power of that truth (Mark 7:13) by teaching that we still have our old self, or sin nature, which are constantly being resurrected from the dead. There is no scripture that mentions a daily or even periodical resurrection of our old man. Only Jesus has that power. Satan has no power to accomplish resurrection of any kind.

This common belief that we still have our old man, or sin nature, does not come from scripture but through observation. People observe a drive to sin, and they assume that it is their old sin nature that drives them to it.

The Scripture does teach that sin produced death (Gen. 2:17; Rom. 5:12,15,17; 6:23; and Eph. 2:1), and therefore, everyone was born with a spirit that was dead to (or separated from) God. This is the part of us that the Bible calls sin (or the old man). Therefore, the Scriptures do teach that everyone was born with a sin nature, or old man. But Paul is making a very clear presentation in these verses that for the Christian, the old man is dead. We do not have a nature that is driving us to sin.

If that be so, then why do we seem so bound to sin even after we experience the new birth? The reason is that our old man left behind what this verse calls a body. Just as a person's spirit and soul leave behind a physical body at death, so our old man left behind habits and strongholds in our thoughts and emotions. The reason a Christian tends to sin is because of an unrenewed mind, not because of a sin nature.

God made the mental part of us similar to a computer. We can program our minds so that certain actions and attitudes become automatic. For instance, when we were children, it was a major effort to tie our shoelaces or button our shirts, but as adults, we can now perform those duties without even thinking about what we are doing. It's like it is just a part of us, but in actuality, it was an acquired trait.

Likewise, our old man ruled our thinking before we were born again. He taught us such things as selfishness, hatred, and fear, as well as placed within us the desire for sin. The old man is now gone, but these negative parts of the old man remain. Just as a computer will continue to perform according to its programming until reprogrammed, so our minds continue to lead us on the course that our old man charted until renewed (Rom. 12:2).

Therefore, a Christian does not have a part that is still of the devil and is driving him or her to sin. Instead, the Christian has been liberated from the part that was dead in sin (i.e., old man Eph. 2:1), and the rest of the Christian life is a renewing of the mind that results in the resurrection life of Jesus being manifest in our physical bodies (2 Cor. 4:11).

Someone might say, "What's the difference? Whether it's my old man or an unrenewed mind, I still struggle with the desire to sin." The difference is enormous! If we still have a sin nature, then we are doomed to a life of schizophrenia (literally a split mind), but if it is just our unrenewed minds that cause the problem, then we can see the situation improve as we renew our minds.

If we retained a sin nature, even after the new birth, then a person who was bound by a particular sin before salvation would still be bound to it after salvation. They would just have to refrain from the physical act, but in their hearts they would continue to be guilty of committing that sin in thought. Yet, there are millions of examples of people who experience the new birth and are so changed that the very sins that used to enslave them before salvation are now so repulsive to them that they have no desire to commit those acts. They can't even relate to the old self that did those things, because they are a new person (2 Cor. 5:17) with a renewed mind.

It is truly liberating to learn that I don't have to commit sins, I chose to do so. Therefore, I can change through the renewing of my mind (Rom. 12:2) because there is no longer a part of me that is a sinner by nature. This is the point that Paul is making in this verse. To experience the resurrection life of Jesus, we have to know that our old man is dead, and through the renewing of our minds we destroy the body that the old man left behind, with the end result being that we will not serve sin any longer.

Romans 6:7 - For he that is dead is freed from sin.

(Rom. 6:7) There is a difference between being freed and being free. In the 1800's, President Lincoln issued the Emancipation Proclamation which freed the American slaves, but many slaves continued to serve their masters in slavery because the truth was hidden from them, or in some cases, the slaves were afraid that they couldn't make it on their own.

Likewise, Christians have been freed from sin, but that doesn't automatically mean all Christians experience that freedom. Through ignorance and deception, Satan continues to maintain mastery over those who have not yet realized their death and resurrection with Christ.

Romans 6:8-9 - Now if we be dead with Christ, we believe that we shall also live with him: 9) Knowing that Christ being raised from the dead dieth no more; death hath no more dominion over him.

(Rom. 6:9) Our death to sin and resurrection to life with Christ is already a reality in our spirits, but it will only become a physical reality as we know and believe these truths. In this verse, Paul is stressing that this resurrection life is dependent on knowing that our death with Jesus to sin is a one-time death that does not have to be repeated.

Much current theology believes that we died unto sin but that we resurrect unto sin every morning and, therefore, must continually repeat this process. That is not what happened to Jesus, and these verses are comparing our death to sin unto Jesus' death to sin. It is true that we continually have to appropriate this death to sin, but there is a big difference between dying over and over and over and just renewing your mind with an accomplished fact.

In the same way that Jesus died unto sin once (v. 10) and now death has no more dominion over Him, the person who recognizes one's death with Christ unto sin will not have sin rule over him or her anymore either (verse 14). Any Christian who is struggling with sin has not recognized that he or she is dead unto sin.

Romans 6:10-11 - For in that he died, he died unto sin once: but in that he liveth, he liveth unto God. 11) Likewise reckon ye also yourselves to be dead indeed unto sin, but alive unto God through Jesus Christ our Lord.

(Rom. 6:11) Our old man is dead. However, because there is still a lust to sin present even after the new birth, many teach that the old man is constantly being resurrected. That's not so.

This verse makes it very clear that we are to reckon ourselves dead to sin in the same manner as Christ is dead to sin. The Greek word that was translated "likewise" in this verse is the word "houto," meaning in this way (referring to what precedes or follows). The dictionary defines "likewise" as, "in the same way; similarly." Therefore, we are dead to sin in the same way that Christ is dead to sin.

Of course, Jesus only died to sin once, so therefore, we only die to sin once (vv.9-10). After that, we simply reckon ourselves dead to sin and alive unto God.

The Greek word "logizomai," which was translated "reckon" here is explained in detail. The word conveys no causative meaning but rather only an inventory, or assessment, of a condition that already exists. Therefore, the state of being dead to sin already exists for the Christian, but we have to seize this benefit by reckoning it to be so. The use of the word "indeed" in this verse further establishes that this is already an accomplished work of Christ that we are simply appropriating.

Many people focus on the death to sin that is mentioned in this verse and omit or, at least, put secondarily, the being alive unto God part. It is assumed that if we will just die to sin, then life with Christ comes automatically. That's no more so than physical death automatically producing physical resurrection. God doesn't need dead people; He needs people who have risen from the dead spiritually.

People who are preoccupied with dying to themselves will not experience new life with Christ. This verse emphatically states that we are to believe unquestionably, without a doubt, that we are in fact, in reality, already dead to sin in the same way that Christ is already dead to sin.

Being dead to sin is not a struggle against nor victory over sin that we are accomplishing, but it is deliverance from our old man that enslaved us to sin. Our old man no longer exists and, therefore, no longer can dominate us if we know the truth.

It is wrong to teach that dying to sin is something that we still have to accomplish by acknowledging all our sinfulness and forsaking it. This actually causes people to focus on self (sinful self) more than ever before and, therefore, actually strengthens the hold of what's left of the old man in our lives. The way to get rid of the residual effect of the old man in our lives is not to focus on our sins but to focus on our resurrected union with Christ.

Therefore, according to the instruction of this verse, we are to unquestionably count on the fact that our old man is gone and, just as certainly, reckon that our new man is alive with Christ, desiring only those things that please the Father. Doing this will transform us outwardly, in our flesh, into a person who reflects on who we already are inwardly in our spirits.

Romans 6:12 - Let not sin therefore reign in your mortal body, that ye should obey it in the lusts thereof.

(Rom. 6:12) If this sentence was to be diagrammed the way we were taught in school for the purpose of identifying the subject and verb, then the understood subject of this sentence would be you. Paul is saying, "You let not sin therefore reign in your mortal body." You have the power to stop the reign of sin in your life or the Lord would not have given you this command.

A mistaken belief that we can't help but sin is one of the biggest reasons that we do sin. The power of sin has been broken in our lives, and the only reason a Christian sins is because he or she hasn't renewed their mind with the reality of this new life with Christ.

The word "therefore" makes our ability to end sin's reign in our lives that this verse speaks of dependent on the truth that was just expressed in verse 11. We have to know beyond any doubt that our old man is dead and gone. Then, and only then, will we be able to renew our minds and end the dictatorship of sin in our lives.

Romans 6:13-14 - Neither yield ye your members as instruments of unrighteousness unto sin: but yield yourselves unto God, as those that are alive from the dead, and your members as instruments of righteousness unto God. 14) For sin shall not have dominion over you: for ye are not under the law, but under grace.

(Rom. 6:14) The old man is dead and gone. Yet there is a residual old man, or the unrenewed mind and emotions, that the old man left behind. It is these lingering effects of the old man, or sin, to which Paul is referring.

Paul makes a very clear statement that the reason this sin shall not have dominion over us is because we are not under Law but under grace. However, most Christians today are still operating under the Law, so it's no surprise that sin is still having dominion over them. Understanding our freedom from the Old Testament Law is a prerequisite to breaking the dominion of sin in our lives.

The reason this is so is because the Law strengthened sin by producing guilt that condemned us and killed us. The Law also brought the wrath of God against our sin. However, once we accept the atonement of Christ for our sin, we no longer need to fear the wrath of God. That was placed on Jesus. We also don't need the Law to condemn us and kill us. We have already come to Christ for salvation, which is what the Law was designed to do (Gal. 3:24-25).

Knowledge of this frees a person from sin: it doesn't free a person to sin. As Christians, we all continue to sin to some degree, not because we have to, but because we are still in the process of renewing our minds. However, when we aren't condemned and feeling separated from God because of our sin, we are free to run to God for help instead of away from God in fear. Therefore, understanding God's grace and our freedom from the Law is the key to breaking the dominance of sin in our lives

Romans 6:15 - What then? shall we sin, because we are not under the law, but under grace? God forbid.

(Rom. 6:15) Paul had started this sixth chapter with a similar question about whether or not his teaching was encouraging people to sin. He spent the first thirteen verses of this chapter explaining that Christians don't sin, because they are dead to sin. Then in verse 14, he brings up our deliverance from the Law again, which prompts this similar question. He then goes on through the rest of this chapter to explain that the second reason Christians don't sin is because it gives Satan an inroad into our lives.

Romans 6:16 - Know ye not, that to whom ye yield yourselves servants to obey, his servants ye are to whom ye obey; whether of sin unto death, or of obedience unto righteousness?

(Rom. 6:16) This is the second argument that Paul presents in this chapter, why Christians don't live in sin. The legalistic Jews were seeking a life without sin so that they could earn God's favor. Paul had conclusively proven that no one could keep the precepts of the Law and that the Law was never given for the purpose of justification. Therefore, he is explaining that Christians still seek to live holy lives, but for different reasons.

This second reason that Paul gives for holiness in the life of the believer is that when we obey sin, we yield ourselves to Satan, the author of that sin. Notice the use of the personal pronoun whom in this verse. Yielding to sin is yielding to a person, Satan. God doesn't impute the sin to us but the devil does . Our actions either release the power of Satan or the power of God in us.

Therefore, although God is not imputing our sins unto us, we cannot afford the luxury of sin, because it allows Satan to have access to us. When a Christian does sin and allows the devil opportunity to produce his death in the person's life, then the way to stop that is to confess the sin, and God is faithful and just to take the forgiveness that is already present in our born-again spirits and release it in our flesh, thereby removing Satan and his strongholds.

The Greek word that was translated "servants" twice in this verse is "doulos" denoting a slave. Therefore, Paul is not speaking of an infrequent error on our part but rather a servile condition where a person gives one's self up wholly to another's will (Thayer's Gk.-Eng. Lexicon). So, Paul is stating that a person who abandons one's self to sin is, in actuality, becoming a slave of the devil, while a person who obeys righteousness is actually yielding one's self to the Lord. This is the second reason in this chapter as to why a Christian should live holy.

Romans 6:17-18 - But God be thanked, that ye were the servants of sin, but ye have obeyed from the heart that form of doctrine which was delivered you 18) Being then made free from sin, ye became the servants of righteousness.

(Rom. 6:18) Jesus said, "No man can serve two masters: for either he will hate the one, and love the other; or else he will hold to the one, and despise the other. Ye cannot serve God and mammon" (Matt. 6:24). We cannot become the servant of righteousness until we are made free from serving sin.

The Greek word used for "servant" here denotes slavery. Christians still sin (1 John 1:7, 9), but they aren't the slaves of sin anymore. Those who believe that the old man still lives and exerts mastery in their lives will not experience the joy of being servants to righteousness.

Romans 6:19-20 - I speak after the manner of men because of the infirmity of your flesh: for as ye have yielded your members servants to uncleanness and to iniquity unto iniquity; even so now yield your members servants to righteousness unto holiness. 20) For when ye were the servants of sin, ye were free from righteousness.

(Rom. 6:20) Paul had just made a statement in the previous verse that we should serve the Lord with the same fervor that we served the devil before we were born again. He continues that comparison through verse 22 and makes an amazing point. He is saying that in the same way that our good acts could not change our sinful nature before we were born again, likewise our sinful acts cannot change our righteous nature now that we have become a new creature in Christ Jesus.

In this verse, the phrase "servants of sin" is describing a person before he or she is born again. The phrase "free from righteousness" is not saying that a lost man cannot do anything that is right, but rather, all of an individual's good acts aren't enough to change his nature. He must be born again.

Most Christians have accepted this truth unquestionably. They were saved as a result of believing that. Yet this exact terminology is used again in verse 22 in a way that very few Christians accept. The same logic that was used in verse 20 is reversed in verse 22.

If "servants to sin" in verse 20 signified a person before salvation, then "servants to God" in verse 22 denotes just the opposite, a person who has been saved through faith in Christ. If "free from righteousness" in verse 20 described a lost man who was incapable of changing his sinful nature by his own good works, then "free from sin" in verse 22 describes a Christian as being unable to change his righteous nature through his sins.

This is a powerful truth. In the same way that our sinful nature could not be changed by our own actions, now our new born-again spirits cannot be changed by our actions either. If we are going to accept one of these truths, we have to accept the other. We cannot honestly accept verse 20 and reject verse 22 when the exact same terminology is used in the same context.

Actions cannot produce the new birth, and actions cannot destroy the new birth. We had to believe to receive salvation, and we have to willfully reject that faith in Christ to become reprobate.

Romans 6:21-22 - What fruit had ye then in those things whereof ye are now ashamed? for the end of those things is death. 22) But now being made free from sin, and become servants to God, ye have your fruit unto holiness, and the end everlasting life.

(Rom. 6:22) Notice that holiness is a fruit and not a root of salvation. That is to say that holiness is a by-product of relationship with God, it does not produce relationship with God.

Romans 6:23 - For the wages of sin is death; but the gift of God is eternal life through Jesus Christ our Lord.

(Rom. 6:23) The dictionary defines "wages" as "a fitting return; recompense; requital." Sin has a wage that it pays, and no one can avoid payday without faith in Jesus.

The sin spoken of here is not an individual act of sin but rather the sin nature, or old man, itself. Anyone who does not receive the new birth will be held liable for all the wrongs committed as a result of their sinful nature . However, for those who receive the new birth through faith in Jesus, they don't have a sin nature and will therefore not receive this payment of death.

The physical death of our bodies is not really what is being spoken of here. Physical death as well as every result of the sin nature (i.e., sickness, depression, fear, etc.) are only by-products of the spiritual death that was already present on the inside of us. The Lord told Adam that in the day he ate of the forbidden tree, he would surely die (Gen. 2:17). Adam didn't die physically that day, but he did die spiritually. Physical death came when Adam was 930 years old (Gen. 5:5) as a by-product of spiritual death.

The wages (plural) of death that those who are not born again will receive, can be broken into two categories. The Bible speaks of a second death (Rev. 2:11, 20:6,14, and 21:8), which is banishment to the lake of fire on judgment day. The first death is this separation from God (or spiritual death), which was inherited through Adam.

So, this verse is specifically speaking of the spiritual death which was inherited through Adam, and then the second death, which is eternal banishment from God and torment in the lake of fire. However, any negative result of sin, which was not a part of God's original plan for man, can also be included in the term "death," since it is a direct result of this spiritual death.

Eternal life is a gift. The dictionary defines "gift" as "something that is bestowed voluntarily and without compensation; a present." We have nothing to do with earning this gift; eternal life would cease to be a gift if we had to earn it (Rom. 11:6). We simply receive it by faith

Romans 6:1-23
Discipleship Questions

. . . .

Answer the following questions by reading the corresponding discipleship commentary lesson and using your Bible.

1. Read Romans 5:20 in the New International Version. According to the context (thoughts that precede or follow), why is the question in Romans 6:1 being asked?

   _____

   _____

2. What key phrases and words are found in Romans 6:1-2 that indicate that Paul is speaking about a lifestyle of sin?_____

   _____

3. How were Paul's questions in Romans 6:1 answered in Romans 6:2?

   _____

4. Read Romans 6:6 & 6:7. What does the phrase "dead to sin" mean?

   _____

   _____

5. How does 1 John 3:9-10 and 1 Peter 1:14-15 give understanding to the phrase "dead to sin"? Read the New International Version.

   _____

   _____

   _____

6. Read Romans 6:3. When Paul uses the phrase "know ye not," he implies that there is something that these Christians should know but don't know. What is it that they don't know, or realize?_____

   _____

7. According to Romans 6:3 there has been a "death to sin" (v. 2) caused by what?

   _____

8. Read Romans 6:3. This "baptism" was into what?

   _____

9. How does 1 Corinthians 12:12-13 describe being "baptized into Jesus Christ"?

   _____

   _____

   _____

   _____

10. Read Acts 2:38. How does this verse relate to the phrase "baptized into Jesus Christ"?

_____

11. Read Romans 6:3. When people are "baptized into Jesus Christ," what also happens to them according to Romans 6:3?

_____

12. Read Romans 6:4-5. Besides being baptized into Jesus' death, what other two things happened to us? _____

_____

13. Read the last phrase in Romans 6:4. Being identified with Jesus in His death, burial and resurrection results in what?

_____

14. Read Romans 6:5,10. What is the "likeness of his resurrection"?

_____

15. Does the term "old man" also imply that there is a "new man"?

_____

16. Read the last phrase in Romans 6:6. The "old man" being crucified with Christ results in what for us?_____

_____

17. Read Romans 6:7. Is there a difference in being "freed" and in being "free"? If so, what is the difference? _____

_____

_____

18. Jesus paid the wages of our sins, which was death. How is this death described in John 3:16? _____

19. How is death described in 2 Thessalonians 1:9?

_____

20. Read Romans 6:23. Because death hath no more dominion over Jesus Christ, what can God now offer us? _____

21. Jesus became sin on our behalf (2 Cor. 5:21). Does Jesus Christ have any relationship to sin now? _____

22. Read the last phrase in Romans 6:10. How is His life lived?

_____

23. How are we to consider ourselves according to Romans 6:11?

_____

_____

24. What is the command given to believers in Romans 6:12?

_____

25. Read Romans 6:12. What does the word "reign" imply?

_____

26. Read Romans 6:12. Where is sin not to reign?

_____

27. Read Romans 6:12 and Hebrews 11:24-25. Does sin have its own lusts and desires?

_____

28. What are the two commands given to believers in Romans 6:13?

_____

_____

29. What is it that you are not to yield as instruments of unrighteousness?

_____

30. Name some of these members.

_____

31. How is the word "righteousness" used in Romans 6:13?

_____

32. How does Romans 13:14 describe yielding your members as instruments of righteousness unto God?

_____

_____

33. In what ways could we make provisions for our flesh?

_____

_____

34. Read Ezekiel 18:20 and Revelation 20:13-14. If sin has dominion over you, according to the Law, what is the result? _____

35. Read Ephesians 2:4-5. What is the result of being under grace?

_____

36. How are the questions in Romans 6:15 different from the questions in Romans 6:1-2?

_____

_____

37. Being slaves to the master of sin pays us what wages according to Romans 6:16 and 6:23?

_____

38. Read Romans 6:17. In the past we were slaves of sin, but then what happened?

_____

_____

39. Read Romans 6:18. When we obeyed from the heart the truth of the Gospel, what was the result? _____

_____

40. Read Romans 6:19. Paul has been using the illustration of slaves and masters so that human nature can grasp the truth more readily. Define what it means to "yield."

_____

41. Read Romans 6:19. What was it that we yielded our bodies to in the past?

_____

42. Read Romans 6:19. What is it that we are to yield our bodies to now?

_____

_____

43. Read Romans 6:20. What relationship did you have with righteousness in the past?

_____

_____

44. Read Romans 6:20. Was righteousness your master?

_____

45. Read Romans 6:21. What kind of harvest, or result, do you get from the things you now are ashamed of doing? _____

_____

46. Read Romans 6:21. The end of those things results in what?

_____

47. Read Romans 6:22. Now that sin is no longer your master and you have become the servants of God, you reap the fruit of what?

_____

48. Read Romans 6:22. The end result of repentance toward God is what?

_____

49. Read Romans 6:23. What are the wages for what you've done?

_____

50. Read Romans 6:23. What is the free gift of God?

_____

Romans 6:1-23
Discipleship Answer Key

. . . .

Do not look at the answer key until you have completed the questions.
Compare your answers with the following answers.

1. Read Romans 5:20 in the New International Version. According to the context (thoughts that precede or follow), why is the question in Romans 6:1 being asked?
   It was prompted by Paul's statment, "Where sin increased, grace increased all the more."

2. What key phrases and words are found in Romans 6:1-2 that indicate that Paul is speaking about a lifestyle of sin?
   "Continue in sin" (v. 1), and "live any longer therein."

3. How were Paul's questions in Romans 6:1 answered in Romans 6:2?
   "God forbid, certainly not, by no means!"

4. Read Romans 6:6 & 6:7. What does the phrase "dead to sin" mean?
   Freed from sin, i.e., sin is no longer our master, that henceforth we should not SERVE sin.

5. How does 1 John 3:9-10 and 1 Peter 1:14-15 give understanding to the phrase "dead to sin"? Read the New International Version.
   Anyone born of God will not continue in a lifestyle of sin. 1 John 3:10 states, "Anyone who does not do what is right (showing repentance is lacking in one's life) is not a child of God." "Dead to sin" in 1 Peter means not conforming to the evil desires you had when you lived in ignorance.

6. Read Romans 6:3. When Paul uses the phrase "know ye not," he implies that there is something that these Christians should know but don't know. What is it that they don't know, or realize?
   As many as were baptized into Jesus Christ were baptized into His death.

7. According to Romans 6:3 there has been a "death to sin" (v. 2) caused by what?
   Baptism.

8. Read Romans 6:3. This "baptism" was into what?
   Jesus Christ.

9. How does 1 Corinthians 12:12-13 describe being "baptized into Jesus Christ"?
"Our bodies have many parts, but the many parts make up only one body when they are all put together. So it is with the 'body' of Christ. Each of us is a part of the one body of Christ. Some of us are Jews, some are Gentiles, some are slaves and some are free. But the Holy Spirit has fitted us all together into one body. We have been baptized into Christ's body by the one Spirit, and have all been given that same Holy Spirit" (1 Cor. 12:12-13, Living Bible).

10. Read Acts 2:38. How does this verse relate to the phrase "baptized into Jesus Christ"?
Acts 2:38 states, "Be baptized every one of you in the name of Jesus Christ."

11. Read Romans 6:3. When people are "baptized into Jesus Christ," what also happens to them according to Romans 6:3?
They are baptized into His death.

12. Read Romans 6:4-5. Besides being baptized into Jesus' death, what other two things happened to us?
1. We are buried with Him.
2. Identified with His resurrection.

13. Read the last phrase in Romans 6:4. Being identified with Jesus in His death, burial, and resurrection results in what?
Walking in newness of life.

14. Read Romans 6:5,10. What is the "likeness of his resurrection"?
Living your life unto God.

15. Does the term "old man" also imply that there is a "new man"?
Yes.

16. Read the last phrase in Romans 6:6. The "old man" being crucified with Christ results in what for us?
That henceforth we should not serve sin, i.e., sin is no longer our master.

17. Read Romans 6:7. Is there a difference in being "freed" and in being "free"? If so, what is the difference?
"Freed" is the believers position, "free" is the result of the believer's choice to believe his or her identity with Christ and to yield one's members as instruments of righteousness unto God.

18. Jesus paid the wages of our sins, which was death. How is this death described in John 3:16?
To perish.

19. How is death described in 2 Thessalonians 1:9?
Everlasting destruction from the presence of the Lord.

20. Read Romans 6:23. Because death hath no more dominion over Jesus Christ, what can God now offer us?
Eternal life.

21. Jesus became sin on our behalf (2 Cor. 5:21). Does Jesus Christ have any relationship to sin now?
No.

22. Read the last phrase in Romans 6:10. How is His life lived?
Unto God.

23. How are we to consider ourselves according to Romans 6:11?
In the same way (as verse 10), dead to sin and alive to God.

24. What is the command given to believers in Romans 6:12?
Do not let sin reign in your mortal body so that you obey it.

25. Read Romans 6:12. What does the word "reign" imply?
To rule as a king. To be predominant, or prevalent.

26. Read Romans 6:12. Where is sin not to reign?
In your mortal body.

27. Read Romans 6:12 and Hebrews 11:24-25. Does sin have its own lusts and desires?
Yes.

28. What are the two commands given to believers in Romans 6:13?
   1. **Don't yield any part of your body to sin.**
   2. **Offer yourselves to God, i.e., the parts of your body as instruments of righteousness (right doing).**

29. What is it that you are not to yield as instruments of unrighteousness?
Your members.

30. Name some of these members.
Hands, eyes, feet, mind, etc.

31. How is the word "righteousness" used in Romans 6:13?
As doing right.

32. How does Romans 13:14 describe yielding your members as instruments of righteousness unto God?
Putting on the Lord Jesus Christ and making no PROVISION for the flesh.

33. In what ways could we make provisions for our flesh?

34. Read Ezekiel 18:20 and Revelation 20:13-14. If sin has dominion over you according to the law, what is the result?
Death, or the second death.

35. Read Ephesians 2:4-5. What is the result of being under grace?
Being made alive and in union with Christ.

36. How are the questions in Romans 6:15 different from the questions in Romans 6:1-2?
Romans 6:1-2 is asking the question, "shall we continue in sin" i.e., live in sin or make sin our lifestyle? Romans 6:15 is asking, shall we commit an act of sin?

37. Being slaves to the master of sin pays us what wages according to Romans 6:16 and 6:23?
Death.

38. Read Romans 6:17. In the past we were slaves of sin, but then what happened?
"But thanks be to God! For at one time you were slaves to sin; but then you obeyed with all your heart the truths found in the teaching you received" (Romans 6:17, Today's English Version).

39. Read Romans 6:18. When we obeyed from the heart the truth of the Gospel, what was the result?
We were made free from sin (it no longer is our master), and we became the servants of righteousness (we received a new master).

40. Read Romans 6:19. Paul has been using the illustration of slaves and masters so that human nature can grasp the truth more readily. Define what it means to "yield."
To give up; surrender; submit.

41. Read Romans 6:19. What was it that we yielded our bodies to in the past?
Uncleanness, i.e., impurity and iniquity, i.e., wickedness.

42. Read Romans 6:19. What is it that we are to yield our bodies to now?
We are to offer our bodies in slavery to righteousness and holiness.

43. Read Romans 6:20. What relationship did you have with righteousness in the past? **"When you were slaves of sin, you felt no obligation to righteousness" (Rom. 6:20, The Jerusalem Bible).**

44. Read Romans 6:20. Was righteousness your master?
No.

45. Read Romans 6:21. What kind of harvest, or result, do you get from the things you are now ashamed of doing?
"Evidently not good, since you are ashamed now even to think about those things you used to do" (Romans 6:21, The Living Bible).

46. Read Romans 6:21. The end of those things results in what?
Those things, i.e., that behavior, results in death!

47. Read Romans 6:22. Now that sin is no longer your master and you have become the servants of God, you reap the fruit of what?
Holiness.

48. Read Romans 6:22. The end result of repentance toward God is what?
Everlasting life.

49. Read Romans 6:23. What are the wages for what you've done?
Death.

50. Read Romans 6:23. What is the free gift of God?
Eternal life.

OVERVIEW OF ROMANS CHAPTER 7

by Don Krow

Turn in your Bible to Romans 7:1: *"Know ye not, brethren, (for I speak to them that know the law,) how that the law hath dominion over a man as long as he liveth?"* I have often wondered about Romans 7 because in chapters 1-3 there was universal guilt and condemnation of man. Jesus stepped in and justified us, and then we see very positive things in Romans 5-6, how the old man has been crucified. We see victory, victory, victory. Then when we get to chapter 7 we see defeat again.

Some people say, "Well, Romans 7 is talking about Paul before he became a believer." There might be some sections of the chapter that indicate that, but there certainly is a lot that indicates he is talking about a believer.

I'm going to tell you a little secret that has taken me 25-30 years to learn: Anytime we go back to the Law as a means of trying to establish some kind of righteousness, or right-relationship with God, we will plunge into defeat and despair, which is exactly what happened in the church at Galatia in the New Testament. It has happened in many churches, and is what is happening in Romans 7.

Paul is saying, "I want to tell you a little bit about the Law. It has jurisdiction and authority over an individual only as long as that person is alive."

Verse 2-3: *"For the woman which hath an husband is bound by the law to her husband so long as he liveth; but if the husband be dead, she is loosed from the law of her husband. So then if, while her husband liveth, she be married to another man, she shall be called an adulteress: but if her husband be dead, she is free from that law; so that she is no adulteress, though she be married to another man."* Paul is not trying to teach on marriage here. He is using an illustration of the divine ideal of marriage, that it is to be a permanent relationship until death do them part. He says that the husband is bound in marriage until the wife dies and vice versa, but at death, they are free from that law of marriage so they can be married to another individual. There is no adultery involved in that. We can all understand that. Here Paul is taking that principle and applying it to our relationship with the Law and with Jesus Christ.

I want you to notice what he says in verse 4: *"Wherefore, my brethren, ye also are become dead to the law by the body of Christ; that ye should be married to another, even to him who is raised from the dead, that we should bring forth fruit unto God."* He is saying that we used to have a relationship with the Law, it was like the Law was our husband. The Law says, "Do this, do that, do this, and if you don't do it right and correctly, you'll die." It has a curse attached to it.

I want to tell you something about the Law being our husband. All the things the Law told us to do, he (the Law) never offered any help to do them. He was a terrible husband—it was terrible being married to the Law because he was saying, "perfection, perfection, and if you don't do it, you will surely die."

The Bible says the only way to be released from that is death. The Law isn't going to die because it is righteous, holy, and just. The answer is in our union with Jesus Christ—we were crucified with Him. When He died, we died, and it forever released us from the jurisdiction of the Law. Now we are free to be married to another, and it says here that we are married to the person who rose from the dead. We are married to the Lord Jesus Christ and now, in union with Him, we can really bring forth fruit unto God, because everything God asked us to do will be done with His ability, power, and strength.

Let's go down to verse 22 for the sake of time: *"For I delight in the law of God after the inward man."* I know the Law of God is the right thing—the way I should live—but there is a problem.

Verses 23-24: *"But I see another law* [principle] *in my members* [the limbs of my body], *warring against the law of my mind* [attacking my mind], *and bringing me into captivity* [into slavery] *to the law of sin which is in my members. O wretched man that I am! who will deliver me from the body of this death?"* I never understood it. Victory, victory, victory in the chapters before, and in chapter 7, suddenly, we are bound. He said earlier, "The things I want to do, the things I hate, I end up doing. There is a principle that when I want to do good, evil is with me."

Does that sound pretty normal to you? Paul said the problem is what he called in verse 23, a law of sin that works in your members. What is a law of sin that works in your members? Let me ask this: What is the law of gravity? If I released my Bible, it would fall down. I didn't push it down, didn't have to hold it down. A law has its own natural ability and power. If I stepped off a building, I would go down. If I was in Russia, Australia, or China and went up instead of down, I would say gravity is not a law, because sometimes it works this way, and sometimes it doesn't. A law is consistent. It works the same way all the time, has its own natural ability, has it own natural power.

Paul is saying that sin is a law of sin that works in our members. It beats and defeats us. We don't have the power to defeat it. Verse 18 says, *"For I know that in me (that is, in my flesh) dwelleth no good thing: for to will is present with me; but how to perform that which is good I find not."* The will is present: "bless God, I'm going to defeat this law!"

If I drop my Bible and say, "I'm going to defeat this law of gravity. Look at that Bible—it's not going down to the ground now." Do you know what the law of gravity would be doing? It would be laughing at me, saying, "Hold that Bible out there five minutes, ten minutes, an hour, or eight hours." Do you know what will happen? After eight hours, we'll call 911, and they will wrap my arm in a sling, because gravity is a law. It's pulling on my arm. Will power is not enough to defeat it. I have to have a higher law in operation.

If you go to the airport, you can get on a jet plane and fly across the sea—I've done it many times. Is the law of gravity pushing on the plane? Yes, it is. It is trying to defeat it and push it down, but there is a higher law in operation called the law of aerodynamics, the law of lift. If someone builds an airplane, it can supersede the law of gravity and fly even overseas. Gravity is still pushing on it, but a higher law is in operation that has beaten and defeated it.

In Romans 7 Paul is saying he has tried to live the Christian life by the principle of the law—doing, earning, achieving, trying the best he can in his own strength. The things he wanted to do, he couldn't do. He hated the things he was doing. *"O wretched man that I am! who shall deliver me?"* Does that sound pretty normal to you in your Christian life?

Paul finally came to the end of himself. He didn't say, "God, give me another formula. Give me more will power." He said, "I can't do it. Who will deliver me from the body of this death," and the answer came through the Lord Jesus Christ. I don't thank Don Krow and his ability; I thank Jesus Christ my Lord. He is the only one who has the power to live the Christian life. There is a law that is more powerful, more dynamic than the law of sin that works against us.

Go to Romans 8:2 to read about it: *"For the law of the Spirit of life in Christ Jesus hath made me free from the law of sin and death."* The devil is stronger than I am. Sin has more power over me than I have in my will power. It is stronger than I am, but Jesus Christ's power supersedes sin.

Do you know how to really understand Romans 7? Look at it: I want to do this … I can't do it … the things that I want to do, I can't do … I try ... and I fail. Where is the Holy Spirit? He is not in Romans 7. It is man living by the Law, man living by his own ability. Paul says we have to abandon our ability and trust the ability of God's Spirit, the Spirit of life that is in Christ Jesus. He is the only one who has the power to live the Christian life.

Why don't you trust Him and quit trusting yourself and your own ability? Why don't you trust Him today? God bless you.

Romans 7:1-25
Discipleship Commentary

Read the entire lesson and then answer the questions that follow.

Romans 7:1 - Know ye not, brethren, (for I speak to them that know the law,) how that the law hath dominion over a man as long as he liveth?

(Rom. 7:1) Remember that Paul wrote this epistle to all the saints in Rome (Rom. 1:7). Therefore, even though this term "brethren" can be used to designate fellow countrymen as in Romans 9:3, here it is specifying fellow believers, especially the Jewish believers who were knowledgeable of the Law.

Paul is saying that the only way to get out from under the Old Testament Law is through death. He had just taught that the old man is, once and for all, dead. Now he uses the natural illustration of marriage to further make this point.

In the same way that the marriage vow was intended by God to be binding until death do us part, so our bondage under the tyranny of the sin nature was inescapable except through death. Therefore, this knowledge of our death to the old man is crucial to escaping the carnal life that the old man put in place in our lives.

Romans 7:2 - For the woman which hath an husband is bound by the law to her husband so long as he liveth; but if the husband be dead, she is loosed from the law of her husband.

(Rom. 7:2) Paul likens our death to sin, which he had explained in chapter 6, to the laws governing a marriage relationship. The husband is our old man, the wife is the soul and body part of us, or our personality, and the binding civil and moral code that enforces a marriage is like the Old Testament Law.

We, the wife, were enslaved to a wicked husband, the old man. In Old Testament times, the Law gave the wife no option of divorce. The man could divorce his wife (Deut. 24:1), but the wife could not divorce her husband. Therefore, the only hope a woman could ever have of being delivered from that situation was that her "old man" would die. Then she was delivered from that moral and civil code that kept her from having relationship with someone else.

Likewise, we were in bondage to our old man. We wanted out of the relationship, but we were by nature slaves to sin (Eph. 2:3). The Old Testament Law only made the situation worse. It strengthened the control of the old man over us. The Law actually empowered sin, or our wicked husband, against us.

Then Jesus entered the scene. He took our old man with Him to the cross and when He died, our old man died too. But Jesus rose from the dead, and our old man didn't. Now we are free from the old man and the Law that bound us to him so that we can be married to Him who is risen from the dead.

Romans 7:3 - So then if, while her husband liveth, she be married to another man, she shall be called an adulteress: but if her husband be dead, she is free from that law; so that she is no adulteress, though she be married to another man.

(Rom. 7:3) In this comparison, it is clearly understood that a woman who has two husbands would be living in adultery. Likewise, Paul is saying that a Christian who has two natures would be living in adultery. A Christian who does not understand that our old man is dead will constantly feel the guilt of the Old Testament Law that bound us to our first husband, the old man.

Romans 7:4 - Wherefore, my brethren, ye also are become dead to the law by the body of Christ; that ye should be married to another, even to him who is raised from the dead, that we should bring forth fruit unto God.

(Rom. 7:4) Through Jesus, not only is our old man dead, but we are dead to the Law that enforced the tyranny of the old man over us. The Law was only made for the old man (1 Tim. 1:9-10). Once he is dead, we are no longer under the Law. Failure to understand this will produce the same end results as if our old man was not dead.

Christ didn't free us from the relationship to our first husband, the old man, so we could just run around and do whatever we want, but He freed us from that first marriage so we could marry Him. A Christian's freedom is not freedom to do our own thing, but it is freedom from the old nature so that we can now serve Christ in newness of spirit (v. 6).

Just as it is normal for a physical marriage to produce children, so our marriage to Christ is intended to bring forth fruit.

Romans 7:5 - For when we were in the flesh, the motions of sins, which were by the law, did work in our members to bring forth fruit unto death.

(Rom. 7:5) A Christian is not in the flesh even though he or she walks after the flesh at times. There is a difference, and Paul makes a major point in the difference between being in the flesh and after the flesh in chapter 8.

Notice that the emotions, or influences, of sin were by the Law. The Law actually made sin come alive in us.

This is the same phrase that was used in the last part of verse four. In the same way that relationship with the old man produced death, now realizing our new relationship with Christ produces the fruit of holiness.

Romans 7:6 - But now we are delivered from the law, that being dead wherein we were held; that we should serve in newness of spirit, and not in the oldness of the letter.

(Rom. 7:6) In these first six verses of Romans 7, Paul says we are loosed from the Law (v. 2), free from the Law (v. 3), dead to the Law (v. 4), and delivered from the Law (this verse). Romans 6:14 says that we are not under the Law. How could it be made any clearer that the Law was not made for a born-again man (1 Tim. 1:9).

The dictionary defines "spirit," when used as in this verse, as "the real sense or significance of something" (American Heritage Dict.). Just as Jesus taught against ritualistic observance of laws, so Paul is saying a Christian is someone who fulfills the real sense or significance of the Law, not every detail. God is more pleased with someone who has a pure heart, and yet fails Him in actions, (Lk. 7:36-50) than someone who does the right things with an impure heart (1 Sam. 16:7). Second Corinthians 3:6 says that the letter kills, but the spirit gives life.

True Christianity is not the observance of a different set of rules than some other religion. It is a change of the heart (2 Cor. 5:17; Ezek. 11:19, and 36:26). Once a person's heart is changed, the person will serve God, not because one has to but because he or she wants to.

Romans 7:7 - What shall we say then? Is the law sin? God forbid. Nay, I had not known sin, but by the law: for I had not known lust, except the law had said, Thou shalt not covet.

(Rom. 7:7) Remember that in context, the sin that is being spoken of here is not an individual act of sin but rather the sin nature that compelled us to sin. Paul is asking, is the law that compelled us to sin? The answer to this is no.

Paul had just spoken of being "loosed from," "free from," "dead to," and "delivered from" the Law. Now Paul is clarifying his statements so that someone doesn't think that he is saying that the Law is the thing that drove us to sin. The Law of God simply made clear to us that we already had a depraved nature. When the Law said, thou shalt not covet, that commandment didn't make covetousness come, but it made the lust that was already present revive (v. 9), and strengthened it (1 Cor. 15:56) so that we could not be deceived any longer into thinking that we could produce salvation on our own.

God's commandments are holy, just, and good (v. 12), but man, apart from God, is sinful. Therefore, it was impossible that a revelation of God's true standards could change our nature; only a new birth could do that. The Law simply stripped our sinful nature of its disguise so that we could properly assess exactly how bad the situation was.

There is an intuitive knowledge of right and wrong on the inside of every person. How does that harmonize with Paul's statement here? The answer is that the Law brought sin into focus.

Every person has an intuitive picture of what sin is, but the hardness of our hearts caused this image to become blurred. Once the Law comes to an individual, all blindness is removed, and it is very clear what God's standard of right and wrong is.

Romans 7:8-9 - But sin, taking occasion by the commandment, wrought in me all manner of concupiscence. For without the law sin was dead. 9) For I was alive without the law once: but when the commandment came, sin revived, and I died.

(Rom. 7:9) Paul is stating that there was a time in his life when he (his soulish, emotional, or personality part) was not separated from God. This was before the Law came. But the Law of God was communicated thousands of years before Paul was born, so what does this mean?

When Paul speaks of the Law coming, he is speaking of the time in every person's life when he recognizes that he is violating a command of God. A child may know he's been told not to do certain things and that if he does, he or she will be punished. However, there comes a time when the child realizes that it is not just Mom or Dad or society that he is disobeying, but this is disobedience to God. That's when the Law comes, and God imputes that person's sins from that time. Prior to that time, the sin nature of that individual is not being imputed to the person and he or she can fellowship with God.

Notice, Paul said that when the commandment came, sin revived. He did not say, sin came. You cannot revive something that doesn't already exist. The sin nature already exists in every human at birth, but until the Law comes, that nature is dead (v. 8). This does not mean that it is not functional. Observation tells us that very young children have a functional sin nature. But God is not imputing sin unto us until the time when every person knowingly violates God's law.

This is why children can receive from God even before they are born again, and this is also the reasoning behind why infants who die go to heaven. Until the time that Paul calls "when the commandment comes" or what many call "the age of accountability," the sin nature does exist, but God is not imputing that sin. Therefore, they are not bearing God's judgment against sin. But once the commandment comes, then the wrath of God against sin is released, and unless they receive Jesus as their Savior, they will bear the eternal punishment of God.

It is impossible to set a certain age of when this accountability for children occurs. That varies from person to person, and for some, such as in cases of retardation, it is possible that this age of accountability is never reached. We can be sure that our all-knowing God will be righteous in His judgment of each individual.

Every individual is born with a nature that is dead in trespasses and sin (Eph. 2:1), but until the person reaches an understanding where he or she is accountable to God, that sin is not imputed unto the person. Until that time, people are alive, in the sense that they can communicate with God without the barrier of sin. But once the Law comes and sin is imputed, there is a separation (or death) from God which can only be remedied by the new birth through faith in Jesus.

Romans 7:10-11 - And the commandment, which was ordained to life, I found to be unto death. 11) For sin, taking occasion by the commandment, deceived me, and by it slew me.

(Rom. 7:11) The ministry of the Law actually gave sin an occasion against us. The corrupt rebellious nature of man will always lust for what it cannot have. Forbid a man to do something that he was only mildly interested in before, and he will develop an uncontrollable lust for that very thing.

This is how the Law worked. Sin was already at work in man, but when the Law came and condemned man's actions, sin came alive (v. 9) in a way that man hadn't realized before. The reason God did this is because mankind had been blinded to what sin was and its consequences. Sin had already beaten and enslaved us, and we didn't realize it. We thought we were good enough until the Law came. Once we were forbidden to do and think certain ways, sin began to abound (Rom. 5:20), and we became aware that we were by nature children of the devil (Eph. 2:3) and needed a Savior. That was the purpose and ministry of the Old Testament Law.

Failure to understand this truth has led many well-meaning religious people to try and get others to stop sinning through the proclamation of God's laws and punishments for sin. The Law wasn't for that purpose. According to these verses, sin actually revives and gains an occasion against us when the Law is used. The right use of the Law is to give a knowledge of sin (Rom. 3:19) and convince us that we are doomed without a Savior. The Law is powerless to overcome sin. Only the grace of God can cause us to overcome sin (Rom. 6:14).

Romans 7:12-13 - Wherefore the law is holy, and the commandment holy, and just, and good. 13) Was then that which is good made death unto me? God forbid. But sin, that it might appear sin, working death in me by that which is good; that sin by the commandment might become exceeding sinful.

(Rom. 7:13) Even though the Law was called "the ministration of death" (2 Cor. 3:7), the Law itself was not death. Death was already at work in us through the sin nature. The Law simply drew out what was already there so that we could see how sinful we were and realize that we needed a Savior. The deceitfulness of sin evaporates in the presence of the Law, and sin becomes exceedingly sinful.

Romans 7:14 - For we know that the law is spiritual: but I am carnal, sold under sin.

(Rom. 7:14) This is why the Law could not produce life for us. It is because the Law is spiritual, but we are carnal. Another way of saying this is, the Law is perfect, but we aren't. If we could have lived up to every detail of the Law, then we could have obtained salvation through it. But all have sinned and come short of God's perfect standard (Rom. 3:23)—All except for one, and that is Jesus.

The Law did provide life for one man, the man Christ Jesus, because He was the only man who was ever perfect. Jesus was without any sin whatsoever, and therefore, He deserved eternal life as a payment, not a gift. Those who put their faith in Jesus as their Savior, benefit from His keeping of the Law (Rom. 8:4).

Romans 7:15 - For that which I do I allow not: for what I would, that do I not; but what I hate, that do I.

(Rom. 7:15) Many debates have occurred over whether Paul was describing himself before his conversion in these verses or whether he was describing the carnality that still existed in him after all those years of walking with the Lord. Is Paul describing a condition that has already been taken care of through the new birth, or is he saying that even mature Christians are doomed to a life of schizophrenia (literally a split mind) where part of us wants to serve God and part of us wants to serve the devil?

Actually, Paul is not stating either one of those positions. He is expounding the impossibility of serving God in our own power, whether lost or saved. The flesh is unwilling and unable to fulfill the Law of God, and if a Christian tries to fulfill the righteousness of the Law through one's own will power he or she will fail just the same as an unregenerate man or woman. Paul is describing the futility of trying to obtain favor with God through our own goodness, whether Christian or non-Christian. That has been the theme throughout the book of Romans.

Paul only used the term "spirit" once in Romans 7 (v. 6)—a chapter that described the hopelessness of man to ever keep the righteousness of the Law in his own strength. In contrast, the word "spirit," or "Spirit," is used 21 times in Romans 8—a chapter that gives the answer to the hopelessness of Romans 7.

In these verses of Romans 7, Paul is not describing a warfare that wages between the new man and the old man. He is contrasting the complete inability of man to save himself because of his corrupted flesh versus the life-transforming power of Christ described in chapter 8.

The Apostle Paul was not living a life of constant failure, where the good that he wanted to do he was unable to accomplish, but the evil that he didn't want to do, he did. He wasn't living that kind of life, because it was no longer him living, but Christ living in him (Gal. 2:20). Christ in Paul was manifesting a holiness in Paul's life that was second to none.

However, if he would have abandoned his dependency upon Christ and would have started trying to live the Christian life out of his own resources, then the condition described in Romans 7:15-24 would have been his experience.

Our flesh has been corrupted through sin, and though we can renew our minds through God's Word (Rom. 12:2), we can never elevate our flesh to a place where it can fulfill the Law of God. Hence, the good news of Romans 8 is that what the Law couldn't do because of the weakness of our flesh (Rom. 8:3), God did for us, and all we have to do is receive by faith.

Romans 7:16-17 - If then I do that which I would not, I consent unto the law that it is good. 17) Now then it is no more I that do it, but sin that dwelleth in me.

(Rom. 7:17) This sin is not speaking of an individual act of sin, but of the old man or sin nature, itself. This looks like a direct contradiction of Paul's statements in Romans 6 about the old man being dead.

To harmonize these apparently opposite accounts, most people have said that the death spoken of in Romans 6 is not a one-time experience but an ongoing process. Experience and Paul's testimony here seem to bear that out.

However, Romans 6:9,10, and 11 make a specific point of comparing our death to sin to Christ's death to sin. Verse 10 clearly states that Christ died unto sin once, and verse 11 says we should likewise reckon ourselves to be dead unto sin. To further strengthen this point, Paul begins Romans 7 with the illustration of marriage. In the same way that a woman cannot have two husbands, a Christian cannot have two natures.

So, in context, there is a very strong case for our old man being dead in the absolute sense. But, what about Paul's statements in verses 17 and 20 about sin dwelling in him? The key is in verse 23 where Paul speaks of a law (influence) of sin that dwelt in his members, not sin itself.

Therefore, this passage is referring to the force, or influence, of the old man, which does still exist, but not the old man himself. The argument for the complete abolishment of the sin nature is further strengthened in verse 24 where Paul refers to the body of this death, which is referring to the same thing that Paul spoke of in Romans 6:6 where he used the terminology "the body of sin."

Romans 7:18 - For I know that in me (that is, in my flesh,) dwelleth no good thing: for to will is present with me; but how to perform that which is good I find not.

(Rom. 7:18) The term "flesh" comes from the Greek word "sarx." Sarx was translated "flesh" 147 times, "carnal" two times (Rom. 8:7 and Heb. 9:10), "carnally" one time (Rom. 8:6), and "fleshly" one time (Col. 2:18). There are many ways that the word "flesh" was used in the New Testament, but for simplification, we will group its usage into three main categories.

First, it can refer to the physical flesh of man (Luke 24:39) or beasts (1 Cor. 15:39). When used in that context, the term is descriptive of only the physical makeup of man and is neither good nor bad, as can be seen by the fact that Jesus was made flesh (John 1:14).

Second, flesh can describe the weakness and frailty of man, or man apart from God. This is the way Paul used the term in Romans 8:3 when he said, "For what the law could not do, in that it was weak through the flesh." Paul is saying that man, without the quickening power of God in his life, was unable to keep the Law. Paul described his own efforts at holiness without the power of Christ as works of the flesh (Phil. 3:3-9). The flesh is weak (Matt. 26:41).

Third, flesh can refer to all that is sinful in man. In Galatians 5:19-21, Paul describes the works of the flesh as adultery, fornication, uncleanness, lasciviousness, idolatry, witchcraft, hatred, variance, emulations, wrath, strife, seditions, heresies, envyings, murders, drunkenness, revellings, and such like. In this sense, the term "flesh" can be used almost interchangeably with the sin nature of man when describing those who are not born again, or the effects of the residual old man on those who are born again.

In this instance, when Paul used this parenthetical phrase "that is, in my flesh" he was specifying the natural part of his person, or the second category of flesh described above. He was stating that in himself, apart from his born-again spirit, there was no good thing. He had to include this explanation, or his statement would not have been accurate, for in his spirit there was a good thing (i.e., Christ).

Romans 7:19-21 - For the good that I would I do not: but the evil which I would not, that I do. 20) Now if I do that I would not, it is no more I that do it, but sin that dwelleth in me. 21) I find then a law, that, when I would do good, evil is present with me.

(Rom. 7:21) This law (force or influence) was present, but Paul was not living under the dominance of it (Rom. 6:14). He clearly states in Romans 8:2 that the law of the Spirit of life in Christ Jesus had made him free from the law of sin and death.

Romans 7:22-23 - For I delight in the law of God after the inward man: 23) But I see another law in my members, warring against the law of my mind, and bringing me into captivity to the law of sin which is in my members.

(Rom. 7:23) The Greek word translated "law" three times in this verse is "nomos," meaning "a force or influence impelling to action" (W.E. Vine). So, these verses are not speaking of the old self or sin nature directly, but rather of its influence.

In verse 22, this same Greek word was used to refer to the Law of God. In that instance it is clear that this is speaking of the influence of God through His precepts and not the divine person Himself. Likewise, in verse 23, the influence of the old man is what is being spoken of.

The old self is dead and gone, but it left behind a body. Attitudes and emotions, which still influence us until we renew our minds, are the body of the old man. We are not dealing directly with the old sin nature but with its influence that is still being exerted through our unregenerate flesh. So, the Christian life is a renewal of our minds to who we have become in Christ, not a hatred for who we are in our old self.

Romans 7:24 - O wretched man that I am! who shall deliver me from the body of this death?

(Rom. 7:24) Paul was not describing his spiritual condition when he said, "O wretched man that I am," he was speaking of his flesh. He made this distinction clear in verse 18 when he said, "I know that in me (that is, in my flesh,) dwelleth no good thing." So, Paul was describing the absolute wretchedness of his flesh.

In context, Paul is summarizing his statements from verses 14 through 23. He didn't say, "Who shall deliver me from this death," for the Christian has already been delivered from death that is the wage of sin. He made special mention of the body of this death.

The terminology "the body of this death" corresponds to what Paul called "the body of sin" in Romans 6:6. He was not speaking of the sin nature itself, for a Christian no longer has a sin nature, but he is rather speaking of the old man, or the lingering influence of the sin nature, that still exerts itself through the unrenewed mind.

So, death, or the old man, is gone but the body that it left behind (i.e., the thoughts, attitudes, and emotions) still poses a problem to the Christian. How do we overcome this flesh? The answer is stated in verse 25 and then explained in Romans 8.

Romans 7:25 - I thank God through Jesus Christ our Lord. So then with the mind I myself serve the law of God; but with the flesh the law of sin.

(Rom. 7:25) Paul is not just stating that he is thanking God through Jesus Christ, but he is specifically thanking God for the deliverance from this body of death, which only comes through our Lord Jesus Christ.

Here is the conclusion of Paul's arguments from verses 14 through 24. He desires to serve the Law of God but his flesh is incapable of doing so. How then can we overcome this frustration? The answer is given in Romans 8, as Paul explains how to escape the flesh and walk after the Spirit.

Romans 7:1-25
Discipleship Questions

Answer the following questions by reading the corresponding
discipleship commentary lesson and using your Bible.

1. Read Romans 7:1. How long does the Law exercise authority over an individual?
   _____

2. If a man was speeding in a car, had an accident, and was killed, what offense would he be charged with?_____

3. Read Romans 7:2. If a woman's husband dies does the law of marriage apply to her any longer?_____

4. Read Romans 7:2. What looses a married individual from the law of marriage?
   _____

5. Read Romans 7:3. If a woman's husband dies and she marries another man, is she an adulteress? _____

6. Why isn't she an adultress?_____
   _____

7. Read Romans 7:4. The Living Bible states, "Your 'husband,' your master, used to be the Jewish law; but you 'died,' as it were, with Christ on the cross" (Romans 7:4). Are you married to the Law any longer?_____

8. Read Romans 7:4. Who are you now free to be married to?
   _____

9. Read Romans 7:4. What is the result of your union with Jesus Christ?
   _____

10. Read Romans 7:5, 6:21, and Galatians 5:19-21. Paul states that when we were "in the flesh" (probably meaning before conversion) the motions of sins (i.e., the sinful passions), which were by the Law (i.e., unsubdued by the Law), brought forth fruit resulting in what (which in the Greek is present tense, meaning continuous, uninterrupted or habitual action)?

11. The Phillips translation in Romans 7:6 states, "But now that we stand clear of the law, the claims which existed are dissolved by our 'death,' and we are free to serve God." How is this so? _____
    _____
    _____

12. Read Romans 7:7 and Romans 3:20. The Law is not sinful, but the Law showed me what?

_____

_____

13. When there is no law, sin is what?

_____

14. Read and explain Romans 7:9.

_____

_____

_____

15. Read Romans 7:10 and Matthew 19:16-17. The Law was ordained to give what?

_____

16. Read Romans 7:10. Instead of the Law giving me eternal life, it resulted in what?

_____

17. Read and explain Romans 3:19-22.

_____

_____

_____

18. Read Romans 7:13. Sin results in spiritual death (it slew me) v. 11. The Law is holy, just and good. Sin, by the law, or commandments, did what two things?

_____

_____

19. The Law is spiritual (a spiritual force, holy, just, and good). What two ways am I described?

_____

_____

20. How does Romans 7:15 describe being "sold under sin"?

_____

_____

21. Read Romans 7:18 (NIV). How far will your own willpower carry you in doing good?

_____

_____

22. Read Romans 7:21. When I want to do evil, evil is present with me. When I want to do good, what is present with me? _____

_____

23. Read Romans 7:23. Every true believer delights in the Law of God or the ways of God. However, another principle is at work in a person's members attacking his or her mind bringing the person into captivity to what?_____

_____

24. Read Romans 7:23. This is the first time Paul uses the expression "law of sin." What do you think "the law of sin" is?_____

_____

_____

25. Read Romans 8:2. The only way to overcome a law, such as gravity, is to apply another law, such as lift, or aerodynamics, to overcome it. The only way to overcome "the law of sin" is to apply what law?_____

_____

26. Read Romans 7:24-25. The personal pronoun "I" is used all throughout Romans chapter 7. The Holy Spirit is absent. Paul discovers that the Christian life is not only hard to live, it is impossible to live. He is now calling on **Whom** to deliver him from the law of sin and its dominion?_____

_____

Romans 7:1-25
Discipleship Answer Key

．．

Do not look at the answer key until you have completed the questions.
Compare your answers with the following answers.

1. Read Romans 7:1. How long does the Law exercise authority over an individual?
   As long as he is alive.

2. If a man was speeding in a car, had an accident, and was killed, what offense would he be charged with?
   None.

3. Read Romans 7:2. If a woman's husband dies, does the law of marriage apply to her any longer?
   No.

4. Read Romans 7:2. What looses a married individual from the law of marriage?
   Death.

5. Read Romans 7:3. If a woman's husband dies and she marries another man, is she an adulteress?
   No.

6. Why isn't she an adultress?
   Because she is free from the law of marriage (death has freed her).

7. Read Romans 7:4. The Living Bible states, "Your 'husband,' your master, used to be the Jewish law; but you 'died,' as it were, with Christ on the cross" (Romans 7:4). Are you married to the Law any longer?
   No.

8. Read Romans 7:4. Who are you now free to be married to?
   Him who is raised from the dead, i.e., Jesus Christ.

9. Read Romans 7:4. What is the result of your union with Jesus Christ?
   Producing good fruit, or deeds, for God, being productive for God.

10. Read Romans 7:5, 6:21, and Galatians 5:19-21. Paul states that when we were "in the flesh" (probably meaning before conversion) the motions of sins (i.e., the sinful passions), which were by the Law (i.e. unsubdued by the Law), brought forth fruit resulting in what (which in the Greek is present tense, meaning continuous, uninterrupted or habitual action)?
    Fruit resulting in death.

11. The Phillips translation in Romans 7:6 states, "But now that we stand clear of the law, the claims which existed are dissolved by our 'death,' and we are free to serve God." How is this so?
In union with Christ, in the new way of the Spirit (empowered by Him), not by legalism.

12. Read Romans 7:7 and Romans 3:20. The Law is not sinful, but the Law showed me what?
The knowledge of sin, i.e., to make man know that he has sinned.

13. When there is no law, sin is what?
Dead, having no life of its own.

14. Read and explain Romans 7:9.
"That is why I felt fine so long as I did not understand what the law really demanded. But when I learned the truth, I realized that I had broken the law and was a sinner, doomed to die" (Romans 7:9, Living Bible).

15. Read Romans 7:10 and Matthew 19:16-17. The Law was ordained to give what?
Life.

16. Read Romans 7:10. Instead of the Law giving me eternal life, it resulted in what?
Death.

17. Read and explain Romans 3:19-22.
Through the Law, all the world is aware that they are guilty before God. God's way of putting people right with Him is not through keeping the Law (or any religious law). God puts men in right-relationship with Himself through their faith in Jesus Christ.

18. Read Romans 7:13. Sin results in spiritual death (it slew me) v. 11. The Law is holy, just and good. Sin, by the law, or commandments, did what two things?
1. It appeared as sin.
2. It became exceeding sinful.

19. The Law is spiritual (a spiritual force, holy, just, and good). What two ways am I described?
1. Carnal (unspiritual).
2. Sold under sin.

20. How does Romans 7:15 describe being "sold under sin"?
I don't do what I would like to do but instead do what I hate.

21. Read Romans 7:18 (NIV). How far will your own willpower carry you in doing good?
Not very far. Even though the desire to do good is with me, I am not able to do it.

22. Read Romans 7:21. When I want to do evil, evil is present with me. When I want to do good, what is present with me?
Evil.

23. Read Romans 7:23. Every true believer delights in the Law of God or the ways of God. However, another principle is at work in a person's members attacking his or her mind bringing him into captivity to what?
The law of sin which is in my (his) members.

24. Read Romans 7:23. This is the first time Paul uses the expression "law of sin." What do you think "the law of sin" is?
A law of defeat that works the same way all the time and seems to have its own natural ability, or power—much like gravity, a principle that works everywhere, the same way all the time and has its own natural ability, or power. If you step off a building you will go down.

25. Read Romans 8:2. The only way to overcome a law, such as gravity, is to apply another law, such as lift, or aerodynamics, to overcome it. The only way to overcome "the law of sin" is to apply what law?
The law of the Spirit of life in Christ Jesus.

26. Read Romans 7:24-25. The personal pronoun "I" is used all throughout Romans chapter 7. The Holy Spirit is absent. Paul discovers that the Christian life is not only hard to live, it is impossible to live. He is now calling on **Whom** to deliver him from the law of sin and its dominion?
God through Jesus Christ our Lord.

OVERVIEW OF ROMANS CHAPTER 8

by Andrew Wommack

In the previous lesson, Don Krow did a tremendous teaching with great insight on the last part of Romans 7, which ends by saying, *"O wretched man that I am! who shall deliver me from the body of this death? I thank God through Jesus Christ our Lord."* Romans 7 talks about the futility of trying to please God through self-effort; Romans 8 is a contrast, showing the abundance of the Spirit-filled life.

In Romans 7 the word "spirit" is used one time and isn't even referring to the Holy Spirit but rather to a mental disposition, or attitude. In contrast, the word "Spirit" (capital "S," Holy Spirit) is mentioned 21 times in Romans 8. So it is very easy to see that the frustration, disappointment, and wretchedness described in Romans 7 is because the person is into self-effort. There is absolute victory in Romans 8, which is one of the greatest, most victorious chapters in all of the Word of God. It is no coincidence that the Holy Spirit is referred to 20 times in this chapter.

Verse 1: *"There is therefore now no condemnation to them which are in Christ Jesus, who walk not after the flesh, but after the Spirit."* There is no condemnation. This word "no" in the Greek actually means none, nada, zilch. It is an overemphasis on this word and is saying there is absolutely no condemnation. The word "condemnation" here means an adverse sentence, a sentence that is against you. My layman's definition would be like when you condemn a building and say it is not inhabitable, no longer fit for use. So in my terminology, this is what the word is talking about—there is no sense of guilt or shame, nothing to make you non-usable. There is nothing to prevent God from using you, answering your prayers, or loving you if you are in Christ Jesus.

Verse 2: *"For the law of the Spirit of life in Christ Jesus hath made me free from the law of sin and death."* In the Old Testament, there was a law that when you sinned, you got death. You can see this very clearly in Deuteronomy 28 where the first 14 verses list the blessings that a person will receive if they keep the Law, and verses 15-68 list the curses that will come on a person who doesn't keep the Law. This verse is saying that the law of the Spirit of life in Christ Jesus has given you Deuteronomy 28:1-14 instead of Deuteronomy 28:15-68. In other words, you are not receiving the curse, the punishment for your sins. It's imperative that you understand this.

The law of sin and death still exists, but it no longer has any effect or dominance over you once you come into Christ. I liken it to flying in an airplane. When you fly, the law of gravity doesn't cease to exist; it's just that you are exerting a superior law of thrust and lift (aerodynamics) that allows you to fly. If you ever doubt that the law of gravity is still at work, all you have to do is step outside the plane, and you will instantly go down, because gravity is still working.

This is the same thing. Condemnation, guilt, and shame are still working in this world. If you get outside of Christ, quit trusting Him and walking in the revelation He gave in the Word of God, and go out on your own, you will be condemned. But when you are abiding in Christ (not talking about doing everything right) and trusting in Him, all of the shame, guilt, condemnation, and failure that should come as a result of your sin, doesn't, because you are in Christ like a person who is in the plane. That is a powerful scripture.

How could this be? Verse 3 says, *"For what the law could not do, in that it was weak through the flesh, God sending his own Son in the likeness of sinful flesh, and for sin, condemned sin in the flesh."* You could say that He condemned sin in the flesh of His Son, Jesus. God put your condemnation on Jesus—put your judgment, your separation, your shame, your guilt on Jesus. If Jesus has borne that for you, there is no reason you should bear it. That is the reason God set you free from the law of sin and death. It's not that you don't sin or that there isn't a law of death as a result of sin, but that law of death has been placed on Jesus.

Romans 6:23 says, *"The wages of sin is death."* The wages for your sin was placed on Jesus so that instead of you reaping death, which is what you deserve, you reap the life that Jesus deserves. Verse 4 says, *"That the righteousness of the law might be fulfilled in us, who walk not after the flesh, but after the Spirit."* You not only have been freed from the punishment you deserve, but you have inherited the righteousness you don't deserve. You have not only been freed from the terrible results of your sin but have obtained the blessings that go with the holy life Jesus lived. He accepted your sin, punishment, guilt, and condemnation, and you accept His righteousness, holiness, and right-standing with God. This says that the righteousness of the Law is fulfilled in you who walk not after the flesh but after the Spirit.

This terminology, "walk not after the flesh, but after the Spirit," isn't talking about you living perfectly. Some people interpret this to say that you keep the Word, and when you are living right, then these blessings are yours, but when you are in the flesh and sin, they aren't. No, the context of Romans is teaching the unmerited, unearned, undeserved favor of the Lord, showing that God doesn't deal with you proportional to your obedience or goodness. That would violate the whole context of Romans.

What Paul is talking about is that when you walk in the Spirit, you are relating to God by grace. When you are in the flesh, you are relating to God by Law. It doesn't matter if you are relating to God and doing better than someone else. If you are living a relatively holy life, it doesn't matter how holy you are, it's not holy enough, and you fail. But if you are relating to God on the basis of grace, trusting in His grace, even if you are failing, sinning, and making mistakes, then you are walking after the Spirit, and therefore the righteousness of God has been fulfilled in you.

There is no way to teach Romans 8 in just a few moments, because there are some powerful things here. Let's just hit some of the highlights.

Verse 6: *"For to be carnally minded is death; but to be spiritually minded is life and peace."* This doesn't say that carnal mindedness tends toward death for certain types of people. It says carnal mindedness equals death. On the other hand, spiritual mindedness equals life and peace. John 6:63 says, *"The words that I speak unto you, they are spirit, and they are life."* So, to be spiritually minded is to be Word minded, specifically minded about the grace of God. When you are thinking and relating to God based on grace—what he has done for you in your positive faith response to Him—then you have life and peace. Anything contrary to that is carnal mindedness. Carnal mindedness is not necessarily terrible sin and rebellion, but just being religious, legalistic, and trying to relate to God by Law is carnal mindedness, and it will produce death. This is one of the most powerful chapters in the Bible, and I encourage you to really spend time studying it.

Verse 9: *"But ye are not in the flesh, but in the Spirit, if so be that the Spirit of God dwell in you. Now if any man have not the Spirit of Christ, he is none of his."* This shows us that having Christ in you is part and parcel of being born again. If you don't have the Spirit of Christ in you, then you aren't born again. This is what separates true Christianity from religion, where you go to a church and go through the motions but there is no change, no transformation. A true Christian literally has Christ come live on the inside of him or her.

Verse 18: *"For I reckon that the sufferings of this present time are not worthy to be compared with the glory which shall be revealed in us."* This is a tremendous statement.

Verses 26-27 talk about the intercession of the Holy Spirit. Let me finish by reading these last verses: *"Who shall separate us from the love of Christ? shall tribulation, or distress, or persecution, or famine, or nakedness, or peril, or sword"* (verse 35). Verses 37-39 say, *"Nay, in all these things we are more than conquerors through him that loved us. For I am persuaded, that neither death, nor life, nor angels, nor principalities, nor powers, nor things present, nor things to come, Nor height, nor depth, nor any other creature, shall be able to separate us from the love of God, which is in Christ Jesus our Lord."*

All of that is because of the Gospel, the grace of God. If you are living under works, you are separated, but if you are in the grace of God, walking after the Spirit, nothing can separate you from the love of God.

. . . .

Read the entire lesson and then answer the questions that follow.

Romans 8:1 - There is therefore now no condemnation to them which are in Christ Jesus, who walk not after the flesh, but after the Spirit.

(Rom. 8:1) The dictionary defines the word "therefore" as "for that reason; consequently; hence." This word ties Paul's statement here in Romans 8:1 to the previous verses. Paul is now giving us the answer to the hopeless situation he described in Romans 7:14-24.

Prior to Romans 8, the Holy Spirit was only mentioned once in this epistle (Rom. 5:5). In this chapter alone, the Holy Spirit is referred to 20 times. Paul is making the point that the only way to overcome the effects of sin in our lives is through the indwelling presence and power of the Holy Spirit.

There are 11 Greek words used in the New Testament that were translated "now." Some of these words simply provide a transition between thoughts. However, the Greek word translated "now" in this verse is "nun," which is "a primitive particle of present time; now" (Strong); "the immediate present" (W.E. Vine). Thus, Paul's use of this word makes it very clear that living with no condemnation is a present tense experience of the believer, not something reserved for the future.

The Greek word that was translated "no" in this verse is "oudis." This is an emphatic term meaning "none; not even one" (Strong). Wuest translated this as, "There is not even one bit of condemnation" (Galatians in the Greek New Testament by Kenneth S. Wuest).

The Greek word translated "condemnation" here is "katakrima," meaning "an adverse sentence (the verdict)." Paul is stating that God has no adverse sentence against us once we accept Him. All our punishment has been placed on Jesus, and we don't bear it. Christians who still walk in condemnation are being condemned by the devil or are condemning themselves. It's not God who condemns us (Rom. 8:34).

Second Corinthians 3:9 called the Law a "ministration of condemnation." It was the Law that brought God's adverse sentence against us. Romans 3:19 says the Law was given to make us guilty before God. Guilt is the emotional response to condemnation.

This can be illustrated by the way we condemn buildings. When the government condemns a building, it is declared unfit for use and must be destroyed. Likewise, when Satan condemns us, he makes us feel unfit for use and ready to be destroyed. Since the Christian is no longer under the Law, he or she should no longer be condemned, or feel unfit for use. We have been accepted by the Father through Jesus (Eph. 1:6).

God placed the judgment that the Law prescribed against us upon His Son. Therefore, those who accept Jesus as their Savior will not be condemned, because Jesus was condemned for us (v. 3). This truth and the fact that this phrase, "who walk not after the flesh but after the Spirit" is not in some of the old Greek manuscripts has led many scholars to believe that this phrase does not belong here. They say it was borrowed from verse 4 by some scribe who was copying out the Scriptures.

Condemnation still exists as any Christian knows. This verse has rightly portrayed that only those who are living in the power of the Holy Spirit escape that condemnation. Compare this to the law of gravity. Gravity is a law that never quits exerting its power, but it can be overcome. Through the laws of aerodynamics, man can actually fly and send spaceships beyond earth's gravity. But it takes power to do this. If the power is shut off, the law of gravity is still at work and will cause the vehicle to fall.

Likewise, the law of sin and death still exists. If a Christian shuts off the power of the Spirit of life and begins to start walking in the power of one's own flesh, Satan will use this law of sin and death to make sure the person crashes and is condemned.

God convicts of sin but He doesn't condemn (Rom. 8:34). Conviction is solely for our profit with no malice, while condemnation includes punishment. Satan is the one who condemns the Christian, but the Holy Spirit has given us the power to escape that condemnation.

Romans 8:2 - For the law of the Spirit of life in Christ Jesus hath made me free from the law of sin and death.

(Rom. 8:2) Romans 7:14-24 described the hopelessness of anyone overcoming the law of sin and death in his or her own ability or holiness. But Romans 8, and specifically this verse, brings us the good news that what could not be done by human effort has been done through the power of the Holy Spirit. We are no longer slaves to the law of sin and death.

According to Romans 6:23, death is the wages of sin. Therefore, this phrase, "the law of sin and death" is referring to the influence of sin and the resulting wages of that sin. Another way of saying the law of sin and death is to say that it is the law that when we sin we receive death instead of life, or when we sin we reap the curse instead of the blessing.

Deuteronomy 28:1-14 lists the blessings that come if a person keeps the whole Law. Verses 15-68 list all the curses that come as the wages of not keeping the Law. Because the law of the Spirit of life has set us free from the law of sin and death, we no longer reap Deuteronomy 28:15-68, even though we haven't kept every precept of the Law. Christ redeemed us from these curses of the Law (Gal. 3:13). Praise God that we don't have to receive the wages of sin, which is death.

Not only have we been redeemed from the curses of Deuteronomy 28:15-68, but through Jesus we have the righteousness of the Law fulfilled in us so that the blessings of Deuteronomy 28:1-14 are now ours. So, through Christ, we receive what we don't deserve (the blessings of Deut. 28:1-14), and we don't receive what we do deserve (the curses of Deut. 28:15-68).

Romans 8:3 - For what the law could not do, in that it was weak through the flesh, God sending his own Son in the likeness of sinful flesh, and for sin, condemned sin in the flesh:

(Rom. 8:3) The Law itself was not weak. In Romans 7:12 Paul said, "the law is holy, and the commandment holy, and just, and good." The Law wasn't weak but our flesh was. The Law and our flesh were linked together like a chain, and a chain is no stronger than its weakest link. Our flesh was the weak link in the chain. Although the Law was strong, it couldn't accomplish righteousness because of the weakness of our flesh.

This is speaking of the flesh of Jesus. God placed the condemnation that was directed toward us upon the flesh of His Son Jesus.

The Law was strong enough to produce life if anyone would have been able to keep it, but our human flesh rendered us impotent. This was a dilemma. The Law was ordained to life (Rom. 7:10), but no one could keep it (Isa. 59:16). So, God Himself became flesh (John 1:14;,1 Tim. 3:16). He did what no sinful flesh had ever done. He kept the Law thereby winning the life of God as the prize for keeping the Law.

This granted Him eternal life, but before He could give it to us, we still had a debt that had to be paid. This is similar to someone receiving the death penalty for some hideous crime, then some man who ie a billionaire leaves his whole estate to him. It would do the condemned man no good. But if that same billionaire could somehow take that man's place and die for him, then the other could go free and enjoy his new wealth. That's what Jesus did for us. He took our sins and gave us His righteousness.

Jesus did much more than just obtain eternal life for us, He also paid all the wages of our sins (Rom. 6:23). God literally placed the condemnation, or judgment, that was against us upon His own Son. Jesus' perfect flesh was condemned so our defiled flesh could go free. What a trade!!

Since Jesus bore our sentence (condemnation), we don't have to bear it. The debt has already been paid. It would be double jeopardy if we also had to bear any condemnation.

Romans 8:4 - That the righteousness of the law might be fulfilled in us, who walk not after the flesh, but after the Spirit.

(Rom. 8:4) This verse is saying that through the sacrificial death of Jesus, we can now fulfill the righteousness of the Law. There are two ways that we need to understand this.

First, the righteousness of the Law is now fulfilled in our new born-again spirits. Jesus fulfilled the Law (Mt. 5:17) and has given us His righteousness. Every believer's spirit is righteous and truly holy.

Second, through the Holy Spirit, we are now empowered to live the holy lives outwardly in our actions that the Law demanded, but we were unable to do in our own strength. That's what Paul is referring to when he says, "who walk not after the flesh, but after the Spirit." It needs to be pointed out that although a Spirit-filled believer will live a holy life, he or she will never keep every detail of the Law. That could not be done before salvation, and it cannot be done after salvation.

In Luke 1:6, the same Greek word that was translated "righteousness" was translated "ordinances" in this verse. Luke was speaking of Zacharias and Elisabeth, that they were both righteous before God, walking in all the commandments and ordinances of the Lord, blameless. Notice that they were both righteous and blameless before the Lord, but not sinless. So, the righteousness of the Law can be fulfilled without keeping every commandment.

The purpose of the Law was to make us despair of saving ourselves and point us to a Savior. When a person comes to put faith in Jesus as their Savior, then they are fulfilling the purpose of the Law. So, this verse is speaking of the believer being empowered to live a holy life, but fulfilling the righteousness of the Law is not the same as keeping every detail of the Law.

Therefore, every Christian has fulfilled the righteousness of the Law in his spiritual man through Jesus. But only those Christians who are under the control of the Spirit of God are fulfilling the spirit of the law in their actions.

The word "walk" in this phrase is translated from the Greek word "peripateo," meaning, "to tread all around, i.e. walk at large; figuratively to live, deport oneself, follow." The dictionary defines it as "to conduct oneself or behave in a particular manner; to live." Therefore, this phrase, "who walk not after the flesh, but after the Spirit" is speaking of those who do not conduct their lives according to the flesh but follow the leading of the Spirit.

The next verse goes on to further explain this and uses the terminology "mind the things of the flesh" to describe those who "walk after the flesh" and "mind the things of the Spirit" to describe those who "walk after the Spirit." So, "walking after the flesh" is simply having your mind focused on carnal things, and "walking after the Spirit " is having your mind stayed on spiritual things (John 6:63).

Romans 8:5 - For they that are after the flesh do mind the things of the flesh; but they that are after the Spirit the things of the Spirit.

(Rom. 8:5) Verses 5-8 explain to us why only those who walk after the Spirit are seeing the righteousness of the Law fulfilled in their lives. It is because, whatever a person thinks on is what he or she is going to become or do (Prov. 23:7). Those who are after the flesh think on carnal things and, therefore, do carnal things. Thinking carnally can only produce death, while thinking spiritually (according to the Word John 6:63) can only produce life.

This verse gives us a test so we can determine if we are walking after the flesh or after the Spirit. Just judge what you are thinking about. If you consistently are thinking on the things of the Spirit (John 6:63), then you are walking after the Spirit. If you are dominated with carnal thoughts, then you are walking after the flesh.

Romans 8:6 - For to be carnally minded is death; but to be spiritually minded is life and peace.

(Rom. 8:6) The same Greek word "sarx" that was translated "flesh" in verses 1,3,4,5, and 8 was translated "carnally" in verse 6 and "carnal" in verse 7. So, these terms can be used interchangeably.

The death that is spoken of here is not only physical death, although that is included. It refers to all the effects, or wages, of sin. The Amplified Bible translates this verse, "death that comprises all the miseries arising from sin, both here and hereafter." Sickness, depression, loneliness, hatred, poverty, fear, and everything else that came as a result of sin would be included in this term "death."

This is a powerful statement. Being carnally minded doesn't just tend toward death; it is death. Likewise, being spiritually minded doesn't just tend toward life, it is life and peace. A person who says he or she is spiritually minded and yet is experiencing death is deceived. If we would just dominate ourselves with the spiritual truths of God's word, we would receive only life and peace.

Romans 8:7 - Because the carnal mind is enmity against God: for it is not subject to the law of God, neither indeed can be.

(Rom. 8:7) This word "carnal" is translated from the same Greek word as "flesh." Just as with the word "flesh," there is more than one way that the word "carnal" is used. All sin is carnal, but not all carnality is sin. Carnal can also refer to human ability or natural things.

Trying to live the Christian life from our own ability is carnal. In context, Paul is contrasting the hopeless struggle of the flesh to live holy, which he portrayed in Romans 7:15-24 with the Spirit-filled life that he presents in this chapter. Therefore, he is portraying trying to obtain holiness through the flesh as being carnal. It is inaccurate to think that only sin is carnal. All our self-righteousness is carnal too.

The carnal mind is hostile, or opposed, to God. The carnal mind hates the things of God. Therefore, no one just naturally pleases God. It is impossible for the natural mind to think in the ways of God (1 Cor. 2:14). As Paul said in 1 Corinthians 2:14, "But the natural man receiveth not the things of the Spirit of God: for they are foolishness unto him: neither can he know them, because they are spiritually discerned." We have to deny our natural way of thinking and be led by the Spirit of God to walk pleasing to God.

Romans 8:8 - So then they that are in the flesh cannot please God.

(Rom. 8:8) Hebrews 11:6 says, "without faith it is impossible to please him." This verse also could read, "So then they that are in the flesh cannot have faith, because faith is the only way to please God." Faith is a fruit of the Spirit (Gal. 5:22) and cannot be produced by human effort.

This is the sum of what Paul was saying in Romans 7:14-24 and the reason no one can ever trust in his or her own holiness to be justified in the sight of God. The Christian life is not just hard to live; it is impossible to live in our own ability. Christianity only works when the Spirit of God indwells and controls an individual, thereby giving him or her supernatural ability. Without the quickening power of the Holy Spirit, no one can believe God and receive salvation.

Many religions of the world believe in one God, and some of them even worship the God of Abraham, but they don't believe in Jesus as their Savior. Without Jesus, they are in the flesh and cannot please God. They may even live a holier life than someone who has put faith in Jesus as his or her Savior, but their flesh will fail to be holy enough to earn salvation.

Romans 8:9 - But ye are not in the flesh, but in the Spirit, if so be that the Spirit of God dwell in you. Now if any man have not the Spirit of Christ, he is none of his.

(Rom. 8:9) Paul makes a clear distinction between being "in the flesh" and "after the flesh" and "in the Spirit" and "after the Spirit." A born-again person cannot be "in" the flesh, but he or she can walk "after" the flesh. A lost person cannot be "in" the Spirit although one seeks to walk "after" the ways of the Spirit.

The word that was translated "in" here is the Greek word "en" and it denotes "a (fixed) position (in place, time or state)" (Strong). In contrast, the word that was translated "after" in verses 1,4,5,12, and 13 denotes "according to anything as a standard; agreeable to" (Thayer's). Therefore, when Paul speaks of being "in" the flesh or Spirit, he is referring to a fixed position, or state. When he speaks of being "after" the flesh or Spirit, he is referring to whatever we are using as a standard of conduct, or whatever we are agreeing to at any given time.

A Christian can agree to, or conduct his or her actions according to some standard other than God's and still keep one's position in Christ. So, a Christian can walk "after" the flesh but is never considered "in" the flesh.

According to Jesus' statement in John 14:17, no one can receive the Holy Spirit unless the persom has first received Jesus as his or her Savior. Therefore, anyone who has the Spirit of God dwelling in him or her is a born-again person and is not in the flesh.

This passage makes an emphatic statement that every believer receives the Spirit of Christ at salvation. The supposition that the "Spirit of Christ" and the "Spirit of God" are synony-mous terms has led many to believe that every Christian receives the baptism of the Holy Spirit at salvation. However, this seems to be in contradiction to the examples given in the book of Acts .

It is very likely that the phrase "Spirit of Christ" refers to the born-again spirit that every believer receives at salvation. The phrase "Spirit of God" possibly refers to the Holy Spirit that only indwells the believer if he or she receives the baptism of the Holy Spirit.

Romans 8:10 - And if Christ be in you, the body is dead because of sin; but the Spirit is life because of righteousness.

(Rom. 8:10) Based on the previous verse as well as John 14:20, 2 Corinthians 13:5, and Colossians 1:27, Christ is in every born-again believer. Therefore, Paul is saying that for every one of us who are Christians, our bodies are dead because of sin.

The body is dead because of sin, but the Spirit is life because of righteousness. The Greek word translated "because" here is "dia" which denotes "the channel of an act; through (Strong). Therefore, our bodies are dead through, or because, of the influence of sin in our lives.

In the same way that some people who have recovered from the polio virus still have crippled bodies, so Christians who have been delivered from the old man still have to deal with the corruption that the old man released into their physical bodies and minds. That's why no one can please God in the flesh. The flesh has been corrupted and is therefore dead, or inca-pable of living up to, God's standard.

To counter this, the Spirit of God is releasing life because of the new righteous spirit that we received through faith in Jesus. Sin has left its mark on our bodies, but the Spirit of life within us is more than enough to overcome these problems. That's why it is imperative that the Christian learn how to walk after the Spirit and not after the flesh.

Romans 8:11 - But if the Spirit of him that raised up Jesus from the dead dwell in you, he that raised up Christ from the dead shall also quicken your mortal bodies by his Spirit that dwelleth in you.

(Rom. 8:11) This verse is speaking of more than just the quickening of our bodies at the second return of Christ, although that is included. In the previous verse, Paul had spoken of the body being dead because of sin but the Spirit being life because of righteousness. This is speaking of the current situation we face in this life.

Our flesh has been rendered incapable of serving God correctly because of the effect sin had on it. But our situation isn't hopeless. God has given us His Spirit, and we can overcome this deficit by letting Him live through us (Gal. 2:20). In this verse Paul is commenting on this quickening power of the Holy Spirit for this life as well as the ultimate victory when our physical bodies will be resurrected.

Romans 8:12 - Therefore, brethren, we are debtors, not to the flesh, to live after the flesh.

(Rom. 8:12) Paul is saying that our flesh never helped us. It has been rendered powerless through sin. It is only through the indwelling power of the Holy Spirit that the Christian has any hope of living in victory. Therefore, we are indebted to the Spirit and should yield to Him.

Romans 8:13 - For if ye live after the flesh, ye shall die: but if ye through the Spirit do mortify the deeds of the body, ye shall live.

(Rom. 8:13) Paul is speaking of death in a figurative sense rather than a literal sense. He is addressing believers who have already received eternal life through the new birth, and he is not saying that they will lose their salvation if they walk "after" the flesh.

"Death" is a term that refers not only to physical death, but it also can denote all the effects of sin in our lives. Therefore, Paul is speaking about experiencing defeat as we walk after the flesh compared to experiencing victory when we walk after the Spirit.

The word "mortify" was translated from the Greek word "thanatoo," meaning "to kill." The dictionary defines "mortify" as, "to discipline (one's body and appetites) by self-denial." If we deaden ourselves to the flesh by self-denial and follow the leadership of the Holy Spirit, we will live.

Romans 8:14 - For as many as are led by the Spirit of God, they are the sons of God.

(Rom. 8:14) Being led by the Spirit of God is the ultimate standard whereby we may know someone is a son of God. This raises the question, "If you aren't led by the Spirit of God, are you not born again?" It is true that everyone who is not born again is not led by the Spirit of God and that everyone who is born again is led by the Spirit of God, but that needs some explanation.

First, there are varying degrees of being led by the Holy Spirit. No believer is following the leading of the Lord as much as he or she could be and if an absolute standard was applied to this verse, no one would qualify to be a son of God. With this in mind, believers have been led by the Spirit to some degree, in making Jesus their Lord if nothing else.

Second, being led by the Spirit does not cause us to be sons of God, but being sons of God causes us to be led of the Spirit. Every believer does have the Spirit of God to lead him or her but that doesn't mean every believer heeds His leading. In context, Paul has just spoken about denying the flesh through the power and leading of the Holy Spirit. Now he is simply pointing out that every Christian has the leading of the Holy Spirit available to accomplish this.

Some people have tried to make a distinction between being a "child of God" and a "son of God." They say a "child of God" is any born-again believer, while a "son of God" refers only to a mature Christian. This looks good on the surface, but further study will reveal there is no difference.

In Galatians 4, these same terms are used and "son" or "sons," is applied to all believers. Galatians 4:6 says, "And because ye are sons, God hath sent forth the Spirit of his Son into your hearts, crying, Abba, Father," and Romans 8:9 says, "Now if any man have not the Spirit of Christ, he is none of his." Since every believer has to have the Spirit of Christ (Rom. 8:9) and every son of God has the Spirit of God's Son in them crying, "Abba, Father" (Gal. 4:6), then we can clearly see that every born-again believer is a son of God. Therefore, these terms are used interchangeably, and no doctrine about different levels of maturity can be drawn.

Romans 8:15 - For ye have not received the spirit of bondage again to fear; but ye have received the Spirit of adoption, whereby we cry, Abba, Father.

(Rom. 8:15) This spirit of bondage is a reference to the old sin nature. The fact that Paul says "ye have not received the spirit of bondage again" is a further testimony that our old sin nature is not just ceremonially dead, but that it is gone in the life of the believer.

We are sons of God by adoption. Jesus was the Son of God by nature. As Jesus said to the Jews, we were of our Father the devil (John 8:44, Eph. 2:3), but Jesus purchased us and made us adopted sons of God.

Romans 8:16 - The Spirit itself beareth witness with our spirit, that we are the children of God:

(Rom. 8:16) First John 5:10 says, "He that believeth on the Son of God hath the witness in himself." John goes on to say in verse 13, "These things have I written unto you that believe on the name of the Son of God; that ye may know that ye have eternal life." So, the Spirit bearing witness with our spirits is to assure us that we are the children of God (1 John 3:19).

Romans 8:17 - And if children, then heirs; heirs of God, and joint-heirs with Christ; if so be that we suffer with him, that we may be also glorified together.

(Rom. 8:17) We are not just heirs, we are joint-heirs with Christ. How wonderful it would be to inherit any amount of God's glory and power. But to think that we share equally with the one who has inherited everything God is and has, is beyond comprehension. This is an awesome blessing, but it places a tremendous responsibility on us too.

In the same way that a check that is made out to two people cannot be cashed without the endorsement of both parties, so our joint-heirship with Jesus cannot be taken advantage of without our cooperation. Unaware of this, many Christians are just trusting that the Lord will produce the benefits of salvation for them. They are acutely aware that they can do nothing without Him, but don't realize that He will do nothing without us (Eph. 3:20).

The way we place our endorsement on the check is to believe and act like what God promised in His Word is true. Jesus has already signed His name to every promise in the Word. We aren't waiting for Him; He is waiting for us.

Romans 8:18 - For I reckon that the sufferings of this present time are not worthy to be compared with the glory which shall be revealed in us.

(Rom. 8:18) This is a very important statement. Paul did not say that this glory would be revealed "to us" but rather "in us." The complete glory of God that Christians dream of receiving in eternity is already in us here on this earth!

Paul said in 2 Thessalonians 2:14, "he called you by our gospel, to the obtaining of the glory of our Lord Jesus Christ." And in 1 Peter 5:1, Peter said he was a (present tense) partaker of this glory, which shall be (future tense) revealed. Paul also prayed for the Ephesians that the Lord would grant them the spirit of wisdom and revelation in the knowledge of Him so they would see the glory of His inheritance, which was already in the saints.

This leaves no doubt that the Christian's spirit is already complete. We don't need more faith, more power, or more anointing. We simply need to use more of what we have already received. Many Christians will be shocked when they stand before God and realize that all the things they prayed for were inside of them ever since they believed.

Romans 8:19 - For the earnest expectation of the creature waiteth for the manifestation of the sons of God.

(Rom. 8:19) The two English words "earnest expectation" were translated from the Greek word "apokaradokia." The word was only used twice in the New Testament (here and Phil. 1:20). This is a compound word meaning "intense anticipation" or as other scholars have translated it, "to strain forward" or lit. "await with outstretched head" (Sanday and Headlam); "to expect on and on, to the end" (Cremer). Fritz Rienecker says this word "denotes diversion from all other things and concentration on a single object."

Therefore, this verse makes it very clear that the whole creation is eagerly and intensely anticipating the day when the glory of God that is already deposited within God's saints will be revealed. That day won't completely arrive until the second return of the Lord. but it is logical to think that creation rejoices to some degree every time some saint manifests His glory here on this earth.

The Greek word "ktisis" was translated "creature" in verses 19-21. This same word was translated "creation" in verse 22. It literally means "that which is created."

The American Heritage Dictionary defines manifestation as "the demonstration of the existence, reality, or presence of a person, object, or quality." You cannot manifest something that does not already exist. As the Apostle John said, "Beloved, now are we the sons of God, and it doth not yet appear what we shall be" (1 John 3:2). We are already the sons of God. This is not something that has yet to transpire. The whole creation is waiting for us to manifest what is already in us.

Romans 8:20 - For the creature was made subject to vanity, not willingly, but by reason of him who hath subjected the same in hope,

(Rom. 8:20) Many people have thought that the part of creation that is being spoken of here is human beings. However, the contrast made in verses 22-23 clearly exempts the saints from this group. In verse 21 it speaks of the creature being delivered from the bondage of corruption into the glorious liberty of the children of God. If "creature" was referring to unsaved people, then this would mean ultimate reconciliation of the human race to God, which is not the teaching of Scripture. Therefore, it is most probable that the part of creation being spoken of here is all of creation, living and non-living, excluding humans. Paul is speaking of how all of creation did not choose to rebel at God. It was just mankind that sinned. Yet the Lord brought all the rest of creation against their choice into our cursed state with us so He could also redeem them with mankind.

Take, for example, the animal creation. Genesis 1:30 says that all the animals were given the green herbs of the field for their food. There were no carnivorous beasts. Yet after man's rebellion, parts of the animal creation began to devour one another as we see today. This was not God's original plan, and it was not because of a specific sin on the animal's part that this happened. God subjected the animal creation to the same vanity that man had come into, in the hope of redeeming them also.

The animal creation as well as the inanimate creation will be delivered from the corruption that we now see to walk in the glorious liberty of the children of God. It is not clear that every animal that has ever lived will be resurrected, but it is clear that the animal creation will be represented.

The Scriptures declare this freedom for the creation when it speaks of the child playing with the snake (Isa. 11:8); the wolf and the leopard dwelling peacefully with sheep; and the lion and lamb, cow and bear dwelling together and eating straw like the ox (Isa. 11:6-7, also Isa. 65:25). We know that in heaven there are animals since the saints ride white horses at the second return of Jesus (Rev. 19:14).

So, in summary, the animal creation was plunged into the same degenerate state as mankind so that they could also be redeemed with us into liberty. Therefore, it can be expected that on the new earth where the saints will live for eternity (Rev. 21:1-7), there will be animals living in harmony with each other and mankind as God originally designed in His first creation.

The Greek word that was translated "vanity" here is the word "mataiotes," which means "emptiness as to results." In this verse it specifically means "failing of the results designed, owing to sin" (W.E. Vine). This is speaking of the non-human creation being subjected to a corruption (v. 21) that was not God's original design.

Romans 8:21 - Because the creature itself also shall be delivered from the bondage of corruption into the glorious liberty of the children of God.

(Rom. 8:21) God made creation involuntarily subject to the same corruption that mankind voluntarily entered into so that He could reunite us through redemption back into the glorious creation He originally intended us to be.

Romans 8:22 - For we know that the whole creation groaneth and travaileth in pain together until now.

(Rom. 8:22) Many times we are awestruck at the perfect balance that we see in all of nature. As glorious as it may seem, it is not God's best. Creation as we see it today has been corrupted and is far less than what God originally intended it to be. The whole creation is groaning and travailing together in pain and will not be relieved until the manifestation of the children of God.

Romans 8:23 - And not only they, but ourselves also, which have the firstfruits of the Spirit, even we ourselves groan within ourselves, waiting for the adoption, to wit, the redemption of our body.

(Rom. 8:23) The Holy Spirit is called the firstfruit of our salvation. Where there is a firstfruit, there has to be more fruit. Paul spoke of the Holy Spirit as being the earnest, or down payment, of our salvation with more to come (2 Cor. 5:5, Eph. 1:14).

As wonderful as our salvation is right here in this life, it is not complete. Our flesh is a constant source of trouble and even victorious Christians groan for the time when we will be delivered from this flesh at the redemption of our bodies (2 Cor. 5:1-4).

The word "adoption" is used five times in the New Testament (Rom. 8:15,23, 9:4; Gal. 4:5; Eph. 1:5). People draw many analogies from this term that have merit, but this verse makes it very clear that the term "adoption" is referring to the time when we will receive our glorified bodies.

Jesus purchased redemption for us—spirit, soul, and body. But our redemption is not completed yet. Our spirits are the only part of us that have experienced total redemption.

The English word "redemption" is translated from the Greek word "apolutrosis," which means, "to ransom in full" (Strong). However, it is not only specifying more than just the payment of a ransom but the releasing that comes as a result (W.E. Vine). Paul is speaking of the time when we will experience in our bodies what Jesus has already purchased for us.

This can be illustrated by the way we use trading stamps. First, the stamps have to be purchased, then they are redeemed for the desired product. The purchase is essential, but so is the redemption. No one really wants the stamps; they want what the stamps can be redeemed for.

The purchase for our total salvation has already been made with the blood of Jesus, but our bodies are not redeemed yet. That is to say that we have not received all the benefits of that transaction in our physical bodies yet. That will take place at the second coming of the Lord when we receive our new, glorified bodies.

Romans 8:24 - For we are saved by hope: but hope that is seen is not hope: for what a man seeth, why doth he yet hope for?

(Rom. 8:24) Ephesians 2:8 says, "For by grace are ye saved through faith." Is there a contradiction between these two scriptures? Not at all. Putting faith in God's provision is what saves us, but hope is an important part of faith.

This verse makes it very clear that hope is not based on what is seen. Someone who says, "I have no reason to hope" doesn't understand what hope is. Hope comes directly from God (Rom. 15:13) through His Word (Rom. 15:4).

Romans 8:25 - But if we hope for that we see not, then do we with patience wait for it.

(Rom. 8:25) This verse definitely links patience and hope together. Hope produces patience. When we are in need of patience, we are in need of hope.

Romans 8:26 - Likewise the Spirit also helpeth our infirmities: for we know not what we should pray for as we ought: but the Spirit itself maketh intercession for us with groanings which cannot be uttered.

(Rom. 8:26) The word "likewise" is stressing that in the same way that hope helps us to endure until the redemption of our bodies (v. 23), so the Holy Spirit helps us through the frailties of our flesh by interceding for us.

The word "helpeth" was translated from the Greek word "sunantilambanomai," meaning, "to take hold of opposite together; i.e. cooperate (assist)." It describes a union, not the Holy Spirit doing all the interceding for us. The Holy Spirit helps us as we are interceding, but He doesn't automatically do it for us.

The Greek word that was translated "infirmities" in this verse is "astheneia," meaning "feebleness (of body or mind); by implication malady; moral frailty" (Strong). This same word was translated "weakness" five times (1 Cor. 2:3, 15:43; 2 Cor. 12:9, 13:4; and Heb. 11:34), so it is easy to see that this word is describing mental and moral weakness, not sickness.

Paul goes on to describe what these infirmities are when he says, for we know not what we should pray for as we ought. The infirmities this scripture is speaking of are the weaknesses that come from not knowing how we should pray.

This has been an encouraging scripture for countless believers. It is certain that none of us knows exactly how to pray in every situation. Therefore, it is comforting to know the Holy Spirit is there to help us. He doesn't do the interceding for us but through us.

Even Jesus drew on this ministry of the Holy Spirit. It is written in John 11:33 and 38 that Jesus groaned in the Spirit twice when He raised Lazarus from the dead. What infirmity did Jesus have that He needed this ministry of the Holy Spirit? Jesus had no sin but He did have an infirmity. It was His physical mind. Even a sinless human mind could not comprehend raising a man from the grave after four days. If Jesus needed the Holy Spirit to help Him when He didn't know how to pray, then certainly this should be an important ministry of the Holy Spirit in our lives.

This intercession of the Holy Spirit is with groanings that cannot be uttered. Some Spirit-filled Christians have said that this means groanings that cannot be uttered in normal speech and that this is referring to speaking in tongues. Yet this is referring to an intercession different from speaking in tongues.

In John 11:33 and 38, Jesus groaned in the Spirit twice. This is the exact terminology that is used here in Romans 8:26, and in those cases it is easy to see that there were no words uttered. It was exactly as the scripture states, a groaning in the Spirit.

Everyone who has the indwelling presence of the Holy Spirit has or will have this happen to them. Paul was referring to this in Galatians 4:19 when he spoke of travailing in birth for the Galatians. This groaning of the Holy Spirit is not just a grief but a groan of anger and resistance against Satan's devices in our lives. Many times Christians don't discern this, because they think it is just them grieved with their situation. But this is the Holy Spirit desiring to get into intercession with us against our problems.

Although the groaning is unutterable, you can discern it, and many times people react to this with audible groans, or other outward acts. This has led to religious doctrines and traditions that are unscriptural and offensive to many people. There is nothing wrong with us reacting to the inner working of the Holy Spirit as long as we don't confuse our reactions with the Holy Spirit's actions. This intercession cannot be uttered.

Any counterfeits that religion may have produced only serve to illustrate that there has to be a genuine. The genuine groaning in the Spirit is priceless.

Romans 8:27 - And he that searcheth the hearts knoweth what is the mind of the Spirit, because he maketh intercession for the saints according to the will of God.

(Rom. 8:27) He that searcheth the hearts is a reference to God. God knows our hearts and He knows that the Holy Spirit will only intercede for the will of God to be done. The Holy Spirit is never at a loss of knowing how to convey our needs to the Father as we sometimes are. That's the reason this ministry of the Holy Spirit is so important. There is such oneness between the Father and the Holy Spirit that even His groanings are perfectly understood.

Romans 8:28 - And we know that all things work together for good to them that love God, to them who are the called according to his purpose.

(Rom. 8:28) This is a very powerful verse with a wonderful promise, but it has been greatly abused and misapplied. This verse is not saying that everything that happens to us is from God and is used by Him to accomplish His purposes in our lives. The Bible doesn't teach that.

Second Peter 3:9 makes a clear statement that the Lord is "not willing that any should perish, but that all should come to repentance." Yet many men and women are perishing, because they have a choice. So, regarding salvation, God's will is not being done in the lives of many people.

Concerning physical healing, the Bible states that Jesus has already provided healing for us (Isa. 53:5) and that it is God's will for us to be healed (3 John 2). Yet not everyone is healed and their sicknesses are not automatically working some redemptive purpose in their lives.

Verse 28 begins with the word "and." This means that the statement about everything working together for our good is made after Paul had spoken of the Holy Spirit making intercession for us. If we are not cooperating with the Holy Spirit so that He can make intercession for us, then everything will not work together for our good.

This verse also says this happens for those "that love God, to them who are the called." That means this doesn't apply to everyone. However, this verse has been used to try to convince even unbelievers that God is controlling the circumstances of their lives. That is not the message of this verse.

Also, this verse did not say that everything that comes our way is from God but rather that the Lord can work it together for our good through the intercession of the Holy Spirit. Romans 6:16 clearly states that if we yield to the devil, we become his slaves. The false teaching that nothing happens to us but what God wills or allows has caused many people to yield to Satan's bondage instead of resisting him (James 4:7).

People may cite experiences where they learned great lessons through tragedy and argue that these negative experiences are the only way the Lord could have accomplished His will in their lives. Again, that is not what the Bible teaches.

Second Timothy 3:16-17 says, "All scripture is given by inspiration of God, and is profitable for doctrine, for reproof, for correction, for instruction in righteousness: That the man of God may be perfect, throughly furnished unto all good works." Verse 17 says that God's Word will make us perfect, thoroughly furnished unto all good works. That means we don't have to learn through hardships. God's Word is for correction and reproof.

Although not ordained by God for our good, each of us will experience tribulation. Therefore, we can and should learn from trials, but God's Word could have taught us the same thing with less grief. A man who submits to his problems because he believes God has brought them to teach him something is making a great mistake. That mistake is allowing the devil to inflict much pain in his life.

Verse 28 is really promising that when we let the Holy Spirit intercede through us with these groanings that cannot be uttered, then we can rest assured that regardless of what the devil brings across our path, God can turn that situation around and work it together for our good.

Romans 8:29 - For whom he did foreknow, he also did predestinate to be conformed to the image of his Son, that he might be the firstborn among many brethren.

(Rom. 8:29) The word "foreknowledge" refers to God knowing who would accept His offer of salvation in advance of them actually doing it. The Scriptures teach that we (believers) were chosen in Christ before the foundation of the world (Eph. 1:4). That's how infinite God's ability is to know our choices in advance.

The Scriptures also reveal that there are some things God does not know. Twice in the book of Jeremiah God said that the fact that people would offer their children as sacrifices to demon gods never even came into His mind (Jer. 19:5; 32:35). There are some things that God Himself said He had never foreseen.

It is most probable that the Lord has the ability to know everything in advance, but He simply doesn't choose to exercise that ability in every situation. He told us to be wise concerning that which is good and simple (or innocent) concerning that which is evil (Rom. 16:19). He also told us to think on things that are true, honest, just, pure, lovely, of good report, and things that have virtue and praise. That's the way He desires us to be, because that's the way He is.

As we have already pointed out from Ephesians 1:4, God chose us in Christ before the foundation of the world. He knew there would be a transgression and a need for redemption before man was even created. But apparently, He did not utilize His foreknowledge to the extent that He knew every move that man was making. No reason is given for this, but certainly one reason is that an absolute use of God's foreknowledge would hinder His relationship with man.

God sent two angels to Sodom and Gomorrah to see if their actions were really as bad as had been reported to Him (Gen. 18:20-19:29). The Lord tested Abraham (Gen. 22:1-10). After the test He said, "For now I know that thou fearest God, seeing thou hast not withheld thy son, thine only son from me" (Gen. 22:12). The Lord repented that He had chosen Saul to be king when he saw the way he turned out (1 Sam. 15:11). There are many other examples in Scripture.

God's ability to know all things in advance is limitless, but God does not know every detail by His choice. Understanding foreknowledge provides the foundation for understanding predestination, calling (v. 30), and election (1 Pet. 1:2).

This verse provides the key for unlocking the answer to the doctrine of predestination. Predestination is dependent on foreknowledge.

Romans 8:28 - And we know that all things work together for good to them that love God, to them who are the called according to his purpose.

The word, "predestinate" means, "to predetermine." "Predestinate" and its variant "predestinated" are only used four times in the New Testament (Rom. 8:29-30; Eph. 1:5,11). Men have interpreted this doctrine as saying that God predetermines everything in an individual's life, including whether he or she will be saved or lost. This interpretation is not consistent with other doctrines or examples in Scripture. This belief will destroy a person's motivation to fight evil and do good. If God predetermines everything that happens in your life, then everything that happens to you is God's will, even sin. That is not true.

This verse limits God's predestination to only those whom He foreknew. This means that only those people whom God knew would accept His offer of salvation have been predestined. He does not predestine people to be saved or lost. Those whom He foreknew in Christ have been predestined to be conformed to the image of Christ. As we can tell by observation, God doesn't even force that to happen. With some Christians, this will not occur until they receive their glorified bodies, but it will occur.

God gave every individual a free will, and God will not violate that free will except in judgment. Even in judgment, God is only enforcing the choices that each individual has already made of his or her own free will. Each person has a God-given right to go to hell if he or she wants to.

Just as in the previous verse, Romans 8:28, God works everything together for good for those who already love God. And even then He does not take away our free will. Everything that happens to us is not good, and it is not from God. However, God in His infinite wisdom can work it together for good. Verse 29 is simply continuing to develop the truth that God is for us and has predetermined that those who have come to Him for salvation will be saved to the uttermost.

Understood correctly, this verse provides great reassurance to the believer that God is for them and working with them to bring them to the complete stature of the Lord Jesus Christ (Eph. 4:13).

This English word "firstborn" was translated from the Greek word "prototokos." This is a compound Greek word comprised of "protos," meaning "foremost (in time, place, order or importance)" and "tikto," meaning, "to produce (from seed)." Therefore, this word "firstborn" could refer to either first in order or importance. Both of these applications are true of Jesus.

Although others were raised from the dead before, Jesus was the first one to be raised from the dead, never to die again. Jesus was also the firstborn in the sense of importance since His resurrection made all other resurrections possible.

In context, Paul is stressing that we are predestined to be just like Jesus, then he draws from Scripture that prophesied Jesus being the firstborn (Ps. 89:27). Therefore, the point that is being made is the extent that we will be conformed to the image of Jesus. There are other children who will become just like Jesus, and it is in this sense that "firstborn" is used here.

Romans 8:30-31 - Moreover whom he did predestinate, them he also called: and whom he called, them he also justified: and whom he justified, them he also glorified. 31) What shall we then say to these things? If God be for us, who can be against us?

(Rom. 8:31) The eighth chapter of Romans came as the answer to the hopelessness of the flesh ever pleasing God which Paul declared in the seventh chapter. The eighth chapter is full of victory through the indwelling presence and power of the Holy Spirit.

Paul had just spoken of the Holy Spirit making intercession for us (vv. 26-27), God working all things together for our good (v. 28), and us being predestined to be conformed to the image of Jesus (v. 29). Now he is drawing a conclusion from all these things. If God be for us (which is exactly what he has been saying) then no one can successfully be against us. This is an exclamation of victory for the Spirit-controlled life that Paul continues through the end of this chapter.

Romans 8:32 - He that spared not his own Son, but delivered him up for us all, how shall he not with him also freely give us all things?

(Rom. 8:32) Paul had already used this same reasoning in Romans 5:6-10.

Romans 8:33 - Who shall lay any thing to the charge of God's elect? It is God that justifieth.

(Rom. 8:33) If Almighty God has dropped all charges against us because of our faith in Christ, then why should we let the accusations of others bother us?

Romans 8:34 - Who is he that condemneth? It is Christ that died, yea rather, that is risen again, who is even at the right hand of God, who also maketh intercession for us.

(Rom. 8:34) Jesus is making intercession for us. Therefore, Jesus couldn't be the one ministering condemnation to us. Intercession and condemnation are opposites.

Romans 8:35 - Who shall separate us from the love of Christ? shall tribulation, or distress, or persecution, or famine, or nakedness, or peril, or sword?

Rom. 8:35) Neither people nor things external can separate us from the love of Christ. The only way for a believer to be exempted from the love of Christ is to deny his or her faith in Christ.

Romans 8:36-39 - As it is written, For thy sake we are killed all the day long; we are accounted as sheep for the slaughter. 37) Nay, in all these things we are more than conquerors through him that loved us. 38) For I am persuaded, that neither death, nor life, nor angels, nor principalities, nor powers, nor things present, nor things to come, 39) Nor height, nor depth, nor any other creature, shall be able to separate us from the love of God, which is in Christ Jesus our Lord.

(Rom. 8:37) How can you be more than a conqueror? A conqueror has the victory and the spoils of war, but they have to be fought for. We are more than conquerors, because we have victory and all the spoils of war, but we didn't do the fighting. Jesus fought and won this battle for us, and all we have to do is receive the benefits. That's being more than a conqueror.

Romans 8:1-39
Discipleship Questions

. . . .

*Answer the following questions by reading the corresponding
discipleship commentary lesson and using your Bible.*

1. There is therefore now no condemnation or judgment awaiting those that are in Christ Jesus. How does Romans 8:33-34 express this truth?
   _____
   _____

2. The word "walk" (Rom. 8:1) means "to live" and is in the present tense in Greek. This means "to do something continuous as a lifestyle." Read 1 Corinthians 6:9-11. How does 1 Corinthians 6:9-11 describe a life lived after the flesh and after the Spirit?
   _____
   _____
   _____

3. Read Romans 2:7-11. How does Romans 2:7-11 describe a life lived after the flesh and one after the Spirit?
   _____
   _____
   _____

4. "After the flesh" and now "after the Spirit" is another way to describe one who has come to "conversion." How does Acts 26:18 state this?
   _____
   _____

5. Read Romans 8:2. God's Spirit and Christ's life have set me free from the law of sin, resulting in what? _____

6. Read Romans 8:3. What is it that "the law could not do"? Read Galatians 3:21 and Galatians 2:21. _____
   _____

7. Read Romans 8:4. The Law and its ability to bring spiritual life and righteousness was weakened by our own sinful flesh. So God brought judgment against sin in the human body of Jesus Christ on the cross (2 Cor. 5:21). This act accomplishes what according to Romans 8:4? _____
   _____

8. Read Romans 8:5. "Do mind" is from a Greek word meaning, "to be of the same mind, i.e. to agree together, to cherish the same views and be harmonious" (Thayer's Lexicon). Paul is describing what two kinds of people?

_____

_____

9. Read Romans 8:6. To be "carnally minded" means that a person's thoughts and purposes are of the lower human nature, apart from God. Paul says that the end result of this is what?

_____

_____

10. The thoughts and purposes of those whose hearts are set on God results in what?

_____

11. Read Romans 8:7. The carnal mind, fleshly mind, is what?

_____

12. Read Romans 8:7. The carnal mind is not subject to what?

_____

13. Read Romans 8:8. Who does "in the flesh" describe ?

_____

14. Read Romans 8:9 and 2 Corinthians13:5. To belong to God, you must have what?

_____

15. According to Romans 8:10, our bodies will die because of sin, but if Christ is in us our spirits, we are alive because of what? _____

_____

16. Read Romans 8:11. If the Spirit of God dwells in you, what will He do to your mortal body?

_____

17. Because God's Spirit brings life to deliver us from the body of death (where the law of sin is in our members, Rom. 7:24), what are we not debtors to?

_____

18. Read Romans 8:12. We are not obligated to live what way?

_____

_____

19. Read Romans 8:13. For if you do what, shall you die?

_____

_____

20. Read Romans 8:13. What does the word "mortify" mean?

_____

21. How do you put to death the deeds prompted by the flesh?

   _____

22. What is this called in Romans 8:14?

   _____

23. Read Romans 8:15. Before you had the Spirit of God in your life, what kind of spirit did you have? _____

   _____

24. Read Romans 8:15. Through Christ, what kind of Spirit did you receive?

   _____

25. Read Romans 8:15. We now cry, "Abba," meaning what?

   _____

26. God's Spirit and our spirits bear witness that we belong to God (Rom. 8:16). How does Galatians 4:6 express this truth?_____

   _____

27. If we are God's children, we are heirs of God and joint-heirs with Christ (Rom.8: 17). How does Romans 8:32 also express this truth?

   _____

   _____

28. Read Acts 14:22. According to Romans 8:17, is the Christian life always going to be easy?

   _____

   _____

29. Read Romans 8:18. How does 1 Peter 4:12-14 describe "the sufferings of this present time"?_____

   _____

30. Read Romans 8:18; 2 Corinthians 4:17-18. How does Paul describe the future of the believer?_____

   _____

31. Read Romans 8:19. Everything that God made is waiting for what?

   _____

   _____

32. How does 1 John 3:2 describe this manifestion of God's children?

   _____

33. The Living Bible in Romans 8:20-21 states, "For on that day (the day of the manifestation of the sons of God) thorns and thistles, sin, death, and decay - the things that overcame the world against its will at God's command - will all disappear, and the world around us will share in the glorious freedom from sin which God's children enjoy." How does 2 Peter 3:13 describe this? _____

34. Read Romans 8:22. All creation has been groaning like a woman experiencing what?

35. Read Romans 8:23. For what is the Christian waiting for?

36. What does "redemption" in Romans 8:23 mean?

37. Faith is defined as what, according to Hebrews 11:1?

38. Invisible things hoped for are grasped by faith. According to Romans 8:25, hope calls us to be what? _____

39. Read Romans 8:25. The Christian life involves patient waiting in hope for what, according to Romans 8:23? _____

40. What is the context of Romans 8:26-27 (i.e., the thoughts that the preceding or following verses add)? _____

41. What does Romans 8:26 say about our prayers?

42. Read Romans 8:26. Who must help us in prayer?

43. Read Romans 8:27. The Spirit pleads on behalf of whom?

44. Read Romans 8:28. All things work together for good for whom?

45. For whom God did "foreknow" He did predestinate. What does "foreknow" mean?
_____
_____

46. What does "predestinate" mean?
_____

47. What are believers predestinated to in Romans 8:29?
_____

48. What are believers predestinated to in Ephesians 1:4-5?
_____

49. Why did God predestinate the believers according to Ephesians 1:5?
_____
_____

50. Read Romans 8:30. What four things will God do for the believer?
_____
_____

51. Read Romans 8:30. Define these four terms of our salvation?
_____
_____
_____

52. What is the questions being asked in Romans 8:31?
_____
_____

53. What is the question being asked in Romans 8:32?
_____
_____

54. What is the question being asked in Romans 8:33?
_____

55. Read Romans 8:33. What is the answer to that question?
_____
_____

56. Read Romans 8:34. Who can condemn and bring judgment against the believer?
_____

57. Why is it that no one can condemn or bring judgment against the believer?
_____
_____

58. What does intercession mean?

_____

_____

59. Who shall separate us from the love of Christ?

_____

60. Read Romans 8:35. What seven hardships are mentioned that cannot separate us from Christ's love?

_____

_____

61. Read Romans 8:38-39. In all these things (the hardships in verses 35-36), we are more than conquerors through God that loves us. Why?

_____

_____

Romans 8:1-39
Discipleship Answer Key

. . . .

Do not look at the answer key until you have completed the questions.
Compare your answers with the following answers.

1. There is therefore now no condemnation or judgment awaiting those that are in Christ Jesus. How does Romans 8:33-34 express this truth?
   Read Romans 8:33-34.

2. The word "walk" (Rom. 8:1) means "to live" and is in the present tense in Greek. This means "to do something continuous as a lifestyle."? Read 1 Corinthians 6:9-11. How does 1 Corinthians 6:9-11 describe a life lived after the flesh and after the Spirit
   The wicked, i.e., unrepentant live after the flesh and practice a lifestyle discribed in 1 Corinthians 6:9-10. The converted are described in 1 Corinthians 6:11 and are now washed, sanctified and justified.

3. Read Romans 2:7-11. How does Romans 2:7-11 describe a life lived after the flesh and one after the Spirit?
   Those that are converted and live after the Spirit persist in doing good: they seek glory, honor, and immortality; they receive eternal life. The unconverted live after the flesh and are self-seeking, rejecting the truth and following evil. One has repentance, the other does not.

4. "After the flesh" and now "after the Spirit" is another way to describe one who has come to "conversion." How does Acts 26:18 state this?
   This is stated as one turning from darkness to light, from the power of Satan unto God, so that they may receive forgiveness of sins.

5. Read Romans 8:2. God's Spirit and Christ's life have set me free from the law of sin, resulting in what?
   Death.

6. Read Romans 8:3. What is it that "the law could not do"? See Galatians 3:21 and Galatians 2:21.
   The Law could not give life, i.e., eternal life (Gal. 3:21). The Law could not give us the righteousness that we needed (Gal. 2:21), a right relationship with God.

7. Read Romans 8:4. The Law and its ability to bring spiritual life and righteousness was weakened by our own sinful flesh. So God brought judgment against sin in the human body of Jesus Christ on the cross (2 Cor. 5:21). This act accomplishes what according to Romans 8:4?
   That the righteousness of the Law might be fulfilled in us. (Note: Walking after the flesh or after the Spirit denotes direction, not perfection. This is another way of describing repentance).

8. Read Romans 8:5. "Do mind" is from a Greek word meaning, "to be of the same mind, i.e. to agree together, to cherish the same views and be harmonious" (Thayer's Lexicon). Paul is describing what two kinds of people?
Believers and non-believers. To further illustrate this, Paul is speaking in the present tense, which means that those he is describing are behaving in a continuous, or habitual, lifestyle.

9. Read Romans 8:6. To be "carnally minded" means that a person's thoughts and purposes are of the lower human nature, apart from God. Paul says that the end result of this is what?
Death. "Death that comprises all the miseries arising from sin, both here and here-after" (Romans 8:6, The Amplified Bible).

10. The thoughts and purposes of those whose hearts are set on God results in what?
Life and peace.

11. Read Romans 8:7. The carnal mind, fleshly mind, is what?
Enmity against God, i.e., hostile to God.

12. Read Romans 8:7. The carnal mind is not subject to what?
The Law of God, or God's ways.

13. Read Romans 8:8. Who does "in the flesh" describe?
The unconverted.

14. Read Romans 8:9 and 2 Corinthians13:5. To belong to God, you must have what?
The Spirit of God, or the Spirit of Christ, dwelling in you.

15. According to Romans 8:10, our bodies will die because of sin, but if Christ is in us our spirits, we are alive because of what?
Righteousness, or because we have been put right with God.

16. Read Romans 8:11.If the Spirit of God dwells in you, what will He do to your mortal body?
Quicken your mortal bodies, i.e., give life to your mortal bodies.

17. Because God's Spirit brings life to deliver us from the body of death (where the law of sin is in our members, Rom. 7:24), what are we not debtors to?
We are debtors not to the flesh, to live after the flesh.

18. Read Romans 8:12. We are not obligated to live what way?
According to the flesh, or after the flesh.

19. Read Romans 8:13. For if you do what, shall you die?
Live after the flesh. "Live" is present tense in the Greek meaning "continuous and habitual action."

20. Read Romans 8:13. What does the word "mortify" mean?
To put to death, or make to die.

21. How do you put to death the deeds prompted by the flesh?
    Through the power of the Holy Spirit.

22. What is this called in Romans 8:14?
    Being led by the Spirit.

23. Read Romans 8:15. Before you had the Spirit of God in your life, what kind of spirit did you have?
    The spirit of bondage that reigned in fear.

24. Read Romans 8:15. Through Christ, what kind of Spirit did you receive?
    The Spirit of sonship.

25. Read Romans 8:15. We now cry, "Abba," meaning what?
    Daddy.

26. God's Spirit and our spirits bear witness that we belong to God (Rom. 8:16). How does Galatians 4:6 express this truth?
    The Spirit of God's Son in our hearts cries, "Abba, Father."

27. If we are God's children, we are heirs of God and joint-heirs with Christ (Rom.8: 17). How does Romans 8:32 also express this truth?
    God with, or through, Jesus freely gives us all things.

28. According to Romans 8:17, is the Christian life always going to be easy? See Acts 14:22.
    No. We must suffer with Him. We must through much tribulation enter into the kingdom of God.

29. Read Romans 8:18. How does 1 Peter 4:12-14 describe "the sufferings of this present time"?
    As a fiery trial and being reproached for the name of Christ.

30. Read Romans 8:18; 2 Corinthians 4:17-18. How does Paul describe the future of the believer?
    The glory which shall be revealed in us and a far more exceeding and eternal weight of glory.

31. Read Romans 8:19. Everything that God made is waiting for what?
    The manifestation of all that it means to be a son of God.

32. How does 1 John 3:2 describe this manifestion of God's children?
    We shall be like Him.

33. The Living Bible in Romans 8:20-21 states, "For on that day (the day of the manifestation of the sons of God) thorns and thistles, sin, death, and decay - the things that overcame the world against its will at God's command - will all disappear, and the world around us will share in the glorious freedom from sin which God's children enjoy." How does 2 Peter 3:13 describe this?
According to God's promise, there will be a new heaven and a new earth where righteousness will dwell. See also Revelation 21:1-5.

34. Read Romans 8:22.   All creation has been groaning like a woman experiencing what?
Childbirth.

35. Read Romans 8:23. For what is the Christian waiting for?
The redemption of our bodies.

36. What does "redemption" in Romans 8:23 mean?
Release, deliverance, and liberation of the body. See Philippians 3:21.

37. Faith is defined as what, according to Hebrews 11:1?
Being sure of what we hope for and certain of what we do not see.

38. Invisible things hoped for are grasped by faith. According to Romans 8:25, hope calls us to be what?
Patient.

39. The Christian life involves patient waiting in hope for what, according to Romans 8:23? See also Romans 8:25.
The redemption of our bodies.

40. What is the context of Romans 8:26-27 (i.e. the thoughts that the preceding or following verses add)?
That the Holy Spirit is helping us in our present limitations and weaknesses.

41. What does Romans 8:26 say about our prayers?
We know not what we should pray for as we ought.

42. Read Romans 8:26. Who must help us in prayer?
The Holy Spirit. The Spirit Himself expresses our plea in a way that could never be put into our own words.

43. Read Romans 8:27. The Spirit pleads on behalf of whom?
The saints.

44. Read Romans 8:28. All things work together for good, to who?
To them that love God and have been called according to His purpose and plan.

45. What does "foreknow" mean?
To know in an intimate way. See Jeremiah 1:5.

46. What does "predestinate" mean?
Pre = beforehand; Destinate = To give a destiny to.

47. What are believers predestinated to in Romans 8:29?
To be conformed to the image of His Son.

48. What are believers predestinated to in Ephesians 1:4-5?
To be adopted as His sons.

49. Why did God predestinate the believers according to Ephesians 1:5?
We don't know His reasons, but it was according to the kind intention and good pleasure of His own will.

50. Read Romans 8:30. What four things will God do for the believer?
Predestinate, call, justify, and glorify.

51. Read Romans 8:30. Define these four terms of our salvation?
Predestinate = To beforehand give a destiny to.
Call = To invite to belong to Jesus Christ.
Justify = To declare to be in right relationship with God.
Glorify = To be in Christ likeness in all aspects (1 John 3:2).

52. What is the questions being asked in Romans 8:31?
What can we ever say to such wonderful things as these? (Living Bible). If God be for us, who can be against us?

53. What is the question being asked in Romans 8:32?
How will God not also, along with Jesus, graciously give us all things?

54. What is the question being asked in Romans 8:33?
Who shall lay any charge against those whom God has chosen?

55. Read Romans 8:33. What is the answer to that question?
It is God that justifieth. The Jerusalem Bible states, "Could anyone accuse those that God has chosen? When God acquits" (Romans 8:33).

56. Read Romans 8:34. Who can condemn and bring judgment against the believer?
No one.

57. Why is it that no one can condmn or bring judgment against the believer?
Because of Christ's death and His intercession on our behalf.

58. What does intercession mean?
To keep back the judgment (for our sins) that we deserve. The word actually means "to light upon a person."

59. Who shall separate us from the love of Christ?
   No one.

60. Read Romans 8:35. What seven hardships are mentioned that cannot separate us from Christ's love?
   1. Tribulation = trouble.
   2. Distress = mental anguish.
   3. Persecution
   4. Famine = lacking food.
   5. Nakedness = lacking clothes.
   6. Peril = danger
   7. Sword = threatened with death, or possibly war.

61. Read Romans 8:38-39. In all these things (the hardships in verses 35-36), we are more than conquerors through God that loves us. Why?
   Because Paul had an eternal perspective of God's love that will be manifested to him throughout all eternity.

OVERVIEW OF ROMANS CHAPTER 9

by Don Krow

Turn to Romans 9:1-4a: *"I say the truth in Christ, I lie not, my conscience also bearing me witness in the Holy Ghost, That I have great heaviness and continual sorrow in my heart. For I could wish that myself were accursed from Christ for my brethren, my kinsmen according to the flesh: Who are Israelites."* Paul here is telling about his great compassion for his fellow Israelites, how he with all his heart is saying the truth and not lying, that he would be willing to be cut off from Christ if it would mean the Jews' salvation. As he goes on, he begins to describe the people of Israel and the advantages and blessings God had given them.

Verse 4b: *"to whom pertaineth the adoption, and the glory, and the covenants, and the giving of the law, and the service of God, and the promises."* Israel had a lot of advantages. They saw the *Shekinah* glory of God. They had covenants that were given to them, agreements between them and God, the receiving of the Law, the way to worship God, and the promises.

Verse 5: *"Whose are the fathers, and of whom as concerning the flesh, Christ came, who is over all, God blessed for ever. Amen."* Jesus Christ, the promised Messiah, came through the nation of Israel.

Verse 6: *"Not as though the word of God hath taken none effect. For they are not all Israel, which are of Israel."* Paul is reasoning here and saying that there were promises given to Israel, but not everyone, because they were physical descendants of Abraham, are really of Israel. The true Israelite in God's perspective is the one we saw in Romans 2 that had a changed heart. The real Jew is one inwardly, who had circumcision of the heart.

Verse 7: *"Neither, because they are the seed of Abraham, are they all children: but, In Isaac shall thy seed be called."* In other words, it is not the natural children who are God's children, but the children of the promise who are regarded as Abraham's offspring.

Verse 9: *"For this is the word of promise: At this time will I come, and Sarah shall have a son."* So Abraham's true offspring, the true children of God, are not children of God because they came through a certain lineage but are children of God because they came through a promise.

Paul further states this in verses 10-13: *"And not only this; but when Rebecca also had conceived by one, even by our father Isaac; (For the children being not yet born, neither having done any good or evil, that the purpose of God according to election might stand, not of works, but of him that calleth;) It was said unto her, The elder shall serve the younger. As it is written, Jacob have I loved, but Esau have I hated."* We're getting into a subject over which there has been great controversy for hundreds of years, I suppose. I'm sure there are questions all of us have, and we're not going to explain all of it in this overview.

I just want to say that we're talking about a subject that is not talked about very much: God's divine election. It started in Romans 8:29 where it says, *"For whom God did foreknow, he also did predestinate to be conformed to the image of his Son."* The remainder of chapter 8 talks about predestation and election, and then chapter 9 talks about it even more. It is one of the most difficult passages in the entire New Testament, especially if you have a certain persuasion.

For many years I couldn't understand Romans 9. I never made an attempt to understand it, because I came with a preconceived idea of what I thought it meant. So I tried to read my interpretation into it, and I could never understand it. The way to really look at the chapter and begin to come to an understanding of it is this: look at the questions that are being asked, the conclusions that are being stated, and then the questions that are being asked. If you come to the same questions that these people are asking in Romans 9, then you probably will have a correct interpretation.

Let me say two things about predestation and election. There are basically two views regarding this. I'm not here to tell you what to believe. I'm here to ask you to work through the material we have supplied for you and to come to your own conclusions. I'm not trying to read anything into the passage. I want it to read for itself.

Romans 8:29 says, *"Whom he foreknew, he did predestinate to be conformed to the image of his Son."* In Romans 8, predestation is saying that people God knew in an intimate way He predestinated, and we must define that term. What does the term actually mean? "Predestination" comes from two words: "pre" means "beforehand" and "destination," or "destinate," means "destiny." God beforehand gave a destiny.

Romans 8:29 says that the destiny of the believer is to be conformed to the image of Jesus Christ, to be just like Him. Ultimately we as believers will be heirs and joint heirs of Jesus Christ. We don't know everything that involves, but we will be like Him.

The two views of predestation are this: (1) God saw down the corridors of time those who would believe on the Lord Jesus Christ. Based on that, He chose, or elected, them. That is one way people look at predestation. Let me tell you the shortcoming of that particular view: it is not God doing the choosing, but man. As I understand Romans 9, it appears that the choice is God's, not man's choice. If you take that view you are going to have to deal somehow with the passages in Romans 9. (2) The other view of predestation is that God makes the choice, but if He chooses, or elects, then that is not fair. How could He choose one and not another? So you have to deal with the fairness of God. When we look at Romans 9, the questions asked there are exactly those being asked: Is God just? Can God be fair? In the verses we just read concerning the twins, Jacob and Esau, they came from the same mother, from the same father, had the same genes, were totally identical in those ways, yet the Bible says that even before they were born, before they did anything good or bad, God's purpose in electing them was not their works. He didn't look down and say, "Hey, look at that person and all the good works they do. I will set my grace on him." It isn't based on that. When God sets His grace and mercy on an individual, do you know why He does it? He does it because of what is in Him, not what's in them.

I'm a believer in the Lord Jesus Christ. I believe you are a believer in the Lord Jesus Christ. I believe you have repented of your sins; you have turned in faith to Him. Do you know what that means? It means you are God's elect! God has manifested His grace to you.

In order to understand this, we have to understand the total depravity of man. We talked in Romans 3 (and we didn't deal with it very extensively) about the total depravity of man. The Bible says there is none that seeks after God, none righteous—no, not one. What does that mean? It means that if none seeks after God, if no man will seek after God, then God must seek man out.

Jesus made a statement in John 6:44, "No man can come to me except something happens first. The Father which sent me must draw him." That word "draw" means actually "to drag." It is used of dragging fish caught in a net to the shore. I don't know if it is a correct statement that man can't seek God, but he won't seek Him. Why, because in his sinful condition he is like a sheep that goes astray. He wants to go his way, not God's way, so God has to intervene in his life. The way God intervenes is through preaching of the Gospel, and as the Gospel is preached, the Holy Spirit takes the message of Christ and begins to draw an individual. So really we are saying that God is helping us along. We wouldn't make the right choice.

I think of all the garbage I used to be in as a kid, where I have come from, and here I am today preaching the Gospel of the Lord Jesus Christ. How did it ever happen? Was it any one step I took, a decision I made; what was it? When I really examine it, I must say this. It was the mercy and grace of God that intervened in my life, and that is what we see in Romans 9, the grace of God intervening in someone's life.

God owes grace to no one, because grace means it is undeserved. It is undeserved, unmerited favor. If it is undeserved and unmerited—if God gives it to people who actually deserve the opposite—then we can make no claim on the grace of God. God is reaching down to us in His love and mercy because of who He is, not because of who we are. I think that is the whole basis and interpretation of Romans 9, that God is not doing things based on our works but setting His love on us because of who He is.

God bless you, open your eyes, and help you as you meditate on this particular chapter. The same subject is also dealt with to some degree in chapters 10-11.

Romans 9:1-33
Discipleship Commentary

. . . .

Read the entire lesson and then answer the questions that follow.

Romans 9:1 - I say the truth in Christ, I lie not, my conscience also bearing me witness in the Holy Ghost,

(Rom. 9:1) Paul is going to great lengths to verify that what he is saying is the truth. This needs to be stated, because Paul's statement in verse 3 would certainly have been interpreted as an exaggeration, if there had not been some clarification.

Romans 9:2 - That I have great heaviness and continual sorrow in my heart.

(Rom. 9:2) This is not a contradiction to other statements by Paul (2 Cor. 7:13; Gal. 5:22-23; Phil. 1:4,18, 2:2,18, 4:4; Col. 1:24; 1 Th. 3:9, 5:16; and Philemon. 1:7). Paul did operate in the joy of the Holy Ghost just as he told others to do. However, there was this continual heaviness and sorrow in his heart when it came to the unbelieving Jews.

This is comparable to someone who has lost a loved one who is very dear to them. In the process of time, they get over it to the point that they may be considered a very joyful person. But there is always that vacancy in their heart. Similarly, Paul was rejoicing in the Lord, but he always had this great longing in his heart for the salvation of the Jews.

Romans 9:3 - For I could wish that myself were accursed from Christ for my brethren, my kinsmen according to the flesh:

(Rom. 9:3) What a statement! Paul is saying that he would go to hell in the place of the Jews if that would accomplish their salvation. This is nothing less than the perfect agape love that Jesus demonstrated when He died for our sins.

Although this desire is commendable on Paul's part, there is nothing that he could accomplish that Jesus hadn't already accomplished completely. Paul was specifically commissioned by the Lord to go to the Gentiles, yet we see him repeatedly going to the Jews, even after he said he wouldn't do that anymore. Paul even went to Jerusalem apparently against the instruction of the Holy Ghost and was more than willing to lay down his life for the sake of the Jews (Acts 21:13). This illustrates his great love for the Jewish people that he is describing here.

Romans 9:4-6 - Who are Israelites; to whom pertaineth the adoption, and the glory, and the covenants, and the giving of the law, and the service of God, and the promises; 5) Whose are the fathers, and of whom as concerning the flesh Christ came, who is over all, God blessed for ever. Amen. 6) Not as though the word of God hath taken none effect. For they are not all Israel, which are of Israel:

(Rom. 9:6) Paul had just expressed a compassion for the Jewish race that was so strong that he was willing to be damned in their place if that would have produced their salvation. As he said in verse 2, this produced great heaviness and continual sorrow.

According to verses 4 and 5, one of the reasons he longed for the salvation of the Jews so intensely is because he himself was a Jew, and he was acutely aware that Christ was the Jewish Messiah. How ironic it was that Jesus came unto His own and His own did not receive Him (John 1:11). Now he begins to relate the reasoning that had enabled him to cope with the Jews' tragic rejection of Jesus.

The promises made to Abraham and his descendants were not made to his physical descendants, but to his spiritual seed (vv. 6-8). Therefore, the true people of God have not rejected their Messiah. There is a body of believers comprised of believing Jews and Gentiles, which are the true Israel of God. To back this up, Paul cites the two Old Testament examples of Isaac (v. 9) and Jacob (vv. 10-13) to illustrate how the blessing of God was not passed on through the normal method of inheritance but through election.

Paul had expressed some of these same thoughts twice before in this epistle, and he used the same reasoning in his letter to the Galatians.

Romans 9:7-8 - Neither, because they are the seed of Abraham, are they all children: but, In Isaac shall thy seed be called. 8) That is, They which are the children of the flesh, these are not the children of God: but the children of the promise are counted for the seed.

(Rom. 9:8) Paul cites six Old Testament references to make his point that God's promises to Abraham and his seed were made to the spiritual offspring of Abraham, not the physical.

First, Isaac was not the firstborn son of Abraham entitled to the birthright and blessing, yet he obtained both, because he was chosen by God. Next, Jacob was not the firstborn either, yet he was chosen by God. These two examples confirm that God's promise was not inherited by birth.

Paul also points out that before Jacob and his twin brother Esau were born, God told Rebecca that the elder would serve the younger. They weren't even born yet, so they had not done any good or evil that caused God to make this choice. This meant that the blessing of Abraham was not obtained by individual performance either but was based solely on God's choosing by grace.

Romans 9:9-11 - For this is the word of promise, At this time will I come, and Sara shall have a son. 10) And not only this; but when Rebecca also had conceived by one, even by our father Isaac; 11) (For the children being not yet born, neither having done any good or evil, that the purpose of God according to election might stand, not of works, but of him that calleth;)

(Rom. 9:11) Paul is citing these Old Testament examples to show that those who were considered the children of Abraham were not his physical sons and daughters, but they were chosen by God, in this case, before they were born. This proves God's election is not based on birth or performance.

However, some people have interpreted this verse and the quotation from Malachi 1:2-3 in the next verse as an example of extreme predestination. They reason that Esau was hated by God before he was born. Therefore, some people are predestined by God for damnation, while some are elected to salvation before they are ever born. This means a person has no choice in the matter. That is not what these verses are saying.

God's predestination is based on His. Only those whom God foreknew would accept Him have been elected and predestinated. God did not force Jacob and Esau to make the choices they made. But through His foreknowledge He was able to foresee who would respond to Him, and that is the one He chose.

The doctrine of election is based on God's foreknowledge the same way that predestination is based on God's foreknowledge. This can be clearly seen in 1 Peter 1:2, which says we are, "Elect according to the foreknowledge of God the Father." God does not choose an individual independent of his or her free will. Instead, through His foreknowledge, He knows who will choose Him, and those are the individuals He elects to be His own.

Romans 9:12 - It was said unto her, The elder shall serve the younger.

(Rom. 9:12) There is no record in Scripture that the individual Esau ever served the individual Jacob. However, Esau's posterity did serve Jacob's posterity (1 Chr. 18:13). Although Paul is making reference to the actual birth of these two individuals, the prophecy given to Rebecca and its fulfillment are referring to the nations which came from these men.

Romans 9:13 - As it is written, Jacob have I loved, but Esau have I hated.

(Rom. 9:13) God did not hate Esau and love Jacob while they were still in their mother's womb. He did choose Jacob over Esau as the inheritor of Abraham's blessing before they were born, but Esau could have walked with God and have been blessed by God if he would have chosen to do so.

The scripture from Malachi that says, "I loved Jacob, and I hated Esau," was written in approximately 557-525 B.C., thousands of years after the birth of Esau and Jacob. So, this is not speaking of God hating Esau at birth. There is not any mention in Scripture that God hated the individual Esau. This reference to Esau is referring to the nation of Edom (Esau's descendants) in the same way that the term Israel often referred to the entire nation of Israel, not the individual. So, God is saying that He had rejected the nation of Edom and had chosen the nation of Israel.

Paul quotes from Malachi, not to show that God hated Esau and loved Jacob while they were still in their mother's womb, but rather to confirm that the choice God made before they were born based on His foreknowledge was the right choice. Jacob went on to become a mighty man of God, and Esau despised the things of God. God's choice of Jacob didn't cause this to happen. This quotation from Malachi simply confirms that God's foreknowledge was accurate.

Jacob was called to a higher position than his brother Esau before they were born, but that does not display any rejection of Esau on God's part. That is comparable to God choosing one person to be a pastor, while another is called to be a deacon. The deacon is not inferior to the pastor. They are simply called to different positions. Jacob and Esau were called to different positions before they had done any good or evil to illustrate that election was not based on performance but choice.

Romans 9:14 - What shall we say then? Is there unrighteousness with God? God forbid.

(Rom. 9:14) Paul is seeking to stop anyone from interpreting his statements in a way that would make it look like God was unfair in his dealings with man. God can extend mercy to an individual without treating others unjustly. Just as in the parable that Jesus gave in Matthew 20:1-16, God treats everyone fairly, but to some He chooses to give extra mercy. Does that mean He was unjust? Not at all.

If God chooses to call a man to account for his actions and choices he has made of his own free will, He is completely justified to do that at any time. In Luke 13:1-9, Jesus mentioned the people whom Pilate had killed and mingled their blood with the sacrifices, and the people on whom the tower in Siloam fell and who were killed. He raised the question, "Were these people worse sinners than others to suffer this judgment?" He answered His own question by saying that all of them deserved such judgment, but God in His mercy had spared them.

He then immediately follows with the parable about the man with an unproductive tree in his vineyard. He was going to cut down this dead tree and replace it, but the vine dresser interceded for the tree, and the owner gave him some extra time to see if he could revive it. Likewise, we all deserve judgment, but through things such as the intercession of others, God will sometimes show extra mercy to certain individuals.

However, if He chose not to extend mercy to anyone and He called all of our accounts due, He would be completely justified in doing so. It's His choice. God has never brought judgment on anyone without being righteous in doing so. Likewise, He has never extended mercy to any individual that made His treatment of someone else unfair.

Romans 9:15-16 - For he saith to Moses, I will have mercy on whom I will have mercy, and I will have compassion on whom I will have compassion. 16) So then it is not of him that willeth, nor of him that runneth, but of God that sheweth mercy.

(Rom. 9:16) There is a very subtle trap which many people who have been used of God fall into. They see what God has accomplished through them and they begin reasoning, "God must use me because of my great faithfulness." But that is not the case. God has never had anyone qualified working for Him yet. God is a lot more merciful than we are faithful.

Romans 9:17 - For the scripture saith unto Pharaoh, Even for this same purpose have I raised thee up, that I might shew my power in thee, and that my name might be declared throughout all the earth.

(Rom. 9:17) Some people have taken this word from God about Pharaoh and have made a paragraph out of it. They have drawn conclusions that God predetermines everything in our lives to the degree that our free will doesn't exist. That is not what the Lord is speaking of here.

We can be assured that Pharaoh had already had ample opportunity to respond to God prior to the time that God began to harden his heart. Since Pharaoh had already made his choice, even to the point that he proclaimed himself to be deity and commanded the Egyptians to worship him, God was not unrighteous in bringing him into judgment for this.

God did not make Pharaoh the way he was, but God used the way Pharaoh had chosen to be for His glory. God exalted Pharaoh and gave him leadership of the nation knowing full well how he would respond to His demands to let His people go. Since Pharaoh had already hardened his heart toward God, God was not unjust in continuing to harden his heart further until His glory was manifest completely.

This verse is depicting God as using Pharaoh's hardened heart for His glory, but Pharaoh had already had his chance. God simply upheld his choice and received glory through His triumph over Pharaoh and all his host.

Romans 9:18 - Therefore hath he mercy on whom he will have mercy, and whom he will he hardeneth. 19) Thou wilt say then unto me, Why doth he yet find fault? For who hath resisted his will?

(Rom. 9:19) The argument that Paul is refuting here is not a correct interpretation of what he had said. This is comparable to his statement in Romans 6:1 where he said, "What shall we say then? Shall we continue in sin, that grace may abound?" Just as he knew someone would interpret his teaching on grace to be an advocation of sin, therefore, he spoke their wrong conclusion and then refuted it; it's likewise here.

Romans 9:20 - Nay but, O man, who art thou that repliest against God? Shall the thing formed say to him that formed it, Why hast thou made me thus?

(Rom. 9:20) The truth that Paul is expressing here is the overall point that is made in the book of Job. God never did explain Himself to Job as Job had insisted that He do. Instead, God rebuked Job for his know-it-all attitude (Job 38:18). God basically asked Job what right he had to maintain his own integrity at the expense of God's (Job 40:8). Job got the message when God spoke to him from a whirlwind, and Job humbled himself (Job 42:2-6). Paul's message should bring the same response from us

Romans 9:21 - Hath not the potter power over the clay, of the same lump to make one vessel unto honour, and another unto dishonour?

(Rom. 9:21) Paul is drawing an illustration from an Old Testament passage of Scripture from Jeremiah 18:3-6. In that passage, God sent Jeremiah to the potter's house to learn a lesson. The potter was making a vessel and it was marred, so he remade it. The Lord spoke to Jeremiah and said, "O house of Israel, cannot I do with you as this potter? . . . Behold, as the clay is in the potter's hand, so are ye in mine hand, O house of Israel."

From this illustration, some people have drawn a wrong conclusion that the Lord creates some people evil and predestined to a life of damnation, not by their choice, but by God's. However, a closer look at the passage in Jeremiah and its context will show that is not the case.

First of all, the potter started to create a good vessel, but the clay was marred. Whose fault was that? It wasn't the potter's fault. The clay was faulty. So, the potter took this imperfect clay and, instead of discarding it, refashioned it into another vessel that may not have been worth nearly as much as his original design but was still useful.

Likewise, the Lord does not create certain individuals for destruction; however, some do become marred by their own choice, not due to any fault of the Creator. Instead of just removing them from the earth, the Lord will endure (v. 22) their atrocities. He may even put them in great positions of authority, such as He did with Pharaoh, so that He may manifest His great power through His victory over them and their devices. God can still use someone who has rejected Him in the same way that a potter can take a marred piece of clay and find some use for it.

It can be clearly seen that the Lord does not do these things against the will of the individual by continuing to read the context of Jeremiah's experience with the potter. In verses 7-10, the Lord says that when He purposes evil or good against a nation, if that nation repents, then God will change His plans for them. That undeniably states that our choice influences God's choice.

Romans 9:22-24 - What if God, willing to shew his wrath, and to make his power known, endured with much longsuffering the vessels of wrath fitted to destruction: 23) And that he might make known the riches of his glory on the vessels of mercy, which he had afore prepared unto glory, 24) Even us, whom he hath called, not of the Jews only, but also of the Gentiles?

(Rom. 9:24) Paul had started explaining in verse 6 that there was a true people of God not based on nationality but on faith in God. He now gives four quotes from two Old Testament prophets to show that this is not a new concept, but it had been prophesied hundreds of years before.

Romans 9:25-27 - As he saith also in Osee, I will call them my people, which were not my people; and her beloved, which was not beloved. 26) And it shall come to pass, that in the place where it was said unto them, Ye are not my people; there shall they be called the children of the living God. 27) Esaias also crieth concerning Israel, Though the number of the children of Israel be as the sand of the sea, a remnant shall be saved:

(Rom. 9:27) This verse could read, "Only a remnant shall be saved." That is the point that Paul is making. His next reference from Isaiah (v. 29) complements this one, and it is clearly stressing that there will be very few Jews who are truly God's people.

Romans 9:28-30 - For he will finish the work, and cut it short in righteousness: because a short work will the Lord make upon the earth. 29) And as Esaias said before, Except the Lord of Sabaoth had left us a seed, we had been as Sodoma, and been made like unto Gomorrha. 30) What shall we say then? That the Gentiles, which followed not after righteousness, have attained to righteousness, even the righteousness which is of faith.

(Rom. 9:30) Paul is saying that this is the conclusion, or the summary, of his point in this chapter. This is another one of Paul's radical statements. People who are not seeking to be righteous can become righteous? How can this be? The answer to this question lies in God's grace.

By grace, God has provided righteousness for everyone, regardless of their actions. If a person will believe and receive this gift, God will reckon that person righteous. This is what happened to the Gentiles. They had a reputation for not seeking God (Eph. 4:17-19 and 1 Pet. 4:3), and yet the Gentiles as a whole accepted God's gift of salvation while the Jews as a whole, who were seeking after God, rejected His gift. The reason for this is given by Paul in verses 32-33.

People who don't understand God's grace will always be confused and unbelieving that a person who hasn't lived a morally good life can be righteous in the sight of God, while a morally good person can be unrighteous in His sight. Righteousness is based on faith, not actions.

Romans 9:31-32 - But Israel, which followed after the law of righteousness, hath not attained to the law of righteousness. 32) Wherefore? Because they sought it not by faith, but as it were by the works of the law. For they stumbled at that stumblingstone;

(Rom. 9:32) Why is it that a person who is seeking so hard to please God can be rejected, while a person who has not sought God at all can come into a righteous relationship with Him? This is an important question, and its answer is one of the most profound doctrines in Scripture.

Paul gives the answer to his own question. The answer is faith and its object. The Jews were zealous (Rom. 10:2) for the things of God, but their faith was in themselves. They were trusting that they could earn God's favor by their acts of righteousness. On the other hand, the Gentiles had no holiness to trust in. So, when they heard the Gospel which said that Jesus paid our debt for us, they readily accepted His gift of salvation, while the religious Jews could not abandon their trust in themselves for salvation. This same problem exists today. Millions of church people are trying to live holy lives, but they do not have a true faith in Jesus as their Savior. If they were to stand before God and He was to ask them what they had done to deserve salvation, they would immediately start recounting all their acts of holiness: church attendance, giving receipts, etc. Regardless of how good our actions are compared to others, they always come short of the perfect standard of God. The only response to this kind of question that would grant us entrance to heaven is to say, my only claim to salvation is faith in Jesus as my Savior. Anything more or less is damned.

There is a difference between works of faith (1 Thess. 1:3, 2 Thess. 1:11) and works of the Law (Gal. 2:16, 3:2,5, and 10). The difference is not in the action but in the attitude. A work of the Law is some act of righteousness or holiness that is being done to earn the favor of God. A work of faith may be the same act of righteousness or holiness, but it is done as a labor of love (1 Thess. 1:3). It is done not to obtain favor but in gratitude for the favor that has already been extended to us in Christ. Works of the Law and faith in Jesus are opposites (Gal. 2:16).

Jesus is the stumblingstone that Paul is speaking of. God has placed Jesus directly in the path of every person. Those who fail to put their complete trust in Jesus because they are trusting in themselves will stumble and fall into hell while those who believe in Him will never be ashamed (v. 33).

Romans 9:33 - As it is written, Behold, I lay in Sion a stumblingstone and rock of offence: and whosoever believeth on him shall not be ashamed.

(Rom. 9:33) Those who are offended at Jesus are the ones who are trusting in themselves. They feel they will be accepted with God, because they are holy enough on their own. It is humbling to admit that all of of our righteousness is as filthy rags (Isa. 64:6). This is why the religious people have always been the persecutors of true Christians.

This quotation does not appear in the Old Testament in these exact words. It is most probable that Paul is quoting the last part of Isaiah 28:16. If so, Paul substituted the words "be ashamed" for Isaiah's words "make haste." In the context of war, making haste is descriptive of a person who has been shamed in battle.

Romans 9:1-33
Discipleship Questions

....

Answer the following questions by reading the corresponding discipleship commentary lesson and using your Bible.

1. Read Romans 9:1. Do you think Paul could have passed a lie detector test?_____

2. What three statements indicate Paul's truthfulness? _____
   _____

3. What was Paul feeling in Romans 9:2? _____
   _____

4. Why did Paul feel that way? Read Romans 9:3._____
   _____

5. Read Romans 9:4-5. What privileges did the Israelites have?
   _____

6. Read Romans 9:6 (NIV). Has God's Word to Israel failed? _____

7. Why has it not failed? Read Romans 9:6 (last part of the verse). _____
   _____

8. Read Romans 9:7-8. Because someone descends from Abraham, does that make him or her a child of God? _____

9. Read Romans 9:8-9. Isaac was a child of God and the true descendant of Abraham simply because of God's what? _____

10. Isaac married Rebecca, and she bore him twin sons. God chose Jacob over Esau. How does Romans 9:12 state this? _____

11. How does Romans 9:13 state that God chose Jacob over Esau?
    _____

12. Read Romans 9:11. Is it true that God made this choice because He knew beforehand that Jacob's behavior would be good and Esau's would be evil? _____
    _____

13. Read Romans 9:11 and 11:5-6. Is election an act of God's grace?
    _____

14. What is grace? _____

15. Read Romans 9:14. What is the objection to what Paul has just stated?

_____

16. Read Romans 9:14. If men did the choosing instead of God, would this question have been raised? _____

17. Is God unrighteous or unfair? _____

18. How does Romans 9:14 prove this? _____

19. Read Romans 9:14. Even if we don't understand God's election, is God unfair? _____

20. Read Romans 9:15. God will have mercy and compassion on whom?

_____

21. Man's desire and effort counts for everything. Does Romans 9:16 teach this? _____

22. Read Romans 9:17. God gave Pharaoh the kingdom of Egypt for what purpose?

_____

_____

23. Read Romans 9:18. God is kind and merciful to us. Why?

_____

24. What are the questions being asked in Romans 9:19?

_____

25. How does Paul answer those questions in Romans 9:20-21?

_____

_____

26. What two kinds of vessels are mentioned in Romans 9:22-23?

_____

27. Read Romans 9:24. The vessels of mercy whom He hath called consist of whom?

_____

28. No man can come to Christ except something happens first. What must happen according to John 6:44? _____

29. Read Romans 9:25. People who were not beloved are now called what?_____

30. Read Romans 9:26. People who were not God's people are now what?

_____

31. Read Roman 9:27. Out of the large number of the children of Israel, who only will be saved?

_____

32. Read Romans 9:29. Unless God had left descendants, all would have ended up like what?

_____

33. What is the conclusion of Romans 9, according to verses 30-31?

_____

_____

34. What kind of righteousness is God offering us, according to Romans 9:30?

_____

35. Read Romans 9:31. What kind of righteousness did Israel try to obtain?

_____

36. The stumbling stone that Israel stumbled over was whom? _____

Romans 9:1-33
Discipleship Answer Key

. . . .

Do not look at the answer key until you have completed the questions.
Compare your answers with the following answers.

1. Read Romans 9:1. Do you think Paul could have passed a lie detector test?

2. What three statements indicate Paul's truthfulness?
   1. I say the truth in Christ (in union with Christ).
   2. I lie not (I am not lying).
   3. My conscience in union with the Spirit assures me of it too.

3. What was Paul feeling in Romans 9:2?
   Great heaviness and continual sorrow.

4. Why did Paul feel that way? Read Romans 9:3.
   He wanted those of his own race to be won to Christ.

5. Read Romans 9:4-5. What privileges did the Israelites have?
   The privilege of being adopted as sons, being led about with a great cloud of glory, and God made covenants with them, He gave them His Law, the temple worship, and gave them mighty promises.

6. Read Romans 9:6 (NIV). Has God's Word to Israel failed?
   No.

7. Why has it not failed? Read Romans 9:6 (last part of the verse).
   Because not all who are descended from Israel are Israel, i.e., the chosen people of God.

8. Read Romans 9:7-8. Because someone descends from Abraham, does that make him or her a child of God?
   No.

9. Read Romans 9:8-9. Isaac was a child of God and the true descendant of Abraham simply because of God's what?
   Promise.

10. Isaac married Rebecca, and she bore him twin sons. God chose Jacob over Esau. How does Romans 9:12 state this?
    The older will serve the younger.

11. How does Romans 9:13 state that God chose Jacob over Esau?
    Jacob have I loved, but Esau have I hated.

12. Read Romans 9:11. Is it true that God made this choice because He knew beforehand that Jacob's behavior would be good and Esau's would be evil?
No. God's choice is based on His call, not upon anything good in man.

13. Read Romans 9:11 and 11:5-6. Is election an act of God's grace?
Yes, it is not of works.

14. What is grace?
Unmerited favor and mercy, not justice (giving us what we deserve).

15. Read Romans 9:14. What is the objection to what Paul has just stated?
That God is unrighteous, that God is unfair (it is unfair to choose one and not another).

16. Read Romans 9:14. If men did the choosing instead of God, would this question have been raised?
No.

17. Is God unrighteous or unfair?
No.

18. How does Romans 9:14 prove this?
By the phrase "God forbid."

19. Read Romans 9:14. Even if we don't understand God's election, is God unfair?
May it never be!

20. Read Romans 9:15. God will have mercy and compassion on whom?
God owes grace to no one, or it would not be grace.

21. Man's desire and effort counts for everything. Does Romans 9:16 teach this?
No.

22. Read Romans 9:17. God gave Pharaoh the kingdom of Egypt for what purpose?
To use Pharaoh to show God's power and to make God's name known in all the world.

23. Read Romans 9:18. God is kind and merciful to us. Why?
Because of who He is, not because of who we are.

24. What are the questions being asked in Romans 9:19?
Why does God still blame us?
For who resists his will?

25. How does Paul answer those questions in Romans 9:20-21?
Who are you to talk back to God? A clay pot does not ask the man who made it, "Why did you make me like this?" The man who makes the pots has the right to use the clay as he wishes.

26. What two kinds of vessels are mentioned in Romans 9:22-23?
Vessels of wrath and vessels of mercy.

27. Read Romans 9:24. The vessels of mercy whom He hath called consist of whom?
Even us, whom he hath called.

28. No man can come to Christ except something happens first. What must happen according to John 6:44?
The Father must DRAW them.

29. Read Romans 9:25. People who were not beloved are now called what?
Beloved.

30. Read Romans 9:26. People who were not God's people are now what?
Children of the living God.

31. Read Roman 9:27. Out of the large number of the children of Israel, who only will be saved?
Only the remnant will be saved.

32. Read Romans 9:29. Unless God had left descendants, all would have ended up like what?
Sodom and Gomorrah.

33. What is the conclusion of Romans 9, according to verses 30-31?
The Gentiles, who did not pursue righteousness, obtained it (through faith).
Israel who pursued righteousness by keeping the Law did not obtain it.

34. What kind of righteousness is God offering us, according to Romans 9:30?
The righteousness which is of faith.

35. Read Romans 9:31. What kind of righteousness did Israel try to obtain?
Righteousness derived from keeping the Law.

36. The stumbling stone that Israel stumbled over was whom?
Jesus Christ.

OVERVIEW OF ROMANS CHAPTER 10

By Don Krow

In Romans 9, we discovered that Israel was seeking righteousness as an outcome of keeping the Law. However, they did not attain it. The reason for this was that they sought righteousness by works and stumbled over the stumbling stone of Christ (Rom. 9:30-33).

We are going to discover in Romans 10 that the righteousness that makes men acceptable before God is the righteousness that comes through faith.

Paul begins this chapter by stating that his desire and prayer to God is that Israel might be saved (Rom. 10:1). Paul further states that Israel has a zeal for God, but it's not according to correct knowledge and understanding, for they being ignorant or unaware of the righteousness that God has provided, they went about to establish their own righteousness, or a righteousness belonging to themselves. In so doing, they did not submit themselves to the righteousness that God had provided for them. (Rom. 10:2-3) Paul now states that the righteousness God has provided that makes men acceptable is Jesus Christ Himself. Paul states in Romans 10:4 that "Christ is the end of the law for righteousness to every one that believeth." Notice that the scripture did not say that Christ is the end of the Law as a part of the Word of God, or that Christ is the end of the Law as a part of Israel's history, but Christ is the end of any kind of law-keeping as a means of obtaining righteousness.

In Romans 10:5-6it says that Moses described the righteousness of the Law as a righteousness that is obtained by *doing*, but the righteousness of faith is not a righteousness of *doing* but a righteousness that has been provided, that is *done*.

Christ has already died, was buried, and rose again to provide the righteousness that we need. We simply have to confess with our mouths Jesus as Lord and believe in our hearts that God has raised Him from the dead, and we shall be saved. The word, "Lord," (Greek, *kurios*) is a word that means "someone who is supreme in authority, someone who has the right to control" (Strong's). It also has the idea of "master, owner, or a possessor of property" (Lexical Aids to the N.T.). In other words, in confessing Jesus as Lord, we are giving Him the control of our hearts and our lives. Another biblical word for this would be "repentance," a change of heart that has turned toward God and received all the benefits of His grace.

Romans 10:10 further states that with our hearts, we believe unto justification, or right-standing with God, and with our mouths, confession is made unto our salvation.

The progression of our salvation experience, as described in Romans 10, is that we first of all hear the message of the Gospel. As a result, we believe upon Christ. As a result of our faith, we then call upon His name, for the Bible states that whosoever shall call upon the name of the Lord shall be saved (Rom. 10:13). Faith came because we heard the message of Christ (Rom. 10:17).

Paul states that this message of Christ has gone out unto all the earth and that the Gentiles accepted it and found the salvation that they were not even looking for. But Israel stumbled over the stumbling stone, which was Christ. Even though God stretched out His hands all day long to the Jews, they kept arguing and refusing to come to Christ and the salvation that He has provided (Rom. 10:18-21).

Romans 10:1-21
Discipleship Commentary

Read the entire lesson and then answer the questions that follow.

Romans 10:1-2 - Brethren, my heart's desire and prayer to God for Israel is, that they might be saved. 2) For I bear them record that they have a zeal of God, but not according to knowledge.

(Rom. 10:2) This scripture goes contrary to many religious teachings. Many people believe that it's not necessary to believe the right thing, just as long as we believe something, we'll be all right. However, Paul disproves this kind of thinking in this passage by saying that their zeal was without knowledge, and therefore they were not saved (v. 2).

The Jews were very zealous about their religion, but that wasn't enough. It's not enough just to believe; we have to believe the truth. Even a person who is sincere can be sincerely wrong. Jesus said, "Ye shall know the truth, and the truth shall make you free" (John 8:32).

Romans 10:3 - For they being ignorant of God's righteousness, and going about to establish their own righteousness, have not submitted themselves unto the righteousness of God.

(Rom. 10:3) This verse describes the condition of much of the church today. Most people are unaware that there are two kinds of righteousness. Only one type of righteousness is acceptable to God.

One form of righteousness that Paul describes here is our own righteousness (also Phil. 3:9). These are the acts of holiness that we do in an attempt to fulfill the commands of the Old Testament Law. This is an imperfect righteousness, because human nature is imperfect and incapable of fulfilling the Law. Therefore, our own righteousness, which is according to the Law, is inadequate. Isaiah said it this way in Isaiah 64:6, "All our righteousnesses are as filthy rags."

In contrast, God's righteousness is perfect. Also, God's righteousness is not something that we do but something that we receive as a gift through faith in Christ.

Paul makes it very clear in this verse that it's not possible to trust in our own righteousness and in God's righteousness also. A person who believes that he or she must earn God's acceptance by one's holy actions cannot be believing in God's righteousness, which is a gift. It has to be one or the other; we cannot mix the two. Righteousness is not what Jesus has done for us plus some minimum standard of holiness that we have to accomplish (Rom. 11:6).

Romans 10:4 - For Christ is the end of the law for righteousness to every one that believeth.

(Rom. 10:4) The Greek word that was translated "end" here is "telos," which means, "the point aimed at as a limit; i.e. (by implication) the conclusion of an act or state (termination)."

This verse does not say that Christ is the end of the Law but rather that Christ is the end of the Law for the purpose of righteousness. This means that no one any longer becomes righteous, or justified in the sight of God, by how well they perform the deeds of the law. However, there are still useful purposes of the Law for the New Testament believer.

The Old Testament Law still reveals to us God's holiness, which we should seek to emulate. It must be understood, however, that our failure to comply does not bring the punishments pronounced in the Law, since Jesus bore those for us (Gal. 3:12). Our compliance does not earn the blessings of God either; those only come by faith in Christ (Rom. 4:8-13). We also need to be acquainted with the Old Testament Law so we will better understand our new covenant and God's historical dealings with mankind.

Also, Paul said to Timothy, "But we know that the law is good, if a man use it lawfully" (I Tim. 1:8). He then says that the Law was not made for a righteous man (i.e., a Christian 2 Cor. 5:21), but rather for an unbeliever (1 Tim. 1:9-10). So, a Christian can still use the Law when ministering to unbelievers to show them their sin and their need for a Savior.

As Christians, we should not discard the Old Testament Law. When understood in the light of the new covenant, the old covenant provides us with invaluable revelation of God. Paul is simply stressing that the time when anyone sought to be justified through the keeping of the Old Testament Law is over. Now, everyone must put their faith in Christ, and Christ alone, for salvation.

Someone might ask, "Was anyone ever justified by the keeping of the Law?" The answer is, "yes." One person did become righteous through His keeping of the Old Testament Law. That person was Jesus. One of the reasons the Old Testament Law was given was so that Jesus could legally earn man's redemption. Now that the purchase has been completed, that function of the Law is over.

This phrase, "to every one that believeth" limits this benefit to only believers (Christians). To those who do not receive God's gift of salvation, the Law is still in effect. A person who fails to believe on Jesus will have to answer to God for each and every one of his or her transgressions of the Law.

Romans 10:5 - For Moses describeth the righteousness which is of the law, That the man which doeth those things shall live by them.

(Rom. 10:5) In verses 5-9, Paul contrasts those who seek righteousness by the Law with those who seek the righteousness of God as a gift. Those who seek to earn righteousness through keeping the Law are consumed with "doing" (this verse), while those who receive righteousness by faith are simply confessing what has already been done (v. 9).

This is a simple and yet profound difference. If we are still "doing" acts of holiness to get God to move in our lives, then we are still operating under a "law" mentality that is not faith (Gal. 3:12). When we simply believe and confess what has already been provided through Christ, then that's grace.

A person who is living under the Law and a person who lives under grace should have very similar actions of holiness, but their motivations are completely opposite. The legalist has his or her attention on what he or she must do, while the person living by faith has his or her attention on what Christ has already done for them.

For instance, the scriptures teach to confess with the mouth and believe with the heart and the results will be that a person will receive from God (Rom. 10:9-10; Mark 11:23-24, etc.). The legalist thinks, "That means I can get God to heal me by confessing 'By His stripes I am healed.'" However, the person who understands God's grace will not confess the Word to get healed. He or she will confess, "By His stripes I am healed," because he or she really believes it has already been done.

Analyzing our mind set is the simplest way of discerning whether we are operating in true Bible faith or a legalistic counterfeit. If the motive for our actions is to be accepted with God, that's legalism. If we live holy out of faith and gratefulness for what God has already done, that's grace.

The Greek word that was translated "live" here is "zao," which means, "to live." However, that definition by itself doesn't fully convey Paul's intent in quoting this Old Testament passage from Leviticus 18:5. It is clear from the context that Paul is contrasting the effort to keep the Old Testament Law with New Testament faith in Christ. He is concluding that the observance of the Old Testament law for producing righteousness is inferior to the New Testament method of obtaining righteousness by putting faith in Jesus as our Savior.

This quote from Moses is intended to illustrate the harshness of living by the Old Testament Law. Paul quotes this same Old Testament passage in Galatians 3:12 and so does Nehemiah in Nehemiah 9:29. In each case the context clearly reveals that the writer was quoting this verse to speak of the negative effects of living by the Law.

The word "live" in the English language can mean many different things as can be seen by the multiple definitions of this word in any dictionary. In the American Heritage Dictionary, there is one meaning that communicates Paul's meaning here. The word "live" can mean "to continue to remain alive."

Using this definition, this quote from Leviticus 18:5 is saying that once a person starts trying to fulfill the law to earn righteousness he or she will have to subsist, or remain alive, by his continued adherence to the precepts of that Law. In other words, once someone decides to "earn" right standing with God, then God is going to give that person what they deserve. The thing that is dreadfully wrong with this thought is that no one really deserves righteousness. We don't need justice—We need mercy!

This is what Paul is communicating through quoting this scripture from Leviticus. Trying to achieve righteousness by keeping the Law doesn't bring peace because it puts the burden of salvation on our shoulders. In contrast, salvation by grace through faith places the burden on Jesus, and allows us to walk free.

Romans 10:6 - But the righteousness which is of faith speaketh on this wise, Say not in thine heart, Who shall ascend into heaven? (that is, to bring Christ down from above:)

(Rom. 10:6) Paul is saying that failure to understand justification by grace produces an attitude that, in effect, denies Christ's substitutionary work for us. A person who still believes that his performance is essential for salvation is denying that Christ is in heaven making intercession for us (Rom. 8:34). This belief dethrones Christ from His present position. It is like denying that Christ has ascended into heaven for us.

Likewise, a belief that we have to bear the punishment for our sins is like denying Christ's death was sufficient by itself. If we are to be punished for our sins, then Christ might as well not have died for us.

All of this is continuing the contrast that Paul began in verse 5 between the doing of the Old Testament Law and the believing of New Testament grace. The Law mentality puts us under an unbearable load of performance to obtain righteousness; faith simply receives the righteousness that has already been provided through Christ.

Romans 10:7-8 - Or, Who shall descend into the deep? (that is, to bring up Christ again from the dead.) 8) But what saith it? The word is nigh thee, even in thy mouth, and in thy heart: that is, the word of faith, which we preach;

(Rom. 10:8) In verses 6-8, Paul was again quoting from Moses, this time from Deuteronomy 30:11-14. However, in this verse, he adds, "that is, the word of faith, which we preach," which provides us with a commentary on Moses' statements.

A reading of Deuteronomy 30:11-14 by itself might lead someone to suggest that Moses was saying that the Law was not hard to keep. Yet, that is against everything Paul taught, and the context of this verse in particular. Paul was saying that Moses' statements in this quotation were actually prophesying the day of justification by faith that Paul was preaching.

Paul revealed in Galatians 3:22-25 that the purpose of the Old Testament Law was to "shut us up" unto the faith which should afterwards be revealed. The Law was our schoolmaster to bring us to Christ. From Paul's use of Moses' statements to make his point, it is possible that Moses had revelation of the day when faith in Christ would supersede the law (Deut. 18:15-18).

Romans 10:9 - That if thou shalt confess with thy mouth the Lord Jesus, and shalt believe in thine heart that God hath raised him from the dead, thou shalt be saved.

(Rom. 10:9) Remember that in context, Paul had been contrasting two types of righteousness. The righteousness of the Law binds a person up in "doing" while the righteousness of faith simply receives what Christ has already done.

This verse is stressing the simplicity of receiving righteousness by faith as opposed to the bondage of trying to produce our own righteousness that is by the Law (Phil. 3:9). An attempt to amplify on the conditions of this verse too much would counter the point that Paul is making. However, in the light of other scriptures, some explanation needs to be given.

This verse is not saying that anyone who just says the words, "Jesus is Lord" and believes that He rose from the dead is born again. The Greek word "homologeo" that was translated "confesseth" here means more than just saying words. It literally means, "to assent; i.e., covenant; acknowledge." By looking at Jesus' statement in Luke 6:46, a true confession of Jesus as Lord has to be heartfelt enough to involve a person's actions.

There are some groups that interpret the word "Lord" in a way that denies the deity of Jesus. This confession of Jesus as Lord has to be a declaration of faith in Jesus as "God manifest in the flesh" (1 Tim. 3:16). A Jesus who is less than God could not provide salvation for the whole human race.

Therefore, this verse is a promise to those who believe on Jesus to the extent that they are willing to change their actions accordingly, and confess Him as Lord (God) with their mouths, so that they might be saved.

Romans 10:10 - For with the heart man believeth unto righteousness; and with the mouth confession is made unto salvation.

(Rom. 10:10) For true salvation to take place, there must be confession with the mouth and belief from the heart. People tend to major on one or the other of these requirements, failing to obtain the desired results.

Confession is scriptural, but it is a result of faith in the heart. Only when a person has already believed with his or her heart will confession release the power of God. Confession without sincere belief in the heart is dead works (Heb. 9:14).

Likewise, faith without works is dead (James 2:17). When a person really believes in his or her heart, they will speak what they believe (Matt. 12:34; Luke 6:35). A faith that won't confess what is believed is not God's kind of faith.

Failure to properly combine these two truths has caused some people to fail in their attempts to receive from God and reject "faith teaching" or "confession teaching." However, if one of these truths is presented without the proper emphasis on the other, it isn't scriptural teaching. The truths of faith and confession will work when used according to the instructions in this verse.

Romans 10:11 - For the scripture saith, Whosoever believeth on him shall not be ashamed.

(Rom. 10:11) The emphasis here as well as in verse 13 is on the word "whosoever." In the first chapter of Romans, Paul had started making the point that Gentiles did not have to become Jews to be saved (Rom. 1:16). He developed that truth all the way through this epistle and is making it once again.

Romans 10:12 - For there is no difference between the Jew and the Greek: for the same Lord over all is rich unto all that call upon him.

(Rom. 10:12) The differences between Jew and Gentile do not mean much to the Christian church today. Therefore, many church people may feel that they agree with this verse. However, Paul is speaking of more than just racial differences.

Paul is saying that there is no difference between moral and immoral people. There is no difference in the sight of God between the religious and the non-religious. Everyone is a sinner and in need of the same salvation. This point still aggravates the religious people today as much as it did in Paul's day.

Romans 10:13 - For whosoever shall call upon the name of the Lord shall be saved.

(Rom. 10:13) Paul is quoting from Joel 2:32. Paul used the word "saved" for the word "delivered" that Joel used. There is no contradiction. Salvation includes deliverance.

Romans 10:14 - How then shall they call on him in whom they have not believed? and how shall they believe in him of whom they have not heard? and how shall they hear without a preacher?

(Rom. 10:14) Paul had just conclusively proven that salvation was not according to a person's performance but according to his or her acceptance of God's grace by faith in Christ Jesus. This was great news! Yet, this great news will not do anyone any good if they don't know it. The Gospel has to be heard to release its power (Rom. 1:16).

Verses 14 and 15 show a number of things that must happen in order for a person to be born again. The individual must believe, but he or she needs to have something or someone to believe in. Therefore, someone has to share the Gospel with him. But in order for that to happen, others have to send the ministers to the uttermost parts of the earth.

There are three areas of responsibility for salvation: An individual has to believe, someone has to preach, and others have to send. Satan works in all three of these areas to stop people from receiving God's gift of salvation.

Satan tries to harden a person's heart through the deceitfulness of sin (Heb. 3:13) to the point that the Gospel will not penetrate. If people are faithful to the two other responsibilities, salvation still will not occur if the individual rejects the good news.

Many times people are hungry and ripe for salvation and there is no one to share the good news with them. If Satan can stop people from preaching the Gospel because of a lack of preachers or a lack of people who will send them, then he can stop individuals from being saved.

As Christians we cannot take responsibility for a person's reaction to the Gospel but we must take the responsibility of preaching the Gospel, and giving, so others can preach the Gospel.

Romans 10:15 - And how shall they preach, except they be sent? as it is written, How beautiful are the feet of them that preach the gospel of peace, and bring glad tidings of good things!

(Rom. 10:15) When a person understands that sharing the Gospel is as important a part of salvation as the individual's acceptance of the message, then he will rejoice with Isaiah about the beauty of the person who shares this good news.

Romans 10:16 - But they have not all obeyed the gospel. For Esaias saith, Lord, who hath believed our report?

(Rom. 10:16) Contrary to popular belief, an anointed messenger with an anointed message is not always well received. This quotation from Isaiah shows that not everyone received his message about the coming Messiah. The same thing was true of many other prophets that the Lord sent to Israel including Jeremiah, Ezekiel, and even Jesus.

A misbelief that if we really minister in the power of the Holy Spirit, we will always succeed in converting the hearers has brought undeserved condemnation on many Christians. We cannot take responsibility for the actions or reactions of other people.

Romans 10:17 - So then faith cometh by hearing, and hearing by the word of God.

(Rom. 10:17) Faith comes by hearing God's Word because God's Word is His faith. A person cannot be born again through human faith. He has to use God's supernatural faith to receive God's supernatural gift of salvation.

The only place to obtain God's kind of faith is from God's Word. Therefore, we cannot compromise God's Word. It must be proclaimed boldly to make God's faith available to those who choose to believe.

Notice that this verse says "faith comes by hearing," not by "having heard." A person cannot rest on a revelation he received from God years ago unless he is still hearing the Lord speak that same truth to him now.

It is not the Lord who fails to speak, it is we who fail to hear. Therefore, anyone can keep their faith in the present tense if they will open their spiritual ears to hear what God's Word is saying (Prov. 4:20-22).

Romans 10:18-21 - But I say, Have they not heard? Yes verily, their sound went into all the earth, and their words unto the ends of the world. 19) But I say, Did not Israel know? First Moses saith, I will provoke you to jealousy by them that are no people, and by a foolish nation I will anger you. 20) But Esaias is very bold, and saith, I was found of them that sought me not; I was made manifest unto them that asked not after me. 21) But to Israel he saith, All day long I have stretched forth my hands unto a disobedient and gainsaying people.

(Rom. 10:19) What was it that Israel knew? Paul is saying that Israel knew the Gospel of salvation by faith which he had expounded on in this epistle. One way this truth was revealed in the Old Testament was through the prophecies concerning the Gentiles becoming the people of God. If God was going to embrace nationalities that didn't adhere to the rites and ceremonies that were delivered to the Jews, then it should have been evident that these things were not prerequisites to salvation.

Paul quotes a prophesy of Moses and two additional passages from Isaiah to verify that this truth was revealed in the Old Testament. The truth was there but the Jewish heart had become so hardened through legalism that it couldn't perceive this truth.

Romans 10:1-21
Discipleship Questions

. . . .

*Answer the following questions by reading the corresponding
discipleship commentary lesson and using your Bible.*

1. Read Romans 10:1. What was the Apostle Paul's heart's desire and prayer?

    _____

2. Read Romans 10:2. Israel, the Jews, were devoted to God and had a zeal, but it was not according to what?_____

3. Read Romans 10:3.The Jewish people were ignorant of what?

    _____

4. Read Romans 10:3. What were the Jews going about to establish?

    _____

5. According to Titus 3:5, can the righteousness that belongs to us save us?

    _____

6. According to Titus 3:5, how does God save us?_____

7. Does mercy ask that we get what we deserve, or that we get what we don't deserve?

    _____

8. How was the criminal in Luke 23:39-43 saved?_____

9. How was the tax collector in Luke 18:9-14 saved?_____

10. Read Romans 10:3. In going about to establish our own righteousness, to what did we fail to submit? _____

11. Read Romans 10:4. Christ is the end of what? (for those who believe in Him).

    _____

12. Read Romans 10:5. How did Moses describe the righteousness which is of the Law?

    _____

13. Read Romans 10:6-8. The righteousness which is of faith can be described as what?

    _____

14. What are the necessary elements of salvation according to Romans 10:9?

    _____

    _____

15. What does it mean to confess Jesus as Lord? _____
_____
_____

16. How does Luke 6:46 show us that confessing Jesus' Lordship is not just saying the words, "Jesus is Lord"? _____

17. What does Luke 6:47-49 reveal about Jesus Lordship?
_____

18. Read 1 Corinthians 15:14-17 and Romans 4:25. What is the importance of believing God has raised Jesus from the dead?_____

19. Read Romans 10:10. With the heart man believes. What is the result of this?
_____

20. With the mouth **confession** is made unto salvation (Rom.10:10). What was the eunuch's confession in Acts 8:35-38? _____

21. The Lord is rich unto all that call upon Him (Rom.10:12). Describe how the tax collector called on the Lord in Luke 18:9-14. _____

22. Describe how Saul called on the Lord in Acts 22:16.
_____
_____

23. Read Romans 10:14. What must a person do first before he or she calls upon the Lord?
_____

24. Read Romans 10:14. What must happen before a person believes?
_____

25. Read Romans 10:14. One cannot hear about Christ without what happening first?
_____

26. Read Romans 10:15. The Gospel is synonymous with hearing what?
_____

27. Read Romans 10:16. To obey the Gospel you must what?_____

28. Read Romans 10:17. How does faith come?_____

29. Read Romans 10:17. Faith comes by hearing what?
_____

30. Read Romans 10:18-19. Did the Jews hear the message of Christ? _____

31. God was found by people not even looking for Him. Does Romans 10:20 teach this?

_____

_____

32. Read Romans 10:21. How did the Jews respond to God's offer of salvation?

_____

Romans 10:1-21
Discipleship Answer Key

. . . .

Do not look at the answer key until you have completed the questions.
Compare your answers with the following answers.

1. Read Romans 10:1. What was the Apostle Paul's heart's desire and prayer?
That the Israelites might be saved.

2. Read Romans 10:2. Israel, the Jews, were devoted to God and had a zeal, but it was not according to what?
True knowledge.

3. Read Romans 10:3.The Jewish people were ignorant of what?
God's righteousness, i.e., that Christ died to make them right with God (2 Cor. 5:21).

4. Read Romans 10:3. What were the Jews going about to establish?
Their own righteousness, i.e. a righteousness belonging to themselves.

5. According to Titus 3:5, can the righteousness that belongs to us save us?
No. Not by works of righteousness which we have done are we saved.

6. According to Titus 3:5, how does God save us?
According to His mercy.

7. Does mercy ask that we get what we deserve, or that we get what we don't deserve?
What we don't deserve.

8. How was the criminal in Luke 23:39-43 saved?
By Jesus' mercy.

9. How was the tax collector in Luke 18:9-14 saved?
By God's mercy and grace.

10. Read Romans 10:3. In going about to establish our own righteousness, to what did we fail to submit?
The righteousness that comes from God.

11. Read Romans 10:4. Christ is the end of what (for those who believe in Him)?
The Law as a means of achieving righteousness before God.

12. Read Romans 10:5. How did Moses describe the righteousness which is of the Law?
With the word "doeth" or "doing" (things that we do).

13. Read Romans 10:6-8. The righteousness which is of faith can be described as what?
Done.

14. What are the necessary elements of salvation according to Romans 10:9?
    (1) Confess Jesus as Lord.
    (2) Believe that God has raised Him from the dead.

15. What does it mean to confess Jesus as Lord?
    We don't make Him Lord; He is already Lord. We set our lives in agreement with His Lordship. He is boss, He is Lord, He is the one who has the right to control our lives. Not that we do everything perfectly, but it is a change of direction.

16. How does Luke 6:46 show us that confessing Jesus' Lordship is not just saying the words, "Jesus is Lord"?
    Why say He is Lord if you won't obey Him?

17. What does Luke 6:47-49 reveal about Jesus Lordship?
    It is not enough to hear God's Word you must also do it (that is, put it into practice), because you trust and believe Him.

18. Read 1 Corinthians 15:14-17 and Romans 4:25. What is the importance of believing God has raised Jesus from the dead?
    It is essential to salvation (Rom. 10:9).

19. Read Romans 10:10. With the heart man believes. What is the result of this?
    Justification.

20. With the mouth **confession** is made unto salvation (Rom.10:10). What was the eunuch's confession in Acts 8:35-38?
    "I believe that Jesus Christ is the Son of God."

21. The Lord is rich unto all that call upon Him (Rom.10:12). Describe how the tax collector called on the Lord in Luke 18:9-14.
    "God be merciful to me a sinner!"

22. Describe how Saul called on the Lord in Acts 22:16.
    It is time you were baptized and had your sins washed away while invoking his name (Acts 22:16b, Jerusalem Bible).

23. Read Romans 10:14. What must a person do first before he or she calls upon the Lord?
    Believe.

24. Read Romans 10:14. What must happen before a person believes?
    He must hear about Christ.

25. Read Romans 10:14. One cannot hear about Christ without what happening first?
    Christ being preached, testified of, or proclaimed.

26. Read Romans 10:15. The Gospel is synonymous with hearing what?
    Glad tidings of good things.

27. Read Romans 10:16. To obey the Gospel you must what?
Believe it.

28. Read Romans 10:17. How does faith come?
By hearing.

29. Read Romans 10:17. Faith comes by hearing what?
The Word of God or the Word of Christ (the Gospel).

30. Read Romans 10:18-19. Did the Jews hear the message of Christ?
Yes.

31. God was found by people not even looking for Him. Does Romans 10:20 teach this?
Yes, the scripture states, "I (God) was made manifest unto them that asked not after me."

32. Read Romans 10:21. How did the Jews respond to God's offer of salvation?
By being disobedient and refusing to come to Him.

OVERVIEW OF ROMANS CHAPTER 11

by Andrew Wommack

We are drawing toward the end of the book of Romans. The major doctrine being presented is that the grace of God *is* the Gospel. The point has already been made that the Gospel and the grace of God are interchangeable. In the ninth and tenth chapters Paul began talking about the application of this to the nation of Israel. They prided themselves on being God's chosen people, not because they were walking in faith with Him and believing Him, but because they thought they had access to Him through their physical birth and genealogy.

Paul began to disprove this belief in the ninth chapter and continues in 11:1: *"I say then, Hath God cast away his people? God forbid. For I also am an Israelite."* What he begins to say is; "As a whole, yes, the Jewish nation fell from favor because they were trusting in the fact that they were born Jews rather than believing God." He goes on to make the point that it is the people who have faith in God who are the true people of God. He made that same point in Romans 2:28 very clearly, saying, *"For He is not a Jew, which is one outwardly, neither is that circumcision, which is outward in the flesh."* True circumcision is that which is in the heart.

The true people of God today are those Jews or Gentiles who have put their faith in Jesus. Does that mean there is no benefit to the nation of Israel? No, because he goes on in this chapter to say there will be a time that the nation of Israel as a whole turns back to their faith in the Lord. He also issues a warning to the Gentiles that they, like a wild olive tree, were grafted into the good tree and have become a part of it (God's Kingdom), while the others were broken off because of unbelief. He says if God can graft a wild branch into this olive tree, how much more could he take the original (the nation of Israel) and graft it back in, and we could be broken off. The point is, don't be proud thinking, "Now the church has replaced and displaced the nation of Israel," and trust in something other than God. The same thing could happen to you that happened to the nation of Israel.

I want to point out some things in verse 6 where he is talking again about how the election of God, that is, who He chooses and who is accepted—whether on an individual or national basis, is not based on good works, or on genealogy, but rather on faith. *"And if by grace, then it is no more of works: otherwise grace is no more grace. But if it be of works, then is it no more grace: otherwise work is no more work."* That's a little confusing to some because it's Elizabethan (or old) English.

Paul is basically saying you are either saved and in right standing with God by grace or by works. It is either by grace without any work-effort on your part, or it is by work without any grace on God's part. He is saying you can't mix faith and works together—faith in the grace of God and faith in your own works. You are saved by one or the other, but not by a combination of the two.

This is very important because there are a lot of people today who would say, "Oh, yes, I know that I can't really earn the favor of God. It is by God's grace that everything is available to me—but it's not only grace. God's grace makes everything available, but then I have to work and do a certain measure. Maybe I don't have to be perfect, as good as Jesus was, but I have to be pretty good—better than this person over here." That's what the Pharisees and scribes did in the time of Jesus.

One Pharisee prayed, "Father, I thank you that I'm not like other men, like this publican over here." He was comparing himself with other people and there are lots of people today who do the same thing. They have a sense of pride in their own actions and say, "Well, I'm not only trusting in myself. It is the grace of God, but it is also my goodness that makes God answer my prayers."

This verse is totally dispelling that, saying it is either grace without works or works without grace. You have to put faith in what God did for you (grace), not works (what you do for God). It is completely God's grace. That is a scripture God has used to minister to me, and I have shared it with a lot of people.

Paul then talks about how the nation of Israel got out of faith—trusting in their own genealogy, performance, religious observances, hour of prayer, and synagogues—and was basically like a theocracy. They trusted in all of the religious trappings instead of trusting in a personal relationship with God, but he does say that in the end the entire nation will be gathered back to the Lord.

Verses 25-27: *"For I would not, brethren, that ye should be ignorant of this mystery, lest ye should be wise in your own conceits; that blindness in part is happened to Israel, until the fullness of the Gentiles be come in. And so all Israel shall be saved; as it is written, There shall come out of Sion the Deliverer, and shall turn away ungodliness from Jacob. For this is my covenant unto them, when I shall take away their sins."* He says the nation of Israel is coming back. I don't understand all of this. It is a prophetic statement and there are people who claim to understand it completely, but actually there is no way to verify whether they understand it because it hasn't happened yet.

In the future, there will be a restoration of Israel back to faith in God, and some people will be upset saying, "That doesn't seem fair to take a nation that has basically renounced the Lord and gone contrary to Him all this time yet, because at one time Abraham was faithful, there will be this restoration and God is going to do something special and bring all these people back to Himself." All this does is once again heighten the fact that it is not according to good works, but according to the grace of God. He extended grace towards Abraham and his descendants, and though as a whole they rejected that grace and suffered greatly for it, there is coming a future time of restoration. This amplifies once again that it is the grace of God that does these things, not our own goodness.

Verse 29: *"For the gifts and calling of God are without repentance."* In context, this is specifically talking about the nation of Israel coming back into relationship with God, but there is a great application of this to all kinds of things. I have had many people come to me who at one time were really in love with the Lord, seeking Him, and had Him working in their life. They felt His call on their lives and flowed in the gifts of the Spirit, but fell into sin, or discouragement, and renounced Him. They had been away from Him for years, then came back, talked to me, and made a new commitment, but are lamenting, "I've lost everything God gave me. What do I do now? One time it was so good and now I have lost it."

This says the gifts and callings of God are without repentance. You may have stepped out from the blessings God has placed on your life, turned your back on your call and obedience to God, and gone through all these things, but God has never changed His call or His purpose for your life. Anything you ever had with Him, no matter what you have gone through, you can reactivate if you repent and get into faith again. It may seem that you are so far off track that you say, "No, God couldn't get me back on track from where I am." But God in His wisdom can plot a course from where you are right back into the center of His will.

Another application of this is that if you have had healing in your body, walked away, and the sickness returned, you think, "What am I going to do? I was healed at one time, but I've lost it." This verse says the gifts and callings of God are without repentance. The same power that flowed in your body at one time to bring you absolute, total health is still in you. It's just a matter of releasing it once again by faith.

The tremendous things spoken here lead into Romans 12, which will be dealt with next. That is the chapter God used to transform my life.

Romans 11:1-36
Discipleship Commentary

. . . .

Read the entire lesson and then answer the questions that follow.

Romans 11:1 - I say then, Hath God cast away his people? God forbid. For I also am an Israelite, of the seed of Abraham, of the tribe of Benjamin.

(Rom. 11:1) Paul's message of grace and his announcement that Gentiles could now become a part of the true Israel of God through the new birth without becoming Jews was a startling revelation. Paul had systematically dealt with objections that a legalistic Jew would have to such a message. Now he answers the criticism that this would mean God has forsaken the Jewish nation.

Basically, Paul is saying that Jews are not excluded, they just aren't favored over the Gentiles. He cites himself as an example of a believing Jew and compares the status of Israel to that of the Jewish nation in the days of Elijah. In the same way that there were 7,000 true worshipers of God left in Israel in Elijah's day (1 Kings 19:18), so there was a remnant of believing Jews in Paul's day.

The rest of this chapter is Paul's explanation of Israel's current relationship to God during the church era.

Romans 11:2-6 - God hath not cast away his people which he foreknew. Wot ye not what the scripture saith of Elias? how he maketh intercession to God against Israel, saying, 3) Lord, they have killed thy prophets, and digged down thine altars; and I am left alone, and they seek my life. 4) But what saith the answer of God unto him? I have reserved to myself seven thousand men, who have not bowed the knee to the image of Baal. 5) Even so then at this present time also there is a remnant according to the election of grace. 6) And if by grace, then is it no more of works: otherwise grace is no more grace. But if it be of works, then is it no more grace: otherwise work is no more work.

(Rom. 11:6) Paul stated the doctrine of justification by grace through faith so clearly in his writings that any person who claims to believe the Bible has to acknowledge this truth. However, one of Satan's cleverest deceptions is to take a truth and add to it until it is no longer the truth. Lest that happen with this doctrine of grace, Paul states emphatically that we cannot combine anything with God's grace as a requirement for salvation.

In the same way that gasoline and water don't mix, so grace and works will not mix. Justification has to be all works or all grace, but not a combination of the two.

In this epistle, Paul had repeatedly made his point of justification by grace through faith. He had repeatedly stressed that faith is the only requirement on our part. He is repeating that point once again in perhaps his clearest words yet. Still, there is an abundance of religious people today who cannot accept the fact that all we have to do is to believe to receive God's grace (Rom. 5:2). This verse leaves no alternatives.

Romans 11:7-8 - What then? Israel hath not obtained that which he seeketh for; but the election hath obtained it, and the rest were blinded 8) (According as it is written, God hath given them the spirit of slumber, eyes that they should not see, and ears that they should not hear;) unto this day.

(Rom. 11:8) This appears to be a paraphrase of a Bible truth that is expressed in many scriptures.

Romans 11:9 - And David saith, Let their table be made a snare, and a trap, and a stumblingblock, and a recompence unto them:

(Rom. 11:9) This quotation from David comes from Psalm 69:22-23 (below). In this psalm, David was prophesying about the suffering of Christ in the first person as if David himself was actually describing his own suffering. Additionally, there are seven other very clear references to Christ in this chapter which were quoted in the New Testament as having a direct fulfillment in Jesus (1st - Ps. 69:4 fulfilled in John 15:25; 2nd - Ps. 69:9a fulfilled in John 2:17; 3rd - Ps. 69:9b fulfilled in Rom. 15:3; 4th - Ps. 69:21a fulfilled in Matt. 27:34; Mark 15:23; Luke 23:36; 5th - Ps. 69:21b fulfilled in Matt. 27:48; Mark 15:36; John 19:28-30; 6th - Ps. 69:22 fulfilled in Rom. 11:9; and 7th - Ps. 69:25 fulfilled in Acts 1:20). Also Psalm 69:8 was certainly fulfilled in Jesus (John 7:5) although this passage was not quoted in the New Testament.

Therefore, Psalm 69 is a prophetic psalm where Christ is describing His earthly ministry and crucifixion. The denunciation of Psalm 69:22-23 is given by Christ against those who crucified him. When understood in this context, it is easy to see that this blindness and deafness didn't cause the Jews' rejection, but it was the Jews' rejection that caused this pronouncement.

All of this is to say that God is not unjust and has never taken away a person's freedom of choice unless that individual or nation had already exercised that choice against Him.

Romans 11:10-11 - Let their eyes be darkened, that they may not see, and bow down their back alway. 11) I say then, Have they stumbled that they should fall? God forbid: but rather through their fall salvation is come unto the Gentiles, for to provoke them to jealousy.

(Rom. 11:11) The Greek word translated "fall" here is "pipto" signiying "a complete irrevocable fall" (Rienecker's). Paul is saying, "Is this rejection of Jesus by the Jews irrevocable?" The answer is no.

The Amplified Bible reads, "So I ask, have they stumbled so as to fall to their utter spiritual ruin, irretrievably? By no means!" The New International Version reads, "Again I ask: Did they stumble so as to fall beyond recovery? Not at all!"

Paul then begins to relate how the Jews can still be saved during this "church age," and he cites Old Testament scriptures to declare a future time when the whole nation of Israel will once again come back into God's fold (vv. 26-27).

Romans 11:12-15 - Now if the fall of them be the riches of the world, and the diminishing of them the riches of the Gentiles; how much more their fulness 13) For I speak to you Gentiles, inasmuch as I am the apostle of the Gentiles, I magnify mine office: 14) If by any means I may provoke to emulation them which are my flesh, and might save some of them. 15) For if the casting away of them be the reconciling of the world, what shall the receiving of them be, but life from the dead?

(Rom. 11:15) Paul had conclusively proven that the Jews did not have a monopoly on God. The Gentiles could now come directly to God without becoming Jews. He had also stated that the Jewish nation as a whole had rejected God, because they denied the concept of a Savior. They had become their own savior.

This could leave some Jew wondering if the Jews had been forsaken by God. Paul answers this question in this chapter. There was still a remnant of Jews who were heirs through faith (Rom. 11:5).

In this passage of Scripture, Paul draws a conclusion. If the Jews rejection of Christ opened up salvation to the rest of the world, then what would happen when the Jews turned back to God? It will be resurrection from the dead! Paul's statement that the return of the Jews to their God will be life from the dead could be an analogy. That is, Paul could be comparing the Jews return to God to the joy and blessing that would come from seeing a friend raised from the dead. Or Paul could be speaking literally, saying that the time the Jews return to God will be at the end of the world and the return of Christ when the dead shall be raised.

In either case, Paul is stressing the facts that there will be a future spiritual restoration of Israel and great blessing on the world as a result.

Romans 11:16-18 - For if the firstfruit be holy, the lump is also holy: and if the root be holy, so are the branches. 17) And if some of the branches be broken off, and thou, being a wild olive tree, wert graffed in among them, and with them partakest of the root and fatness of the olive tree; 18) Boast not against the branches. But if thou boast, thou bearest not the root, but the root thee.

(Rom. 11:18) Paul is warning the Gentiles against gloating in the fact that salvation had now been opened unto them as though it happened because of some goodness on their part. It wasn't earned; it was God's grace. Paul explains that the Jews' unbelief (v. 20) caused them to be broken off and that the same thing could happen to the Gentiles (v. 21) if they didn't stand strong through faith.

Romans 11:19-22 - Thou wilt say then, The branches were broken off, that I might be graffed in. 20) Well; because of unbelief they were broken off, and thou standest by faith. Be not highminded, but fear: 21) For if God spared not the natural branches, take heed lest he also spare not thee. 22) Behold therefore the goodness and severity of God: on them which fell, severity; but toward thee, goodness, if thou continue in his goodness: otherwise thou also shalt be cut off.

(Rom. 11:22) Even in the midst of God's judgment there is mercy. The people who suffered destruction, for instance, during Noah's flood and the overthrow of Sodom and Gomorrah, experienced the severity of God. But these judgments were actually an act of mercy upon the world as a whole. During those times, sin was so rampant on the earth that it was like a cancer. God did radical surgery on mankind by removing these vile sinners and, therefore, allowed the human race as a whole to survive.

Likewise, God's turning from the Jewish nation to the Gentiles had both severity and goodness in it. It had severe consequences for the Jews, but it blessed the rest of the world.

Romans 11:23 - And they also, if they abide not still in unbelief, shall be graffed in: for God is able to graff them in again.

(Rom. 11:23) God is not only "able" to restore the Jewish nation, but Paul goes on to say in verse 26 that all Israel "will" be saved.

Romans 11:24-25 - For if thou wert cut out of the olive tree which is wild by nature, and wert graffed contrary to nature into a good olive tree: how much more shall these, which be the natural branches, be graffed into their own olive tree? 25) For I would not, brethren, that ye should be ignorant of this mystery, lest ye should be wise in your own conceits; that blindness in part is happened to Israel, until the fulness of the Gentiles be come in.

(Rom. 11:25) This phrase "fulness of the Gentiles" is only used here. A similar expression, "times of the Gentiles" is used in Luke 21:24. There are two obvious ways this phrase could be interpreted.

First, the fullness of the Gentiles could be referring to all the Gentiles which are foreordained to come to Christ and experience salvation. Then there would be a wonderful move of God among the Jews, in which the Jewish nation as a whole would come to the Lord (v. 26). The Amplified Translation would lend itself to this interpretation: "a hardening (insensibility) has temporarily befallen a part of Israel to last until the full number of the ingathering of the Gentiles has come in."

This phrase could also be referring to the time when the Gentiles would no longer be dominating the Jewish nation, specifically referring to the occupation of Jerusalem by the Gentiles. This is apparently what Luke 21:24 is referring to. If so, then there will have to be a future fulfillment of the scriptures that prophesied the end of Gentile control of Jerusalem, since Israel has physically possessed Jerusalem since the Israel-Arab War of 1967, and yet, the nation as a whole has not come to God.

Romans 11:26-36 - And so all Israel shall be saved: as it is written, There shall come out of Sion the Deliverer, and shall turn away ungodliness from Jacob: 27) For this is my covenant unto them, when I shall take away their sins. 28) As concerning the gospel, they are enemies for your sakes: but as touching the election, they are beloved for the fathers' sakes. 29) For the gifts and calling of God are without repentance. 30) For as ye in times past have not believed God, yet have now obtained mercy through their unbelief: 31) Even so have these also now not believed, that through your mercy they also may obtain mercy. 32) For God hath concluded them all in unbelief, that he might have mercy upon all. 33) O the depth of the riches both of the wisdom and knowledge of God! how unsearchable are his judgments, and his ways past finding out! 34) For who hath known the mind of the Lord? or who hath been his counsellor? 35) Or who hath first given to him, and it shall be recompensed unto him again? 36) For of him, and through him, and to him, are all things: to whom be glory for ever. Amen.

(Rom. 11:29) In context, this is speaking about the future restoration of the Jewish nation. Paul is saying that even though the Jews had rejected God, the Lord was still going to bring His promises to the Jews to pass. This is an act of total grace on the Lord's part.

This scripture has a broader application too. Any calling, or gift to accomplish that calling, that the Lord gives an individual is without repentance. This means that regardless of what an individual does, God doesn't withdraw His gifts and callings. This is why some ministers who fall into sin can still see the supernatural gifts of God flow in their ministries.

That is not to say that living a life separated unto God is not important; it is very important. A person who is living in sin is going to have their faith made shipwreck through their conscience (1 Tim. 1:19). They will begin to lose effectiveness. However, as much as they can operate in faith, the gifts and callings of God that they received are still there and will function.

Anything you've ever received from God is still there; it just needs to be activated by faith.

Romans 11:1-36
Discipleship Questions

. . . .

*Answer the following questions by reading the corresponding
discipleship commentary lesson and using your Bible.*

1. Read Romans 11:1. What is the question being asked in Romans 11:1?
   _____

2. Read Romans 11:1. What is the answer to that question?
   _____

3. Read Romans 11:1. Paul's proof that God has not cast away the Israelites is what?
   _____

4. Read Romans 11:2-4. What is further proof that God did not reject the Jews?
   _____

5. At this present time (according to Romans 11:5), God has done what?
   _____

6. Read Romans 11:5-6. His choice is based upon what? _____
   _____

7. What is the conclusion to Paul's statements in Romans 11:7? _____
   _____

8. Read Romans 11:11. The Jews stumbled at Christ as their righteousness. Did they fall
   beyond recovery? _____

9. Read Romans 11:11. Who did the fall of the Jews open salvation to?
   _____

10. What is Paul's conclusion in Romans 11:12? _____
    _____
    _____

11. How does Acts 13:43-48 echo the words in Romans 11:14?_____
    _____

12. Read Romans 11:15. The Jews' rejection of Christ opened the Gospel (reconciliation) to the
    world. Their acceptance of Christ will be like what?_____

13. Read Romans 11:16-24. What illustrations does Paul give to explain what has happened to the Jews and the Gentiles?_____

_____

_____

14. How does Romans 11:25 explain the previous verses? _____

_____

15. Read Romans 11:25-26 and Romans 2:28-29. How shall we interpret the phrase "so all Israel shall be saved"? _____

_____

16. Read Hebrews 8:7-13. What is the covenant described in Romans 11:27? What does Romans 11:28-29 mean? Also read Romans 9:6-8 and Romans 11:1-4.

_____

_____

_____

_____

_____

17. What is the key word found in Romans 11:30-32?_____

18. What is mercy? _____

_____

19. In Romans 11:30, to whom is God showing mercy? _____

20. In Romans 11:31, to whom is God showing mercy?_____

21. In Romans 11:32, to whom is God showing mercy?_____

_____

22. In Romans 1:16-17, to whom is the Gospel of Christ offered?_____

23. In Romans 11:33-36, Paul gives God praise for His wisdom, shown to us in salvation. How does 1 Corinthians 2:7-8 show us this? _____

_____

24. The New Century Version translates Romans 11:33-36 in the following way: "Yes, God's riches are very great, and his wisdom and knowledge have no end! No one can explain the things God decides or understand his ways. As the Scripture says, 'Who has known the mind of the Lord, or who has been able to give him advice?' (Isaiah 40:13). 'No one has ever given God anything that he must pay back.' (Job 41:11). Yes, God made all things, and everything continues through Him and for Him. To Him be glory forever! Amen." How could you summarize this doxology?_____

_____

_____

Romans 11:1-36
Discipleship Answer Key

1. Read Romans 11:1. What is the question being asked in Romans 11:1?
   Did God reject His own people?

2. Read Romans 11:1. What is the answer to that question?
   God forbid, certainly not, by no means!

3. Read Romans 11:1. Paul's proof that God has not cast away the Israelites is what?
   That he himself is an Israelite.

4. Read Romans 11:2-4. What is further proof that God did not reject the Jews?
   God kept for Himself seven thousand Jews who did not worship false gods.

5. At this present time (according to Romans 11:5), God has done what?
   Chosen a small number because of His mercy and grace.

6. Read Romans 11:5-6. His choice is based upon what?
   Grace: not based upon what men have done or do, otherwise it would not be true mercy (grace).

7. What is the conclusion to Paul's statements in Romans 11:7?
   Israel did not find the right-standing with God that it was looking for, but a small group, chosen by God did.

8. Read Romans 11:11. The Jews stumbled at Christ as their righteousness. Did they fall beyond recovery?
   God forbid!

9. Read Romans 11:11. Who did the fall of the Jews open salvation to?
   The Gentiles, the whole world.

10. What is Paul's conclusion in Romans 11:12?
    The Living Bible states, **"Now if the whole world became rich as a result of God's offer of salvation, when the Jews stumble over it and turned it down, think how much greater a blessing the world will share in later on when the Jews, too, come to Christ."**

11. How does Acts 13:43-48 echo the words in Romans 11:14?
    "When the Jews noticed the crowds, they became terribly jealous"

12. Read Romans 11:15. The Jews' rejection of Christ opened the Gospel (reconciliation) to the world. Their acceptance of Christ will be like what?
Life from the dead.

13. Read Romans 11:16-24. What illustrations does Paul give to explain what has happened to the Jews and the Gentiles?
An offering of the firstfruits, and a tree with roots and branches. Grafting a wild olive branch into a good olive tree (Gentiles receiving what was first meant for the Jews).

14. How does Romans 11:25 explain the previous verses?
That blindness in part has happened to Israel, until the full number of the Gentiles come in (are saved).

15. Read Romans 11:25-26 and Romans 2:28-29. How shall we interpret the phrase "so all Israel shall be saved"?
"A hardening has come upon a part of Israel, until the full number of the Gentiles come in." Giving the Gentiles the opportunity to hear and receive the Gospel.

16. Read Hebrews 8:7-13. What is the covenant described in Romans 11:27? What does Romans 11:28-29 mean? Also read Romans 9:6-8 and Romans 11:1-4.
As concerning the Gospel (of Jesus Christ), they (the Jews) are enemies for your sakes (which is to the Gentiles' advantage). But as touching the election (those Jews that God has chosen), they are beloved (the object of God's love) for the fathers' sakes (for the sake of Abraham, Isaac, and Jacob to whom God gave the promise of a spiritual seed). For God's gifts and His call can never be withdrawn; He will never go back on His promises.

17. What is the key word found in Romans 11:30-32?
Mercy.

18. What is mercy?
To give you what you don't deserve—kind, compassionate, and forgiving treatment.

19. In Romans 11:30, to whom is God showing mercy?
The Gentiles.

20. In Romans 11:31, to whom is God showing mercy?
The Jews.

21. In Romans 11:32, to whom is God showing mercy?
All of mankind, both Jews and Gentiles.

22. In Romans 1:16-17, to whom is the Gospel of Christ offered?
To the Jew first and also to the Greek.

23. In Romans 11:33-36, Paul gives God praise for His wisdom, shown to us in salvation. How does 1 Corinthians 2:7-8 show us this?
God's hidden wisdom was ordained before the world began for our benefit. None of the princes of this world knew about it. If they had known it, they would not have crucified the Lord of glory.

The New Century Version translates Romans 11:33-36 in the following way: "Yes, God's riches are very great, and his wisdom and knowledge have no end! No one can explain the things God decides or understand his ways. As the Scripture says, 'Who has known the mind of the Lord, or who has been able to give him advice?' (Isaiah 40:13). 'No one has ever given God anything that he must pay back.' (Job 41:11). Yes, God made all things, and everything continues through Him and for Him. To Him be glory forever! Amen." How could you summarize this doxology?

OVERVIEW OF ROMANS CHAPTER 12

by Andrew Wommack

We now come to Romans 12. God used the first few verses of this chapter to transform my life. I have come to love the entire Word of God, but this is one of the very first supernatural revelations God gave me. When I was only 18 years old and seeking Him for His will for my life, I came across these verses, and they totally changed my life. I have hours and hours of teaching on just the first two verses, and of course the whole chapter is powerful, but let me emphasize these verses.

Romans 12:1-2: *"I beseech you therefore, brethren, by the mercies of God, that ye present your bodies a living sacrifice, holy, acceptable unto God, which is your reasonable service. And be not conformed to this world: but be ye transformed by the renewing of your mind, that ye may prove what is that good, and acceptable, and perfect, will of God."* The phrase at the end of verse 2 is what got my attention, because I wanted to know God's will for my life. It says if you will do these things then you will prove God's will. The word "prove" means to make manifest to your physical senses or, in other words, to make evident, to reveal, to take off the cover.

I knew God had a purpose for my life, but I didn't know what it was. I was seeking desperately, and here the Lord said to do these things and I will make manifest to my physical senses the good, acceptable, and perfect will of God. That grabbed my attention, and I just began to study these verses until I received revelation from them.

The Lord taught me in verse 1 that the first thing you have to do is make yourself a living sacrifice, which is only your reasonable service. This isn't just for those who want to go deeper into God than the average. Every born-again Christian should have this attitude that you should be a living sacrifice to God. It isn't just for the super saints but also for Joe-Blow-Christian. God wants every person to be a living sacrifice.

Notice it also says in the first part of the verse, *"I beseech you by the mercies of God."* This isn't something He is doing because He is going to get you if you don't. It's because of His goodness. If you truly understood how good God is, if you truly understood that He has a perfect plan for your life, you would be willing to submit yourself to Him as a living sacrifice.

In the Old Testament, when they bound an animal to the altar, it had zero rights, zero ability to do anything—it was about to be killed. This says that you are supposed to be a living sacrifice, which is a continual process. It isn't something you do one time in a crisis situation where you say, "God, if you get me out of this, I promise I will serve you." You don't just make the commitment one time … you make a commitment that is continual—a living commitment, something you do over and over and over.

The problem with a living sacrifice is that it keeps crawling off the altar. It has to be done over and over, and you need to constantly make yourself a living sacrifice. Actually, what the Lord taught me through this is that God's will for my life, and actually for all our lives, is to be a living sacrifice. That is His will for your life, and how He uses you, such as me being a minister or you being an electrician or Wall Street trader, this is actually a secondary thing. The number one will, the general will of God for every person, is to be a living sacrifice.

If you make yourself a living sacrifice and are totally committed to God, you won't have to worry about how He is going to use you. That's like a person building a great ocean liner. Once it is built, what do you do with it? You immediately put it out to sea. The builder who builds it can use it. If you make yourself available to God as a living sacrifice and let Him work His nature and character into your life, as soon as you become usable, you will be used.

The Lord told me that. He told never again to pray, "God, use me," but instead to say, "God, make me usable." That is a wonderful truth, a wonderful revelation. You need to pray, "O God, make me a living sacrifice."

The second step in verse 2 says, *"And be not conformed to this world."* That word "conformed" means to be poured into the mold of this world. Nobody goes through life unchanged. You come into life absolutely innocent, ready to be molded and changed, and life's pressures, experience, peer pressure, desires, etc. begin to melt you. You are going to be melted and fitted into the mold of something. You can't go from cradle to grave without being shaped and molded, but the good news is that you get to choose what mold you fit into. You don't have to let your negative circumstances ruin your life. You don't have to become bitter because of bad circumstances; you can become better. You have a choice. He is telling you not to be conformed (poured into the mold) to this world.

How do you keep from doing that? It says, *"But be ye transformed by the renewing of your mind."* It's the way you think that determines your actions, your attitudes, everything else, and you can be transformed. This word "transformed" is the Greek word "metamorphoo," and it's where we get the word "metamorphosis" from. If you want to be like a little worm that spins a cocoon and comes out a butterfly, if you want to change from a creepy, crawly thing to something that is beautiful and flies, then the way to do it is by renewing your mind.

Everything you will need from God was placed in you when you were born again. You already have it. The rest of your Christian life is not trying to obtain more from God but rather is a renewing of your mind so you can begin thinking like a winner, so you can believe, operate in faith, and release the life of God inside you—not go get it. That is a wonderful truth, a tremendous revelation, and most people haven't seen it. You will be transformed by the renewing of your mind. Your little heart is perfect, and the only problem is your head.

I'm not ministering to your spirit. If you are born again, you know the truth in your heart, and in your spirit, but you need your mind renewed. If you have a problem today, it is right between your ears, and if you will renew your mind as you are going through this series, the truth will set you free (John 8:32). God's Word is the truth that sets you free (John 17:17).

Let's go to verse 3. Paul is talking about not being arrogant, not thinking of yourself more highly than you ought, but to think soberly. The end of the verse says, *"According as God hath dealt to every man the measure of faith."* The King James Bible says "the measure of faith." There are some translations that say "a measure of faith," but I really believe it's correctly translated in the King James when it says that God has dealt to every man (and it's understood that he is talking about every Christian man or woman) the measure of faith.

If I was serving soup and had just one ladle, when I dipped soup and poured it into the bowls, everyone would get the same measure because I only had one ladle. The importance of this is for you to recognize that God didn't give us different amounts of faith. When you were born again, you were given the same faith I have, that anybody has. You were given the same faith Paul had, and he said in Galatians 2:20 that the faith he had was the faith of the Son of God. You were given the exact same measure of faith Jesus had when He walked on this earth and performed His miracles. It isn't a matter of different measures of faith—it's just learning to use the faith. You have to renew your mind and start releasing the faith of God, but we all have the same faith.

He then goes on to say that we have different gifts, but we can all operate with the faith that God gives us and see things work. There are gifts listed here that are different from those in 1 Corinthians 12—gifts of administration, exhortaton (lifting others up), etc., which are spiritual giftings from God that are just as important as the gifts of miracles and healing. They all function in the body, and you may have one of these gifts.

The book of Romans, specifically chapter 12, is a life-changing teaching that has revolutionized my life. I encourage you to let God open it up and change your life through this study.

Romans 12:1-21
Discipleship Commentary

Read the entire lesson and then answer the questions that follow.

Romans 12:1 - I beseech you therefore, brethren, by the mercies of God, that ye present your bodies a living sacrifice, holy, acceptable unto God, which is your reasonable service.

(Rom. 12:1) Paul was speaking to Christians. It is possible to commit our lives to the Lord for the purpose of salvation, and yet not be yielded to the Lord in our daily lives. It is only when we are total sacrifices that we begin to see God's perfect will manifest through our lives.

Paul uses the mercies of God to encourage these Romans to give themselves totally to God. Today, most preachers use the wrath of God to try and drive men to God. There are some people who need the condemnation of the Law to make them aware of their need for a Savior, but as a whole, we could "draw more flies with honey than with vinegar." It's the goodness of God that leads men to repentance (Rom. 2:4).

Notice that we are the ones who have to make this presentation of our bodies to the Lord. He will not do it for us. Many people pray, "Lord, you do what you have to do to make me serve you." That is not a proper prayer. You cannot have someone lay hands on you to impart this commitment to you. You cannot just rebuke the flesh and expect it to disappear. You have to give your bodies to God as a living sacrifice daily.

This sounds like a contradiction of terms. How can we be a living sacrifice when sacrifices are always dead? This is speaking of the fact that offering ourselves to God is not just a one-time deal. We have to die to our own desires daily. This has to be a living, on going commitment to the Lord.

The Apollo spacecraft traveled to the moon, but it was not just as simple as blasting off and landing on the moon. There were course corrections made every ten minutes or so, for the entire trip. And then, they only landed a few feet inside the targeted landing area of 500 miles. Yet the missions were a success.

Likewise, there has to be a starting place for this decision to be a living sacrifice. We have to blast off, or start our journey, sometime. We don't ever "arrive" in this life. We just leave and start toward the goal (Phil. 3:12-14). We may be making course corrections every ten minutes for the rest of our lives.

You see, living sacrifices have a tendency to keep crawling off the altar. Every minute of every day, we have to reaffirm this decision to be totally separated unto God. This is what Paul is referring to by the term "living sacrifice."

Many Christians think that living a totally consecrated life to God is something that only preachers or a few lay people do. They see it as "extra" and not "normal" Christianity. However, Paul says this level of commitment is our reasonable service. Jesus died for each one of us. Each one of us ought to live for Him.

Romans 12:2 - And be not conformed to this world: but be ye transformed by the renewing of your mind, that ye may prove what is that good, and acceptable, and perfect, will of God.

(Rom. 12:2) Many people would think that if we fulfill the conditions of verse 1 that everything else would automatically work out. Yet Paul goes on to state that we also have to renew our minds. There have been many people who have had a genuine commitment to the Lord, but they didn't renew their minds through God's Word, and they suffered many problems that they didn't have to.

The Greek word that was translated "conformed" here is the word "suschematizo," meaning "to fashion alike; i.e., conform to the same pattern." This scripture is telling us that we should be different than the unbelievers. Most Christians recognize this, but they seem at a loss as to how to accomplish it. This verse goes on to give us the answer. The key is our minds. "As he thinketh in his heart, so is he" (Prov. 23:7).

If we think on the same things that the world thinks on, we are going to get the same results. If we keep our minds stayed upon God through the study of His Word and fellowship with Him, then we'll have perfect peace (Isa. 26:3). It's that simple.

The Greek word that was translated "transformed" here is the word "metamorphoo" and is the same word that we get our word "metamorphosis" from. It is describing a complete change like to that of a caterpillar changing into a butterfly. This word is also the same word that was used to describe Jesus' transformation when His garments became white as the light (Matt. 17:2).

Making our thinking line up with God's Word will effect this complete transformation in our lives.

When anyone is born again, the person becomes a totally new creation in his or her spirit. Their spiritual salvation is complete. They don't need any more faith, joy, or power. They are complete in Him (Col. 2:9-10).

However, it is not God's will that we just be changed on the inside; He wants to manifest this salvation in our physical lives. That takes place through the renewing of our minds.

Man is a spirit, soul, and body (1 Thess. 5:23). Our spirits are as perfect as they will ever be in heaven. If we will change our thinking so that we believe what God says in His Word about who we are, and what we have, then this agreement between our spirit and soul forms a majority and our flesh will experience the life of God that has been deposited in our spirits.

If we fail to renew our minds, we can live our entire time on this earth without experiencing the abundant life that Jesus provided for us (John 10:10).

The dictionary defines "prove" as "to establish the truth or validity of by evidence or argument; to be shown to be; turn out." Therefore, this is speaking of how to physically display God's will in our lives. This is a promise that if we fulfill the requirements of these two verses, we will prove, not might prove, but "will" prove the good and acceptable and perfect will of God.

Finding God's will for our lives is not hard when we do what these verses instruct us to do. As a matter of fact, it would be impossible to miss God's will once we commit ourselves to God as a living sacrifice and begin to renew our minds. Finding God's will for our lives only becomes hard when a person is not totally committed to God.

There is a difference of opinion among scholars, whether Paul is using "good, and acceptable, and perfect" to describe the will of God or if Paul is saying that there are stages in walking in the will of God (i.e., good, then acceptable, then the perfect will of God). Either of these cases would be doctrinally correct.

God's will certainly is good and acceptable and perfect. It is also true that no one moves immediately into everything that God has for them, but there is always growth into the things of God.

This is a wonderful promise that we can prove God's will in our lives. The first step is to make a total commitment of our lives to the Lord (a living sacrifice - v. 1). Actually, this is the will of God for everyone. Our vocation is secondary. God's will for every individual is to be a living sacrifice to Him. Once that is accomplished, more specific direction will come as we renew our minds.

If we try to find God's vocation for us, but don't present ourselves to God as a living sacrifice, then we are frustrating God's plan. God doesn't just want our service, He wants us. Once He gets us, He'll get our service.

Romans 12:3 - For I say, through the grace given unto me, to every man that is among you, not to think of himself more highly than he ought to think; but to think soberly, according as God hath dealt to every man the measure of faith.

(Rom. 12:3) Paul begins this sentence with the conjunction "for." This means that the point he is making in verse 3 is a continuation, or result, of what was said in verse 2. Many times the word "because" can be used interchangeably with "for."

Paul had just admonished them about humility and submission (a living sacrifice) being the way to true success. He now continues that thought by giving these people another reason for humility—the fact that every man has been dealt the "measure of faith."

In other words, there is a perfect plan for every believer's life, which they can "prove" if they will totally yield themselves to God. We may have a different gift but it is not a better gift than someone else's. He then continues in verse 4 with the word "for" again and draws a comparison from the way our bodies have different parts but all work together to make one body.

Religion has interpreted this verse to say that we should think of ourselves in a lowly manner, but that is not what Paul is saying. It would be proper to say that we shouldn't think of ourselves more highly or more lowly than we ought to think. We need to remember that any good thing that we have is a gift from God (1 Cor. 4:7). Paul is admonishing us to have the correct viewpoint, not a lowly viewpoint.

The dictionary defines "according as" as "in proportion to." Paul is saying that we need to remember that God has given every believer "the" measure of faith. The reason this sobers us up is because we recognize that what we have is a gift from God that every child of God possesses. Some live up to more of their potential than others, but it's all God's mercy that makes it possible for any of us to accomplish anything.

God has dealt to every man "the" measure of faith, not "a" measure of faith. There are not different measures with God. The Lord doesn't give one person great faith, while another person is given small faith. We were all given an equal amount of faith at salvation. The problem is not that we don't have faith, but rather we don't know how to use our faith because of our unrenewed minds.

Peter said we had like precious faith with him (2 Pet. 1:1). That same faith that he used to raise Dorcas from the dead (Acts 9:36-42) is in us too. The same faith that Peter used is the same faith that we have.

Paul said he was living his Christian life by the faith of the Son of God (Gal. 2:20). Since we all have been given "the" measure of faith, then that means we all have the faith of the Son of God in us. Our faith is sufficient. It's our minds that don't know what we have that are giving us the problem.

In the same way that a car battery transfers its power to the starter through battery cables, so our minds allow this faith of God that is in our spirits to flow into our bodies. If our minds are not renewed, then it's like having corroded cables. The power is there but it won't flow. Likewise, every believer has the same faith that Jesus has, but it won't flow through us until we renew our minds through the Word of God.

Romans 12:4 - For as we have many members in one body, and all members have not the same office:

(Rom. 12:4) This verse starts with the word "for," which is a conjunction just as in verse 3. This is linking Paul's following statements with his previous statements.

Paul had encouraged these people to experience the perfect will of God (Rom. 12:2) through humbling themselves (being a living sacrifice). This was vastly different than the world's formula for success and needed some further explanation. Therefore, in verse 3, Paul explains that every believer has been given the same opportunity for success through "the" measure of faith.

Now in verse 4, Paul continues to explain that although every believer has been given "the" measure of faith, not every believer has been given the same job in the body of Christ. He uses our physical bodies to illustrate this.

We have many different parts of our body, and they all have a different purpose, or function. Yet, it takes all the parts operating in unity to make one body. Likewise, it takes all the different people in the church performing their different functions to make up Christ's body.

So, in verses 1-2, Paul gave a foolproof formula for success. However, to keep anyone from gloating at the tremendous potential of these promises, he makes it clear in verse 3 that everyone has been given the same potential. And in verses 4 through 8, he reveals that we all have different functions, and we all need each other.

Romans 12:5-6 - So we, being many, are one body in Christ, and every one members one of another. 6) Having then gifts differing according to the grace that is given to us, whether prophecy, let us prophesy according to the proportion of faith;

(Rom. 12:6) It must be remembered that Paul is not teaching on the function and administration of these seven gifts that he mentions here as he taught on the nine gifts of the Spirit in 1 Corinthians 12-14. He is simply mentioning these gifts to illustrate his point that different people in the body of Christ have different positions, or functions. However, there are some truths concerning these gifts that we can glean from these scriptures.

First, it needs to be pointed out that all believers can operate in the gifts listed here, but that doesn't mean that is their ministry. For instance, we can and should be able to teach others, but that doesn't make us a teacher. Paul said we could all prophesy one by one (1 Cor. 14:31), but he also made it clear that we are not all called to be prophets (1 Cor. 12:29). It is definite that we should all show mercy and be a giver, but there are some people who are given a supernatural gift in these areas, which Paul is describing here.

Concerning the gift of giving, Paul says that we should do our giving with simplicity. He that rules should be diligent about it, and the person who has the gift of mercy should administer it with cheerfulness.

The Greek word that was translated "prophecy" here is "propheteia," which "signifies the speaking forth of the mind and counsel of God" (W.E. Vine's). This originally applied to Old Testament prophets who were predicting future events, but it came to apply to any messenger who was inspired by God as he spoke. This would apply to a preacher today if he was speaking under the anointing of the Holy Spirit.

This verse is saying essentially the same thing that Peter said in 1 Peter 4:11. If we are going to prophesy, let's do it according to the ability that God gave us—the measure of faith.

Romans 12:7 - Or ministry, let us wait on our ministering: or he that teacheth, on teaching;

(Rom. 12:7) The Greek word that was translated "ministry" here is "diakonia" and means, "attendance (as a servant, etc.)." It is a variation of the Greek word "diakonos" where we get our English word "deacon" from.

This same Greek word was translated "serving" in Luke 10:40; "service" (referring to charitable giving) in Romans 15:31; "relief" in Acts 11:29; and "office" in Romans 11:13. The Amplified Bible translates this verse as "He whose gift is practical service, let him give himself to serving."

Therefore, we can surmise from these things that this is referring to those who have been given a ministry of serving others as Paul described the house of Stephanas (1 Cor. 16:15). This gift is not often recognized and even more often not appreciated, but it is listed in good company. Paul mentions this between prophecy and teaching, two gifts which are recognized and accepted.

The ministry gift of a teacher was placed third in authority in the church behind the ministry of the apostle and prophet (1 Cor. 12:28). The basic difference between a teacher and a preacher is that a preacher proclaims and a teacher explains.

Romans 12:8 - Or he that exhorteth, on exhortation: he that giveth, let him do it with simplicity; he that ruleth, with diligence; he that sheweth mercy, with cheerfulness.

(Rom. 12:8) The Greek word for "exhorteth" is "parakaleo." It was translated "beseech" in Romans 12:1, 15:30, and 16:17. It can also mean "to comfort or encourage" and it probably is used that way here.

Our English word "exhort" comes from the Latin "exhortari." This is a compound word comprised of "ex," meaning "completely," and "hortari," meaning "to encourage." Therefore, the word "exhort" literally means "to completely encourage." One of the purposes of prophesy is exhortation (1 Cor. 14:3). Exhortation is also a part of preaching the Word (2 Tim. 4:2). However, this verse shows that there are individuals who have a special ministry of encouraging people. This is a supernatural gift.

The Greek word used here is "haplotes" and means "sincerity, uprightness, or frankness;" but it can also mean, "generosity or liberality." Most scholars agree that in this case, it is expressing "generosity or liberality." Therefore, Paul is saying to those who have a ministry of giving that they should be generous in their giving.

The Greek word that was translated "ruleth" here is "proistemi," and it means "to stand before; i.e., (in rank) preside." The Amplified Bible translates this phrase as "he who gives aid and superintends, with zeal and singleness of mind." This could be speaking of any one of many positions of authority in the church. This does reveal that although everyone has some degree of authority, there are individuals who are given a ministry gift of ruling, or what might be commonly called administration today.

The Greek word that was translated "cheerfulness" here is "hilarotes" and means, "cheerfulness." It comes from the Greek word "hilaros," which is where we get our word "hilarious" from. Therefore, Paul is admonishing those who show mercy to be hilarious in their administration of this gift.

Romans 12:9 - Let love be without dissimulation. Abhor that which is evil; cleave to that which is good.

(Rom. 12:9) The dictionary defines "dissimulate" as "to disguise under a feigned appearance." The Greek word that was used was "anupokritos" meaning, "without hypocrisy, unfeigned." This Greek word was only used six times in all the New Testament. In James 3:17 it was translated "without hypocrisy," and four times it was translated "unfeigned" (2 Cor. 6:6, 1 Tim. 1:5, 2 Tim. 1:5, and 1 Pet. 1:22).

Paul is still talking about love when he said, "Abhor that which is evil; cleave to that which is good." Part of true love is hatred. If we don't hate the things that oppose the one we love, then it is not God's kind of love. If we don't hate evil, then our love for God is with dissimulation. It is hypocritical.

It has become customary in our society to conceal our real feelings behind a hypocritical mask. Although we should be tactful and not purposely say things to offend people, there is a time and a place for speaking the truth, even if it isn't popular.

In Leviticus 19:17, the Lord said, "Thou shalt not hate thy brother in thine heart: thou shalt in any wise rebuke thy neighbour, and not suffer sin upon him." That verse is saying that if we fail to rebuke our neighbor when we see sin approaching, then we hate the person. Many people have concealed their true feelings about evil under the pretense of "I just love them too much to hurt their feelings." The truth is, they just love themselves too much to run the risk of being rejected. That's hypocrisy.

This scripture commands us to abhor that which is evil. We need to love the sinner, but hate the sin. We need to be outspoken on what is right and wrong. Jesus illustrated this scripture when He drove the moneychangers out of the temple with a whip (John 2:14-17).

The Greek word that was translated "abhor" here is "apostugeo" meaning "to detest utterly."

Sometimes people have misunderstood and misapplied God's kind of love so that they no longer hate evil. However, Proverbs 8:13 says, "The fear of the LORD is to hate evil." Those who love the Lord hate evil (Ps. 97:10). Only the wicked don't abhor evil (Ps. 36:4).

Jesus got angry, and the Scriptures say, His hatred for sin was the reason God anointed Him with gladness above His fellows (Ps. 45:7, Heb. 1:9). It is impossible to truly love someone with God's kind of love without hating anything that comes against that person. There is a righteous type of anger which is not sin (Eph. 4:26).

Romans 12:10 - Be kindly affectioned one to another with brotherly love; in honour preferring one another;

Rom. 12:10) The word that was translated "brotherly love" here in Romans 12:10 is "philadelphia" meaning "fraternal affection" and comes from the Greek word "phileo." The Greek word that was translated "kindly affectioned" in this verse is a compound of "phileo" and "storge" meaning "cherishing one's kindred."

There is much confusion on the subject of love today, because we have only one English word (love) to describe a broad aspect of meanings. For example, if I said, "I love my wife, I love apple pie, and I love my dog," obviously I am not talking about love in the same degree or definition from one to the other.

In the New Testament, there were three major Greek words that described the various kinds of love. One of these words "eros," was not actually used in the New Testament, but it was alluded to. The following is a brief definition of these three major words.

EROS: sexual passion; arousal, its gratification and fulfillment. The Greek word is not used in the New Testament probably because its origin came from the mythical god Eros, the god of love. It is inferred in many scriptures and is the only kind of love that God restricts to a one-man, one-woman relationship within the bounds of marriage (Heb. 13:4; Song 1:13; 4:5-6; 7:7-9; 8:10; Eph. 5:31).

PHILEO: friendly love based on feelings or emotions. We could describe PHILEO love as "tender affection, delighting to be in the presence of; a warm or good feeling towards someone that may come and go with intensity."

This verb with its other related Greek words are found around 72 times in the New Testament. Although PHILEO love is encouraged in the Scripture, it is never a direct command. God never commands us to PHILEO love anyone, since this type of love is based on feelings. Even God did not PHILEO the world. He operated in AGAPE love toward us.

The following are some scriptures in which PHILEO or a form of it is used (John 5:20, 11:3,36, 12:25, 16:27, 20:2, Acts 28:2; Rom. 12:10 [kindly affection]; 1 Tim. 6:10; 2 Tim. 3:4; Titus 2:4, 3:4; Heb. 13:1; 3 John 1:9; and Rev. 3:19).

AGAPE: God's type of love; the highest kind of love. AGAPE is "seeking the welfare or betterment of others even if there is not affection felt" (a paraphrase of Happiness Explained by Bob Rigdon). AGAPE love does not have the primary meaning of affection nor of coming from one's feelings.

Jesus displayed this AGAPE kind of love by going to the cross and dying even though He didn't feel like dying. He prayed, "O my Father, if it be possible, let this cup pass from me: nevertheless, not as I will, but as thou wilt" (Matt. 26:39; Mark 14:36; Luke 22:41-43; John 18:11). Jesus sought the betterment of you and me, regardless of His feelings.

We, too, can AGAPE love our enemies even though we don't have a warm feeling of affection for them (Luke 6:35). If they are hungry we can feed them; if they thirst we can give them a drink (Rom. 12:20-21). We can choose to seek the betterment and welfare of others, regardless of how we feel.

The Apostle John said, "Let us not love in word, neither in tongue; but in deed and in truth" (1 John 3:18). Jesus referred to His love for others (John 13:34, 15:9, and 12), but He never directly told anyone, I love you.

The dictionary defines "preferring" as "to choose as more desirable; like better." That means, this verse is admonishing us to desire the welfare of others more than our own, to like others better than ourselves. That is an awesome command that is only obtainable through God's supernatural love.

If this very simple yet very profound truth could be understood and applied, then strife would cease (Prov. 13:10), the world would see Christianity as never before, and we would discover the true joy that comes from serving someone besides ourselves (Matt. 10:39, 16:25).

Romans 12:11 - Not slothful in business; fervent in spirit; serving the Lord;

(Rom. 12:11) There are many scriptures that teach against slothfulness, or laziness. Paul even went so far as to say, "This we commanded you, that if any would not work, neither should he eat" (2 Thess 3:10).

It is interesting that Paul speaks about not being slothful right after he mentions brotherly love and preferring one another. This adds a very important balance to brotherly love, which many today are missing. While it is true that we have a responsibility to help others, it is also true that a handout doesn't help a lazy person.

When we support those who are living in direct disobedience to God's instructions regarding slothfulness, we are hurting that person. Charity should be reserved for those who need it, not those who abuse it.

The Amplified Bible's rendering of this verse indicates that the "spirit" that is being spoken of here is the Holy Spirit - "Never lag in zeal and in earnest endeavor; be aglow and burning with the Spirit, serving the Lord"). The New American Standard - "not lagging behind in diligence, fervent in spirit, serving the Lord," and the New International Version - "Never be lacking in zeal, but keep your spiritual fervor, serving the Lord." These refer to "spirit" as our attitude.

The Greek word that was translated "spirit" is "pneuma." This word was used to distinguish the Holy Spirit many times (Examples: Matt. 3:16, 10:20, 12:28; Luke 4:18; 11:13; John 7:39; and Acts 2:4) but it was also translated "spirit" when the context clearly indicates it is speaking of our attitudes (Matt. 5:3; 1 Cor. 4:21; 2 Cor. 4:13; Eph. 1:17, 4:23; Phil. 1:27; 1 Tim. 4:12; and Rev. 19:10).

"Pneuma" can mean "mental disposition." In this application "spirit" is speaking of our attitudes. The American Heritage Dictionary defines spirit as "a prevailing mood or attitude."

This same point was made in Ephesians 6:6-7 where Paul said, "Not with eyeservice, as menpleasers; but as the servants of Christ, doing the will of God from the heart; With good will doing service, as to the Lord, and not to men." Paul is emphasizing that even in our business endeavors, we are serving the Lord and not man. He repeated this same thought in Colossians 3:23 when he said, "Whatsoever ye do, do it heartily, as to the Lord, and not unto men."

Romans 12:12-14 - Rejoicing in hope; patient in tribulation; continuing instant in prayer; 13) Distributing to the necessity of saints; given to hospitality. 14) Bless them which persecute you: bless, and curse not.

(Rom. 12:14) Many people think of a curse only in relation to witchcraft. However, it should go without saying that a Christian should not practice witchcraft against someone who has done them harm. That is not the type of curse that is being spoken of here.

The Greek word used for "curse" is "kataraomai" meaning "to execrate; by analogy to doom."

The word "execrate" means "to protest vehemently against; denounce." W.E. Vine says "kataraomai" means, "to pray against; to wish evil against a person or thing."

Therefore, our vicious talk about others is actually a curse. Without realizing it, many Christians curse others and thereby, allow the devil access to the lives of those they are denouncing.

Proverbs 18:21 says, "Death and life are in the power of the tongue: and they that love it shall eat the fruit thereof." Every word we speak either releases life or death. Our negative talk releases death. When we speak against others, we are actually releasing Satan against them.

Once a person understands this, it should make one pray this prayer with David, "Set a watch, O LORD, before my mouth; keep the door of my lips" (Ps. 141:3).

Romans 12:15 - Rejoice with them that do rejoice, and weep with them that weep.

(Rom. 12:15) A self-centered person will not rejoice at someone else's prosperity, but will be jealous instead. Likewise, a selfish person will not weep with those that weep, because the person really doesn't care about anyone but oneself. The Lord is continuing the thought about preferring one another.

Romans 12:16 - Be of the same mind one toward another. Mind not high things, but condescend to men of low estate. Be not wise in your own conceits.

(Rom. 12:16) This is not saying that Christians should never occupy a prominent position. If that were true, then Paul would not need to admonish these people to be willing to associate with those of low estate. They wouldn't have any other choice.

Many Bible people were people of renown, even among the non-believers (Abraham, Isaac, Joseph, David, Solomon, Paul [Acts 28:7], John [John 18:15], etc.). Paul is just saying that we shouldn't seek out prestigious people and snub those whom the world doesn't consider important. God doesn't evaluate people the way the world does. Those who are greatest in His kingdom are the greatest servants.

We will miss some of the most beautiful people who could bless our lives if we judge people by the world's standards. We also run the risk of destroying our faith when we seek the honor that comes from man.

Romans 12:17 - Recompense to no man evil for evil. Provide things honest in the sight of all men.

(Rom. 12:17) There is an unwritten but widely understood code in human relations that says we should treat people the way they treat us. Jesus taught just the opposite, and Paul is reaffirming that same teaching. If we are to be Christlike, then we cannot give people what they deserve.

It is not enough to just be honest in the sight of God. This scripture commands us to also have integrity in the sight of man. This corresponds to "abstain from all appearance of evil" (1Thess. 5:22). We not only need to be right, but we need to appear right as much as possible.

Romans 12:18 - If it be possible, as much as lieth in you, live peaceably with all men.

(Rom. 12:18) This verse is advocating living peaceably with all men. Yet, the very wording reveals that this is not always possible. We are not responsible for other people's actions. We must pursue peace, even when we are not at fault, but the other person does have a choice. Be sure that you are at peace with all men. Whether or not they are at peace with you is their decision.

Romans 12:19 - Dearly beloved, avenge not yourselves, but rather give place unto wrath: for it is written, Vengeance is mine; I will repay, saith the Lord.

(Rom. 12:19) Verses 19-21 are humanly impossible. It takes the supernatural power of God's faith at work in the heart to fulfill these scriptures. Letting God be the one who defends us is a matter of faith. If there is no God who will bring men into account for their actions, then turning the other cheek would be the worst thing we could do. But if there is a God who promised that vengeance is His and He will repay, then taking matters into our own hands shows a lack of faith in God and His integrity.

Romans 12:20 - Therefore if thine enemy hunger, feed him; if he thirst, give him drink: for in so doing thou shalt heap coals of fire on his head.

(Rom. 12:20) These coals of fire are not coals of punishment or torment, but rather conviction. If this was urging us to be kind to our enemies because that would hurt them more than anything else, then that would be violating the context of this verse. Paul is telling us to live peaceably with all men (v. 18) and to render to no man evil for evil (v. 17). God's kind of love is being promoted, not some scriptural way to hurt those who hurt you.

When we walk in love toward those who hurt us, it heaps conviction on them. They know what their reaction would be if they were in our place, and to see us walk in love under adverse circumstances shows them that we have something special that they don't have.

Paul should know. He saw Stephen forgive and pray for the very people who stoned him to death. When Jesus appeared to Saul (Paul) on the road to Damascus, He told him that it was hard to kick against the pricks. The Lord was saying it was hard for Saul to resist the conviction that had come to him through Stephen's witness.

Romans 12:21 - Be not overcome of evil, but overcome evil with good.

(Rom. 12:21) We cannot fight evil with evil. Evil has to be overcome with good. It is frustrating to see the schemes of Satan and his kingdom. However, we must never let our frustration drive us to using their tactics. The wrath of man does not accomplish the righteousness of God (James 1:20). Instead of cursing the darkness, turn on a light.

Romans 12:1-21
Discipleship Questions

. . . .

Answer the following questions by reading the corresponding discipleship commentary lesson and using your Bible.

1. Read Romans 12:1. Paul beseeches the Christians, i.e., makes an appeal to them in view of what? _____

2. What does Paul beseech them to do in Romans 12:1?
   _____

3. Read Romans 12:1 in the New International Version. According to Romans 12:1, how can we worship God? _____

4. According to Romans 12:2, how should a Christian not act?
   _____

5. Read Philippians 4:8. According to Romans 12:2, how should a Christian think?
   _____

6. Read Romans 12:2. Your minds must be renewed and your bodies presented to God in order to correctly prove or judge what?
   _____

7. Read Romans 12:3. As Christians, how are we to think of ourselves?
   _____

8. God has dealt to every man the measure of faith and gifts that differ. How are we to operate our spiritual gifts according to Romans 12:6?
   _____

9. Read Romans 12:4. There are many members in the physical body, but what don't all the members have? _____

10. In the same way (as the physical body), we are many, but one body in Christ. According to Romans 12:6, how do we differ?_____

11. Read Romans 12:6. We have these gifts according to what?
    _____

12. Read Romans 12:6-8 and 1 Corinthians 12:7-11. Describe some of the various gifts God gives individuals. _____
    _____
    _____
    _____

13. Read Romans 12:9. What instructions did Paul give about love?

_____

14. Read 1 John 3:18. What does it mean to love?

_____

15. What further instructions did Paul give in Romans 12:9?

_____

16. How are we to love one another according to Romans 12:10?

_____

17. Read Romans 12:10. What should our attitudes be toward each other?

_____

18. Read Romans 12:11. How should we work and serve the Lord?

_____

19. What three instructions are given to us in Romans 12:12?

_____

_____

_____

20. According to Romans 12:13, if God's people are in need, what should we do?

_____

21. Read Romans 12:14. How are we to respond to those who persecute us?

_____

22. Read Romans 12:14 and James 3:8-10. What must we not do?

_____

23. According to Romans 12:15, we are to share in one another's joy and share in one another's grief. How does Galatians 6:2 express this?

_____

24. What four instructions does Paul give us in Romans 12:16?

_____

_____

_____

_____

25. What two examples can we follow from Romans 12:17?

_____

_____

26. As much as possible, what are we to do according to Romans 12:18?

_____

27. Read Romans 12:19. What does the phrase "dearly beloved, avenge not yourselves" mean? _____

28. Read Romans 12:19. Who are we to allow to take wrath, vengeance, and to repay?

_____

29. Read Romans 12:20. If your enemy is hungry, what are you to do?

_____

30. Read Romans 12:20. If your enemy is thirsty what are you to do?

_____

31. How does Proverbs 21:22 state what Romans 12:20 says?

_____

32. According to 1 Corinthians 13:4, what is love? _____

33. Who are we to love, according to Luke 6:35?_____

34. How are we to overcome evil, according to Romans 12:21?

_____

Discipleship Answer Key
Romans 12:1-21

. . . .

Do not look at the answer key until you have completed the questions.
Compare your answers with the following answers.

1. Read Romans 12:1. Paul beseeches the Christians, i.e., makes an appeal to them in view of what?
    God's great mercy that has been shown to them.

2. What does Paul beseech them to do in Romans 12:1?
    To present, or offer, their bodies unto God, holy, set apart unto Him.

3. Read Romans 12:1 in the New International Version. According to Romans 12:1, how can we worship God?
    By offering our bodies as living sacrifices.

4. According to Romans 12:2, how should a Christian not act?
    A Christian should not be conformed to the world, i.e., he or she should not act or behave like people of this world.

5. Read Philippians 4:8. According to Romans 12:2, how should a Christian think?
    With a transformed and renewed mind.

6. Read Romans 12:2. Your minds must be renewed and your bodies presented to God in order to correctly prove or judge what?
    The good, acceptable, and perfect will of God.

7. Read Romans 12:3. As Christians, how are we to think of ourselves?
    "Don't cherish exaggerated ideas of yourself or your importance" (Phillips translation).

8. God has dealt to every man the measure of faith and gifts that differ. How are we to operate our spiritual gifts according to Romans 12:6?
    According to the faith given us.

9. Read Romans 12:4. There are many members in the physical body, but what don't all the members have?
    The same office, or the same function.

10. In the same way (as the physical body), we are many, but one body in Christ. According to Romans 12:6, how do we differ?
    We differ according to our gifts.

256

11. Read Romans 12:6. We have these gifts according to what?
According to the grace that is given to us.

12. Read Romans 12:6-8 and 1 Corinthians 12:7-11. Describe some of the various gifts God gives individuals.
Prophecy, ministering (practical service), teaching, exhortation, giving, ruling (administrative ability), showing mercy, the word of wisdom, the word of knowl edge, gifts of healing, the working of miracles, discerning of spirits; divers kinds of tongues, and the interpretation of tongues.

13. Read Romans 12:9. What instructions did Paul give about love?
It is to be without dissimulation, i.e., sincere, not pretending, but really loving others.

14. Read 1 John 3:18. What does it mean to love?
To seek the welfare and benefit of another regardless of how we feel.

15. What further instructions did Paul give in Romans 12:9?
Hate evil and hold on to what is good (or upright).

16. How are we to love one another according to Romans 12:10?
With kind affection and brotherly love, i.e., in a way that you feel close to each other like brothers.

17. Read Romans 12:10. What should our attitudes be toward each other?
To give you more honor than we give ourselves. To give deference to others.

18. Read Romans 12:11. How should we work and serve the Lord?
Work hard, not be lazy, and serve the Lord enthusiastically.

19. What three instructions are given to us in Romans 12:12?
1. Rejoicing in hope, i.e., be glad for all God is planning for you.
2. Be patient in tribulation, i.e., don't give up when trials come.
3. Continue instant in prayer, i.e., keep on praying, maintain a habit of prayer.

20. According to Romans 12:13, if God's people are in need, what should we do?
Help them out.

21. Read Romans 12:14. How are we to respond to those who persecute us?
We are to bless them, i.e., speak good things to them and over them.

22. Read Romans 12:14 and James 3:8-10. What must we not do?
Curse them, i.e., to speak doom or evil over them.

23. According to Romans 12:15, we are to share in one another's joy and share in one another's grief. How does Galatians 6:2 express this?
Bear one another's burdens.

24. What four instructions does Paul give us in Romans 12:16?
    1. Be of the same mind toward one another, i.e., have the same concern for all, treat everyone equal, live in harmony.
    2. Mind not high things, i.e., don't be proud, snobbish, high-minded, or try to act big.
    3. Condescend to men of low estate, i.e., associate with the lowly, poor, or ordinary people.
    4. Be not wise in your own conceits, i.e., don't think you know it all!

25. What two examples can we follow from Romans 12:17?
    1. If someone does evil to you, do not pay back with evil.
    2. Do things in such a way that everyone can see you are honest.

26. As much as possible, what are we to do according to Romans 12:18?
    Live peaceably with everyone.

27. Read Romans 12:19. What does the phrase "dearly beloved, avenge not yourselves" mean?
    Never take your own revenge.

28. Read Romans 12:19. Who are we to allow to take wrath, vengeance, and to repay?
    The Lord.

29. Read Romans 12:20. If your enemy is hungry, what are you to do?
    Feed him.

30. Read Romans 12:20. If your enemy is thirsty what are you to do?
    Give him a drink.

31. How does Proverbs 25:22 state what Romans 12:20 says?
    "For thou shalt heap coals of fire upon his head."

32. According to 1 Corinthians 13:4, what is love?
    Kind.

33. Who are we to love, according to Luke 6:35?
    Our enemies.

34. How are we to overcome evil, according to Romans 12:21?
    By doing good.

OVERVIEW OF ROMANS CHAPTER 13

by Andrew Wommack

Romans 13 is a very interesting passage of scripture. Again, the whole context of the book of Romans is talking about grace, the Gospel being the power of God unto salvation. Paul has done a masterful work explaining the grace of God. In this chapter he begins to give instructions to the believers of the church in Rome about their relationship to the government system that is over them.

There are many ways to teach on this. For the sake of time, there are two main applications: submission to the physical, carnal government over you (the nation you live in) and submission to church government. Every person who is born again should be involved in the church and should be submissive to the leadership. When God brings two or more people together, someone has to be in leadership. That's the way He established it.

Paul says in verse 1, *"Let every soul be subject unto the higher powers. For there is no power but of God; the powers that be are ordained of God."* If you live in a country with a good government system, a democracy or something similar with good leadership, you really don't have a problem with this. But if you look at it from the universal perspective, some government systems in the world today have had dictators who were mass murderers. You can go back in history to Hitler, Mussolini, Idi Amin in Uganda, the things that happened in Rwanda and other African nations, and see the bloodshed and the terrible things that have happened.

People read a verse like this that says there is no power but of God, that the powers that be are ordained of God, and say, "How could this be? Is this saying God is the one who put all these people in power?" No, that's not what it says, but that is the way it is often interpreted. Let me clarify. He didn't say that all the people who are in power are ordained of God, but that the power is ordained of God. There is a difference, a distinction there.

God ordained government, and even if it is poor, is always superior to anarchy. You can see an example of this in the fall of the former Soviet Union. When they were under communism—Lenin and Stalin—millions of people were mass murdered. There were terrible atrocities committed, yet there was stability because there was a government system. I don't believe it was the right type of government—it was an oppressive government—but there was stability there. When communism fell and the Berlin wall came down in 1989, all the Soviet republics began to break away and become independent and there was a tremendous amount of anarchy for a period of time. There have been civil wars in different places, and things that were happening were worse than when the strict government was in place.

I am not advocating communism or any other bad system of government, but Scripture says that God ordained government. He didn't necessarily ordain the way people use government. It can be misused. Some people might debate on the secular systems, but let's look at the church situation.

In the church God said we should submit to the elders and not take an accusation against an elder except before two or three witnesses (1 Tim. 5:19). In 1 Peter 5:2-3, Peter said to take the oversight of the church, not as lording it over them, but as an example. He was talking about a government system. In 1 Corinthians12, Paul said that God set in the church first apostles, second prophets, third teachers, and after that government, helps, etc. He also talked about a system of government in the church.

Although God ordained in the church a governmental power, does that mean every pastor functions exactly the way He designed it to function? Certainly not. You may have seen pastors who have abused their power, did wrong things, misappropriated funds, and manipulated and controlled people. Most of you would agree that God ordained church government, but some pastors have not followed God's standard and missed the mark. He ordained the government, but not the person.

It is the same in the civil sense. God ordained government, but not necessarily the way it always functions. He did not ordain people killing others, manipulating, and unrighteousness, but He did ordain the power.

In verse 2 Paul says, *"Whosoever therefore resisteth the power, resisteth the ordinance of God; and they that resist shall receive to themselves damnation."* Again, there is a right and wrong way to interpret this. Some people have interpreted this as, "one is supposed to follow every command government gives," but Scripture teaches differently. In Acts 3 and 4, Peter healed a man at the gate of the temple and as a result a crowd came together. Peter and John preached Christ to them and people were born again. The Scribes and Pharisees, the government system that was over them, came and took them, beat them, and commanded them not to preach any more in the name of Jesus. Peter looked right at them and said, *"Whether it be right in the sight of God to hearken unto you more than unto God, judge ye. For we cannot but speak the things which we have seen and heard"* (Acts 4:19-20).

They disobeyed the command of the government system over them, yet Peter is the same man who wrote in 1 Peter 2:13, *"Submit yourselves to every ordinance of man for the Lord's sake: whether it be to the king, as supreme; or unto governors, as unto them that are sent by him."* How does one harmonize these things? The answer is that submission and obedience are not synonymous. Most people believe they are, but you can disobey an ungodly command and still be submitted to the power of that government system.

Some people don't understand that, but Mahatma Ghandi actually demonstrated it in India. He did not form violent protests, did not overthrow the government, did not form a rebellion and get people to throw off the government's power. He staged peaceful protests, though some of his followers did not always follow his teaching. Martin Luther King was the same way with the civil rights movement in the United States. Those are modern examples, but in New Testament days the disciples suffered even to the point of being crucified and burned at the stake, yet they never went back to the church and began to form a revolt. They never advocated rebellion. Instead they served and submitted themselves in the sense that they didn't rebel at the power, but they refused to obey ungodly commands. That is what this is speaking about.

Verses 3-4 say, *"For rulers are not a terror to good works, but to the evil. Wilt thou then not be afraid of the power?"* Again, this is talking about the government system, not individual people. It is not telling you to obey an ungodly command, but you do not try and overthrow government. *"Do that which is good and thou shalt have praise of the same: For he is a minister of God to thee for good. But if thou do that which is evil, be afraid; for he beareth not the sword in vain: for he is a minister of God, a revenger to execute wrath upon him that doeth evil."*

There are many applications of this. One way I have used it is when somebody is rebelling against God, causing problems, and hurting other people. I pray and say, "God, these government forces are meant to be your ministers. I'm praying they will fulfill their rightful call and I pray that person will be caught, thrown in jail, punished, fined, or something to stop their behavior," and I have seen it come to pass. That is a rightful use of what he's talking about in these verses.

Verses 6-8 say, *"For this cause pay ye tribute also; for they are God's ministers, attending continually upon this very thing. Render therefore to all their dues: tribute to whom tribute is due* [talking about taxes]*; custom to whom custom; fear to whom fear; honour to whom honour. Owe no man anything, but to love one another: for he that loveth another hath fulfilled the law."* Basically this is saying that Christians should obey civil government, but not obey it more than God. You should never disobey God, but as much as you can obey the government without disobeying Him, you should do it. Taxes are included in that. There are some people who say, "I'm a member of a heavenly kingdom and I am not going to pay these taxes." That's not what the Bible says. Owe no man anything—pay your taxes.

There are many other beneficial things in this chapter. I pray God will continue to open these verses as you study through Romans 13.

Romans 13:1-14
Discipleship Commentary

. . . .

Read the entire lesson and then answer the questions that follow.

Romans 13:1 - Let every soul be subject unto the higher powers. For there is no power but of God: the powers that be are ordained of God.

(Rom. 13:1) The subject of submission to authority is a very basic Bible doctrine. Some of the major areas of submission commanded in the scriptures are: (1) submission to God (Eph. 5:24; James 4:7); (2) submission to civil or governmental authority (Rom. 13:1-7); (3) submission to the church or religious authority (Heb. 13:17); (4) wives are to submit to husbands (Eph. 5:22-24; Col. 3:18); (5) children are to submit to their parents (Eph. 6:1; Col. 3:20); (6) slaves are to submit to masters, which would be today's equivalent of employees submitting to employers (1 Pet. 2:18); (7) the younger are to submit to the older (1 Pet. 5:5); and (8) we are all supposed to submit to each other in love (Eph. 5:21; 1 Pet. 5:5).

The Greek word translated "subject" here, as well as 14 other times in the New Testament is, "hupotasso." This was a military term meaning "to rank under." Although in most cases, obedience is a part of submission, these terms are not synonymous. Just as an enlisted man in the army has limits to his obedience to an officer, so we only obey men as long as their commands do not oppose God.

A failure to understand the difference between submission and obedience has given birth to many false teachings that have caused some people to obey others in matters of sin. That is never commanded in the Word of God.

One of the easiest ways to see that a person can submit without obeying an ungodly command is to look at the life of Peter. Peter made some striking statements in 1 Peter 2:13-14 when he said, "Submit yourselves to every ordinance of man for the Lord's sake: whether it be to the king, as supreme; Or unto governors, as unto them that are sent by him for the punishment of evildoers, and for the praise of them that do well."

This is the same Peter who refused to obey the chief priests when they commanded him to not speak or teach anymore in the name of Jesus (Acts 4:18-19). When Peter and the other apostles continued their teaching and preaching about Jesus, the high priest and the elders of the Jews imprisoned them. However, they were supernaturally freed from prison by an angel of the Lord who told them to go back to the temple and preach again (Acts 5:17-20). This command was a direct contradiction to the commands of the Jews.

The Jews again arrested Peter and the other apostles and said in Acts 5:28, "Did not we straitly command you that ye should not teach in this name?" Peter responded by saying, "We ought to obey God rather than men" (Acts 5:29). This is always the bottom line. We should never obey any man if it would cause us to disobey God.

Yet, we are to submit to every ordinance of man (1 Pet. 2:13). Submission is an attitude, not an action. It will express itself through actions, but a person can have a submissive attitude and yet disobey an ungodly command.

If a government official commanded us to not preach Jesus, we should follow the example of Peter and not obey him. But we should also not rebel at his authority in the same way that Peter and the other apostles did not rebel at the authority of the Jews.

When the apostles were beaten for their obedience to God, they didn't criticize or form a revolt. They praised God and kept right on preaching the Gospel (Acts 5:41-42). They didn't obey ungodly commands but they didn't become ungodly either by cursing those who had hurt them. They submitted to the authority over them to the point that they took a beating without one complaint, but they never did what the Jews had commanded them.

If a man commanded his wife not to go to church anymore, she should not obey that command. The Bible clearly says not to forsake the assembling of ourselves together (Heb. 10:25). However, there is a submissive way and a rebellious way of doing that.

If she said, "You old reprobate. You never have liked me going to church. Well, I'm going to show you that you can't tell me what to do. I'm going anyway and I don't care what you say." That is a rebellious attitude.

Yet, a woman in the same circumstance could affirm her love to her husband and state that she really wants to comply as much as possible. But in this instance, she has to obey God over her husband. If that was her attitude, she would be in submission to her husband even though she didn't do what he said.

Submission is also a voluntary thing. You cannot make another person submit. You can make people obey you, but that doesn't mean they've submitted. Their attitude is totally a matter of choice on their part. This is the reason that a man cannot hear a teaching on submission and go home and make his wife submit. She has to choose to submit.

The book of Daniel has two examples of civil disobedience done through a commitment to God's higher laws (Dan. 3:8-18, 6:10-17). And yet, this disobedience was accomplished with respect and submission to the civil authority. Moses' parents did not obey Pharaoh's command to kill their son and God blessed them for their actions.

Submission is an essential part of true Christianity. However, it is a missing ingredient in most Christians' lives. The root of all lack of submission in our lives lies in pride (1 Pet. 5:4-6).

"For there is no power but of God: the powers that be are ordained of God." This sentence has perplexed many people. Is Paul saying that God wills that there be oppressive governments like the Nazis or even the Roman government that Paul was under? Definitely not. Even though He has used corrupt rulers and governments to punish offences, their governmental authority was not created by God to be oppressive. They were ordained to be ministers of God to us for good (v. 4).

In the same way that God ordains people to the ministry, and yet they fail to fulfill that call as God intended, likewise, God ordains governments but doesn't ordain everything that is done by them. There are countless scriptural examples of rebukes and punishments by God upon civil leaders because they did not submit to His will.

God's original government over man was directly administered by God Himself. Man answered only to his Creator. Even after the fall of man, God worked in cooperation with the conscience of man to refrain him from evil. In the beginning, this was effective, as can be seen through Cain's statement, "My punishment is greater than I can bear" (Gen. 4:13).

However, man seared his conscience (1 Tim. 4:2) through repeated sin. Therefore, since man was no longer responsive to his Creator, God ordained man to begin to police themselves. He told Noah, "Whoso sheddeth man's blood, by man shall his blood be shed: for in the image of God made he man" (Gen. 9:6). This responsibility of corporate man to avenge the wrongs of individual men continued to develop until, through the giving of the Old Testament law, God gave detailed instructions on how mankind was to treat each other and prescribed punishments for failure to do so.

In that context, God did ordain all government, but in more cases than not, governments are not any more responsive to Him than are individuals. However, we are to submit to them and obey them as long as we don't have to violate a clear command of God. Even bad government is superior to anarchy.

Romans 13:2 - Whosoever therefore resisteth the power, resisteth the ordinance of God: and they that resist shall receive to themselves damnation.

(Rom. 13:2) Notice specifically Paul's choice of words here: "Whoso resisteth the power." The word "resist" implies to "actively fight against." You can refuse to comply with ungodly edicts without resisting the government that issued them. The word "power" is referring directly to the authority of the government itself, not just its directives.

Therefore, Paul is instructing us to not fight against the authority of the government we live under. That doesn't mean we have to comply with any law that is in direct opposition to God's laws. But, when we oppose the order of government, we are opposing God's order.

The early Christians were great examples of this. They lived under one of the most corrupt and ruthless governments of all time. The Roman emperors even proclaimed themselves as gods. Yet, nowhere in scripture was there any instruction given to the believers to subvert that government and replace it. On the contrary, Paul commanded the believers to pray for their governmental leaders (1 Tim. 2:1-4). Peter commanded the believers to submit to every ordinance of the king and his governors (1 Pet. 2:13-14).

The early Christians never brought any political pressure to bear on the Roman government or encouraged revolt. Yet in a relatively short period of time, Christianity overwhelmed the pagan Roman government and was adopted as the official state religion. Although this was one of the worst things that ever happened to Christianity, it does illustrate how we can overcome evil with good (Rom. 12:21).

The word that was translated "damnation" here is the Greek word "krima." This same word was translated "judgment" thirteen times; "damnation" seven times; "condemnation" five times; "be condemned" once; "go to law" once; and "avenge" once. It means "judgment; i.e., condemnation of wrong; the decision (whether severe or mild) which one passes on the faults of others: in a forensic sense, the sentence of a judge" (Strong).

In this case, this is not speaking of the eternal damnation or judgment of God. This is saying that if a person resists the power of government, he will come under the judgment of that government.

Romans 13:3 - For rulers are not a terror to good works, but to the evil. Wilt thou then not be afraid of the power? do that which is good, and thou shalt have praise of the same:

(Rom. 13:3) There are certainly scriptural exceptions to this statement. The Egyptian government turned on the Israelites (Ex. 1:8-22), not because of any sin on their part but because of the insecurities and fears of the Pharaoh. James the apostle was killed by Herod just because it pleased the Jews (Acts 12:2). John the Baptist was imprisoned and beheaded by Herod, and Jesus Himself commented on the innocence of John (Matt. 11:9-11).

However, as a whole there is a truth that even corrupt governments do not bother those who are doing good. Paul was an example of this. Many times the Roman government actually came to his defense (Examples: Acts 18:12-16, 19:35-41, 21:31-36, 23:23-24, 25:1-5, and 27:42-44). In the book of Daniel, he and his three friends were repeatedly honored even though the governmental system was corrupt and unjust. Joseph prospered in Egypt despite the injustices some people did to him.

With few exceptions, governments are established to protect the good and punish the evil. If we do good, we have nothing to fear.

Romans 13:4 - For he is the minister of God to thee for good. But if thou do that which is evil, be afraid; for he beareth not the sword in vain: for he is the minister of God, a revenger to execute wrath upon him that doeth evil.

(Rom. 13:4) The word "minister" is the same Greek word that was translated "deacon, and servant." Government officials, including police and army, were ordained by God to minister to us. The Lord uses this civil authority to protect us and execute His wrath on the ungodly. Knowing this gives us added assurance when we pray for justice to be done through the judicial system (1 John 5:14-15).

When an individual fails to respond to the conviction of the Holy Spirit, we can pray that the Lord will use the legal system to stop his evil ways. They are ministers of God. Many thousands of prisoners have praised God for the prison term that finally stopped them and made them come to grips with the real problems of their lives.

The sword that is being spoken of here is symbolic of power to restrain or kill. That is what swords were used for. God has delegated some of His power to rule to governments, even to the extent of taking life.

The Lord told Noah that any man who murdered another man had to die at the hand of mankind (Gen. 9:5-6). Likewise, this verse shows that God has given government the right to use force and execute His wrath, which would include capital punishment. Even some wars can be justified on the basis of this scripture.

Therefore, Christians can serve as police officers or soldiers as long as they are enforcing what is right.

Romans 13:5 - Wherefore ye must needs be subject, not only for wrath, but also for conscience sake.

(Rom. 13:5) In the first four verses of this chapter, Paul had given two reasons for being subject to civil government, which he now summarizes. First, we need to be subject because government has the power to punish us if we aren't. Second, since God has ordained government, we must submit to it or have our consciences condemn us for violating the instruction of God.

Therefore, even if we could break the laws of government and get away with it, we shouldn't because we are also violating God's Word. Laws that are not in direct opposition to God's Word should be kept, whether or not we will get caught, or whether or not we think they are important.

In the next verse, Paul specifically mentions taxes as one of those laws that we should comply with. This could be updated to include speed limits, local ordinances, and a host of other things that many of us may disagree with, but we cannot say they are directly against God's Word. The government has a God-given right and responsibility to regulate and establish order and we should comply for consciences' sake. Our submission to government and our submission to God are intertwined.

Romans 13:6 - For, for this cause pay ye tribute also: for they are God's ministers, attending continually upon this very thing.

(Rom. 13:6) Paul had commanded being subject to the laws of the government we live under as long as they don't cause us to sin against God . In verse 5, Paul said we not only need to do this because of the power of government to punish us, but even if we never got caught, we need to submit because of our submission to God. Then he mentions taxes.

Many Christians feel that taxes and serving God are two different things, but the Lord commanded us to pay our taxes. We cannot be a true servant of God and refuse to obey Him in this area. Jesus as the Creator was not obligated to pay taxes to His creation, but He did. He paid taxes to a corrupt system where much of the tax money went straight into the pocket of the tax collector.

In the United States of America, we are given certain tax deductions for charitable gifts and other exemptions. There is nothing wrong with taking advantage of these, or even using the political process to try and change taxation laws that we feel are wrong. Our government guarantees us those rights. But no Christian has any scriptural ground for refusing to pay taxes. Whether or not we can get away with it is immaterial. God commands us to submit, even in the area of taxes. Failure to do so is rebellion against God.

Romans 13:7-8 - Render therefore to all their dues: tribute to whom tribute is due; custom to whom custom; fear to whom fear; honor to whom honor. 8) Owe no man any thing, but to love one another: for he that loveth another hath fulfilled the law.

(Rom.13:8) In context, Paul is speaking about paying our taxes, respect, and honor (v. 7). However, this principle holds true in every area of our lives. We are to pay our bills.

Some people have interpreted this verse as forbidding a Christian to go in debt. It can be shown in scripture that purchasing on credit is not a blessing but a curse (Deut. 28:12, 44); therefore, it is not God's best. However, it is not a sin to borrow money. Many scriptures speak of lending money and place restrictions on to whom we should lend. The Lord would have us use wisdom and be careful about helping someone sin.

Therefore, being in debt is not a sin. But failure to pay our bills or payments on loans that we have given our word on, is wrong.

Notice that Paul speaks of love for our fellow man as a debt. This is not optional. We are commanded to love one another. Indeed, this is the royal law of God (James 2:8).

Mankind as a whole had misunderstood the purpose of the Law. They thought that God was giving us a list of what we must do to be accepted by Him. The Law was given to convince man that he didn't have a chance of saving himself; he needed a Savior.

However, the Law was accurate, and a perfect description of what God created man to be. The Law portrayed what a person who was walking in God's kind of love would do. We still can't keep the Law perfectly in our flesh but the New Testament believer can now fulfill the spirit of the Old Testament Law as an Old Testament man never could.

Romans 13:9-10 - For this, Thou shalt not commit adultery, Thou shalt not kill, Thou shalt not steal, Thou shalt not bear false witness, Thou shalt not covet; and if there be any other commandment, it is briefly comprehended in this saying, namely, Thou shalt love thy neighbour as thyself. 10) Love worketh no ill to his neighbour: therefore love is the fulfilling of the law.

(Rom. 13:10) Instead of focusing on all the dos and don'ts, all we have to do is let God's kind of love rule in our hearts and we will automatically meet the requirements of the law.

Romans 13:11 - And that, knowing the time, that now it is high time to awake out of sleep: for now is our salvation nearer than when we believed.

(Rom. 13:11) Paul had commanded submission to government and had used two reasons for compliance. The most important reason was not just to avoid being caught and punished by government, but to have a good conscience towards God. He is continuing that thought in this verse.

He is saying that the time left before the Lord's return is growing short and we must therefore be even more sensitive to God. This is the same reasoning that the Lord Jesus used in the parables of the ten virgins and of the stewards and their talents (Matt. 25).

The message of these four verses (vv. 11-14) can be summed up in the words of Jesus from Luke 21:34. The issue of the Lord's imminent return adds even more importance to us walking in love.

Romans 13:12-13 - The night is far spent, the day is at hand: let us therefore cast off the works of darkness, and let us put on the armour of light. 13) Let us walk honestly, as in the day; not in rioting and drunkenness, not in chambering and wantonness, not in strife and envying.

(Rom. 13:13) The dictionary defines "wanton" as "1) immoral or unchaste; lewd; 2) maliciously cruel; merciless; 3) sensual; 4) extravagant; excessive; and 5) unrestrained; frolicsome."

Romans 13:14) But put ye on the Lord Jesus Christ, and make not provision for the flesh, to fulfil the lusts thereof.

(Rom. 13:14) Paul is using the term flesh here as referring to the part of man that has not been changed by Christ, i.e., our sinful appetites and desires. These sinful lusts cannot dominate us if we don't make provision for them. Paul is saying to cut off the flesh's rations and starve it to death.

Many Christians have mistakenly believed that during our life here on the earth, we are doomed to have ungodly lusts and desires. But it doesn't have to be that way. The sin nature that enslaved our flesh is gone, and to the degree that we renew our minds through God's Word, we can experience victory over the flesh. The reason the flesh seems so strong in many people's lives is because they are continually feeding it.

Temptation is linked to what we think on. If we don't think on things that gender temptation, then we won't be tempted and we won't sin.

Romans 13:1-14
Discipleship Questions

. . . .

Answer the following questions by reading the corresponding discipleship commentary lesson and using your Bible.

1. Read Romans 13:1. As believers we should submit ourselves to whom?

    _____

2. Read Romans 13:1. Why should we be submissive? _____

    _____

3. Read Romans 13:2. Those who refuse to obey the laws of the land are refusing to obey whom?_____

4. Read Romans 13:2. What will follow refusing to obey? _____

    _____

5. Read Romans 13:3. Rulers are not to be feared by those who do good, but who should fear them?_____

6. Read Romans 13:3. If we live a law-abiding life, what will come our way?

    _____

7. What is the policeman, judge or civil authority, according to Romans 13:4?

    _____

8. Read Romans 13:4. Civil authorities are God's servants to bring justice. What do they bring the wrongdoers? _____

9. Read Romans 13:5. What are two reasons you should obey the law?

    _____

10. According to Romans 13:6, why do we pay taxes? _____

    _____

11. Read Romans 13:7. What must we pay to those in authority?

    _____

12. Read Romans 13:8. What is the only debt that we are to have?

    _____

13. Read Romans 13:8. When we love others, what do we fulfill?

    _____

14. Read Romans 13:9. In what way does the command, "love your neighbour as yourself" fulfill the other commands? _____

_____

15. Read Romans 13:10. What does love never do to its neighbour?

_____

16. Read Romans 13:10. What does love fulfill?

_____

17. Read Romans 13:11. What is about to arrive for the believer?

_____

18. How does Hebrews 9:28 state this?

_____

_____

19. Read Romans 13:12-13. How does Paul encourage believers to live their lives?

_____

20. What does the word "Lord" mean?_____

_____

21. Read Matthew 1:21. What does the word "Jesus" mean?

_____

22. What does the word "Christ" mean?_____

_____

23. Give some examples of how we make provision for the flesh to fulfill its desires.

_____

_____

_____

24. What are we to do according to 2 Timothy 2:22?

_____

_____

25. Read 1 Corinthians 6:18 and Romans 13:14. How are we to avoid fornication?

_____

_____

Romans 13:1-14
Discipleship Answer Key

. . . .

Do not look at the answer key until you have completed the questions.
Compare your answers with the following answers.

1. Read Romans 13:1. As believers we should submit ourselves to whom?
   Governing and civil authorities.

2. Read Romans 13:1. Why should we be submissive?
   Because all legitimate authority is derived from God. Authorities have been established by God.

3. Read Romans 13:2. Those who refuse to obey the laws of the land are refusing to obey whom?
   God.

4. Read Romans 13:2. What will follow refusing to obey?
   Damnation, i.e., judgment or punishment.

5. Read Romans 13:3. Rulers are not to be feared by those who do good, but who should fear them?
   Those who do evil or wrong.

6. Read Romans 13:3. If we live a law-abiding life, what will come our way?
   Praise or a word of approval.

7. What is the policeman, judge or civil authority, according to Romans 13:4?
   A minister of God, i.e., God's servant working for our own good.

8. Read Romans 13:4. Civil authorities are God's servants to bring justice. What do they bring the wrongdoers?
   Wrath, i.e., punishment on wrongdoers.

9. Read Romans 13:5. What are two reasons you should obey the law?
   1. To keep from being punished.
   2. For conscience sake.

10. According to Romans 13:6, why do we pay taxes?
    To support the authorities who are working for God to bring about social justice.

11. Read Romans 13:7. What must we pay to those in authority?
    Taxes, revenue, fear, honor and respect.

12. Read Romans 13:8. What is the only debt that we are to have?
    To love one another.

13. Read Romans 13:8. When we love others, what do we fulfill?
We fulfill God's laws, commands and requirements.

14. Read Romans 13:9. In what way does the command, "love your neighbour as yourself" fulfill the other commands?
If you love your neighbour, you won't commit adultery with his wife. If you love your neighbour, you won't steal from him, covet his goods, or murder him.

15. Read Romans 13:10. What does love never do to its neighbour?
Love never does harm, wrong or ill will to his neighbour.

16. Read Romans 13:10. What does love fulfill?
All of God's commands.

17. Read Romans 13:11. What is about to arrive for the believer?
His complete salvation.

18. How does Hebrews 9:28 state this?
"Christ died only once as a sacrifice to take away the sins of many people. He will come again but not to deal with our sins again. This time he will bring salvation to all those who are eagerly waiting for him" (NLT).

19. Read Romans 13:12-13. How does Paul encourage believers to live their lives?
We are to put on the Lord Jesus Christ, ie, His thoughts, His actions and walk in love.

20. What does the word "Lord" mean?
Boss, the one who has the right to rule our lives - deity.

21. Read Matthew 1:21. What does the word "Jesus" mean?
God is salvation.

22. What does the word "Christ" mean?
The anointed one, the one anointed to rule, the Messiah, the king.

23. Give some examples of how we make provision for the flesh to fulfill its desires.

24. What are we to do according to 2 Timothy 2:22?

25. Read 1 Corinthians 6:18 and Romans 13:14. How are we to avoid fornication?

OVERVIEW OF ROMANS CHAPTER 14

by Don Krow

Turn to Romans 14:1-12: *"Him that is weak in the faith receive ye, but not to doubtful disputations. For one believeth that he may eat all things: another, who is weak, eateth herbs. Let not him that eateth despise him that eateth not; and let not him which eateth not judge him that eateth: for God hath received him. Who art thou that judgest another man's servant? To his own master he standeth of falleth. Yea, he shall be holden up: for God is able to make him stand. One man esteemeth one day above another: another esteemeth every day alike. Let every man be fully persuaded to his own mind. He that regardeth the day, regardeth it unto the Lord; and he that regardeth not the day, to the Lord he doth not regard it. He that eateth, eateth to the Lord, for he giveth God thanks; and he that eateth not, to the Lord he eateth not, and giveth God thanks. For none of us liveth to himself, and no man dieth to himself. For whether we live, we live unto the Lord; and whether we die, we die unto the Lord: whether we live therefore, or die, we are the Lord's. For to this end Christ both died, and rose, and revived, that he might be Lord both of the dead and the living. But why dost thou judge thy brother? Or why dost thou set at nought thy brother? For we shall all stand before the judgment seat of Christ. For it is written, As I live, saith the Lord, every knee shall bow to me, and every tongue confess to God. So then every one of us shall give account of himself to God."*

I really thank God for Romans 14 because for many years I didn't understand somethings. Some people look at God's word and see only white or black—it has to be this way or that way, and there can't be anything in between. There are many things in God's word that <u>are</u> black and are white. For example, it would be wrong for me or you or anyone to commit adultery. That is an absolute from God's word, and there are no exceptions. It would be wrong for anyone to steal, that is another absolute from God's Word.

There are, however, some things in His Word that are not absolutes, but are according to a man's conscience. Romans 14 deals with Christian liberty and the conscience. What are some of these things of conscience and Christian liberty?

Here it says that one man is a strict vegetarian and goes by dietary laws (probably the Old Testament laws). Another man says, "No, in Christ Jesus we are free to eat anything we want to. We don't have to live by the Levitical dietary laws in the Old Testament." One man says, "Oh, you have to observe the Sabbath." Somebody says Saturday is the Sabbath, another says it has been changed to Sunday, while still another says every day is alike. Some believe it's wrong to drink a glass of wine and some have wine with dinner in their culture.

All of these are areas of Christian liberty are according to the person's conscience. The Bible says we are to be fully persuaded in our own minds about doubtful things, but are not to judge one another about them. I have friends that keep the Sabbath, and I say, "God bless you for keeping the Sabbath—that's great." Other people say we aren't to keep the Sabbath, every day is alike, and I say, "Praise God!"

We stand before God on these issues. Let me tell you something about the conscience. It says here that it isn't a hundred percent right because we could be wrongly informed. If you were a woman and every time you went to church the preacher said only prostitutes in the Bible wore red dresses, you wouldn't go to the closet and put on your red dress because you would feel condemned and evil. Your conscience was weakened because it had wrong information. The Bible doesn't say anything about wearing red dresses.

Many people religiously put other people under bondage, guilt, and condemnation. Paul is saying that there are issues of liberty and issues of conscience. What we need to do is search the scriptures for ourselves to come to a conclusion in our own personal lives about what God would want us to do.

Even though we come to a conclusion and our conscience is stronger than someone else's, we have no right to destroy their conscience by violating their conclusion. If we invite someone to dinner who believes it is wrong to eat meat, and we put meat on the table, and say, "You are just under the Law and you don't understand." We are in error making them feel bad. We don't have the right to make anyone sin or do something they feel is wrong. We have no right to do in front of those, whose conscience is weaker than ours, what they believe is wrong, even though we can do it with a clear conscience. That could make them stumble and sin.

The stronger person in Christ, who understands Christian liberty, is to give way to the weaker brother and not do anything before him that he considers evil, wrong, or sinful. We are not to use our liberty in the wrong way by saying they don't understand, and that they are under the Law, because it could hurt them and cause them to do something they feel is wrong.

Here is where the Apostle Paul draws the line with some people. For instance, if a person who keeps the Sabbath says, "I keep the Sabbath, and you can't be right with God unless you do," Paul would say, "Absolutely not. We are justified through faith in Jesus Christ, not by the works of the law or anything we can do. Our salvation is not based on keeping one day or not keeping one day. It is based only upon Jesus Christ and faith in Him."

This is the problem many churches get into where they take their convictions and try to bind them on someone else. They say, "If you aren't doing it the way we're doing it, then you can't have right standing with God." The Bible says in Galatians 5:4 that if anyone tries to make you be justified by the Law, they have fallen from grace and Christ has become of no effect.

What am I saying here from Romans 14? We are not to do anything that would violate our consciences, but we are to examine the scriptures so our consciences can be strengthened on what is right, what is wrong, what is acceptable before God, and what is not acceptable before Him. The Word of God will guide us in the areas of conscience, so we can come to conclusions based on His Word.

The second thing is if someone has a weaker conscience than yours, never use your strong conscience and do something that would cause them to feel they are doing something sinful. You need to give way to the weaker brother. If they don't eat meat, you are not to eat meat when you are with them. If you are visiting their church and they observe a certain day, then you honor it with them if and don't make a big issue of it.

I believe Romans 14 and all the rest of the Word of God would also be saying that if in any areas of doubtful things we take our convictions, push them on others, and say, "You can't be a Christian, and be right with God unless you do the things I'm doing," then you are totally in error. You have misused your Christian liberty and are actually bringing people under the works of the law, causing them to be separated from God's grace in the sense that grace and the atoning work of Jesus is what makes a person right. It's not the length of my shirtsleeves, how long my hair is, whether I have makeup on or not—these kinds of things are doubtful areas and every-one has their own conviction anout them.

If you have a conviction, walk before God in the light you have. It would be wrong for you to do something that violated your own conscience. But realize that your conscience may not be the conscience of someone else, and we have no right to judge, condemn, or beat down our fellow brothers and sisters if they see something in a different light. It's before God they will answer, not before us. Let's get out of the judging business, start loving people, and point them to Jesus. He can straighten out their lives and show them from the Word of God what they should or should not do.

As you look at Romans 14, I believe the Lord will give you much insight into this area of Christian liberty, the way to use it correctly, and how to avoid doing some very serious damage in the body of Christ. God bless you.

. . . .

Read the entire lesson and then answer the questions that follow.

Romans 14:1 - Him that is weak in the faith receive ye, but not to doubtful disputations.

(Rom. 14:1) Paul wrote this epistle to the saints in Rome. There was a big argument between the Jewish Christians and the Gentile Christians over the issue of grace and works. Paul spent the majority of this letter dealing with the mistaken teaching that Gentiles who became Christians had to keep the Old Testament Law in order to be saved.

The main Old Testament requirement Paul had dealt with up to this point was circumcision (Rom. 4). He conclusively proved that circumcision, or any other point of the Law, was unnecessary for salvation. The only thing that God requires for the born-again experience is faith in what Jesus Christ did for us.

In this chapter, Paul brings up two more points of the Law which were a real stumbling block to Jewish Christians. These are the issues of eating meats which the Law declared unclean and observing special days such as the Sabbath and the feast days. The Jewish Christians were saying that the Gentile Christians had to keep these laws. The Gentile Christians felt no obligation to keep the old Jewish rituals.

Paul stated that the Gentile Christians were correct doctrinally (v. 20), but he warns them against despising their weak Jewish brethren who could not eat meat or skip the observance of special days in good conscience. Therefore, Paul established a principle that those who have the greater revelation of their freedom in Christ have an obligation to try not to display that freedom in a way that offends their weak brethren.

Who is the weak brother referred to here? It is the religious Jew who was converted to Christianity. Verse two refers to the weak one as the one who is eating herbs. This is a reference to the Jewish Christian who had not totally realized his freedom from the Old Testament dietary laws.

The Old Testament Law forbid Jews from eating certain meats (Lev. 11) and blood (Gen. 9:4; Lev. 3:17; 7:26-27, 17:10-14; Deut. 12:16, 23-25, and 15:23). Because the Jews who were in Rome could not always be certain of what type of meat they were buying or if it had been killed properly to drain the blood, many of them had become vegetarians to avoid any possible contamination.

This is very interesting that Paul would cite the religious person as the weak brother. Most religious people think all their religious convictions make them superior to those who come to Christ without any religious background. But that wasn't Paul's assessment.

There is no bondage like religious bondage. A simple pagan background is easy to overcome in comparison to a heritage of legalistic religion. Paul ought to know. He was the Pharisee of the Pharisees.

Paul is saying that we shouldn't be critical of, or discriminate against, those who are weak in their convictions. This has been interpreted by some as inconsistent with some of Paul's actions.

Right here in this epistle, Paul had called the legalistic Jewish Christians impenitent and hardhearted (Rom. 2:5). In dealing with the same subject in the letter to the Galatians, Paul was very uncompromising, saying that they had been bewitched (Gal. 3:1) and that they were fallen from grace if they trusted in circumcision (Gal. 5:2-4). He also said in Galatians 2:5 that he didn't give any place to the legalistic Jews who were advocating circumcision for salvation.

How do Paul's actions harmonize with what he is teaching here?

There are some doctrinal points that are non-negotiable and others that are not. When it came to the doctrine of grace for salvation, Paul didn't compromise. He even said, "But though we, or an angel from heaven, preach any other gospel unto you than that which we have preached unto you, let him be accursed" (Gal. 1:8).

If these Jewish believers had taught abstinence from meats and observance of special days as essential for salvation, Paul would not have tolerated that. But if these Jewish Christians were professing righteousness with God solely on the work of Christ, yet they had a personal conviction about these things, that was okay.

The thought or the motive behind the action is what must be judged.

Paul didn't object to circumcision. Paul objected to faith in circumcision instead of faith in Christ. He even circumcised Timothy to keep from offending the Jews (Acts 16:3). Yet when the legalistic Jews tried to pressure Paul about the circumcision of Titus (Gal. 2:3-5), Paul would not bend.

Likewise, we cannot compromise on the matter of salvation by grace through faith (Eph. 2:8). Yet there should be room for Christians to dwell together and have different ways of conduct.

Romans 14:2 - For one believeth that he may eat all things: another, who is weak, eateth herbs.

(Rom. 14:2) This verse is speaking of the Gentile Christian who didn't have any convictions about eating certain meats and the Jewish Christian who would only eat herbs for fear of breaking an Old Testament dietary law.

Romans 14:3 - Let not him that eateth despise him that eateth not; and let not him which eateth not judge him that eateth: for God hath received him.

(Rom. 14:3) Paul is preaching a tolerance of other believers who have differing views that could appear contradictory to his own actions. However, these are not believers who are putting faith in these actions for salvation; they wouldn't be true Christians if they were. These people were justified by faith but they had a personal conviction about keeping the ceremonial law of their Jewish heritage.

These people are different from the ones that Paul spoke of in his letter to Timothy. In 1 Timothy 4:3, Paul said those who commanded others to abstain from meats were speaking a doctrine of devils. The key difference is the word "command." Those in 1 Timothy 4 were demanding compliance for salvation. The people that Paul is saying to receive in this verse are people who are not judging others for their own personal convictions.

Notice that Paul instructs those who have the revelation of their freedom in Christ not to despise those who don't. He also instructs those who are still emphasizing works to not judge those who aren't.

Paul is revealing that the danger for those who have a revelation of God's grace is to become insensitive to and impatient with their brethren who haven't yet come to that knowledge. We have to temper our freedom in Christ with love for our fellow Christians. "Knowledge puffeth up, but charity edifieth" (1 Cor. 8:1).

Those who have not yet renewed their minds to their freedom from the Old Testament Law tend to be judgmental of others who don't have their standard of holiness. Passing judgment on others is a sure sign of a legalistic mentality.

Romans 14:4 - Who art thou that judgest another man's servant? to his own master he standeth or falleth. Yea, he shall be holden up: for God is able to make him stand.

(Rom. 14:4) We are all servants, not judges. We should let the Lord be the judge. The only thing that we are supposed to judge is ourselves, that we aren't a stumbling block to anyone (v. 13).

Romans 14:5 - One man esteemeth one day above another: another esteemeth every day alike. Let every man be fully persuaded in his own mind.

(Rom. 14:5) On other occasions Paul called it bondage to observe special days (Gal. 4:9-10). Once again, this must be denoting people who were observing certain days as a mere conviction and not a command. Personal convictions and doctrinal truth are two different things.

Romans 14:6 - He that regardeth the day, regardeth it unto the Lord; and he that regardeth not the day, to the Lord he doth not regard it. He that eateth, eateth to the Lord, for he giveth God thanks; and he that eateth not, to the Lord he eateth not, and giveth God thanks.

(Rom. 14:6) This verse verifies that these observances of certain days and abstinence from meats were not done in a legalistic manner that caused the individual to think he was earning salvation. They were doing these things as unto the Lord.

Romans 14:7-11 - For none of us liveth to himself, and no man dieth to himself. 8) For whether we live, we live unto the Lord; and whether we die, we die unto the Lord: whether we live therefore, or die, we are the Lord's. 9) For to this end Christ both died, and rose, and revived, that he might be Lord both of the dead and living. 10) But why dost thou judge thy brother? or why dost thou set at nought thy brother? for we shall all stand before the judgment seat of Christ. 11) For it is written, As I live, saith the Lord, every knee shall bow to me, and every tongue shall confess to God.

(Rom. 14:11) Paul is citing this Old Testament verse to show that each individual is accountable to God (v. 12). Therefore, we don't have to judge our brethren. God will do it.

Romans 14:12-13 - So then every one of us shall give account of himself to God. 13) Let us not therefore judge one another any more: but judge this rather, that no man put a stumblingblock or an occasion to fall in his brother's way.

(Rom. 14:13) We are not supposed to judge our brother or sister. Instead, we are supposed to judge ourselves to make sure that we are not causing others to stumble in their faith through our actions.

Romans 14:14 - I know, and am persuaded by the Lord Jesus, that there is nothing unclean of itself: but to him that esteemeth any thing to be unclean, to him it is unclean.

(Rom. 14:14) This is quite a statement! Nothing is unclean. It is how we use things that makes them unclean.

The Old Testament Law declared many animals unclean (Lev. 11), not because there was anything wrong with the animals, but the Lord was making a point. In the New Testament, Paul reveals that every creature of God is good and nothing to be refused if it is received with thanksgiving (1 Tim. 4:4). Every creature of God was always good, even during Old Testament times. But the Lord wanted His people to be a holy people, separated unto Him even in the things they ate.

Therefore, He gave them dietary laws that pronounced certain animals as unclean so that they would be reminded, even as they ate, that they were not free to do just whatever they wanted to do. They were bought with a price (1 Cor. 6:20) and they were to glorify God in every area of their lives (1 Cor. 10:31).

Colossians 2:16-17 makes it very clear that these dietary laws were shadows of things that are now realities in Christ. Yet, just as with so many other Old Testament truths, the Jews had become engrossed in the observance of the ritual with no understanding as to what it symbolized. Likewise today, some Christians still hold to Old Testament ritual without any idea that the ritual has become reality in Christ.

In Colossians 2:16-17, Paul said these things were shadows of things to come. If I were walking towards you but the corner of a building blocked your view, then my shadow could be very significant. It could show you I was coming and how close I was. But once I came around the corner and was in view, it would be unthinkable that you would fall down and embrace my shadow. My shadow is meaningful only because it represents me. Once you could talk to me, my shadow would be meaningless.

Likewise, Old Testament rituals were significant before Christ came. They illustrated truths that were not yet in full view. But now that Christ has come, the rituals are meaningless and can be oppressive if they are wrongfully thought to be requirements for acceptance with God.

Romans 14:15 - But if thy brother be grieved with thy meat, now walkest thou not charitably. Destroy not him with thy meat, for whom Christ died.

(Rom. 14:15) This ties all of this teaching back in with Romans 13:8-10. Paul had summarized all our duty to mankind as loving our neighbor as ourselves. If we ignore the influence our actions have on others, we are not walking in this law of love.

Romans 14:16-17 - Let not then your good be evil spoken of: 17) For the kingdom of God is not meat and drink; but righteousness, and peace, and joy in the Holy Ghost.

(Rom. 14:17) Man usually focuses his attention on external things such as meat and drink, but God is always concerned with the heart of man (1 Sam. 16:7). God deals with our actions because they indicate the condition of our hearts. It is always the spiritual condition of our inner man that God is seeking to change.

Paul is saying that we need to be like God and focus on the inner condition of our brothers and sisters in Christ. Then we will be able to tolerate minor differences in their actions.

Romans 14:18-20 - For he that in these things serveth Christ is acceptable to God, and approved of men. 19) Let us therefore follow after the things which make for peace, and things wherewith one may edify another. 20) For meat destroy not the work of God. All things indeed are pure; but it is evil for that man who eateth with offence.

(Rom. 14:20) Prior to this verse, Paul had encouraged the believers to consider their weaker brothers based on their obligation to love one another. Now he strengthens that argument by revealing how damaging it could be if the weaker brother follows our actions with a defiled conscience. It is evil for him (v. 20), it will offend him and make him weak (v. 21), it will damn him, and it is sin for him (v. 23).

Romans 14:21 - It is good neither to eat flesh, nor to drink wine, nor any thing whereby thy brother stumbleth, or is offended, or is made weak.

(Rom. 14:21) A casual reading of Paul's instructions here might leave a person with the impression that Paul is only suggesting that we not offend the weak brother in this area. However, this is not the case.

The Jerusalem church had already issued a command to the Gentile Christians that they abstain from meat that had been offered to idols (Acts 15:20, 28-29). Paul agreed with this mandate and became one of the messengers who delivered this decree to the churches (Acts 15:25, 30).

Paul also commented on this same subject in 1 Corinthians 8 and 10. In chapter 8 Paul said, "But when ye sin so against the brethren, and wound their weak conscience, ye sin against Christ" (v. 12). That doesn't sound optional. He also gave a direct command in 1 Corinthians 10:28, "not to eat meat sacrificed to idols for the sake of the weak brother."

However, the greatest proof that this abstinence from meat offered to idols was not optional are the comments of Jesus Himself. In Revelation 2:14 and 20, the Lord rebuked two churches for allowing people to teach in those churches that the people could eat meats sacrificed to idols.

Therefore, even though these scriptures do explain that the actual eating of meats sacrificed to idols is not wrong in itself, it does not give the believers the right to indulge. They are strictly to abstain because of the effect their actions would have upon the weaker Christian's conscience.

Romans 14:22 - Hast thou faith? have it to thyself before God. Happy is he that condemneth not himself in that thing which he alloweth.

(Rom. 14:22) This is specifically speaking of having faith that they could eat meat sacrificed to idols. The Epistles of Paul by W. J. Conybeare renders this verse, "hast thou faith [that nothing is unclean]: Keep it for thine own comfort before God." Therefore, Paul is stating that if anyone has a clear conscience about eating meat sacrificed to idols, he should keep that faith to himself and not practice it openly lest he offend the weaker brother.

Romans 14:23 - And he that doubteth is damned if he eat, because he eateth not of faith: for whatsoever is not of faith is sin.

(Rom. 14:23) The Greek word that was translated "damned" here is "katakrino," meaning "to judge against; sentence." This differs from the Greek word "krino" that is used in 2 Thessalonians 2:12 to designate eternal damnation. "Katakrino," as used in this verse, actually means "to condemn" and is translated that way 17 other times in the New Testament. In contrast, "krino" is only translated as "condemn" once (John 3:17), "condemned" once (John 3:18), and "condemning" once (Acts 13:27).

Therefore, this verse is not saying that any Christian who does something with a defiled conscience is eternally damned. Paul is stating that any Christian who violates his conscience is going to come under condemnation.

This verse provides us with a definition of sin that is applicable to all people of all cultures and different religious backgrounds. Any action is sin for us if we don't have faith in its correctness. Until we can settle our doubts, we aren't to do it. This would provide an infallible system for determining right and wrong for any individual.

Romans 14:1-23
Discipleship Questions

. . . .

Answer the following questions by reading the corresponding
discipleship commentary lesson and using your Bible.

1. Read Romans 14:1. Christians are to welcome all of God's followers, even those who are what?_____

2. Read Romans 14:2, 5. What does it mean to be "weak in the faith"?
_____

3. Read Romans 14:1. What are "doubtful disputations"? _____
_____

4. Read Romans 14:2. One man's faith allows him to eat anything, but another who is weak in faith eats only what? _____

5. Who has God accepted according to Romans 14:3?
_____

6. Read Romans 14:4. Are we to judge God's people in doubtful matters? _____

7. Is everything black and white in these matters?_____

8. Are there some things that are black and white?_____

9. Read Romans 13:9. Romans 13:9. What are some absolutes in the Bible?
_____
_____

10. Read Romans 14:5. Each Christian should reach a conviction in his own mind about what?_____

11. Read Romans 14:6. A person is motivated to celebrate or not celebrate a sacred day, to eat meat or not to eat meat by what? _____

12. Read Romans 14:7. According to this verse, are we our own bosses?_____

13. Read Romans 14:8. Whether we live or die, it must be for whom?_____

14. Read Romans 14:8. Whether we live or die, to whom do we belong?_____

15. Read Romans 14:9. Why did Christ die and rise again?
_____

16. Read Luke 6:46. What does the word "Lord" imply that we do?

_____

17. Read Romans 14:10, 12. How many of us will stand before God to be judged?

_____

18. Read Romans 5:9. How can we be acquitted before God?

_____

19. According to Romans 14:13, what three things are we **not** to do?

_____

_____

_____

20. Read Romans 14:14. There is really no food unclean in itself nor the eating of food that was offered to an idol, but to him who regards it as unclean, it is what?

_____

21. Read Romans 14:15. If another Christian is distressed or grieved by what you do, you are not walking in what? _____

22. What is love? _____

23. What is the instruction in the second part of Romans 14:15?

_____

_____

24. Read Romans 14:16. How would you paraphrase Romans 14:16?

_____

_____

25. According to Romans 14:17, the kingdom of God is not what?

_____

_____

26. According to Romans 14:17, the kingdom is?_____

_____

27. How are we to serve Christ, according to Romans 14:18?

_____

28. How could we paraphrase Romans 14:18? _____

_____

_____

29. Read Romans 14:19. According to this verse, what must we always aim for?

_____

_____

30. What is the instruction Paul is giving us in the first part of Romans 14:20?

_____

31. Read Romans 14:21. Christian liberty becomes wrong when it causes others to do what?

_____

_____

32. Read Romans 14:22. We are to keep what we believe about disputable matters between ourselves and whom?_____

33. Who is happy, according to Romans 14:22? _____

_____

34. Read Romans 14:23. The person who doubts about what he is doing, is what?

_____

35. What does "damned" mean ?_____

36. Read Romans 14:23. If you do anything you believe is not right, what do you do?

_____

Romans 14:1-23
Discipleship Answer Key

. . . .

Do not look at the answer key until you have completed the questions.
Compare your answers with the following answers.

1. Read Romans 14:1. Christians are to welcome all of God's followers, even those who are what?
   Weak in the faith.

2. Read Romans 14:2, 5. What does it mean to be "weak in the faith"?
   To be under dietary laws, keeping of Sabbath days, etc.

3. Read Romans 14:1. What are "doubtful disputations"?
   Matters that can be disputed, such as what day to worship, what we should eat or not eat, the drinking of wine, etc.

4. Read Romans 14:2. One man's faith allows him to eat anything, but another who is weak in faith eats only what?
   Herbs or vegetables.

5. Who has God accepted according to Romans 14:3?
   Both those who eat meat and those who do not (vegetarians).

6. Read Romans 14:4. Are we to judge God's people in doubtful matters?
   No.

7. Is everything black and white in these matters?
   No.

8. Are there some things that are black and white?
   Yes.

9. Read Romans 13:9. Romans 13:9. What are some absolutes in the Bible?

10. Read Romans 14:5. Each Christian should reach a conviction in his own mind about what?
    Doubtful matters such as Sabbath days, etc.

11. Read Romans 14:6. A person is motivated to celebrate or not celebrate a sacred day, to eat meat or not to eat meat by what?
    His conscience.

12. Read Romans 14:7. According to this verse, are we our own bosses?
    No.

13. Read Romans 14:8. Whether we live or die, it must be for whom?
The Lord.

14. Read Romans 14:8. Whether we live or die, to whom do we belong?
The Lord.

15. Read Romans 14:9. Why did Christ die and rise again?
That He might be our Lord.

16. Read Luke 6:46. What does the word "Lord" imply that we do?
That we do the things Jesus commands us to do.

17. Read Romans 14:10, 12. How many of us will stand before God to be judged?
Everyone of us—all people

18. Read Romans 5:9. How can we be acquitted before God?
Through the blood (sacrifice) of Jesus.

19. According to Romans 14:13, what three things are we **not** to do?
   1. Judge one another.
   2. Do anything that would be a stumblingblock to others.
   3. Do anything that would make others fall into sin.

20. Read Romans 14:14. There is really no food unclean in itself nor the eating of food that was offered to an idol, but to him who regards it as unclean, it is what?
Unclean or wrong for him to eat it.

   Statement: Things are not unclean in themselves, but they become unclean when used outside of God's boundaries. Examples are money, sex, wine, etc.

21. Read Romans 14:15. If another Christian is distressed or grieved by what you do, you are not walking in what?
Charity or love.

22. What is love?
To seek the welfare or benefit of another.

23. What is the instruction in the second part of Romans 14:15?
Do not destroy someone's faith by eating food (or do anything else) he thinks is wrong or unclean.

24. Read Romans 14:16. How would you paraphrase Romans 14:16?
Let not your good, i.e., your Christian liberty which is a good thing, be the object of misunderstanding and sin for others.

25. According to Romans 14:17, the kingdom of God is not what?
Issues of religious scruples (what we eat or don't eat, what we drink or don't drink).

26. According to Romans 14:17, the kingdom is?
Righteousness (uprightness in our walk), peace (with God and with others), and joy in and through the Holy Spirit.

27. How are we to serve Christ, according to Romans 14:18?
In righteousness, peace and joy.

28. How could we paraphrase Romans 14:18?
Anyone who serves Christ by living this way is pleasing God and will be respected by people (finding their approval).

29. Read Romans 14:19. According to this verse, what must we always aim for?
1. Things that bring peace.
2. Things that strengthen and build up others.

30. What is the instruction Paul is giving us in the first part of Romans 14:20?
Do not wreck God's work among you by questions such as what to eat or not to eat.

31. Read Romans 14:21. Christian liberty becomes wrong when it causes others to do what?
Stumble, be offended, be weakened or does anything that causes others to fall into sin.

32. Read Romans 14:22. We are to keep what we believe about disputable matters between ourselves and whom?
God.

33. Who is happy, according to Romans 14:22?
Happy are those who do not condemn themselves by doing something they know is alright.

34. Read Romans 14:23. The person who doubts about what he is doing, is what?
Damned.

35. What does "damned" meant?
Condemned or feeling condemned.

36. Read Romans 14:23. If you do anything you believe is not right, what do you do?
Sin.

OVERVIEW OF ROMANS CHAPTER 15

by Andrew Wommack

We now come to Romans 15. We are very close to the end of our study of the book of Romans and it has been powerful talking about the Gospel being the power of God unto salvation. In Romans 14, Paul made some applications about the grace of God, specifying that some people worship on one day and others have special days that they worship on. He said one esteems a certain day and another doesn't. He was talking about how it is a matter of personal faith before God. You can't judge a person based on these outward observances and religious rituals. He ended the chapter by saying, *"He that doubteth is damned if he eat, because he eateth not of faith; for whatsoever is not of faith is sin."*

That leads right into chapter 15. The point he was making is that it's a matter of what you do in faith. There are some people who observe special days, have faith, and are believing for it. There are others for whom that would be a legalistic work of the law. It depends on what your heart attitude is, and only God knows that. So in Romans 15 he is basically talking about having patience with other people and not judging them based on an outward code of conduct or adherence to a set of rules.

Romans 15:1 says, *"We then that are strong ought to bear the infirmities of the weak, and not to please ourselves."* He goes on to explain that this context is referring to a person who doesn't have the faith to eat meat that had been offered to idols. In Bible times people went to the marketplace to buy meat the way we go to a grocery store. Some meat had been offered to an idol and after the sacrifice was taken and sold in the marketplace. When Christians heard about this, many of them wouldn't eat the meat because it had been sacrificed to a devil and they felt it was unholy food. Others would say, "It doesn't matter what someone else did with it, it's just meat and if I pray over it, it's okay."

In 1 Corinthians Paul made a long explanation on this and basically said that technically there was nothing unholy about that meat. There is nothing unholy about money, meat, or anything that has been used by some ungodly person. If you had a gift given you by someone in the Mafia, that doesn't mean it is tainted. It might not be wisdom to take it because of your association there, but the point he is making is that technically the meat itself is not defiled because it had been offered to an idol.

He says, however, that if someone who thinks it is defiled sees you eating it and it causes them to stumble and be offended, then you are wrong in eating it though technically there may be nothing wrong. It is your example, which is what he is talking about here. *"We then that are strong ought to bear the infirmities of the weak, and not to please ourselves. Let every one of us please his neighbour for his good to edification"* (verses 1-2). In context he is talking about this issue over meat sacrificed to idols. The point here is that now that you know this truth, the grace of God might free you to do certain things, to violate religious traditions, which may not be sin for you, but how will it affect other people?

Even Jesus didn't please himself; He pleased other people. Jesus as the Creator could have done all kinds of things, but He didn't. He lived a very holy, separate life so He could benefit others. Verse 3 says, *"For even Christ pleased not himself; but, as it is written, the reproaches of them that reproached thee fell on me."* This is a main point Paul is making here in chapter 15.

Another main point he made as a result of his teaching on the grace of God was regarding the fact that the Jews felt they had an advantage with God, that you had to be a Jew to have a relationship with Him. They believed Gentiles (anyone who wasn't a Jew) had to become proselytes of Judaism to have a relationship with God. So the teaching Paul gave here on the subject of grace showed that it wasn't genealogy or works that produced relationship with God. It was faith in the grace of God, and anybody, Jew or Gentile, could have that. Once again he is saying that the grace of God has now opened the door of salvation to everyone. Gentiles are not excluded. Jews are not excluded. It is for anyone who will come. In Romans 10:13 he said, *"For whosoever shall call upon the name of the Lord shall be saved."*

He begins to quote some verses to verify his point. In Romans 15:9 he quotes from the book of Isaiah, *"And that the Gentiles might glorify God for his mercy; as it is written, For this cause I will confess to thee among the Gentiles, and sing unto thy name."* That passage is talking about the Messiah; Jesus would confess to the Gentiles. In verse 10 he quotes another scripture, *"And again he saith, Rejoice, ye Gentiles, with his people."* That's saying that even in the Old Testament it was prophesied that the Gentiles would be with the people of God. In verse 11 he quotes, *"And again, Praise the Lord, all ye Gentiles; and laud him, all ye people."* And in verse 12, *"And again, Esaias saith, Thee shall be a root of Jesse, and he that shall rise to reign over the Gentiles; in him shall the Gentiles trust."*

All of this is the result of grace. Grace means that God is now available to anybody. You don't have to be holy, have a certain genealogy, and be skilled in all the religious rites and rituals. If you will simply humble yourself and put faith in what Jesus did for you, you can have relationship with God.

Let's go down into verses 25-28. Paul is winding down his teaching here, saying, *"But now I go unto Jerusalem to minister unto the saints. For it hath pleased them of Macedonia and Achaia to make a certain contribution for the poor saints which are at Jerusalem. It hath pleased them verily; and their debtors they are. For if the Gentiles have been made partakers of their spiritual things, their duty is also to minister unto them in carnal things. When therefore I have performed this, and have sealed to them this fruit, I will come by you into Spain."* What this is talking about, is, that Paul was on his way to Jerusalem to bring a collection to the saints there.

There had been a drought in Israel. Some of the saints were impoverished, and when the churches of Macedonia and Achaia heard about it (Macedonia refers to the churches at Thessalonica and Philippi; Achaia to the church at Corinth.), they took up a contribution and Paul was taking it directly to Jerusalem to give to the saints. You have to remember that this was in a day and time when they didn't have organizations like the Red Cross that we are used to seeing minister to such needs. There weren't governmental systems for this. For the Christians in Macedonia whom the Jewish Christians considered to be fringe at the very best (some even doubted if they were true born again believers), this was a tremendous statement of love and faith to give to these collections for the saints in Jerusalem. Scripture doesn't tell us of the impact it made, but I believe it made a positive impact and helped unify the church. This was a major occurrence here.

This same thing should be happening today. We are not only to give to the work of the Lord to build churches and keep preachers going. I'm not saying that is unimportant, but these are saints giving to other saints, Christians helping one another. It doesn't have to be the same denominational people, the same doctrinal bias. If a person is a born again Christian, it is our responsibility to help them.

This is what is discussed in Romans 15, and it leads into Romans 16 where Paul concludes by greeting people and giving his closing arguments. This teaching through the book of Romans has been powerful and I believe God is going to give you revelation as you continue to study through these scriptures.

Romans 15:1-33
Discipleship Commentary

- -

Read the entire lesson and then answer the questions that follow.

Romans 15:1 - We then that are strong ought to bear the infirmities of the weak, and not to please ourselves.

(Rom. 15:1) This verse is the summary of Paul's teaching in chapter 14. He explained that the Christian who is strong in grace, is technically correct, realizing that it is all right to eat meat sacrificed to idols . But just because it's lawful doesn't mean it is the correct thing to do (1 Cor. 6:12, 10:23). He clearly states that the strong believer is supposed to bear the infirmities of his or her weak Christian brother or sister.

This word "bear" was translated from the Greek word "bastazo" meaning "to lift." This gives the picture of the Christian with the weak conscience, being burdened down with guilt or condemnation. We that are strong are supposed to help him or her lift that load. We do that by not offending his or her weak conscience.

The word that was translated "infirmity" here is the Greek word "asthenema" which means "a scruple of conscience." This is saying that the stronger brother or sister needs to help lift the burden of the brother or sister that has a weak conscience.

Paul is summing up his instructions given in chapter 14 on how to get along with a brother or sister who has different convictions than you. It all comes back to love. Love thinks of the other person first. Love is not selfish (1 Cor. 13). If we would seek the pleasure of others more than our own pleasure, we would kill strife. Only by pride cometh contention (Prov. 13:10).

Romans 15:2-3 - Let every one of us please his neighbour for his good to edification. 3) For even Christ pleased not himself; but, as it is written, The reproaches of them that reproached thee fell on me.

(Rom. 15:3) As always, Jesus is the supreme example of God's kind of love. Jesus submitted to things that He didn't have to as God. However, He became a man and submitted Himself lest He should offend people (Matt. 17:27). If Jesus did this for us, how can any of us justify not bearing the infirmities of our weak brother or sister?

Romans 15:4 - For whatsoever things were written aforetime were written for our learning, that we through patience and comfort of the Scriptures might have hope.

(Rom. 15:4) All the Old Testament scriptures were written for our instruction so that we would not make the same mistakes. A person who does not heed the lessons of the Old Testament is like a person who is trying to re-invent the wheel. People have already made mistakes and the Old Testament scriptures were faithful to report the consequences of those sins. We don't have to learn the same lessons by "hard knocks." We can learn at their expense instead of ours.

Patience, comfort, and hope do not come to us by begging and pleading with God. You can not have a lasting measure of these things by having someone just lay hands on you. They come through the scriptures.

A misunderstanding of scriptures like Romans 5:3 and James 1:3 has caused some people to mistakenly think that problems produce patience. However, this verse makes it clear that patience is a product of the Scriptures. If tribulations produced patience, then every Christian would be patient. We have all had tribulation.

Patience comes through God's Word, but problems cause us to exercise or use our patience and thereby become stronger.

Romans 15:5 - Now the God of patience and consolation grant you to be likeminded one toward another according to Christ Jesus:

(Rom. 15:5) Paul is referring back to verse 3 where he used Christ as an example of bearing the infirmities of those who are weak. He is praying that the Lord would work this same grace in us that was displayed in Christ Jesus.

Romans 15:6-7 - That ye may with one mind and one mouth glorify God, even the Father of our Lord Jesus Christ. 7) Wherefore receive ye one another, as Christ also received us to the glory of God.

(Rom. 15:7) How do we determine what doctrines are negotiable and which ones are not. If an individual has been truly born again by Christ receiving him or her, then we should receive that person also, regardless of our differences. If Jesus is able to overlook the doctrinal errors of an individual, who are we to refuse that person.

Romans 15:8 - Now I say that Jesus Christ was a minister of the circumcision for the truth of God, to confirm the promises made unto the fathers:

(Rom. 15:8) In Romans 15:7, Paul concluded his remarks about walking in love towards brethren who had different convictions. He judged that on certain issues that were not critical to salvation, the stronger should bear with the weak.

Now, lest someone should try to cite Jesus' exclusion of the Gentiles during His earthly ministry as proof that we can reject those who don't conform to Jewish traditions, Paul explains why Jesus ministered nearly exclusively to the Jews. He was fulfilling God's promises to the Jews. Jesus could not become the Savior of the Gentiles until He had been the Messiah to the Jews.

Paul then goes on to cite a number of Old Testament scriptures that make it very clear that Jesus' present ministry embraces the Gentiles without converting them to Judaism.

Romans 15:9 - And that the Gentiles might glorify God for his mercy; as it is written, For this cause I will confess to thee among the Gentiles, and sing unto thy name.

(Rom. 15:9) Paul briefly verifies a point that he has already made in this book to the Romans. He quotes four Old Testament scriptures to verify that Christ opened up the door of salvation to the Gentiles.

This is done to make it clear that Gentiles do not have to become Jews to be saved. Salvation to Gentiles as Gentiles does not fall into the category of one of those non-essential doctrines that Paul discussed in chapter 14, on which we compromise for the sake of our weak brother or sister.

Romans 15:10-16 - And again he saith, Rejoice, ye Gentiles, with his people. 11) And again, Praise the Lord, all ye Gentiles; and laud him, all ye people. 12) And again, Esaias saith, There shall be a root of Jesse, and he that shall rise to reign over the Gentiles; in him shall the Gentiles trust. 13) Now the God of hope fill you with all joy and peace in believing, that ye may abound in hope, through the power of the Holy Ghost. 14) And I myself also am persuaded of you, my brethren, that ye also are full of goodness, filled with all knowledge, able also to admonish one another. 15) Nevertheless, brethren, I have written the more boldly unto you in some sort, as putting you in mind, because of the grace that is given to me of God, 16) That I should be the minister of Jesus Christ to the Gentiles, ministering the gospel of God, that the offering up of the Gentiles might be acceptable, being sanctified by the Holy Ghost.

(Rom. 15:16) We cannot just worship God however we want to. Our worship has to be sanctified by the Holy Ghost. Until a person makes Jesus his Lord, the Holy Spirit does not intercede for him. Paul is saying that through his preaching of the Gospel and the Gentiles reception of salvation, then the Holy Spirit was free to work on their behalf.

Romans 15:17 - I have therefore whereof I may glory through Jesus Christ in those things which pertain to God.

(Rom. 15:17) Paul brought the Gospel to the Gentiles, which granted salvation to those who received it. Therefore, he had quite a bit to boast about. However, he said his boasting was through Christ Jesus which clarifies that this was not done in arrogance or pride.

Romans 15:18-19 - For I will not dare to speak of any of those things which Christ hath not wrought by me, to make the Gentiles obedient, by word and deed, 19) Through mighty signs and wonders, by the power of the Spirit of God; so that from Jerusalem, and round about unto Illyricum, I have fully preached the gospel of Christ.

(Rom. 15:19) Paul was known primarily for his preaching of the gospel of God's grace. But Paul had the miraculous power of God working in him, too. Indeed, this should be true of all ministers of the Gospel.

Paul struck Elymas the sorcerer with blindness causing the conversion of Sergius Paulus (Acts 13:6-12). In Lystra, Paul healed a man who had been a cripple from birth (Acts 14:8-10). In Philippi, Paul cast a spirit of divination out of a girl (Acts 16:16-18), and he was also delivered from prison in that city by a miraculous earthquake (Acts 16:25-26).

In Ephesus, the Lord accomplished special miracles through Paul by healing and delivering people as they came in contact with handkerchiefs or aprons that Paul had touched (Acts 19:11-12). In Troas, Paul raised Eutychus from the dead (Acts 20:9-12). And while shipwrecked on the island of Melita, Paul miraculously survived a bite from a poisonous snake (Acts 28:3-6).

Paul was also delivered from death at the hands of the Romans and Jews many times, including one time where he may actually have been raised from the dead. Paul's life, as well as the lives of everyone on his ship, was spared from death at sea through God's intervention (Acts 27:21-26,43-44).

Paul also wrote to the Corinthians that the signs of an apostle were wrought among them by himself (2 Cor. 12:12). Yet there is no record in Acts of any miracles performed by Paul during his visits to Corinth (Acts 18:1-17 and Acts 20:2-3).

Therefore, it can be concluded that there were many miraculous things accomplished by Paul that were not recorded just as in the case of our Lord Jesus (John 20:30, 21:25).

Ancient Illyricum occupied the territory that is modern day Albania and Yugoslavia, just north of Macedonia where Thessalonica and Berea were located. There is no record of Paul preaching in this area, so it can be supposed that he is referring to ministering up to the border of this province.

Some people have interpreted Paul's statement, "I have fully preached the Gospel of Christ," to mean that he had covered all the area of Asia, Macedonia and Achaia with the Gospel. The following few verses would lend itself to that interpretation.

However, the immediate context of this verse specifically mentions "mighty signs and wonders, by the power of the Spirit of God." This would lead us to believe that Paul "fully" preaching the Gospel referred to the confirmation of the Word through demonstration of God's miraculous power.

Therefore, Paul could be making a distinction between just preaching the Gospel and fully preaching the Gospel. A minister hasn't fully preached the Gospel unless there are accompanying signs and wonders . This must be where the phrase "full gospel" came from.

Romans 15:20 - Yea, so have I strived to preach the gospel, not where Christ was named, lest I should build upon another man's foundation:

(Rom. 15:20) Paul had a burning desire to reach the unreached. The greatest legacy that Paul left us is his epistles that were written to those he led to the Lord. This reflected an attitude that Paul had that we should have also. Paul didn't just evangelize, he discipled people.

Romans 15:21-22 - But as it is written, To whom he was not spoken of, they shall see: and they that have not heard shall understand. 22) For which cause also I have been much hindered from coming to you.

(Rom. 15:22) The cause that Paul is referring to is his desire to preach the Gospel to everyone who had not heard. He had wanted to go to Rome, but he felt it was necessary to preach the Gospel to everyone in the areas he had already been first. This is what he refers to in the next verse when he says, "now having no more place in these parts." He was saying there was no place left in those parts that hadn't heard the Gospel. Therefore, he was ready to depart for new, unreached areas.

Romans 15:23 - But now having no more place in these parts, and having a great desire these many years to come unto you;

(Rom. 15:23) In Acts 19:21, Paul purposed in his spirit to visit Rome after he had gone back through Macedonia and Achaia. This happened while he was in Ephesus from 54 to 57 A.D.

Paul was writing this epistle around 57-58 A.D. Therefore, Paul's "many years" is referring to a two-to-three year period of time.

Romans 15:24 - Whensoever I take my journey into Spain, I will come to you: for I trust to see you in my journey, and to be brought on my way thitherward by you, if first I be somewhat filled with your company.

(Rom. 15:24) Paul mentions his intentions to travel to Spain twice in this chapter (this verse and v. 28). These are the only two times in scripture that this is mentioned. There is no scriptural account that Paul ever made it to Spain. Some have speculated that Paul went to Spain after his imprisonment in Rome. There are traditions that support that but no fact.

Paul is referring to the Romans helping him with his expenses for his planned trip to Spain.

Romans 15:25-26 - But now I go unto Jerusalem to minister unto the saints. 26) For it hath pleased them of Macedonia and Achaia to make a certain contribution for the poor saints which are at Jerusalem.

(Rom. 15:26) The account of Paul's travels in Acts do not give us any details about this collection for the poor saints in Jerusalem. However, Paul does mention it as being the reason he made his last trip to Jerusalem (Acts 24:17), and he wrote about it in his letters to the Corinthians.

In 1 Corinthians 16:1-4, Paul gives instructions for the collection for the saints in Jerusalem. In verse 1, he says he gave the same instructions to the churches of Galatia. It is unclear whether he is saying he had also instructed the churches of Galatia to receive an offering for the Jerusalem saints or whether he was simply instructing the Corinthians to receive the collection in the same manner as the Galatians received their offerings. At any rate, Paul was only delivering the offerings from the churches of Macedonia and Achaia during this trip to Jerusalem.

In 2 Corinthians 8:1-5, Paul spoke favorably about the attitude the churches of Macedonia (the churches of Thessalonica and Berea) had towards this offering. He acknowledged that the churches of Achaia (the Corinthian church) had purposed to send an offering a year before the Macedonian churches (2 Cor. 8:10; 9:2). Paul gave the impression that the offering from the Macedonian churches was unsolicited (2 Cor. 8:4).

Paul encouraged the Corinthians to participate generously in this offering reminding them that they would reap proportionally to the way they had sown (2 Cor. 9:6). He stated clearly that they should not give under compulsion (2 Cor. 9:7) or try to give what they didn't have (2 Cor. 8:11-15). And he gave them a tremendous promise of God's physical blessing on them if they participated (2 Cor. 9:8-11).

This must have been a relatively large sum of money for Paul to be carrying to Jerusalem. Even though Paul could have demanded these people's trust since he was the apostle that brought them the Gospel, he made provision for whoever they chose to accompany him to Jerusalem to make sure the money went for what it was intended (2 Cor. 8:20-21 with 1 Cor. 16:3).

This was a benevolence offering for the poor saints in Jerusalem

Romans 15:27 - It hath pleased them verily; and their debtors they are. For if the Gentiles have been made partakers of their spiritual things, their duty is also to minister unto them in carnal things.

(Rom. 15:27) Specifically, the carnal things Paul is referring to here is money.

Romans 15:28-29 - When therefore I have performed this, and have sealed to them this fruit, I will come by you into Spain. 29) And I am sure that, when I come unto you, I shall come in the fulness of the blessing of the gospel of Christ.

(Rom. 15:29) What a statement! Paul had no doubt that he would be walking in the fullness of God. This reveals that walking in the power of the Holy Spirit is our choice.

Some people disagree with this and say you can't make the blessings of God occur. They sometimes happen and other times they don't based on God's choosing. Otherwise, it would be like us being able to turn God on and off.

The answer to that is, God is always on. We are the ones who are on and off. Anytime we choose life (Deut. 30:19), we can be assured that the life of God that was given us through Christ Jesus will flow. The responsibility rests on us to stir up the gift that is in us (2 Tim. 1:6).

Romans 15:30 - Now I beseech you, brethren, for the Lord Jesus Christ's sake, and for the love of the Spirit, that ye strive together with me in your prayers to God for me;

(Rom. 15:30) This shows how important Paul thought prayer was. Paul begs these believers to earnestly intercede on his behalf.

Romans 15:31-33 - That I may be delivered from them that do not believe in Judaea; and that my service which I have for Jerusalem may be accepted of the saints; 32) That I may come unto you with joy by the will of God, and may with you be refreshed. 33) Now the God of peace be with you all. Amen.

(Rom. 15:31) Paul's prayer request was that he would be delivered from the religious unbelievers in Jerusalem. The answer to this prayer came in a way that many of us would not have liked. Instead of not having any problems, he was assaulted and wound up spending many years in prison. Yet, he was delivered from the unbelieving Jews. They had tried to kill him three times (Acts 21:31, 23:20-21, and 25:2-3), but the Lord delivered him through the Roman government.

Paul knew that trouble was waiting for him in Jerusalem. In Acts 20:22-23, Paul said he didn't know exactly what would happen to him in Jerusalem but he knew it would be bonds and afflictions.

Romans 15:1-33
Discipleship Questions

· ·

Answer the following questions by reading the corresponding discipleship commentary lesson and using your Bible.

1. Who are the "strong" referred to in Romans 15:1?
   _____

2. Read Romans 15:1. Who are the "weak"? _____
   _____

3. According to Romans 15:1, the "strong" are to yield to the "weak" and not please themselves. Why? _____
   _____

4. How did Paul yield to the consciences of others in 1 Corinthians 9:20-22? Why?
   _____

5. Read Romans 15:1. What should the strong do for the weak?
   _____

6. What is Romans 15:2 saying? _____
   _____
   _____

7. How does 1 Corinthians 11:23-33 relate to this subject?
   _____
   _____

8. Read Romans 15:3. Did Christ live to please himself?_____
   _____

9. As further proof that Christ did not live to please himself, Paul quotes Psalms 69:9 in Romans 15:3. Who is the word "thee" referring to?_____
   _____

10. Read Romans 15:4. Everything that was written long ago in the Scriptures was written for what purpose? _____

11. What two things do the Scriptures teach us according to Romans 15:4?
    _____

12. Read Romans 15:4. What is the by-product of receiving patience and comfort from the Scriptures? _____

13. God is the source of what, according to Romans 15:5? _____
_____

14. Read Romans 15:5. As we follow Christ Jesus, what attitude are we to portray towards other believers? _____
_____

15. Read Romans 15:6. Why are we to have this attitude? _____
_____

16. For the glory of God, what are we to do according to Romans 15:7?
_____

17. Jesus Christ came as a minister to Jews and Gentiles. What did He do for the Jews, according to Romans 15:8? Also read Galatians 3:6, 16, and 29. _____
_____

18. Read Romans 15:9. What did He reveal to the Gentiles? _____

19. Read Romans 15:9. Romans 15:9-12 are quotations from Psalms 18:49, Deuteronomy 32:43, Psalms 117:1 and Isaiah 11:10. All these Scriptures are quoted to show the Gentiles doing what? _____

20. What is Paul's prayer in Romans 15:13? _____
_____

21. Read Romans 15:14. Paul assures the Roman Christians that his lengthy exposition of the Gospel was not intended to raise doubts about their spiritual condition. He states in Romans 15:14 that he is persuaded or convinced of what? _____
_____
_____

22. Paul has written to the Roman Christians very boldly on some points. According to Romans 15:15-16, why has he done this?_____
_____
_____

23. Read Romans 15:18-19. What two ways did God use the Apostle Paul to make the Gentiles obedient to the Christian faith? _____
_____

24. Read Romans 15:20. Paul's ambition was to preach the Gospel of Christ where?
_____

25. Read Romans 15:21. This verse is a quote from Isaiah 52:15. How does God's Word bear witness that Paul's desire is the leading from the Lord? _____

_____

_____

26. Read Romans 15:22. What had kept Paul from coming to see the Christians in Rome? Also read Acts 26:15-20. _____

27. Read Romans 15:23. What did Paul mean when he said, "But now having no more place in these parts"? Also read Mark 1:38. _____

_____

28. Read Romans 15:24. Where was Paul planning to go?

_____

29. Where was Paul planning to go, according to Romans 15:25?

_____

30. Read 1 Corinthians 16:14 and 2 Corinthians 8:12-15. Why was he planning to go here?

_____

_____

31. Read Romans 15:27. Why was it right for the Gentiles to help these poor Jewish brethren?

_____

_____

32. What was Paul's prayer request in Romans 15:31-32?

_____

_____

_____

Discipleship Answer Key
Romans 15:1-33

. . . .

Do not look at the answer key until you have completed the questions.
Compare your answers with the following answers.

1. Who are the "strong" referred to in Romans 15:1?
   Those who are strong in faith and conscience.

2. Read Romans 15:1. Who are the "weak"?
   Those who esteem one day above another and regard some meats as clean and others as unclean. They are weak in conscience.

3. According to Romans 15:1, the "strong" are to yield to the "weak" and not please themselves. Why?
   The weak can not yield without violating their conscience, but the strong can yield. The weak have to sin to yield.

4. How did Paul yield to the conscience of others in 1 Corinthians 9:20-22? Why?
   By relating to them and accepting them for who they were, that they might be saved.

5. Read Romans 15:1. What should the strong do for the weak?
   Bear the infirmities of the weak, i.e., use their strengths to assist the weak in doctrine.

6. What is Romans 15:2 saying?
   "If we wound or displease our neighbor, we drive him off, and so pull down the work of God. But if, on the other hand, we please him by showing proper respect for his feelings, he remains in the church. Ultimately he grows strong, and so the work of God is built up" (Moses E. Lard).

7. How does 1 Corinthians 11:23-33 relate to this subject?
   In the body of Christ we are all related to, and a part, of one another. We need to value each other and see each other as God does. His love toward others can flow through us when we remember Christ's death, and that we died with Him, no longer living to please ourselves.

8. Read Romans 15:3. Did Christ live to please himself?
   No. Christ did not live to please himself. The welfare and benefit of others was characteristic of His life.

9. As further proof that Christ did not live to please himself, Paul quotes Psalms 69:9 in Romans 15:3. Who is the word "thee" referring to?
   God. Christ endured the reproaches aimed at his Father and did not live for himself.

10. Read Romans 15:4. Everything that was written long ago in the Scriptures was written for what purpose?
For our learning, i.e., to teach us today.

11. What two things do the Scriptures teach us according to Romans 15:4?
1. Patience, i.e., steadfastness or endurance.
2. Comfort or encouragement.

12. Read Romans 15:4. What is the by-product of receiving patience and comfort from the Scriptures?
Hope, i.e., to go on hoping in our present time.

13. God is the source of what, according to Romans 15:5?
1. Patience, i.e., steadfastness and endurance.
2. Consolation or encouragement.

14. Read Romans 15:5. As we follow Christ Jesus, what attitude are we to portray towards other believers?
We are to be like-minded, i.e., live in harmony, unity, and be of the same mind or point of view.

15. Read Romans 15:6. Why?
So that with one heart and mouth we can praise and glorify God together.

16. For the glory of God, what are we to do according to Romans 15:7?
We are to receive or accept one another as Christ has accepted us.

17. Jesus Christ came as a minister to Jews and Gentiles. What did He do for the Jews, according to Romans 15:8? Also read Galatians 3:6, 16, and 29.
He confirmed the promises made unto the fathers, i.e., He showed that God is true to all the promises He made to their ancestors.

18. Read Romans 15:9. What did He reveal to the Gentiles?
His mercy.

19. Read Romans 15:9. Romans 15:9-12 are quotations from Psalms 18:49, Deuteronomy 32:43, Psalms 117:1, and Isaiah 11:10. All these Scriptures are quoted to show the Gentiles doing what?
Glorifying and praising God for His mercy.

20. What is Paul's prayer in Romans 15:13?
"So I pray that God, who gives you hope, will keep you happy and full of peace as you believe in him. May you overflow with hope through the power of the Holy Spirit" (NLT).

21. Read Romans 15:14. Paul assures the Roman Christians that his lengthy exposition of the Gospel was not intended to raise doubts about their spiritual condition. He states in Romans 15:14 that he is persuaded or convinced of what?

    1. That they are full of goodness.

    2. Filled with knowledge.

    3. Able to admonish or teach one another.

22. Paul has written to the Roman Christians very boldly on some points. According to Romans 15:15-16, why has he done this?

    1. To remind them of the truths they already know (v.15).

    2. To bring them the Gospel (v.16).

    3. So that the Gentiles, when offered before God, may be an acceptable sacrifice.

    4. That the Gentiles might be sanctified or hallowed by the working of the Holy Spirit.

23. Read Romans 15:18-19. What two ways did God use the Apostle Paul to make the Gentiles obedient to the Christian faith?

    1. By word, i.e., by what he said.

    2. By deed, this could mean by the way he lived and also by the miracles, signs, and wonders that he did.

24. Read Romans 15:20. Paul's ambition was to preach the Gospel of Christ where?

    Where Christ was not known.

25. Read Romans 15:21. This verse is a quote from Isaiah 52:15. How does God's Word bear witness that Paul's desire is the leading from the Lord? Also read Rom. 15:21.

    The Jerusalem Bible states, "My [Paul's] chief concern has been to fulfill the text: Those who have never been told about him will see him, and those who have never heard about him will understand"

26. Read Romans 15:22. What kept Paul from coming to see the Christians in Rome? Also read Acts 26:15-20.

    His commission to reach the lost

27. Read Romans 15:23. What did Paul mean when he said, "But now having no more place in these parts"?

    That there was no place left that hadn't heard the Gospel. The Conybeare translation states, "But now that I have no longer room enough [for my labors] in these parts." See Mark 1:38.

28. Read Romans 15:24. Where was Paul planning to go?

    Spain, and passing through to see the Christians at Rome also.

29. Where was Paul planning to go, according to Romans 15:25?

    To Jerusalem.

30. Why was he planning to go here? Read 1 Corinthians 16:14 and 2 Corinthians 8:12-15.
To minister unto the saints, i.e. to give a voluntary offering from the churches to help the poor saints in Jerusalem.

31. Read Romans 15:27. Why was it right for the Gentiles to help these poor Jewish brethren?
The Gentiles had received the Gospel first from Jewish Christians. It was only right that the Jews should receive food and clothing from the Gentiles.

32. What was Paul's prayer request in Romans 15:31-32?
   1. **That he may be delivered from the unbelievers in Judaea who rejected the Christian faith.**
   2. **That the relief offering would be accepted in the spirit of love in which it was given.**
   3. **By God's will that he might come to the brethren with joy.**
   4. **That together with the brethren he may be refreshed.**

OVERVIEW OF ROMANS CHAPTER 16

by Andrew Wommack

Today we come to the conclusion of our study through the book of Romans. Paul's teaching in this book is his masterpiece on the subject of grace. I believe this study on the book of Romans has been a life-changing experience for you. By showing you the grace of God, it has taught you a brand new way of relating to the Lord. These truths have changed my life, and have changed the life of Don Krow, my associate, who has done a lot of these lessons. They have impacted us more than anything else.

Chapter 16 is basically Paul's farewell, his closing. There is a lot of incidental material he has already taught. He previously made his points about the grace of God, and yet there are some tremendous truths in this chapter. I am going through a couple of these which you will study in more detail.

Romans 16:1-2 says, *"I commend unto you Phoebe our sister, which is a servant of the church which is at Cenchrea: that ye receive her in the Lord, as becometh saints, and that ye assist her in whatsoever business she hath need of you: for she has been a succourer of many, and of myself also."* This is not a major doctrine, but it is an important point. Today there is still prejudice against women in ministry. Notice in this list that Paul mentions a number of women and talks about how they ministered to him in different ways.

In this instance, he talks about Phoebe, a sister who is a servant of the church at Cenchrea. The word "servant" is the same Greek word we get "deacon" from. In your materials you will be able to study that and go into more detail. Because of this, many people have thought Phoebe was being referred to as a deaconess of the church and that, because that didn't fit the theology of the translators of the King James Bible centuries ago, they translated it "servant." It also can mean servant. Many people take this to say that she was actually a Christian worker, a deaconess in the church.

There are other women mentioned. The next verse says, *"Greet Priscilla and Aquila my helpers in Christ Jesus."* Paul mentions them a number of times in Acts 16 and 18. Priscilla is a woman and was also a minister.

In looking at all of these greetings, there basically are some personal things Paul is saying, but through them you see that he has love for these people. There is a lot to be said for these personal relationships. Paul is writing a letter which has probably impacted the world as much as anything.

It was Romans 3 that changed Martin Luther's life, gave him a revelation of the grace of God, and sparked the Reformation that swept not only through Europe but around the world and is still impacting us today. This letter to the Romans has changed the world, yet as important and weighty as it is, Paul spends time to greet these people individually. They are long since gone, but it teaches us a lesson: Paul, even though he was so powerful, had this great revelation, and wrote these truths that have changed the world, still had personal relationships with these people.

In verse 8 he says, *"Greet Amplias my beloved in the Lord."* He reveals how he loved these people in a personal, intimate way. There are many things you can learn through chapter 16 as Paul talks about these people who had hazarded their lives for the cause of the Lord.

Verse 19: *"For your obedience is come abroad unto all men. I am glad therefore on your behalf: but yet I would have you wise unto that which is good, and simple concerning evil."* The context is that he had just talked about divisions among them, and how to deal with them. About his confidence in their obedience, saying these things because he wants them to be wise concerning what is good and simple concerning what is evil. In a sense, this is a sideline, but it is a profound statement and is diametrically opposite to the way most people are today.

I meet people all the time who feel you can't effectively minister to people unless you really know where they're coming from. In a sense, you have to understand how they think. I have met many ministers who, in an effort to minister to someone from a different culture who is in some type of sin, pour themselves into studying and learning about these things. That is opposite to what this verse says, that he wants us to be wise concerning that which is good and simple concerning that which is evil.

Again, the current intellect of our society tells you that you have to understand all you can about your enemy. Paul is saying just the opposite. He would have you understand a lot about good and be simple concerning evil. Have you heard how they train people who handle money all the time (banks), to recognize counterfeit money? They don't show them counterfeit money and have them study it. They have them take the real thing and study its minutest details, handle it over and over and over. They become so acquainted with the genuine that when a fake comes across their path, they instantly recognize it. It's impossible for a person to totally become acquainted with every kind of counterfeit bill because there are new ones coming out all the time, but they can become so acquainted with the real article that they instantly recognize a fake.

Basically that is what this scripture is saying. It is one of the most powerful scriptures to me. The Lord wants us to be wise concerning that which is good, and simple concerning that which is evil. You don't need to be watching programs, reading books, engaging in conversation or activity so you can see what the rest of the world is involved in to know how to minister to them better. What you need to do is saturate yourself in God and become so God-filled, so God-controlled, that anything contrary to this will immediately be recognizable to you and you will be able to reject it.

This has specifically ministered to me because I grew up without ever saying a word of profanity, without ever taking a drink of liquor. I am now 52 years old and have never done any of those things. Many people would ask how in the world I could minister to people, but what I have done is follow the principle of this verse. I have poured myself into seeking to know God, and as He has revealed Himself to me, it has enabled me to minister to people who have been in adultery and terrible sexual sins. I have been able to help them, yet I have never committed any of those sins. I have been able to help people who were drunks or dope addicts, and set many free—not because I was well acquainted with their situations but because I was well acquainted with God and what His Word has to say.

It is important to recognize this. Satan will constantly try to get you to feel condemned and disqualified, that you have no ability to minister, yet this scripture says that if you will become wise concerning that which is good and simple concerning evil, it will work to your advantage. Not only will it help you individually, but you will still be able to minister to other people.

This is the conclusion of Paul's teaching, but even among these scriptures there are still little nuggets like this. I encourage you to spend the time to go through and look at some of these people, what they have done, and specifically focus on verse 19 to get hold of this. You can make this commitment and reach the place where you can say, "Father, I don't want to know about all these other things. I don't want to be well versed in evil. I want to know you." That's what Paul said in Philippians 3—"I forget everything else … I throw everything else to the side … and I look forward, seeking only this prize of the high calling of God in Christ Jesus."

The key to the Christian life, and actually any aspect of life, is doing one thing well. You can't do multiple things well, but you can focus on God. You can get to where you know Him, and I believe this teaching through Romans has helped acquaint you with the grace of God, has shown you that God loves you independent of your performance. If you will take these truths and meditate on them, I promise that they will bless you and make you a blessing to other people.

Romans 16:1-27
Discipleship Commentary

. . . .

Read the entire lesson and then answer the questions that follow.

Romans 16:1 - I commend unto you Phebe our sister, which is a servant of the church which is at Cenchrea:

(Rom. 16:1) The only mention of Phebe in scripture is Romans 16:1-2 and the subscript in some Bibles at verse 27. From these passages we can see that Phebe was the one who delivered this epistle to the Romans. She had ministered to many including Paul, and therefore Paul instructed the Romans to assist her in whatever way they could in her business.

Because the word "servant" in this verse has also been translated "deacon" in other scriptures, many believe that Phebe was actually a deaconess of the church in Cenchrea.

The Greek word that was translated "servant" here is the word "diakonos." This came from the root word "diako" meaning "to run errands." It specified an attendant, i.e., a waiter (at table or in other menial duties). "Diakonos was specifically a Christian teacher and pastor (technically a deacon or deaconess)" W. E. Vine.

This word was used a total of 28 times in the New Testament. It was translated "deacons" three times (Phil. 1:1; 1 Tim. 3:8,12), "ministers" five times (1 Cor. 3:5; 2 Cor. 3:6, 6:4, 11:15, and 23), "minister" thirteen times (Matt. 20:26; Mark 10:43; Rom. 13:4, 15:8; Gal. 2:17; Eph. 3:7, 6:21; Col. 1:7, 23, 25, 4:7; 1 Th. 3:2; and 1 Tim. 4:6), "servant" four times (Matt. 23:11; Mark. 9:35; John 12:26; and Rom. 16:1), and "servants" three times (Matt. 22:13; John 2:5, 9).

It can be said that the dominant use of this word in the New Testament is to specify a minister or deacon. However, out of the six other times this word was translated "servant" or "servants," it was definitely designating a person who performs menial tasks as a slave. Therefore, it can not be stated emphatically from this verse that Phebe was or was not a deaconess or female minister.

History does supply us with information that there were female ministers in the churches of Bithynia as early as A.D. 100. Pliny wrote the emperor Trajan concerning the Christians and reported that he had examined two old women who were called ministers (Davis Dictionary of the Bible, p. 176).

Romans 16:2 - That ye receive her in the Lord, as becometh saints, and that ye assist her in whatsoever business she hath need of you: for she hath been a succourer of many, and of myself also.

(Rom. 16:2) The archaic meaning of the word "for" was, "because; since" (American Heritage Dictionary). Paul is saying that the reason they should assist Phebe is because she had assisted others, including Paul. This illustrates the law of reaping what you sow (Gal. 6:7, Luke 6:38).

Some people become offended when they do not receive assistance from others, yet they have never helped anyone. That is not what Paul is advocating here. Phebe had earned their help. Salvation is by grace, but respect and help from others has to be earned.

Romans 16:3-4 - Greet Priscilla and Aquila my helpers in Christ Jesus: 4) Who have for my life laid down their own necks: unto whom not only I give thanks, but also all the churches of the Gentiles.

(Rom. 16:4) Paul does not elaborate and the scriptures do not reveal a specific instance where Priscilla and Aquila laid down their own necks for Paul's sake. It is possible they were some of the disciples who restrained Paul from entering into the theatre in Ephesus during the uproar caused by Demetrius (Acts 19:28-41).

Romans 16:5 - Likewise greet the church that is in their house. Salute my wellbeloved Epaenetus, who is the firstfruits of Achaia unto Christ.

(Rom. 16:5) This is the only mention of Epaenetus in scripture. From this reference we can see that Epaenetus was loved very much by Paul. He was Paul's first convert in Achaia.

Romans 16:6 - Greet Mary, who bestowed much labour on us.

(Rom. 16:6) There are a number of Marys mentioned in scripture implying that this was a common name. There is no reason to believe that this Mary in Rome is the same as some other Mary in scripture. This woman had bestowed much labor on Paul and his companions.

Romans 16:7 - Salute Andronicus and Junia, my kinsmen, and my fellowprisoners, who are of note among the apostles, who also were in Christ before me.

(Rom. 16:7) The name "Andronicus" means "conquering men." This is the only mention of Andronicus in scripture. He and Junia were two of six relatives Paul mentions in this chapter. He had been imprisoned, presumably for his faith in Christ. Paul said he was "of note" among the apostles. That probably meant Andronicus and Junia were well known, even to the apostles.

Andronicus and Junia were Christians before Paul's conversion. It is very possible that they witnessed to Paul and this may have been part of the pricks Paul was fighting against at his conversion. Since Junia is a feminine name, it is possible that Andronicus and Junia were married.

This is the only mention of Junia in scripture. The fact that Andronicus and Junia were both imprisoned, both in Christ before Paul, and both Paul's relatives suggests that they were close, possibly man and wife.

They were both "of note" among the apostles, probably meaning that they were well known, even to the apostles. Junia and Andronicus were apparently living in Rome.

The Greek word used for "kinsmen" here is "suggenes" and means "a relative (by blood); by extension, a fellow countryman" (W. E. Vine). In Romans 9:3, Paul used this word to refer to all of the Jews as his countrymen. Therefore, it is not certain whether Paul is using this word to denote blood relatives or fellow Jews. The fact that more of these people were Jews than what Paul designated by the term "kinsmen" would suggest that he was speaking of blood relatives.

There are six (depending on how you interpret v. 21) kinsmen of Paul's referred to in this chapter. These are Andronicus, Junia (this verse), Herodion (v. 11), Lucius, Jason, and Sosipater (v. 21).

It is possible that Tertius is the one speaking in verse 21, and therefore Lucius, Jason, and Sosipater would be his kinsmen.

Romans 16:8 - Greet Amplias my beloved in the Lord.

(Rom. 16:8) The Greek word that was translated "beloved" here is "agapetos," the adjective form of "agape." It is signifying the type of love that God has. Paul said Amplias was "beloved in the Lord" meaning, this was God's love being expressed through Paul.

Romans 16:9 - Salute Urbane, our helper in Christ, and Stachys my beloved.

(Rom. 16:9) The name "Urbane" means "polite." This is the only mention of Urbane in scripture. He had been a companion in work with Paul.

The name "Stachys" means "an ear of grain." This is the only mention of Stachys in scripture.

Romans 16:10 - Salute Apelles approved in Christ. Salute them which are of Aristobulus' household.

(Rom. 16:10) This is the only mention of Apelles in scripture.

The name "Aristobulus" means "best counselor." This is the only mention of Aristobulus in scripture.

Romans 16:11 - Salute Herodion my kinsman. Greet them that be of the household of Narcissus, which are in the Lord.

(Rom. 16:11) The name "Herodion" came from the Greek word "Herodes" meaning "hero." This was the name of a number of kings of Palestine and it is possible that Herodion was named after one of the Herod kings. If so, that would most likely make Herodion a Gentile since it would be very unusual for a Jew to name a child in honor of Herod.

Herodion is the third person Paul mentions in this chapter as being his kinsman. If Herodion was a Gentile as his name could imply, then Paul would have to be referring to him as a brother in the Lord and not a natural blood relative.

The name "Narcissus" came from the flower narcissus or the daffodil. This is the only mention of Narcissus in scripture.

This term "in the Lord" is referring to the members of Narcissus' household who had been born again through faith in Christ. This is a very appropriate and descriptive term since all believers are in Christ Jesus (2 Cor. 5:17; Col. 2:10).

Romans 16:12 - Salute Tryphena and Tryphosa, who labour in the Lord. Salute the beloved Persis, which laboured much in the Lord.

(Rom. 16:12) "Tryphena" meaning "delicate, dainty" and "Tryphosa" meaning "delicate," were women at Rome that Paul saluted and commended for their labor in the Lord.

The name "Persis" means "Persian." He was a Christian at Rome whom Paul greeted. Paul mentioned he laboured much in the Lord. This is the only mention of Persis in scripture.

Romans 16:13 - Salute Rufus chosen in the Lord, and his mother and mine.

(Rom. 16:13) The name "Rufus" means "red." The name Rufus is mentioned twice in scripture (Mark 15:21; and Rom. 16:13). It is unclear whether this is the same Rufus in both instances. If so, then this Rufus whom Paul sent greetings to in Rome would have been the son of Simon of Cyrene who was compelled to bear the cross of Jesus. Paul also sent greetings to the mother of Rufus.

Paul greeted the mother of Rufus and called her his own mother. It is unclear whether this is figurative or literal. Most commentators suspect this was a figurative statement as is the case elsewhere in scripture.

Romans 16:14 - Salute Asyncritus, Phlegon, Hermas, Patrobas, Hermes, and the brethren which are with them.

(Rom. 16:14) "Asyncritus" meaning "incomparable or unlike," "Phlegon" meaning "burning, scorching", "Hermas" a Greek deity, a variation of Hermes, "Patrobas" meaning "father's life," and "Hermes," this was the same name as the Greek god that corresponded to the Roman Mercury. These were all Christians in Rome to whom Paul sent greetings. This is the only mention of these individuals in scripture.

Romans 16:15 - Salute Philologus, and Julia, Nereus, and his sister, and Olympas, and all the saints which are with them.

(Rom. 16:15) The name "Philologus" means "fond of words." The wording of this verse suggest that Philologus was the husband of Julia. This is the only mention of Philologus in scripture.

The name Julia was the feminine form of the Latin "Julius" as in Julius Caesar. Because of the wording of this verse, many people believe Julia was the wife of Philologus. This is the only mention of Julia in scripture.

The name Nereus came from the sea god who, under Poseidon or Neptune, ruled the Mediterranean Sea. This was the name of a Christian in Rome to whom Paul sent greetings. Paul also greets Nereus' sister in this verse who is not named. This is the only mention of Nereus in scripture.

The name "Olympas" means "excess of wine." This was the name of a Christian in Rome whom Paul greeted. This is the only mention of Olympas in scripture.

This is the second consecutive scripture in which Paul greeted a group of people and the brethren or saints which were with them. This is probably referring to a local group of believers who regularly met in the households of these people. This would have made those who were mentioned in these verses leaders of those local bodies of believers.

Romans 16:16 - Salute one another with an holy kiss. The churches of Christ salute you.

(Rom. 16:16) This is one of five times in scripture where we are exhorted to greet other believers with a holy kiss or a kiss of charity.

The culture of Paul's day used a kiss as a greeting just as we still see in the Arab cultures of today. However, Paul's repeated use of this custom in his instructions to the believers would suggest that he advocated it as a Christian custom. It is certain that Christians have more reason to greet one another with a kiss than anyone else.

It needs to be noted that in each reference to this, there is a specific mention of this being a holy kiss or kiss of charity. That qualifies the manner in which this is to be done. This certainly is not an opportunity for someone to exercise his lusts. This should be motivated only by the holiest Christian love for a fellow believer.

If this kiss of charity is misunderstood or not wanted by the person receiving it, then it would certainly be inappropriate to give it.

Romans 16:17 - Now I beseech you, brethren, mark them which cause divisions and offences contrary to the doctrine which ye have learned; and avoid them.

(Rom. 16:17) This is one of many times that Paul makes a very clear statement about withdrawing from individuals who are causing problems in the church (1 Cor. 5:9-11; Phil. 3:17; 2 Th. 3:6, 14-15; 1 Tim. 6:3-5; 2 Tim. 2:16-17, 3:5; 1 John 1:19; and Titus 3:9-10). We also have an example of Paul separating the true believers from the false and meeting in a separate place in Acts 19:9. These are scriptural precedents for separation based on doctrine.

However, Paul did not say to avoid contact with people who simply had different doctrine. He said to avoid those who caused division and offences over doctrine. Some people have doctrines that disagree with the Word, but they aren't disagreeable. These people can be loved and restored. But the person who is causing dissension over doctrine is to be treated as contaminated and infectious.

One example of this that Paul used in this epistle would be the matter of observing dietary laws. Paul made it clear that there was nothing wrong with any food, but it would be sin for an individual to eat certain foods if he or she wasn't eating in faith (Rom. 14:23). Therefore, there can be differences of doctrines but Paul told those that were strong in grace to bear with those who were not. However, if the weak brother or sister became contentious over his doctrine of abstinence from certain meats and began to condemn others, Paul would say to mark that man and avoid him.

The first thing Paul said to do was to mark these people. The Greek word that was translated "mark," is the word "skopeo," meaning "to take aim at (spy) or figuratively, regard." In modern-day terms, we should "keep an eye" on these people. They are not to be trusted and should not be given the freedom to move about freely among the believers and spread the infection.

The way we choose who is to be marked is based on the doctrine of God's Word. There are those who are indifferent to or don't believe the Word of God, but they aren't out to oppose it. Those we simply love and continue to share the Word with, praying for their eyes to be opened. However, those who actively seek to subvert others from following the doctrine of God's Word are the ones to mark. Paul gives some characteristics of these people in verse 18.

Marking these individuals falls into the category of church discipline and should be done consistently with all those instructions.

Romans 16:18 - For they that are such serve not our Lord Jesus Christ, but their own belly; and by good words and fair speeches deceive the hearts of the simple.

(Rom. 16:18) In this verse, Paul gives us some characteristics of the people he said to mark in the previous verse. These people are not truly serving the Lord Jesus Christ; they are serving themselves. That's what this terminology "their own belly" means.

This same description is used in the parallel account of Paul on this same subject in Philippians 3:19. There Paul says that their God is their belly. This is saying that their motive is not the selfless motive of love for God and others, but rather they are motivated by a love for themselves. This is always at the root of all division. Philippians 3:19 gives the further explanation that these people glory in their shame and mind earthly things.

Paul says in this verse, that these individuals use good words and fair speeches and deceive the hearts of the simple. This means that they flatter people (2 Tim. 4:3) and appeal to the same selfish desires as they themselves have, to draw people after themselves (Acts 20:30).

Paul says that the simple are the ones who are deceived by these sowers of strife. If we will quit being simple, we won't be deceived.

What did Paul mean by "simple"? The Greek word that was translated "simple" in this verse is "akakos." It was only used twice in the New Testament; here in Romans 16:18 and in Hebrew 7:26. In Hebrew 7:26, it was translated "harmless" meaning "without guile or fraud; harmless; free from guilt" (Thayer's).

In this verse, the meaning of this word is "fearing no evil from others, distrusting no one" (Thayer's). This is describing those who we today would call "gullible" (Prov. 14:15). Only those who lack discernment between good and evil will fall prey to this deceit.

How do we quit being simple or gullible? It's through God's Word. Many scriptures promise that God's Word will cause the simple to start being wise (Ps. 19:7, 119:130; and Prov. 1:4). A good understanding of God's Word is the greatest defense against deception (John 8:32, 17:17).

The English word "simple" is only used twice in the New Testament; here and in the next verse, Romans 16:19.

Romans 16:19 - For your obedience is come abroad unto all men. I am glad therefore on your behalf: but yet I would have you wise unto that which is good, and simple concerning evil.

(Rom. 16:19) This is the second and last time that the English word "simple" was used in the New Testament. The first time was in the previous verse. However, this one English word came from two different Greek words. The Greek word that was used in verse 18 was "akakos," while the Greek word that was used in this verse is "akeraios" meaning "(1) unmixed; pure as in wines or metals; (2) without a mixture of evil; free from guile; innocent; simple" (Thayer's).

Therefore, when Paul presented being simple in verse 18 as something that is not good, and simple in verse 19 as something that is good, he was speaking of two different things. Verse 18 is speaking against being gullible, while verse 19 is speaking in favor of being pure, focused only on things that are good.

This is a wonderful key that the Lord is giving us for living the Christian life and yet very few people use it. It goes contrary to modern thinking that all knowledge is good, even the knowledge of evil.

Satan used Eve's desire to know about evil to entice her to sin (Gen. 3:5-6). All she knew was good, but Satan convinced her she would be better off if she knew about evil. That definitely was not the case.

God never intended us to know about evil. That's the reason He forbade Adam and Eve to eat of the tree of the knowledge of good and evil. You cannot be tempted with things that you don't think. Therefore, don't think about evil things and you will not be tempted with them.

Of course, since the fall of man, evil is in the world and there needs to be some knowledge about evil so we can avoid its pitfalls. Paul said, "we are not ignorant of his devices" (2 Cor. 2:11). Notice that Paul said we should be "simple," not "ignorant." But most people are indulging in a knowledge of evil that is far beyond what Paul was advocating.

Paul also said, For it is a shame even to speak of those things which are done of them in secret (Eph. 5:12). Yet many Christians feel it is necessary and beneficial to plum the depths of the moral debauchery in our world today. That is not so.

We don't have to know all about Satanism and what his followers are doing to avoid that pitfall and help those who have already fallen in it. A person who is seeking God with his whole heart and thinking on all the good He has to offer, will never fall prey to Satanism. That individual will also have the wisdom of God to deliver anyone who has become possessed by that spirit. The best defense is a good offense.

Bank tellers don't become astute at recognizing counterfeit money by studying counterfeit bills. It would be impossible to school them on all the possible variations they could encounter. Instead, they become so familiar with the genuine that they recognize a fake.

Likewise, Christians should be wise concerning that which is good and simple (or unmixed, separated from) concerning evil. Undue attention to what Satan is doing will actually give the enemy inroads into our lives.

Romans 16:20 - And the God of peace shall bruise Satan under your feet shortly. The grace of our Lord Jesus Christ be with you. Amen.

(Rom. 16:20) The word "amen" does not mean 'the end" as so many people use it in prayer. It means "trustworthy, surely, or so be it." It was used 78 times in the Bible; 56 of those times were in the New Testament.

Romans 16:21 - Timotheus my workfellow, and Lucius, and Jason, and Sosipater, my kinsmen, salute you.

(Rom. 16:21) The name "Lucius" means "illuminative." This name is used twice in scripture (here and Acts 13:1). He is referred to as a kinsman of the Apostle Paul, or possibly Tertius.

It is unclear whether this is the same Lucius that was mentioned in Acts 13:1. If so, Lucius would have been a long-time associate of Paul and would either be a prophet or a teacher.

Some people suspect that this Lucius is the Luke who traveled with the apostle Paul and wrote the books of Luke and Acts.

The name "Jason" means "healing." Jason was a kinsman of the Apostle Paul or possibly Tertius.

The name Jason is used five times in scripture. Four of these times are from an account in Acts 17 (Acts 17:5, 6, 7, and 9). It is not certain that the Jason mentioned here is the same as the Jason mentioned in Acts 17, but it probably is.

If this is the same Jason as the Jason of Acts 17, then this Jason had been an acquaintance of Paul since Paul first came to Thessalonica (Acts 17:1). This would make it hard to understand Jason as being a kinsman of Paul in the sense of a blood relative. This must be referring to these men as being brothers in the Lord, or possibly, these men were Tertius' relatives.

Jason apparently took Paul and his companions into his household. Because of this, the unbelieving Jews assaulted the house of Jason, and when they didn't find Paul they took Jason into custody.

The name "Sosipater" means "savior of his father." He is called a kinsman of Paul or possibly it was Tertius who referred to him as a kinsman.

Most scholars believe that Sosipater is the same man as Sopater of Acts 20:4. If so, this would mean that Sosipater was from Berea and was probably a convert of Paul's missionary work there.

The word "kinsman" has been defined and its normal usage discussed. However, this verse seems to present a problem with the word "kinsman" denoting either a blood relative or a fellow countryman.

There are quite a few scriptures where Paul writes of Timotheus, and nowhere else is it implied that Timothy is related to Paul. Therefore, most scholars exclude Timothy and believe that Lucius, Jason, and Sosipater are the ones being referred to as kinsmen.

However, if these men were the same men as mentioned in Acts , then it would appear that they were converts of the Apostle Paul during his second missionary journey. This would make it doubtful that they were blood relatives as the primary usage of the word "kinsman" would imply.

This could mean that these men were kinsman in the sense of fellow countrymen. This would mean that these men were of Jewish descent, living in these Gentile cities. There is also the possibility that Paul was referring to them as kinsmen in the sense that they were brothers in Christ.

There is also the possibility that Paul had ceased his comments in the previous verse and that Tertius, the writer of Romans was speaking of these men as his kinsmen.

Whether these men were Paul's kinsmen or Tertius' kinsmen, they were definitely Paul's converts and companions in the ministry. This gives us some insight into Paul's methods.

If these men were the same men as listed in the book of Acts, then they were born again during Paul's second missionary journey. This means that these men were converted around A.D. 52 and Paul is writing this letter to the Romans around A.D. 57-58.

That means Paul had been discipling these men for approximately five years. Therefore, we have an example of how long it took for Timothy to progress into a position of leadership. Paul is the one who wrote that a novice should not be given a position of authority (1 Tim. 3:6). Timothy was to be left in charge of the church at Ephesus (1 Tim. 1:3) in just a very short time from the writing of this letter as Paul traveled towards Jerusalem. Some scholars speculate that the church at Ephesus could have had as many as 100,000 members.

Romans 16:22 - I Tertius, who wrote this epistle, salute you in the Lord.

(Rom. 16:22) The name "Tertius" was of Latin origin and means "third." This is the only mention of Tertius in scripture. He actually wrote the book of Romans from the Apostle Paul's dictation.

Romans 16:23 - Gaius mine host, and of the whole church, saluteth you. Erastus the chamberlain of the city saluteth you, and Quartus a brother.

(Rom. 16:23) The name "Gaius" was a common Roman name. This name is used five times in scripture (Acts 19:29, 20:4, here; 1 Cor. 1:14; and 3 Jn. 1) and refers to at least three different men.

Acts 19:29 refers to Gaius as being a man of Macedonia while Acts 20:4 refers to a Gaius who was of Derbe, a city of Asia.

It is probable that the Gaius referred to here is the same man that Paul mentioned in 1 Corinthians 1:14 since the book of Romans was written from Corinth. This would make Gaius one of the few people in Corinth that Paul actually baptized. This verse says that Gaius was not only Paul's host but of the whole church, implying that he had a house church meeting in his residence.

The Apostle John addressed the epistle of third John to Gaius. Some speculate that this is the same Gaius that Paul is referring to here.

The name "Erastus" is mentioned three times in scripture (Acts 19:22; here; and 2 Tim. 4:20). "Erastus" means "beloved."

Most scholars agree that this is the same Erastus that Paul sent with Timothy into Macedonia while Paul remained in Ephesus. Paul later wrote to Timothy that Erastus abode in Corinth (2 Tim. 4:20) where this verse reveals that he was the chamberlain of that city.

The word "chamberlain" is only used six times in the Bible (2 Ki. 23:11; Est. 2:3,14,15; Acts 12:20; and here). Of the two times this word is used in the New Testament, Acts 12:20 uses chamberlain in the sense of an eunuch who keeps the king's bedchamber. In this verse, "chamberlain" was referring to Erastus being the treasurer of the city of Corinth.

The name"Quartus" mean "fourth." This is the only mention of Quartus in scripture. He was a Christian brother in Corinth who sent greetings to the saints in Rome.

Romans 16:24-27 - The grace of our Lord Jesus Christ be with you all. Amen. 25) Now to him that is of power to stablish you according to my gospel, and the preaching of Jesus Christ, according to the revelation of the mystery, which was kept secret since the world began, 26) But now is made manifest, and by the Scriptures of the prophets, according to the commandment of the everlasting God, made known to all nations for the obedience of faith: 27) To God only wise, be glory through Jesus Christ for ever. Amen.

(Rom. 16:27) This subscript was probably not a part of Paul's original letter to the Romans. It was added at a later date by some scribe. However, it does seem to be accurate and is therefore retained.

Romans 16:1-27
Discipleship Questions

. . . .

*Answer the following questions by reading the corresponding
discipleship commentary lesson and using your Bible.*

1. Read Romans 16:2. Paul introduced Phoebe in his letter to the church of Rome. What did he ask the church to do? _____

   _____

2. Read Romans 16:2. Was Phoebe a giver or a taker?

   _____

3. Read Romans 16:3. Who did Paul say were his co-laborers in the Gospel?

   _____

4. Read Acts 18:1-3. How did Paul meet Aquila and Priscilla? _____

   _____

5. Read Acts 18:24-26, 28. Being discipled by Paul, were Aquila and Priscilla good teachers?

   _____

6. Read Romans 16:4. According to this verse, what did Aquila and Priscilla do for Paul?

   _____

7. Read Romans 16:5. According to this verse, where did the churches in Paul's time meet?_____

8. Read Romans 16:5. According to this verse, who was the first convert to Christ in the province of Asia?_____

9. Read Romans 16:6. What does this verse reveal about women working for the cause of Christ? _____

10. Read Romans 16:7. Andronicus and Junia were Paul's kinsmen, i.e., kin or fellow Jews. What experiences did they share with Paul?

    _____

    _____

    _____

11. Read Romans 16:8. According to this verse, how did Paul feel about Amplias?

    _____

12. Read Romans 16:9. What was Urbane to Paul?

    _____

13. What do you think Urbane might have done?

_____

14. Read Romans 16:10. What is said about Apelles?

_____

15. Read Romans 16:11. According to this verse, who was Herodion?

_____

16. Read Romans 16:13. How did the mother of Rufus treat Paul?

_____

17. Read Romans 16:16. How did the early church greet one another?

_____

18. According to Romans 16:17, who are we to avoid? Also read Acts 2:41-42.

_____

_____

19. Was Paul an apostle? _____

20. Read Romans 16:18. People are deceived by what?

_____

21. Read Romans 16:19. What should we be wise and well versed in?_____

22. Give some examples. _____

_____

_____

23. Read Romans 16:19. What should we **not** know much about? _____

24. Read Romans 16:20. If we are wise in things that are good, and innocent in things that are evil, who will God crush under our feet? _____

25. Read Romans 16:22. Who actually wrote down this letter for Paul? _____

26. Read Romans 16:25. How are we established in the Christian faith?

_____

27. Read Romans 16:26. What has God called all the nations to do?

_____

Romans 16:1-27
Discipleship Answer Key

· ·

Do not look at the answer key until you have completed the questions.
Compare your answers with the following answers.

1. Read Romans 16:2. Paul introduced Phoebe in his letter to the church of Rome. What did he ask the church to do?
   1. Welcome her.
   2. Help her with anything she needed.

2. Read Romans 16:2. Was Phoebe a giver or a taker?
   A giver. She helped many people, Paul included.

3. Read Romans 16:3. According to this verse, who were Paul's co-laborers in the Gospel?
   Priscilla and Aquila.

4. Read Acts 18:1-3. How did Paul meet Aquila and Priscilla?
   Paul met them in Corinth. Aquila and his wife Priscilla being Jewish were ordered by Claudius to leave Rome. Paul went to see them and being tentmakers they worked together and he stayed with them.

5. Read Acts 18:24-26, 28. Being discipled by Paul, were Aquila and Priscilla good teachers?
   Yes, they explained to Apollos, who knew only of the baptism of John, "the way of God more adequately."

6. Read Romans 16:4. According to this verse, what did Aquila and Priscilla do for Paul?
   They risked their lives for Paul.

7. Read Romans 16:5. According to this verse, where did the churches in Paul's time meet?
   In people's homes.

8. Read Romans 16:5. According to this verse, who was the first convert to Christ in the province of Asia?
   Epaenetus.

9. Read Romans 16:6. What does this verse reveal about women working for the cause of Christ?
   That they work very hard for the Lord.

10. Read Romans 16:7. Andronicus and Junia were Paul's kinsmen, i.e. kin or fellow Jews. What experiences did they share with Paul?
    1. They were fellow Jews who were in prison with Paul.
    2. They were apostles (Eph. 4:10-12).
    3. They were Christians before Paul became a Christian.

11. Read Romans 16:8. According to this verse, how did Paul feel about Amplias?
He was beloved, a dear friend in the Lord.

12. Read Romans 16:9. What was Urbane to Paul?
A helper in the Lord.

13. What do you think Urbane might have done?

14. Read Romans 16:10. What is said about Apelles?
His loyalty to Christ had been proven.

15. Read Romans 16:11. According to this verse, who was Herodion?
A relative or fellow Jew.

16. Read Romans 16:13. How did the mother of Rufus treat Paul?
She treated him like a son.

17. Read Romans 16:16. How did the early church greet one another?
With a holy kiss.

18. According to Romans 16:17, who are we to avoid? Also read Acts 2:41-42.
Those who cause divisions and upset people's faith. Those who oppose apostolic doctrine.

19. Was Paul an apostle?
Yes.

20. Read Romans 16:18. People are deceived by what?
Smooth talk and flattery.

21. Read Romans 16:19. What should we be wise and well versed in?
Good.

22. Give some examples.

23. Read Romans 16:19. What should we **not** know much about?
Evil.

24. Read Romans 16:20. If we are wise in things that are good, and innocent in things that are evil, who will God crush under our feet?
Satan.

25. Read Romans 16:22. Who actually wrote down this letter for Paul?
Tertius.

26. Read Romans 16:25. How are we established in the Christian faith?
By the Gospel and the proclamation of Jesus Christ.

27. Read Romans 16:26. What has God called all the nations to do?
Believe on and obey Him.